Lectures on Imagination

Lectures on Imagination

Paul Ricoeur

EDITED BY GEORGE H. TAYLOR,
ROBERT D. SWEENEY, JEAN-LUC AMALRIC,
AND PATRICK F. CROSBY

The University of Chicago Press CHICAGO AND LONDON

The University of Chicago Press, Chicago 60637
The University of Chicago Press, Ltd., London
© 2024 by The University of Chicago
All rights reserved. No part of this book may be used or repro-
duced in any manner whatsoever without written permission,
except in the case of brief quotations in critical articles and
reviews. For more information, contact the University of Chicago
Press, 1427 E. 60th St., Chicago, IL 60637.
Published 2024
Printed in the United States of America

33 32 31 30 29 28 27 26 25 24   1 2 3 4 5

ISBN-13: 978-0-226-82053-8 (cloth)
ISBN-13: 978-0-226-82054-5 (e-book)
DOI: https://doi.org/10.7208/chicago/9780226820545.001.0001

Library of Congress Cataloging-in-Publication Data

Names: Ricœur, Paul, author. | Taylor, George H.
(George Howard), 1951– editor. | Sweeney, Robert D., editor. |
Amalric, Jean-Luc, editor. | Crosby, Patrick F., editor.
Title: Lectures on imagination / Paul Ricoeur ; edited by
George H. Taylor, Robert D. Sweeney, Jean-Luc Amalric,
and Patrick F. Crosby.
Description: Chicago ; London : The University of Chicago Press,
2024. | Includes bibliographical references and index.
Identifiers: LCCN 2022007566 | ISBN 9780226820538 (cloth) |
ISBN 9780226820545 (ebook)
Subjects: LCSH: Imagination (Philosophy) | Fiction. |
LCGFT: Lectures.
Classification: LCC BH301.I53 R53 2023 | DDC 128/.3—dc23/
eng/20220304
LC record available at https://lccn.loc.gov/2022007566

♾ This paper meets the requirements of ANSI/NISO Z39.48-1992
(Permanence of Paper).

Contents

Editor's Acknowledgments by George H. Taylor vii
Editor's Introduction by George H. Taylor xi

1 Introductory Lecture 1

PART ONE: CLASSICAL READINGS

2 Aristotle 17

3 Pascal and Spinoza 33

4 Hume 49

5 Kant: *Critique of Pure Reason* 61

6 Kant: *Critique of Judgment* 75

PART TWO: MODERN READINGS

7 Ryle 91

8 Ryle (2) and Price 107

9 Wittgenstein 123

10 Husserl: *Logical Investigations* 137

11 Husserl: *Ideas* 153

12 Sartre (1) 169

13 Sartre (2) 185

14 Sartre (3) 201

PART THREE: IMAGINATION AS FICTION

15 Fiction (1): Introduction 217

16 Fiction (2): Metaphor 231

17 Fiction (3): Painting 245

18 Fiction (4): Models 259

19 Fiction (5): Poetic Language 275

Notes 287
Bibliography 303
Index 319

Editor's Acknowledgments

GEORGE H. TAYLOR

In editing these course lectures for publication, the editors' model has been Paul Ricoeur's *Lectures on Ideology and Utopia*, which Ricoeur had the opportunity to review. The goal has been to create a volume that Ricoeur would have approved for publication. The lecture nature of the text also preserves the distinction from Ricoeur's other works that were written for publication.

Publication of these lectures owes considerably to the original foresight of coeditor Patrick Crosby in realizing the value of recording them, transcribing them in careful, verbatim form, and then preserving the recordings and the transcription. Patrick engaged in the initial editing of the lectures as well. Coeditor Bob Sweeney and I each listened separately to the entire set of recordings and reviewed the transcriptions. Bob and I then engaged together in a close editing of the volume. Coeditor Jean-Luc Amalric, who is based in France, has evaluated the manuscript at several junctures, including in a close reading of its final version. Jean-Luc was also very helpful in locating a number of French bibliographic references. He deserves additional thanks for being the primary translator of the volume into its French edition and for shepherding the translation.

The editors thank Ricoeur's literary executors, the Editorial Committee at the Fonds Ricoeur in Paris, led by Jean-Paul Ricoeur, for permission to publish this volume. To assist the creation of a more definitive edition of these lectures, the Editorial Committee asked for incorporation of Ricoeur's lecture notes on imagination, both to help check the accuracy of the transcription and to add anything substantive to the lectures as presented. Some of these notes appear to refer directly to the 1975 course, while others were taken from various iterations of the course as presented either in the United States or France between 1973 to 1975. We thank the Fonds Ricoeur, Catherine Goldenstein, and Olivier Villemot for having carefully located, classified, and prepared these materials.

The editors also offer our thanks to the Ricoeur family and to Olivier Abel. Nathalie Ricœur-Nicolaï and the entire Ricoeur family have taken over editorial responsibility for publication of works by Paul Ricoeur, and they generously agreed to endorse the present edition. Olivier Abel has been a continuous supporter of this volume and its publication.

The Fonds Ricoeur Editorial Committee invited Jean-Luc and Patricia Lavelle to engage in the initial review of the lecture notes and recommend potential places of insertion in the text. This work required considerable time and effort on their part. I engaged in detailed review of the notes and their suggestions; then working together with Jean-Luc (Patricia having gone on to other projects), we reached agreement on the inclusion of individual notes. In almost all cases, these insertions appear without identification in the text, similar to how notes were incorporated in the *Lectures on Ideology and Utopia*.

Also similar to the prior volume, we have deleted student questions asked of Ricoeur during discussion periods and have integrated Ricoeur's responses into the text. We have also largely deleted Ricoeur's comments on course administration, such as on the course syllabus, and instead present the course syllabus as part of the bibliography at the end of the text. At a few relevant points we have added Ricoeur's comments on the syllabus to the endnotes when they offer a substantive contribution.

We have checked all citations. To assist readers, at a number of places we have added page references in the text to primary material when Ricoeur's reference is sufficiently direct but not explicitly offered by him. We have made no attempt, however, to correlate Ricoeur's many allusions to his book, *The Rule of Metaphor*, in lecture 16. Where Ricoeur offers a general reference to secondary material, we have included the reference in the bibliography but have not added an endnote. Where Ricoeur offers a more specific reference to a secondary text but does not provide pagination, we have added an endnote citation. Interjections in quotations, which are noted by brackets, are by Ricoeur.

All endnotes are additions by the editors, and we have intentionally kept them to a minimum. The titles of the volume's parts and chapters are also the editors' creations.

The bibliography is extended and includes Ricoeur's course syllabus; a chronology of Ricoeur's writings on imagination; other works by Ricoeur cited in this text; and secondary works cited.

For their considerable assistance, we thank Vicki DiDomenico, LuAnn Driscoll, Phyllis Gentile, Karen Knochel, Darleen Mocello, and Barb Salopek, all members at various times of the Document Technology Center at the University of Pittsburgh School of Law, my home institution. We also thank Avinash Ram for assistance with the index and Fernando Nascimento and Trent Taylor for very helpful technical assistance.

My own thanks also extend to Jean-Luc, Fernando, Suzi Adams, John Arthos, Eileen Brennan, Morny Joy, Tom McCormick, and Roger Savage for reading and valuably commenting on the Editor's Introduction, for which I am solely responsible. During the editing process, my ongoing efforts to think through the intellectual contributions of this volume have led to several publications, which I reference in the Editor's Introduction at appropriate junctures.

It is a source of regret that, due to the length of the editing and publication process, coeditors Bob Sweeney and Patrick Crosby are no longer alive to witness the book's publication. Their absence does give me the opportunity to thank them for their individual contributions to the volume. I also take this opportunity to correct a prior error on my part when, as a result of a faulty reading and memory of Patrick's handwritten notation of his name on the recordings of the *Lectures on Ideology and Utopia*, I misidentified Patrick's name in the Editor's Acknowledgments to that volume. Patrick was the source of the recordings in both courses, and readers owe a great debt to him for his prescience in anticipating the value of these lectures.

Prior to his passing, Patrick asked that his contribution be offered in memoriam to a friend who died too young, Christopher Loren Albers. For my part, my contribution is offered in memoriam to both Patrick and Bob.

Editor's Introduction

GEORGE H. TAYLOR

The literature on the human imagination is now vast and continues to increase. The topic has received considerable attention not only in philosophy—the principal focus of this volume—but also in fields such as the arts, cognitive theory, law, literary theory, the natural sciences, psychology, religion, rhetoric, social and political theory, and technology. The present text, Paul Ricoeur's lectures on imagination, dates to lectures Ricoeur gave in 1975 at the University of Chicago. The lectures remain on the cutting edge of current concerns in their development of a theory of productive—and ultimately of creative—imagination.[1] Indeed, their ambition is to show the availability of a productive and creative—rather than simply reproductive—imagination and to argue for its commonality in human thought across the disciplines and so across such fields as poetry and the natural sciences. One of the great powers of Ricoeur's argument, common to his corpus, is his knowledge of diverse fields and his ability to capture and extend their deeper insights into a theory that is creative and innovative in its own right. The lectures should be of interest, then, not only to those more philosophically inclined but also to those oriented to other fields and seeking the insights of a theory of productive imagination applicable to their own arenas. One goal of this Introduction is to render the structure and value of the lectures in ways more amenable to those without significant philosophical training.

During the autumn of 1975, when Ricoeur delivered the present lectures on imagination as a course at the University of Chicago, he also delivered as a separate course a set of lectures on ideology and utopia, later published as the *Lectures on Ideology and Utopia*, where the imagination is a significant subtext. The year of 1975 marked as well the publication of Ricoeur's *La métaphore vive*, later translated as *The Rule of Metaphor*. As the chronology of Ricoeur's works on imagination in the present volume's bibliography attests, Ricoeur was quite immersed in the topic of creativity and the imagination throughout a good part of the 1970s in particular. On the basis of his published works, a number of scholars have written on the significance of the theme of imagination for Ricoeur.[2] Some have gone further, arguing for the centrality of this theme in his corpus.[3] Several of these writers have likewise lamented that Ricoeur did not offer a more systematic presentation of his general argument on the imagination, particularly the productive imagination. Ricoeur's lectures on imagination redress that need and provide this systematic architecture.

The lectures presented here offer his general theory of imagination with the goal of developing a distinct theory of the productive imagination. Ricoeur claims that the productive imagination is divided into four subgroups: the social and political imagination, the poetic imagination, the epistemological imagination, and the religious imagination (243). In addition to providing his general theory, the current volume elaborates both the poetic imagination and the epistemological imagination. Ricoeur contends that the *Lectures on Ideology and Utopia* develop his theory of the social and political imagination, and he leaves discussion of the religious imagination to other of his writings.[4] It is vital, then, to appreciate that Ricoeur's theory of productive imagination runs across both sets of lectures that he gave at Chicago in 1975. The combined structure of the two sets of lectures is quite masterful, just as its reach across different fields is very ambitious in seeking a common theory bridging seemingly quite different domains. It is an unusual thinker whose lectures in one term, let alone across years, encompass intellectual resources as diverse as Marx in one course and, in the other, literary theorist Northrop Frye and philosopher of science Mary Hesse.

This Editor's Introduction proceeds as follows.[5] Part 1 offers an overview of the lectures that follow. Part 2 offers a more delineated view of the themes in each lecture. In the sections prior to Ricoeur's development of his own theory of productive imagination, each lecture displays Ricoeur's engagement with the analysis of imagination of each thinker discussed on its own terms. Each of these lectures also signals elements of a theory of imagination from which Ricoeur will depart, whether to build upon, reject, or transform. In Part 2, the particular objective will be to show how each lecture contributes to Ricoeur's own theory, what that theory contends, and what is its significance. Part 3 returns to elaborate the interrelation between the lectures on imagination and those on ideology and utopia. A claim here is that the ideology lectures inform Ricoeur's more general theory of productive imagination not only in subject area but in substantive conception. Part 4 situates both the lectures on imagination and the lectures on ideology and utopia in relation to Ricoeur's subsequent published corpus, especially

Time and Narrative. Part of the underlying argument of this Introduction is that Ricoeur's work on productive imagination offers a decisive and lasting contribution both to his own corpus and more generally to reflections on the imagination and the productive imagination.

An Overview of the Lectures

The philosophic terrain of the lectures should not and does not obscure that Ricoeur's larger goal is to assess human productivity and creativity across various domains. The first part is composed of five lectures, in which Ricoeur assesses the theory of imagination in five classical philosophers with lectures on Aristotle, Blaise Pascal and Benedict Spinoza, David Hume, and two on Immanuel Kant. The second part turns to more contemporary studies and is divided into three lectures on analytic philosophers of imagination—Gilbert Ryle, H. H. Price, and Ludwig Wittgenstein—and five on continental, phenomenological philosophers of imagination—two lectures on Edmund Husserl and three on Jean-Paul Sartre. Part three consists of the final five lectures and offers Ricoeur's own theory of productive imagination.

In the first, introductory lecture, Ricoeur considers the topic of imagination in light of two coordinate axes. A first, horizontal axis runs from presence to absence (what he will later refine as the nowhere) and typifies the range from reproductive to productive imagination. A second, vertical axis runs from belief at the bottom—as in hallucination, for example—to unbelief or critical distance at the top. For Ricoeur, fiction is the prototype located in the upper right quadrant of these axes, as it offers an alternative to existing reality (to presence) and so is a form of the productive imagination—of the nowhere in existing reality—that can bring the new to bear into reality and at the same time is not bound by belief and so permits critical distance, an innovative vantage point from which to consider reality. Fiction runs across domains and is not reducible to a literary genre.

In his survey of the history of Western philosophy of imagination in the first and second parts of the text, Ricoeur assesses that all of the philosophers discussed (with some exceptions, as we shall see, in Aristotle and Kant) remain caught up in theories of reproductive imagination. Ricoeur builds upon Kant and to a lesser degree on Aristotle to argue for his own theory of productive imagination. The central problem in the history of the philosophy of imagination is that it principally relies upon a restrictive model where the imagination is derived from the model of the image in perception. (Ricoeur will challenge this theory of perception also.) Under this model, something real exists in external reality, and the mental image derives from and therefore is a weaker version of this reality. The image and the imagination, in turn, are reproductive, lesser versions of the real. By contrast, Ricoeur claims that the "nowhere" in fiction allows us to avoid the model of reproduction and bring something new to reality. In one of the concluding paragraphs of the lectures, Ricoeur argues:

> No critical implications concerning reality are implied in the picture, since the picture is the reassertion of reality in an image. The image is entirely dependent on an assumed concept of reality, since the reality of the picture is borrowed entirely from that of its original. Because, however, the fiction has freed itself from the rule of the original, it then provides a new aspect, a new dimension to reality. (285)

It will be the task of the lectures as a whole to detail this argument.

The Lectures

The first, introductory lecture opens with Ricoeur situating his undertaking as a response to what he typifies as the then current "eclipse" of the philosophy of imagination. The lecture moves quickly from this original historical location on to its principal task, which is to set out the hypothesis that the imagination can be assessed across the horizontal and vertical axes already discussed. As the lectures unfold, Ricoeur explicitly returns to the model of the two axes only infrequently. The more overt and continuing discussion in the lectures develops the contrast between reproductive and productive imagination, the subject of the horizontal axis, with the differentiation between belief and critical distance in imagination, the topic of the vertical axis, a more secondary and intermittent source of attention. The lectures offer a framework for a theory of the imagination that remains incisive and innovative in a contemporary period where what was the eclipse of the problem of imagination has itself been eclipsed by the outpouring of attention to the subject.

Lecture 2 is the first of the five lectures on classical philosophies of imagination that constitute Part I. The focus of lecture 2 is Aristotle's *On the Soul* (*De Anima*), which provides the West's "first coherent theory of imagination" (3). Aristotle's theory seeks to answer two questions: what the imagination is, and why it exists. In responding to the first, Aristotle places the imagination as an *intermediary* between sense impressions and intellectual intuitions (of the ideal Forms). While locating imagination on this scale has the positive result of sorting out imagination's distinctiveness, its negative consequence is that imagination is compared negatively to these two functions, each of which is understood to contain truth. Imagination may be false. If philosophy then and now places substantial emphasis on a capacity for truth, then the way is opened for a more disparaging view of imagination as capable of deception or illusion. As to why imagination exists, Aristotle places it within a larger theory of movement and causation. This location also leads to a more critical view of the imagination as a residue or trace of a movement or cause, an image for something else, something *as though* present.

As Ricoeur articulates, it will be his challenge, in part building upon Kant, to argue that the role of the imagination should be understood not as a static intermediary but as a function that acts as more dynamic *mediation* between sensations and concepts and so may have a "double allegiance" (19) with both of them and may indeed be a root of both. Kant will also be helpful in opening the door to a freedom of imagination that moves it beyond adequation to existing truth and allows it, as in the fiction, to disclose new dimensions of reality (30–31). Similarly, to circumscribe imagination within a model of causation does not allow the "nothingness" of fiction— the redescription of reality—because causality is oriented to "actual things generating actual things" (28). Late in the lectures Ricoeur will turn to Aristotle's theory of creative imitation (*mimesis*) in the *Poetics* as a more positive resource for a theory of productive imagination.

In lecture 3, Ricoeur discusses both Pascal and Spinoza. Although their frameworks are different, they share a concentration on imagination as deception, a false presence. For Pascal's Christian apologetics, the charge is to uncover imagination as a deceptive power. Imagination has power over an individual; the individual is in bondage. Deception is more than error, as error allows for correction. Deception requires unmasking of an illusion. Spinoza's philosophy of the fullness of being derives imagination from perception as a quasi-presence, the *as if*, again a presence that is false. Perception is emphasized as primary, and imagination is secondary, a trace. Spinoza's philosophy seeks to awaken us from our ordinary dream state, and imagination represents this dream-like state of life. For Ricoeur, both Pascal and Spinoza offer two of the most prominent characterizations of the role of imagination at the bottom of the vertical axis, imagination as belief, of being captured and deceived, a negative sense of the *as if*. They also narrow the range of imagination. For them imagination covers only its reproductive form. They collapse a distinction between delusion and fiction. Their theories cannot encompass the creative potential of fiction, of an imagination that is not deceived by belief. Moreover, for Spinoza the "nowhere" of fiction is not admissible within his philosophy of the fullness of being. His is a philosophy of presence, and imagination is but an *as if* presence, an illusion of presence.

Hume is the subject of lecture 4, and Ricoeur addresses two central themes in Hume's theory of the imagination. First, Hume represents perhaps the prototype for a philosophical inquiry attempting to derive the image and hence the imagination from experience. Hume begins with what he considers the most actual and present of experience, the sense impression, and the weakened force of the image is derived from and viewed in contrast to the impression's liveliness. If on the one hand a contrast exists between the vitality of image and impression, on the other hand the image also retains a resemblance to the image as a copy. The image acts as a representation. In Ricoeur's view, the potential variability in representation or reduplication opens the space for fictions in ways that Hume's examples seem to permit but that Hume does not adequately incorporate thematically. Part of the intrigue of Ricoeur's analysis here is his careful attention to Hume's examples to show how they do not comport with and so place into question his theoretical framework. In what we shall see to be a continuing motif the implications of which will unfold, Ricoeur also poses whether the impression is a brute fact or, instead, a construct.

The second theme in Hume that Ricoeur discusses is imagination's function of connection. The connecting power of imagination attempts to resolve both the nature of abstract ideas, where in Hume's view the imagination connects separate experiences, and causality, where the imagination as connection offers the solution to the problem of inference from one event to another. Hume seeks through the imagination to support the sense of order that is the subject of the natural sciences; yet at the same time he allows that the imagination permits flexibility in connecting past and future. In this context, imagination is no longer a copy of an original but a freer form of projection between past and future. The freer movement of imagination opens the space for the creative function of fiction, although again Hume does not acknowledge this space. "The productive function of imagination is always there even if without a name" (60). Hume's approach is also notable for its emphasis on imagination as movement, in contrast to the legacy of that part of the Aristotelian model where imagination is a stable intermediary. Imagination now is recognized to have a dynamic quality. What Ricoeur will find to be the decisive approach by Kant to imagination as a synthetic power is a theme introduced by Hume (49).

Lectures 5 and 6 on Kant conclude Ricoeur's discussion of the classic philosophies of imagination, with Kant's *Critique of Pure Reason* (the first *Critique*) the subject in lecture 5 and the *Critique of Judgment* (the third *Cri-*

tique) in lecture 6. In lecture 5, Ricoeur stresses that while in the first *Critique* imagination remains an intermediary between sense and reason, between intuition and thought, Kant decisively reorients imagination as a function of mediation, a function of connection between the poles. Imagination has a function of synthesis. Another major element of the first *Critique* is its restriction to *understanding*, to empirical objectivity. As a consequence, Pascal's and Spinoza's concerns about the illusory character of imagination as the *as if* are set aside as are the potentialities of the fiction. For Ricoeur, attention to the latter will revive in the third *Critique*'s turn to aesthetics.

The first *Critique* marks the advent of a distinction between reproductive and productive imagination. Prior theories had attended imagination as reproductive, such as a copy in Hume. In Kant, the imagination's synthesizing function between intuition and concepts is productive. It is productive even while remaining within the confines of empirical understanding and so, again, not encompassing fiction. The role of imagination as reproductive is reduced to the reproduction of appearances, as in Kant's example of drawing a line in thought, where the manifold representations must be recaptured one after the other. More prototypically, the imagination is productive and as such plays a *constitutive* role in the mediation between the sensible and the intellectual. "Nobody before Kant had thought of a function of imagination related to shaping our world of experience" (69). Characterization of objective reality is a judgment. "The judgment of perception—that this is a tree, that it has such and such characteristics—is an operation of the mind at a high level" (62). The notion of the imagination as copy is fundamentally displaced. Productive imagination is a synthesizing function that is "not at all an alternative to perception but an operation immanent to perception" (67). As we shall see, Ricoeur's own theory of imagination makes much of imagination's productive role within perception and the understanding of objective reality, and he will frame the role of imagination as fiction within this larger perspective.

A significant challenge for the function of the productive imagination is that it needs to encompass a faculty that is homogeneous with the very different domains it mediates, the intuition and the concept. Kant offers the schematism as the solution for this difficulty, but as he acknowledges and Ricoeur presses, the schematism offers only the rules for mediation: "the nature of the power of connecting is beyond the *Critique*'s grasp" (74). A profound subtext of the lectures lies in Ricoeur's attempt to take up this challenge. In lecture 5, for instance, Ricoeur questions the availability of what Kant describes as an intuitive manifold that is separable from the conceptual. In Ricoeur's view, the manifold is never experienced in this fashion but always intertwined with the conceptual. "[T]o put the problem in terms of starting from a manifold and then gathering it, this initial presupposition does not belong to any kind of experience that we may have" (70). Ricoeur argues for a stance that Kant anticipated but retreated from: the imagination acts not only as a mediating function between the sensibility and the understanding but may be "the origin itself of the two functions" (70). There may be a reversal of priority between the imagination and understanding. Productive imagination may precede the understanding; it may be "the source, the matrix, of understanding" (68). We shall follow these hints of Ricoeur's thesis in lecture 5 as they expand in subsequent lectures.

Lecture 6 both concludes and comprises the "culminating point" (75) of Ricoeur's discussion of classical philosophies of imagination. He turns here to Kant's *Critique of Judgment,* and he takes the free play of imagination as the "leading thread" (75) of his analysis. The problem of imagination in Kant is oriented to a contest between rule and play. In the first *Critique* the power of imaginative free play is subordinated to the system of rules that comprise the understanding, while the third *Critique* brings free play to the center. This "wild power" (88) of free play is perhaps most notably exemplified in the experience of the sublime. Yet both Ricoeur and Kant contend that it is misguided to focus in the third *Critique* on the power of imaginative free play alone. The contest between play and rule continues. In the third *Critique* imagination acts as the "interchange between the wild power of imagination and the need for a certain order, for forms" (88). Lecture 6 provides three lessons. First is the availability of imagination as free play. This is a form of productive imagination that goes beyond the confines of empirical understanding and extends imagination's domain. Although Ricoeur does not use the term *fiction* in this lecture, the free play of the imagination provides the space for the imagination as fiction to arise. Second, for both Ricoeur and Kant, we never are dealing with a "naked creativity" (78). Imagination is not a "formless power," because creativity always involves forms (84). Imagination is always enmeshed with "language, structures, and patterns" (88). We shall return to the significance of this thematic in Ricoeur's larger argument as we proceed. Third, building on Hans-Georg Gadamer, Ricoeur critiques Kant's interiorization of aesthetics, his reduction of aesthetics to a subjectivity of order. Although only briefly referenced in lecture 6, Ricoeur's own approach will undertake the challenge of rebuilding the unity of the theory of imagination, which Kant has split between cognitive and aesthetic functions (64), and show the imagination's ontological implications.

Lecture 7 initiates Part II and the first of eight lectures on modern theories of imagination. In this section Ricoeur seeks to compare perspectives in Anglo-American analytic philosophy and continental phenomenology, the latter the tradition from which Ricoeur springs. In the first section of lecture 7, he offers an introduction to Part II and indicates that he will attempt to show connections across the analytic and phenomenological fields at three levels. The first problem area involves "the description of the operation of imagining as such" (92) and will compare Ryle and Sartre.[6] The issue involves what is a mental image and whether the model of an original in reality and mental image as copy is appropriate. A second problem area will turn to a reconsideration of the relation between imagination and perception and lead to a rethinking of the nature of perception. The proposed discussion of Wittgenstein and Maurice Merleau-Ponty will show perception to be an interpretive process itself. In the third problem area, Ricoeur will analyze the contribution that images may offer to thinking through analysis of H. H. Price and Husserl. If the history of philosophy has rendered problematic concepts' origin in images, images may still be used to support and illustrate concepts. There is a separation between the philosophy of logic and the philosophy of mind.

While the central orientation of Ricoeur's outline persists as Part II unfolds, it changes in some significant details. Regrettably, discussion of Merleau-Ponty is dropped, perhaps due to lengthier than anticipated attention to Sartre. Themes that would have been relevant for development of Merleau-Ponty appear to resurface in the third part of the lectures, in the elaboration of the work of François Dagognet. The discussion first of the Anglo-American philosophers and then of the phenomenologists is maintained, but Price is developed before Wittgenstein and Husserl before Sartre.

What remains of particular interest in the opening pages of lecture 7, beyond its outline of the part to come, is its quite intriguing initial comparison of the methods between the analytic and phenomenological fields. For a long period, the two fields were widely considered as having very distinct orientations, and it is one of the tributes of Ricoeur's philosophy that in the present text as elsewhere (as in *Oneself as Another*), Ricoeur has attempted to bridge the gap. In this volume, Ricoeur acknowledges that the analytic tradition has concentrated on language, while the phenomenological tradition has focused on experience, yet he insists that the two approaches overlap "in the attempt both to describe the experience of what occurs in imagination and to describe it in a more proper language" (91). If the analytic tradition seeks to amend our language, the goal is more accurate description, an effort to be more faithful to experience. If phenomenology begins in experience, the concern is what is meaningful, of what we can provide an account. Our experience must be brought to language. Ricoeur intends to show, then, "how a phenomenology is implied in linguistic analysis and how linguistic structures are always implied in experience" (97).

As significant as is Ricoeur's consideration of the overlap between these two traditions, it is even more essential to recognize that the theme that Ricoeur addresses here is one that he takes as his own. "The experiential and linguistic sides of the question [of imagination] will be emphasized together" (91). We saw this point raised also in Ricoeur's lectures on Kant. As in our commentary there, here also we draw out these present clues to where Ricoeur is headed in his own theory of imagination in the third and final part of the lectures. As we shall see, Ricoeur will subsequently offer his own response to the three themes he uses to compare analytic and phenomenological approaches.

Ricoeur's introduction to the modern philosophies of imagination takes up the first half of lecture 7, and the second half is devoted to discussion of Ryle, a discussion that concludes in the first half of lecture 8. As anticipated, Ricoeur attends Ryle because of the latter's development of the operation of imagining. Ryle's discussion of imagination occurs in *The Concept of Mind*, a book more generally engaged in a critique of the concept of mind ("the ghost in the machine"). Ryle similarly rejects that images exist in the mind. The mental image is not a picture, so the notion of the image as a copy must be forsaken. Ryle argues that analysis must turn from nouns—the image—to verbs—how we image, how we imagine. The emphasis is on what we do, a behaviorist account. Ricoeur finds in Ryle a paradigmatic account of imagining as pretending, as an actor in a play or a child with a doll. We do not see an image; we only seem to see one. Ryle places seeing an image within quotation marks: we "see," which is something derivative from actual seeing, as pretending is derivative from and an indirect form of an actual activity. Imaging is a mock action.

Ricoeur views positively Ryle's account of imagining as an activity rather than something merely passive, a reception of an image. This accords with Ricoeur's views of the active nature of perception. He also appreciates Ryle's connection in imagination between not doing, an abstention from performance of the real activity, and an *as if* doing. As we shall elaborate, Ricoeur considers the conjunction between not doing and *as if* doing a fundamental problem in the theory of imagination (110). If previously in Ricoeur's discussion of Pascal and Spinoza we saw the *as if* as something negative, as imagination caught by belief, now the turn is to the *as if* doing as a more positive aspect of the imagination. But Ricoeur finds Ryle's own analysis too restrictive, on two grounds. First, Ricoeur criticizes Ryle's rejection of the imagination as having any form of a mental image. It is quizzical that a philosophy that appeals to ordinary use will simply eliminate the familiar experience of the image as a picture and so as something that appears. It is notable that Price, to whom the lectures will turn, departs from Ryle on this point. The question, Ricoeur argues, is how to arrive at characterization of objects that do not exist, such as the image, and the lectures will lead to the phenomenology of Husserl and Sartre to develop that issue. Second and similarly, Ricoeur objects to Ryle's recharacterization of "I imagine something" as "I imagine that I see." The former has an object, whereas the latter is propositional. The nonverbal element—the object—is eliminated by the verbal expression. Here again, Ricoeur wants to maintain a tension between the verbal and the pictorial—the mental object—that his own theory of imagination will pursue through recourse to phenomenology.

Ricoeur discusses Price in the last half of lecture 8. If in the history of philosophy the relationship between images and concepts has proven to be problematic, Price addresses instead an issue in the philosophy of mind: what it entails to think in or with images. He coins the terms "non-instantive particulars" and "quasi-instantiative particulars" as ways to describe particular examples that are not present, as the drawing or mental image of a dog, that help us think about what the term *dog* means. Price accepts, contrary to Ryle, that in imagining, something in a sense appears without being present in actuality. Price writes of images appearing *as if* they were things. He is comfortable accepting that images appear without being disconcerted by the fact that they do not appear in physical space. In subsequent lectures Ricoeur will seek to extend Price's insights through phenomenological inquiry.

In lecture 9, Ricoeur offers a very sympathetic portrayal of Wittgenstein. He draws on the larger framework of Wittgenstein's *Philosophical Investigations* to inquire more specifically into Wittgenstein's extended development of the nature of *seeing as* in that text. In many of Wittgenstein's examples, such as the famous image of the duck/rabbit, where we see an identical image successively as either a duck or a rabbit, Ricoeur finds Wittgenstein pushing on the limits of language. The examples generate new experiences that dislodge customary linguistic usage. Wittgenstein fights with language that has been significantly "shaped by its use in relation to manipulable objects" (126). Our language "is well adapted to the distinctions available for dealing with objects but not with the mind" (124). The section on *seeing as* offers an "indefinite struggle between language and experience" (125). We must seek a better language.

Ricoeur acknowledges that the theme of Wittgenstein's discussion of *seeing as* is not about the imagination. Nevertheless, the discussion remains important as the third topic of Part II: on the interrelation between perception and imagination. "[A]ll reforms occurring within the problem of perception have, in fact, their counterpart in the theory of imagination" (123). Consider, for example, Wittgenstein's claim that noticing an aspect— noticing that someone's face is similar to someone else's—"seems half visual experience, half thought" (135). The experience and the thought are interconnected but not alike, and it is a challenge for language to give an account. Ricoeur draws from Wittgenstein the insight that we must move beyond a division between thinking and seeing, since the process, Ricoeur says, is one "of thinking in seeing or seeing through thinking." One of the great values for Ricoeur of Wittgenstein is that unlike Kant, who seeks in imagination a third term between the poles of the intuition and the understanding, Wittgenstein begins from the third term, in *seeing as*, these mediating situations "where we are both thinking and seeing" (136). As we are continuing to discern, Ricoeur wants to explore how imagination engages in both the experiential and the linguistic or conceptual. Language and experience are intertwined. "We can no longer oppose imaging or imagining to seeing, if seeing is itself a way of imagining, interpreting, or thinking" (123). Ricoeur ultimately finds Wittgenstein limited, however, as his examples are all restricted to illustrations of reproductive imagination.

In lecture 10, Ricoeur begins the first of five lectures on phenomenology. His discussion of Husserl and more particularly Sartre will provide the foundation for his own phenomenology of imagination, developed in the third and final section of the lectures.[7] The initial pages of lecture 10 offer three themes that at once help define phenomenology and portray its juxtaposition with analytic linguistic analysis. For readers new to phenomenology, Ricoeur's lecture format may prove useful, as he attempts to explain with care the meaning of phenomenology to a more general audience. The first theme of phenomenology is one already anticipated: for phenomenology, the domains of lived experience and language overlap. The second theme explores the nature of phenomenological *reduction* (*epochē*), a suspension of judgment about "the pseudo-evidence of the given" (139) to focus on describing the lived experience. For present purposes, the significance of the reduction is that it engages in critical distance. This critical distance makes language possible; there is a separation between an experience and linguistic signs. The reduction reduces experience to the *meaning* it has for a consciousness. The phenomenological attention to meaning again interrelates experience and language. Phenomenology differs from analytic inquiry in that meaning is not related initially to statements but to experience: "meaning is already an element of perception" (140).

The third theme in phenomenology, on the concept of *intentionality*, is particularly essential for what will become Ricoeur's own analysis. The concept of intentionality addresses that all consciousness is consciousness *of* something. There is a correlation between the *how*—the act—of consciousness and the *what*—the object—of experience. Phenomenology claims this correlation applies in every dimension of experience. When, for instance, we experience fear (the how), objects appear as frightful (the what). The intentional correlation finds linguistic expression in the correlation of verbs and substantives. For Ricoeur, as we shall see, it is particularly illuminating to consider the intentional correlation between imagining and the imagined. Phenomenological analysis will allow for a correlation between imagining—the how—and the imagined—an object whose existence is suspended. For Ricoeur "the image is not the unreal but the like-real."[8] As Ricoeur reiterates, "This connection between *like* and *not* will be the center of the analysis" (143). The phenomenological correlation will help resolve issues that analytic philosophy could not satisfactorily address, such as Ryle's claim that imagining involves no object at all. The analytic tradition seems not to offer a transition between imaging and imagining, and the availability of that transition in phenomenology may offer a principal contribution to the theory of the imagination.

The latter part of lecture 10 begins Ricoeur's discussion of Husserl, which will continue through lecture 11. In lecture 10, Ricoeur focuses on Husserl's *Logical Investigations*. This volume joined similar themes in analytic philosophy rejecting the empiricist claim that concepts can be derived on the basis of their abstraction from images. Yet Ricoeur finds much of value in this text in a positive role for the image that Husserl's language betrays but does not develop. Similar to Price, Husserl recognizes the functioning of thinking in or with images. Husserl allows for the image's illustrative function. While the image does not generate meaning, it offers a form of support to meaning. It can help display the concept and show the concept's range through a variety of images. In the third part of the lectures, Ricoeur will return to the role of imagination as illustrative and correlate it with the question of what it means to imagine something. The role of imagination as depicting will be an innovative crux of that discussion.

Lecture 11 moves to discussion of Husserl's book, *Ideas*, and Ricoeur picks up the question of what it means to imagine or to have an image, the subject also addressed by Ryle. Lecture 11 helps set the stage for the lectures on Sartre that follow, as Sartre builds on Husserl to pursue this issue in a more delineated fashion. In *Ideas* Husserl argues that perception and the image must be sharply distinguished. This argument is based on an *eidetic* reduction, where the effort is to grasp experiences in their typological essences. Husserl claims that images and perception have quite different essences; there is a logical gap between them marked by different modes of givenness. "To perceive is not to have an image of the thing but the thing itself" (156). When, for instance, we mistake an object, the claim is that this was not a mistaken image but a mistaken perception. While perceptions are tied to beliefs in reality, images are linked to the conditional, to the *as if*. The *as if* will play a central role in Ricoeur's own theory of imagination. When we say that we see a centaur, we are "quasi-seeing" it, seeing it as an image. The centaur is an object, but it is an object that is not part of existence, an *as if*. The centaur is *inexistent*. The inexistent is a third category distinguishable from the existent—an affirmation of reality—and the nonexistent—a denial of reality. The inexistent has no referent in reality and so is a "nothing," but it is still an object and has meaning. As Ricoeur relates here and will subsequently pursue, a fiction is a paradigmatic example of the inexistent. Ricoeur will make much of the intentional correlation in imagination between imagining and the imagined as an inexistent object that is "nothing."

Ricoeur addresses Sartre in lectures 12–14, the concluding lectures of Part II. Ricoeur finds both the power and the limit of Sartre's theory in his paradigmatic example of the image of his friend Peter who is absent. The power of the image lies in its ability to help us distinguish, as in Husserl, between the givenness of perception and of imagination. With the image of the absent Peter we are led not to place the image in the mind but to locate it as a relation of intentionality to Peter, the absent object existing elsewhere. The same object is imagined and could be perceived if present. We are turned from a question of an image in the mind to two modes of givenness, in person or in image. Sartre acknowledges that in the image's mode of givenness, something appears. The challenge is to describe an appearance that is not a thing, and Sartre offers the concept of *quasi-observation*. "Sartre is saying with Price that we observe something but with Ryle that it is *as though* we are observing" (179). The object as no-thing is a form of nothingness. In imagination, there is an intentional correlation of the act of imagining—an abstention from reality—with the image, the imagined object—an object that is also an abstention from reality, a nothingness. Unlike in analytic philosophy, the phenomenological concept of intentionality allows a space for the image as nothingness. Ricoeur emphasizes that in the theory of imagination "[i]t may be that the fundamental contribution of phenomenology is to have made of nothingness a phenomenological feature of the imaginary" (181).

Ricoeur finds Sartre extremely insightful in extending Husserl and developing the notion of nothingness on the basis of the example of the absent Peter. Yet Sartre's limitations also rest with this example. Ricoeur argues, "The notion of nothingness is a cloudy term that covers several inconsistent cases" (195). Sartre contemplates that there are four modes of nothingness: the nonexistent, the absent, the existing elsewhere, and the suspended existence. The *nonexistent*—what Ricoeur more precisely terms the *inexistent*—is the fiction, something that is not real. By contrast, the other three modes all involve a real object that is not present, and notably they include Sartre's example of the absent Peter. Ricoeur challenges: "Is there not a radical difference between two dividing lines, Sartre's division between presence and absence and a division between the real and unreal? . . . [I]s the nothingness of absence of the same nature as the nothingness of the unreal, because the unreal is not only absent, but opposed to possible reality?" (195). The greater continuity between presence and absence is evident in their having the same referent, Peter as perceived when present or as imagined when absent.

Ricoeur's own theory of imagination at once builds on but also decisively diverges from Sartre in emphasizing imaginative "nothingness" as juxtaposing the real to the other than real, with the latter typified by fiction. We may draw together as follows Ricoeur's contribution to the phenomenological notion of intentionality as applied to the imagination. Phenomenology's *epoché* allows for a bracketing or suspension of existence. "[I]f we have a correlation between act and object in an intentionality, then if in imagination there is bracketing of the act, there must be some bracketing somewhere of the object" (102). With the concept of intentionality, we have the availability of an act of imagination—that is *as if*—and its object is also an *as if*. "[T]he *as if* of the act is also the *as if* of the object, and we cannot have one without the other" (116). The imagined object appears but as an *as if*. We have an intentional act "with nothing in front of it, but this nothing is a part of what appears" (111). Phenomenology allows for the idea of "objective inexistence" (102), of an "intentional object without existence" (100). The imagined object is "absolutely nowhere" (213). The image is not a thing; it is "no-thing." "[I]f the image is no-thing, then we must construe the concept of consciousness in such a way that it implies this relation to what is no-thing" (208). Ricoeur's insight into the implications of intentionality for a theory of imagination is a decisive contribution. By contrast, while Sartre's four modes of nothingness encompass a potentially broad theory, his orienting conception of imaginative "nothingness" as absence reduces the scope of the field too narrowly. Sartre's model falls on the side of reproductive imagination, because absence is predicated on and derivative from an original already present in reality.

Ricoeur finishes his analysis of Sartre by turning from the axis between reproductive and productive imagination to the axis between belief and critical distance. In the final chapter of *The Psychology of Imagination*, Sartre stresses the role of imagination as one of *fascination*, a magical relation to the image. We are captured by our *belief* in the image; we believe in the *as though.* As in Pascal, imagination has a deceptive power. Imagination here offers an escape from reality. Yet Sartre misses the space for imagination as fiction, where we "are no longer in danger of mistaking fiction for the real" (211). Fictions also avoid the problem of fascination, because in fictions we are not caught up in belief in the reality of objects, because the objects are inexistent. Fiction may in fact help us reorient reality in a new direction. While Sartre's theory is a theory of *reproductive* imagination, where it is vital to separate the image from reality, a *productive* imagination may permit a remaking of reality.

Thus far, Ricoeur's analysis of the intentional structure of imagination has discerned a correlation between imagining and the imagined, where the imagined is a "nothingness" that, going beyond Sartre, allows for its inexistence, its nature as other than real. This stage, Ricoeur claims, is only "a provisional stage, a first stage as the negative condition for remaking reality" (211). The space is opened for remaking reality, and then the task is to show how reality can be remade. "[W]ith inexistence fiction may contribute to reality" (212). It will be the principal challenge of the third and final part of the lectures to show how fiction can indeed contribute to the remaking of reality. By contrast, a reproductive imagination does not contribute to the real, since the original in reality precedes the reproductive image. "With the theory of absence, we are caught in the referent that is already there in the original. When the image has no original, then fiction provides an original of its own" (214).

Lecture 15 begins the third and final part of the lectures, which consists of five lectures on Ricoeur's own theory of productive imagination. Lecture 15 is largely oriented to introducing Ricoeur's path in this final part. In the opening paragraph, he boldly claims that "until this point we have discussed only reproductive imagination and not yet productive imagination" (217). This assertion may seem quizzical, particularly given his prior discussion of Kant on the productive imagination. But as Ricoeur will revisit, his assertion seems to be couched in line with Kant's limitation of productive imagination either to its place within existing empirical reality (in the first *Critique*) or to aesthetics as a subjective function (in the third *Critique*). For Kant the productive imagination does not have ontological implications. Later in the lectures Ricoeur will find a significant line of argument in Aristotle on what could be called the productive imagination, but that derives from different work in Aristotle than what Ricoeur discussed previously.

As the lectures turn toward productive imagination, it is important to appreciate that for Ricoeur the dividing line between productive and reproductive imagination is not stark. Although not much pursued in the last lectures, it is a hallmark of Ricoeur's thought, as he mentions earlier in the lectures and reiterates, as we shall see, in various forms in other works, that productive imagination entails elements of reproduction also. We cannot imagine without some connection to prior experience (54). Productive imagination always begins within existing language and conceptual structures. There is no such thing as "naked creativity" (78). Further, productive imagination may draw on and seek to bring to life hidden, unanticipated, or aspirational elements of reproductive imagination. The interrelation between productive imagination and existing structures will be evident in the final lectures when Ricoeur stresses the role of productive imagination as a work, a work that uses but seeks to transfigure existing structures.

In the opening pages of lecture 15, Ricoeur indicates that his thesis in the final section of the lectures responds to three elements in the model of reproductive imagination. (As we shall later pursue, we shall in fact discern that Ricoeur's own argument responds even more deeply to the three broader points of comparison raised between analytic and phenomenological approaches.) First, as already anticipated, Ricoeur will challenge whether an imaginative referent must already exist or can be a product of "nothingness." In fiction, "a new kind of reference may be opened thanks to the absence of an original" (220). Second, the question is whether the imaginative reference can be productive instead of reproductive, if it can through fiction open new insights into reality. Ricoeur proposes "provisionally" to call this reference a "productive reference." He does not give great weight to the term—it is "a problem for which I offer a name" (219)—and in subsequent work, for reasons we shall discuss, he will use instead the vocabulary of figuration. Third, Ricoeur's emphasis on imagination as a work will counter the standard emphasis on the image considered in isolation, as an object. The imagination as a work will help illuminate it instead as an activity. The word *productive* indicates material shaped by action (*technē*), and it is "only when images are worked . . . that imagination is productive" (221). Imagination as work conceives of imagination more as discourse than as word. As Ricoeur forecasts in an early lecture, the imagination as image has "imposed itself too much on the approach to the problem of imagination" (91). Ricoeur undertakes the challenge that a "phenomenology of fiction" (219), a "phenomenology of discovery" (223), can be accomplished.

It is true, Ricoeur relates, that there is some evidence of a theory of imaginative work in Husserl, in his concept of imaginative variations. Husserl's notion of imaginative variations is something Ricoeur anticipated he would address in his lectures on Husserl but never had the chance to do so. His first substantive elaboration of imaginative variations appears in lecture 15. Imaginative variation permits the testing of a concept through examples to identify what falls within and without its essence. In Husserl, though, imaginative variations remain reproductive because of an assumption of a concept's existing essence that the variations will elucidate. Even when Husserl turns to fiction, he does so for eidetic purposes, to deepen insight into given essences (154). Ricoeur will extend the concept of imaginative variations to be productive, using examples to consider the displacement and transformation of existing concepts. Although not discussed in lecture 15 but only in lecture 1, imaginative variations also retain significance as representative of the top of the vertical axis of imagination, forms of critical distance that are at the opposite pole from capture by belief.

The remainder of the lectures will proceed to develop two forms of productive imagination: the poetic imagination and the epistemological imagination. Toward the end of lecture 15 and then continuing in the beginning of lecture 16, Ricoeur initiates his discussion of poetic imagination by correlating the productivity of imagination with certain uses of language and invokes Gaston Bachelard's work as illustrative. The creativity of imagination arises from language as poetic. Bachelard is particularly instructive because he defines imagination as an element of language rather than of perception. Bachelard's perspective is also valuable because he introduces the notion of newness, of birth, elements that were not part of an image of something already in existence. This birth occurs in language and has an ontological bearing; it redescribes reality. As Ricoeur continues to insist, there is an "ontological dimension of fiction": "if we start with an image without an original, then we may discover a kind of second ontology that is not the ontology of the original but the ontology displayed by the image itself, because it has no original" (231). Bachelard himself, however, offers only a beginning stage in comprehending the poetic imagination, because his description of poetry itself remains poetic, while Ricoeur contends that a more precise philosophical analysis is available.

The bulk of lecture 16 develops Ricoeur's theory of metaphor, drawing on his book, *La métaphore vive* (*The Rule of Metaphor*), published during the same year as the delivery of the imagination lectures. Metaphor theory establishes that the creative use of language does not succumb simply to mystery but is capable of description and analysis. This lecture allows Ricoeur the opportunity to think through the consequences for a theory of imagination of his work on metaphor. Ricoeur argues that in metaphor something similar to the logic of discovery in science can be uncovered. If in the second part of the lectures Ricoeur attended how in Price and Husserl the image played a role in illustrating existing concepts, the transition in lecture 16 is

EDITOR'S INTRODUCTION xxix

to the role that metaphor plays in going beyond illustration to discovery, to extending and transforming concepts. In ascertaining how language itself produces images, Ricoeur's task will be to show more concretely through metaphor the interrelation between the productive capacities of language and of imagination. The operation of metaphor offers insights into the crucial role in imagination of *depiction*.

As readers of Ricoeur's work on metaphor well know, his theory argues that in the metaphoric attribution "X is Y," the metaphor operates not as a matter of an unanticipated naming ("Y") but through the unusual predication that interrelates X and Y and so involves the entire sentence. Metaphoric predication is an act, a movement, and anticipates Ricoeur's discussion on imagination as a work. The logical clash between X and Y as a matter of existent meaning allows a new, metaphoric meaning to emerge. Imagination plays a role in seeing the new likeness between X and Y that is the new meaning. "To see here is to produce, to produce seeing the likeness" (238). Seeing the likeness occurs despite the difference between the terms. The image, which Ricoeur had previously cast out as a weak, reproductive version of reality, now returns as a form of productive imagination through its role as *depiction*.

> Perhaps we could say that an element of depiction is implied in predicative assimilation. The moment of the image arises when we have not only the intellectual insight into the new appropriateness but we read this new appropriateness in a certain picture of the relation. The relation is depicted in pictures. Something appears in which we read the new connection. (240)

The verbal element in language is linked to the quasi-visual in the imaginative depiction of the new metaphoric relation. Ricoeur's description relates back to and now deepens the lecture on the Kantian schema, explicitly recalled in the present lecture, where the schema has elements that are both intellectual—conceptual, verbal, linguistic—and sensible—intuitive, visual. Part of the extension here is that the new connection is not only schematized but depicted, pictured. The productive imagination as depiction also recovers from Kant the notion of the imagination as having a dynamic function of mediation, which here too reiterates the nature of imagination as a work. Ricoeur talks of the imaginative depiction as *iconic*, "the display of the meaning by way of a depiction" (241). Drawing on Marcus Hester's extension of Wittgenstein, Ricoeur claims that productive imagination's depiction, its iconicity, is a form of *seeing as*. "To *think as* and to *see as* are correlative" (241). The linkage between the image and thought is not doomed wreckage, as predominant arguments in the twentieth century would contend but is, instead, capable of recovery. We *see* by means of the depiction, a creative depiction that occurs in language. Ricoeur's analysis here clarifies his early, cryptic comment that imagination belongs more to language than to perception (24).

Lecture 16 remains at the level of productive imagination of meaning, that is, within sentences. Lecture 17 moves to the question of how does productive imagination reshape reality. Ricoeur here addresses the problem of productive reference and describes it, building on Dagognet's work, as iconic augmentation. If the iconic addresses the productivity of imagination at the level of language—at the level of the text's *sense*—iconic augmentation opens imagination's productivity at the level of *reference*, of reality (234). For reasons we shall return to discuss, Ricoeur in later work drops the Fregean vocabulary of sense and reference; he retains that of iconic augmentation. Further, while his discussion of the iconic builds on *The Rule of Metaphor*, his attention to iconic augmentation is new in lectures 16 and 17. He will address productive reference in painting and scientific models in, respectively, lectures 17 and 18 in order to establish the predicates for an argument about the productive imagination of poetic language in lecture 19.

In lecture 17, Ricoeur asserts that what occurs in painting is "the paradigm for all kinds of transfigurations of reality through iconographic devices" (249). An artist's images are not less than reality, not reproductive; instead, they increase reality. Augmentation occurs through painting's iconicity, its quality as depicting. Iconic augmentation in painting adds a pictorial aspect of productive reference to the depiction seen in metaphor. Impressionism, for example, created "a new alphabet of colors capable of capturing the transient and the fleeting with the magic of hidden correspondences . . . [R]eality was remade" (254). The concept of iconic augmentation challenges not only the image as shadow but a "frozen concept of reality" (256). Because of the "shock of fiction, our concept of reality itself becomes problematic" (256–57). Through iconic augmentation, reality can be transfigured.

Ricoeur argues in lecture 18 that iconic augmentation of reality occurs also in the employment of models in the sciences. He types this as a form of epistemological imagination. In lecture 18 he pursues parallelisms for a logic of discovery between metaphor in poetic imagination and models in epistemological imagination. He reserves for lecture 19 discussion of the models' truth claims. Ricoeur finds theoretical models to be exemplary: "the description of the imaginary milieu of the imaginary object provides a formula that is then transposed to reality" (262). A new language is introduced, and the new language changes the domain to which it is applied, similar to metaphor's transposition of linguistic application. Ricoeur draws on Donald Schon's elaboration of conceptual displacement. With conceptual displacement, no overarching category encloses concept and application, and the new category emerges in the productive extension of the concept to the new context. A transformed concept, a displaced concept, emerges, again similar to the work of metaphor. In the process of application, we suddenly see the concept as something else, as transfigured. Ricoeur recalls here the relevance of Wittgenstein on *seeing as*. The "transposition, symbolic relation, or intimation" between concept and new application has already taken place (271). If there remains "a kernel of opacity that is the transposition itself" (273), thought can and does occur in what Schon describes as the three subsequent processes of interpretation, correction, and elaboration of the transposition, the new category. Echoing the concluding pages of both *The Symbolism of Evil* and *The Rule of Metaphor*, Ricoeur claims: "It's this possibility of thinking more that makes of the opaque element of transposition the birthplace of a new language" (273). If traditionally, as in Karl Popper, the logic of discovery analyzes the logic of a discovery that has already occurred, Schon helps to elaborate the logic of the process of discovery itself.

As suggested in the parallelisms Ricoeur draws between metaphor and theoretical models, his larger ambitions in lecture 18 and the transition to lecture 19 are to demonstrate the interrelation between poetic and epistemological imagination. While the terms customarily apply to different domains of application, they partake in a common dimension of thought. "To invent by a creative use of imagination is a general mode of the functioning of thought. The universality of productive imagination implies that we find parallels in the functioning of productive imagination on the sides of both poetry and science" (260). Without explicitly saying so, Ricoeur seeks to show here how the unity of the problem of imagination can be accomplished following the Kantian split between its cognitive and aesthetic modes. The analogy to metaphor helps evince the poetic nature of scientific models, and the more delineated nature of the scientific process of discovery helps unfold the process of poetic imagination, a subject Ricoeur addresses in lecture 19. Further, as Ricoeur also develops in lecture 19, knowledge—in the broad sense of the epistemological—rests not only within the sciences, for the poetic imagination itself extends our understanding of reality. It is mistaken to restrict the poetic and epistemological to distinct arenas. At the end of lecture 18, Ricoeur extends the argument to social and political action, where a similar nature of productive imagination is found in the utopia, the subject of his separate lectures on that topic, to which we return.

A unity exists "in the problem of semantic innovation, in knowing, in acting, and so on" (275).

Lecture 19 concludes the lectures. The beginning of the lecture continues the discussion of models and claims that the displacement of concepts, the subject of the prior lecture, also encompasses an extension of reality. When applied, the new language structures a new, refigured domain of reality. Through the model, "a new dimension of reality is acknowledged, recognized, and witnessed to" (278). The model is in turn valuable for resolving the problem of productive reference outside the scientific domain, because the scientific model offers a truth claim. Evoking language he develops elsewhere, Ricoeur claims that a productive reference, in science and elsewhere, rests not on truth as adequation to existing reality but as a manifestation of new reality.[9] In the last half of the lecture, Ricoeur transfers the implications from the epistemological imagination of the sciences back to poetic imagination. Hearkening to arguments raised in *The Rule of Metaphor* that subsequent to the lectures will become a focal thesis in *Time and Narrative*, Ricoeur builds on Aristotle's notion of mimesis to argue for the productive imagination of poetic language. While usually translated as imitation, and therefore a form of reproductive imagination, Ricoeur urges that mimesis, exemplified for Aristotle in the Greek tragedies, is instead productive and creative.

The lecture finishes with the example of lyric poetry. The example is fruitful because it seems the most extreme case of poetic language that withdraws from reference to the world and instead retreats into itself. Yet, Ricoeur poses, perhaps poetic language's suspension of descriptive reference in actuality says something about a "fundamental relation to the world, because the subject/object relation has been suspended there. It is the pre-objective that is poetically said" (283). Poetic language is not one of description but of evocation. The suspension of the subject/object relation permits an expanded openness to the ontological. As quoted at the outset of this introduction: "Because . . . the fiction has freed itself from the rule of the original, it then provides a new aspect, a new dimension to reality. The paradox is that a theory of imagination has to be connected with an ontology" (285). Ricoeur's vocabulary is replete with identification of the productive imagination as creative in this sense of manifestation (for example, see, 225, 231).

In closing this section on Ricoeur's argument in the *Lectures*, it may be helpful to summarize the volume's themes, including prominent subtexts. As we shall see, the significance of some of these themes will become more apparent in Ricoeur's subsequent work. Ricoeur's principal argument is that

Western thought has given preeminence to reproductive imagination—largely derived from a model of the image as derivative from and reproductive of external reality—while by contrast he wants to advance the availability of a productive, creative imagination that may disclose new aspects of reality. The reproductive imagination renders imagination as something lesser than reality and at its worst an escape or flight from reality (231). The prototypical example of productive imagination lies in fiction.

Ricoeur's argument responds to the three issues he raised in discussing the analytic and phenomenological approaches in Part II. To the question of what does it mean to have an image, Ricoeur extends the phenomenological notion of intentionality to develop the image as nothingness, the nowhere, the "no-thing." To the question of what does it mean to think in images, Ricoeur goes beyond the image as illustration to develop the model of depiction, which intertwines linguistic creation and the visual to produce something new. His model of productive imagination as depiction rests finally not on imagination as image but as work: an act of dynamic mediation. To the question of the differentiation between perception and imagination, Ricoeur argues (in contrast to Husserl and Sartre) that they overlap in "seeing as." Through imagination's productive capacity of iconic augmentation, reality may be transfigured. In this volume, Ricoeur often equates the productive with the creative, with the incorporation of some new dimension of reality.

In his development of intentionality and depiction, Ricoeur asserts that he is able to offer more precise analysis of how creativity and productive imagination occur. Although acknowledging, as we have seen, that a "kernel of opacity" remains (273), the productive imagination is not left simply as a mystery, as what Kant called "an art concealed in the depths of the human soul" (74).[10] If in *Truth and Method* Gadamer claims that artistic "presentation" in word or image offers an "increase in being," Ricoeur develops with greater specificity that this productive imagination occurs as depiction and the increase operates by iconic augmentation.[11]

As a form of mediation between sensation and concept, the imagination may not simply bridge these realms but may undergird both. There may be no such thing as a naked impression; the impression may always be informed by the shaping that we bring to the impression. This claim is also tied to Ricoeur's assertion of the overlay between perception and imagination. In the lectures in this volume, these themes are expressed overtly more rarely but seem part of the deep structure of his argument. In other of Ricoeur's works, as we shall pursue, the themes become more prominent and central and lead to Ricoeur's treatment of two correlative claims, on the inextricable symbolic mediation of human reality and on the constitutive nature of imagination across human reality. The imagination is not marginal or ornamental but permeates thought.

Ricoeur contends that the productive imagination breaks down the division between the cognitive and the aesthetic. The aesthetic—as in fiction—may manifest truth, including in the pre-objective. Ricoeur's attention in this volume and in *The Rule of Metaphor* to the dimensions of the poetic may serve as substitutions for his long-promised book on poetics. Again, the productive imagination applies across domains of thought, from the literary to the scientific.

If the axis between reproductive and productive imagination attends more the "object" side of imagination, the axis between belief and critical distance encompasses more the "subject" side. Imagination may be captured by belief, by deception, illusion, fascination. Critical distance—once more as in fiction—may escape being captured by the imagination and allow, through imaginative variation, critical vantage points from which to assess and compare existing reality.[12] An unexplored tension in the present volume may exist between the *as if* of imaginative variation—the hypothetical, possible—and *seeing as*, where the transfiguration of reality has already occurred. We shall return to this tension in discussion of Ricoeur's subsequent work.

The Lectures on Ideology and Utopia

We now turn, more briefly, to writings by Ricoeur outside the imagination lectures to show how he extends his theory of imagination in other works to locate the role of the present lectures within Ricoeur's larger theory of imagination and to deepen our understanding through this broader frame of what is at stake in these lectures. As previously noted, the *Lectures on Ideology and Utopia* deserve special attention because they were delivered in a separate course during the same semester that Ricoeur presented the imagination lectures. If the present lectures provide Ricoeur's theory of epistemological and poetic imagination, the *Lectures on Ideology and Utopia* offer Ricoeur's theory of social and political imagination. The two sets of lectures compose an integrated whole.

Ricoeur is quite clear in the *Lectures on Ideology and Utopia* that he finds basic parallels between his theory of ideology and utopia and that of reproductive and productive imagination. The "polarity between ideology and utopia may exemplify the two sides of imagination. . . . [I]t may be the dialectics of imagination itself which is at work in the relation between picture and fiction [and so between reproductive and productive imagination], and in the social realm between ideology and utopia" (310–11). Ricoeur generally conceives of ideology as a form of reproductive imagination, while the utopia is a form of productive imagination and hence, for our purposes, the subject of our greater attention.[13]

For our interest in comparison to the imagination lectures, we may divide the traits of ideology and utopia into their negative and positive capacities. Negatively, ideology and utopia as distortion and escape recall from the imagination lectures Ricoeur's attention to the vertical axis between belief and critical distance and the distortive capacity of belief, belief as deception and illusion. The adverse role of belief is also implicated in ideological legitimation, which Ricoeur famously describes as predicated upon a "surplus-value" of belief (201), a belief that goes beyond what the evidence warrants. The negative role of belief in ideology and utopia highlight as well a type of imagination that Ricoeur's model of the horizontal and vertical axes of imagination allows but does not directly address: a form of productive imagination on the horizontal axis that is also caught in belief on the vertical axis. From the perspective of their adherents, for example, political movements such as Nazism offered a utopian form of productive imagination that critiqued and sought to displace the then current political reality. (We see the contest between description of a view as ideological or utopian.) While, as we have observed, Ricoeur does include in the imagination lectures a portrayal of deceptive powers of imagination—as in the critiques of the imagination offered by Pascal and Spinoza—the negative side of the imagination is not his focus in these lectures. He is much more oriented to developing a positive characterization of productive imagination as fiction. The imagination lectures do not offer the systematic division of the layers of imagination as presented in the ideology and utopia lectures.

On the positive side of Ricoeur's depiction of ideology and utopia, we may emphasize three particular points for purposes of comparison to the imagination lectures. First, the utopia literally means the "nowhere" and as such presents the capacity as a fiction (310–11) that offers, as Ricoeur relates in the imagination lectures, "the possibility of the *nowhere* in relation to my social condition" (209). The best function of utopia is "finally the function of the nowhere" (310). Second, Ricoeur's discussion of utopia returns to what we saw in the imagination lectures as the tension between the two positive sides of productive imagination as *as if* and as *seeing as*. While in his discussion of utopia Ricoeur sometimes describes it as an "exploration of the possible" (310), a form of *as if*, the more frequent vocabulary in this text is that utopias can "shatter" existing political and social orders (see, for example, 273). The utopia can "break through the thickness of reality" (309), can "shape a new reality" (309). Just as Ricoeur's work on metaphor shows how we are not caught within the boundaries of existing language, so his work on utopia demonstrates that we are not caught within existing social and political structures.[14] When the utopia shatters reality, reality is transformed; we *see as* differently.[15]

The third positive aspect of ideology and utopia pertains to their structure as a whole. Ricoeur contends that Marx's notion of ideology as distortion could not occur unless there were "a symbolic structure of action"—what he also calls a "symbolic mediation of action"—that could be distorted. What is being distorted must be of the same symbolic structure as the distortion itself (139, 182, 258). Ricoeur considers the symbolic structure of action "absolutely primitive and ineluctable" (77). No social action exists that is not already symbolically mediated (258). Ricoeur identifies the symbolic structuring of action with the imagination (139). "The imaginary is constitutive of our relation to the world" (145, 3, 311).

As previously anticipated, Ricoeur's claims here deepen our insight into themes in the lectures on imagination that were at once subordinate in expression but also fundamental to the structure of his argument. The symbolic mediation of action vivifies the interrelation between perception—now social perception—and imagination. The imagination as constitutive extends this claim of interrelation to argue for the permeation of the imagination across human life.

Ricoeur's Other Work

In discussing Ricoeur's work beyond the present lectures and the *Lectures on Ideology and Utopia*, attention will be restricted to primary themes of the imagination lectures: the nature of productive imagination and the inextricable role and constitutive nature of the imagination in human life. We shall set aside, then, discussion of other of Ricoeur's later works on the imagination, such as his quite illumining discussion in 2000 of the historical imagination in *Memory, History, Forgetting*. While we may find in the historical imagination evidence of traditions the hopes of which remain aspirational and, thus, open to productive imagination, Ricoeur makes evident that the predominant focus of that volume is "the problematic of the representation of the past" (xvi). Instead, our principal attention will be drawn to Ricoeur's three-volume text, *Time and Narrative*. The first volume was published in French in 1983, some eight years after his delivery of the imagination lectures, and was the first book of his to follow publication of his book on metaphor. We shall also briefly discuss a 1985 exchange between Ricoeur and Cornelius Castoriadis, where Ricoeur surprisingly distinguishes sharply between productive and creative imagination.

EDITOR'S INTRODUCTION xxxvii

In considering *Time and Narrative* our task will be to determine what was gained in Ricoeur's thinking on imagination by its publication but also what was lost. The claim is that the imagination lectures, the *Lectures on Ideology and Utopia*, and *The Rule of Metaphor* remain distinctive contributions to Ricoeur's theory of imagination, ones not superseded by *Time and Narrative*. Readers of *Time and Narrative* are well aware that Ricoeur proceeds on the basis of a three-part model of figuration: prefiguration (mimesis$_1$), configuration (mimesis$_2$), and refiguration (mimesis$_3$). The notion of mimesis is drawn from Aristotle, and Ricoeur wants to argue that mimesis is not a form of reproduction—mimesis as imitation, as the term is usually translated—but productive. Ricoeur's brief discussions of mimesis in *The Rule of Metaphor* and in the imagination lectures offer a guide to the continuing thread of Ricoeur's argument that he extends to *Time and Narrative*.

Ricoeur's turn to the theme of figuration in *Time and Narrative* is explicitly a move away from the language of reference—what was metaphoric reference in the metaphor book and productive reference in the imagination lectures. The reasons for the change in vocabulary are several, but two are especially salient for us.[16] First, the terminology of reference derives from Gottlob Frege's juxtaposition of sense and reference, where reference applies to objects. By contrast, as we have seen, Ricoeur wants to propose the interrelation of perception and the imagination and the ability of fiction to bring new reality to life; the language of reference resists this expansion. Ricoeur replaces reference with figuration. Second, in his earlier work, including the imagination lectures, Ricoeur had considered it sufficient to describe the power of literature as a product of the work itself, while in *Time and Narrative* he rightly appreciates the need to add the role of the reader in bringing the fiction to life. If an author *configures* (mimesis$_2$) the text through emplotment, primarily it is the reader who *refigures* (mimesis$_3$) the text through reading it and in acting upon the reading. Ricoeur no longer considers *seeing as* to occur simply through the work of the text.[17]

A point we shall return to, Ricoeur's adoption of the language of figuration has much to commend in its implications for his theory of imagination. But the change also imposes some costs as well. A significant cost is the diminished attention to the role of the configured text to act upon us as readers so that we *see as*, experience a new reality. Instead, Ricoeur's emphasis is much more on fictions as acting *as if*, as "imaginative variations" that project a "world of *possible* objects of communication," a laboratory for "thought experiments" (*Time and Narrative* 2:101; 2:76, emphasis in original; 3:271). The nature of the text *as if* seems to leave refiguration more to a reader's decision whether to integrate the imaginative world that the text deploys into the reader's world. Ricoeur's analysis seems to give less weight and attention to those moments when—as in the *shattering* brought both by metaphor and the utopia—the text's power leads the reader to an experience of *seeing as*, of inhabiting a new world. Ricoeur is correct that the reader needs to be open to and engage with the text and so refigure it, but more significance needs to be drawn to how the imaginative text can also refigure the reader. We lose emphasis on the text's ontological vehemence, the "experience of being seized."[18] While the argument of the imagination lectures, *The Rule of Metaphor*, and the *Lectures on Ideology and Utopia* affirms the transfigurative possibilities of the text, its deep possibilities to recast reality through *seeing as*, the vocabulary and tone of *Time and Narrative* seem generally to project more optional and more modest reworking in the realm of the *as if*.[19]

The much more positive implications of *Time and Narrative* for our understanding of the productive imagination lie in Ricoeur's development there of a third form of figuration, *prefiguration* (mimesis$_1$). Prefiguration should be understood not as a layer of reality prior to figuration but as reality as always already figured. Prefiguration expands upon and deepens Ricoeur's elaboration of the symbolic mediation of action, a theme that, as we have described, was a subtext in the imagination lectures and a significant theme elaborated in the *Lectures on Ideology and Utopia*. In *Time and Narrative*, Ricoeur claims that human action "is always already symbolically mediated" (57). Literature configures "what was already a figure in human action" (64). The symbolic mediation of action entails that the symbolic is not imposed on action from the outside but inherent in action itself. We treat someone raising an arm not first as a physical motion and only subsequently on the basis of its symbolic meaning but more immediately as, depending on the context, a greeting, a vote, or hailing a taxi (57–58).

We can extend even further the implications of Ricoeur's attention to prefiguration and the symbolic mediation of action if we try to extract the underlying nature of figuration itself.[20] While Ricoeur pursues the nature of prefiguration, configuration, and refiguration across the three volumes of *Time and Narrative*, he says little in those texts about these modes' origin in figuration. As noted in our discussion of the imagination lectures, a continuing subtheme there is Ricoeur's interest in locating in imagination a dynamic mediation between intuition and thought. Whereas Kant sought to find a middle term that would bridge these poles, Ricoeur intimates in the lectures that he instead thinks that we never have the pure pole of intuition. We are already located in the middle term (136); every object and every situation are already structured (264). Human action is always already symbolically mediated. Appropriating Ricoeur's later vocabulary, we may say that human action is always already figured. Whereas Kant's system did not allow for a common root between the intuition and thought, Ricoeur, it seems, does find a common root and finds it ultimately in figuration. A theory of figuration at once deepens still further and renders more precise how the productive imagination occurs. On the more intuitive, sensible, impressional side of figuration, figuration shows how the productive imagination can arise and allow for emergent and potentially transfigurative meaning. Figuration here occurs as action, event, a work, something dynamic; it is creative and engendering. On the more structuring, conceptual side, figuration creates figures; it functions "to convey visibility, to make discourse appear."[21] The pictorial—iconic—dimension of metaphor and productive imagination occurs as part of its ability to depict, to offer a figuring.[22] Figuration is a matter of both language and the experiential, reiterating in figuration their common root. As emphasized in the imagination lectures, the interrelation between language and experience goes all the way down. The thesis here may be summarized in a Ricoeur statement in *The Rule of Metaphor*: "[T]o *figure* is always to *see as* . . ." (61). The claim is that this conjunction extends beyond the realm of metaphor to the symbolic mediation of human reality more generally. And Ricoeur will explicitly connect the activity of the imagination with that of figuration.[23] Figuration and the imagination are constitutive of human reality.

One brief final step closes our analysis. It concerns a 1985 discussion Ricoeur had with Castoriadis in a radio program.[24] This occurred some ten years after publication of *The Rule of Metaphor* and presentation of the imagination lectures and the *Lectures on Ideology and Utopia*. Quite strikingly, in this conversation Ricoeur markedly distinguishes between productive and creative imagination and while defending the first criticizes the second. In part, Ricoeur's argument is particular to the context of his engagement with Castoriadis, as Ricoeur criticizes Castoriadis's claim that absolute ruptures with the past are possible. Ricoeur's critique here is similar to his stance in the imagination lectures and elsewhere: transposition is never pure but rather a matter of restructuring and reshaping. We inevitably build on even as we seek to transform prior symbolic mediations of human reality. As we saw in the lectures, transposition is not formless but "proceeds from form to form" (85). Yet Ricoeur's criticism of the creative is a marked departure from his stance ten years prior and seems to reflect an increased modesty about the possibility of transfiguration that we have seen also at work in *Time and Narrative*. It remains a distinctive contribution of the lectures that it pursues what he calls there a "phenomenology of creative imagination" (250, 251), and the vocabulary of that text is replete with endorsement of the positive role of the creative imagination, a stance reinforced in his other works of that period.[25]

It remains unclear why Ricoeur did not decide to publish the imagination lectures himself. (Publication of the *Lectures on Ideology and Utopia* also stemmed from an external request.) As the bibliography to the present volume reinforces, Ricoeur spent several years and published a number of articles on the subject of the imagination in addition to developing these lectures and the *Lectures on Ideology and Utopia*. It may be the case, as discussed, that Ricoeur's focus remained on the arc between *The Rule of Metaphor* and *Time and Narrative*. The hope is that this Introduction offers evidence of the substantial significance of Ricoeur's contributions in this text both to the theories of imagination and productive imagination and to his larger corpus. One of the pleasures of helping bring this volume to life is the anticipation that the text will spark in its readers their own moments of creative insight and response as well.

Lectures on Imagination

1

Introductory Lecture

Our topic is the philosophical problem of imagination. In the first part of this lecture, I shall try to show the main issues raised in this inquiry. I start from the difficulties, obstacles, and paradoxes that plague the field and that perhaps explain why in the existing literature we do not have much of a philosophy of imagination.[1] Then, on the basis of these difficulties, I shall propose an itinerary for our inquiry into the problem.

I thought it would be helpful to start precisely from the eclipse of the problem, and the reasons for this eclipse, and then to unfold or expose the paradoxes that may explain this eclipse. We may speak of an eclipse of the problem if we consider the bibliography of the subject at the present time. There is nearly nothing that could be called a philosophy of imagination. This is why we have to pick up information from different fields. There are three main reasons for this eclipse. The first comes from the use of the term *image* in the empiricist tradition. Too much perhaps was expected of the concept of image. It was viewed as the solution to the problem of abstract ideas. An important part of our philosophical tradition relies on images to solve the problem of signs, abstract thought, and so on. The model for such a claim is the philosophy of Hume. For him, we may proceed step by step from the perception to an impression, to the image as a weak impression, and then through the association of images to abstract ideas. The image is the turning point in this theory of knowledge, since the claim is that in the image we have both some trace of experience and at the same time a distance from experience and therefore the possibility of making abstractions on the basis of experience.

This program has failed, and the main stream of modern epistemology is directed against this overemphasis on the image at least as it is invoked to solve the problem of abstraction. The opposite model can be found in the epistemology of Edmund Husserl and particularly in that of Gottlob Frege. In Frege's philosophy of mathematics and most especially in his famous article "Sense and Reference," to which I shall later return, he discards completely what he calls the *Vorstellung*, the representation, saying that it is private and changes with the individual.[2] By contrast, what he calls the object in thought is common to everyone. The object in thought is an ideal object, whereas the representation is a mental thing that is always shifting. We therefore cannot base an epistemology on the image. On the contrary, we must start from the logical gap between the image as changing and private and what he calls the concept as public, common, universal, and so on. This is not the exact language of Frege, but I summarize in order to present the problem. The fight against psychologism in modern epistemology has as its consequence the first reason for the eclipse of imagination as a philosophical problem. The image is no longer taken as a substitute for conceptual knowledge. So from one side, we have an eclipse of the problem of the image as the solution of the problem of abstraction.

If we examine the other side, that of psychology, we perceive another eclipse, another disappearance of the problem of the image and for one fundamental reason. Modern psychology is mainly behavioristic; it analyzes behavior, observable movements of the organism in the environment.[3] The image lies beyond its attention since, at least at first sight, the image does not appear as a behavior. It seems to be the contrary of a behavior. It seems to be a mental entity in the back of the mind, and for the behaviorist there is nothing like a "mind" that can be studied. Thus, the image appears as a mythical entity of the psychology of introspection. It is private and unobservable and so disappears from the field of inquiry. Later, we shall see that the problem of the image has returned in psychology in different clothing. The subject of inquiry is no longer the mental image as something in the mind but precisely as a kind of behavior. For example, when I take on a role or when I play a game. An important school of psychological inquiry speaks of imagination as mute role-playing.[4] So we must be prepared for what Robert Holt called "the return of the ostracized." Psychologists had ostracized the image. In both epistemology and psychology, the problem of the image, of imagination, was discarded.

A third reason for the eclipse of the problem lies in an inappropriate return of the issue in the literature on creativity. Literature about creativity has made important use of the concept of image but in a very loose way of philosophizing. The disdain accorded this literature by scholarly studies has reinforced the problem. The subject of creativity does not have a good reputation among professional psychologists and philosophers. This is not to say they are right, but we must elaborate a more respectable philosophy of creativity to fill the gap. The problem has been deemed either too psychological and not epistemological or too popular to be considered as a real philosophical problem in the strong sense of the word *philosophical.*

After having surveyed these accidental causes of the eclipse, let us look at the problem itself. Is there in the problem itself something that precisely could or maybe should bring it to a dead end? A first suggestion comes from a study of the word *image* itself. In his book, *Reflections on the Word "Image,"* P. N. Furbank examined English use of the last two centuries to show the occurrences of the word in different contexts. The word is unstable; sometimes it has a narrow referent, sometimes a very wide scope. Or consider, for example, that the Greek of Plato and Aristotle has several words that could be translated by *image* and have been translated by variants of the term. We have the word *eikon*, which has given us the word *icon*, as in Charles Sanders Peirce. Peirce speaks of the icon, either in the narrow sense of the Byzantine icon or in a more philosophical sense of the word that we shall consider later.[5] Or we have the word *eidōlon*, which gave us the word *idol*. Or the word *phantasia*, which was chosen by Aristotle as the technical word to designate what we now call imagination. So perhaps it is not by chance that we have a loose semantic field and maybe several semantic fields that can be considered as raising the problem of what it means to imagine or have an imagination. The Greek is translated into Latin in several ways, but it's the translation of *phantasia* as *imago* that has prevailed in modern culture. As we shall see, Book III of Aristotle's treatise *On the Soul* (*De Anima*) provides the first coherent theory of imagination, and the translation of this treatise into Latin provided us our concepts of the image and imagination.[6]

Yet while Latin narrowed the semantic field down to the word *imago*, modern languages have reopened the field. German, for instance, has several words that have something to do with image or imagination. *Bild*, the main term, means both a portrait—a painting—and an image, as when I have the image of someone elsewhere. But we also have *Phantasie*, which is used by Sigmund Freud, for example, when he speaks of the dream *Phantasien* (*Traumphantasien*). The word *Phantasie* designates the involuntary and more or less absurd emergences of images. Then there's the complex word in Immanuel Kant of *Einbildung*. *Einbildung* underlines more the active process of putting into an image, *Ein-bildung*. Because *Bildung* also means culture, there is a rich semantic field here, since there is the notion of acculturation through an image. *Bilden* is to shape, to give a form. In the concept of formation, there is the notion of cultural formation and in the same word formation of an image. In the *Critique of Pure Reason* (first *Critique)* and the *Critique of Judgment* (third *Critique*), Kant uses the concept of *Einbildungskraft* to emphasize the active process of the faculty of imagination, the power of imagination. It is this concept that has prevailed in philosophy without eliminating that of *Phantasie*. The coexistence of the two terms demonstrates a margin of hesitation in our language. Think also of other words that have to do with the *Vorstellung*, which has been translated by *representation* or sometimes by *presentation*. *Vorstellung* is not unknown to Freud, since in his famous article on "The Unconscious," he speaks of the *Vorstellungen*, the representations that are either ideas or affective representations. *Vorstelllung* therefore has a wider field than *Phantasie* or *image*. We have also *Darstellung*, presentation, the *Darstellung* of a project. We present something but in a schematic way. So we see the richness of the vocabulary surrounding the problem and the word.

English also has several words that cover the field. The word *picture* is closer to the German *Bild*. A picture is first of all a portrait or a photograph, so the physical representation of something else. But we also have *fancy* and *fantasy*. And then there's the word *image*, and it's interesting to see in the modern and the contemporary literature the variations on this term: *imagery, imaging, imagining*, and *imagination*. Each of these expressions refers to a specific approach to the problem.

I wanted to start from the vocabulary to prepare us for the fact that perhaps we have to do not with one function, one faculty, as the classical philosophers would have said, but with a cluster of problems. As we shall later discuss, Gilbert Ryle took this stand in his book *The Concept of Mind*, saying that we have to dismember, to disconnect, the field and to reassign different problems to different areas. This therapeutic action is typical of the approach of an analytical philosopher: we solve philosophical enigmas by dissolving a bad grammar. So perhaps we have to do with a bad grammar at the start. We shall discuss this hypothesis that there is not one problem but a cluster of disconnected problems.

Let me try to place a provisional order onto the uses of the word *image*. And then I shall propose a kind of mapping of the field. We shall proceed from this map, which will be more the map of the difficulties of the field than the schema of its solution. If we begin with ordinary language, when do we use the word *image*? We seem to have at least four main areas of facts or experiences. We may start, first, from the pictures that are in ordinary language what we call an *image*, an image *of* something. Immediately the word *image* is an *image of*. By *picture*, I of course mean not only paintings, drawings, and diagrams, but all kind of designs where a physical object stands for another object, because it reproduces its main trait, its main features. So one sure and very easily identifiable use of the word *image* is as a picture, a *representation* of something else that exists elsewhere and that is not presented but *represented*. This is the function of *representing* by the means of a similar miniature of the thing, the object. This function is already something very complicated, since we have, for example, a photograph which is itself a physical object that we perceive. But by perceiving it we are referred to something else, so in fact we have two objects in one, the object perceived and the other which, precisely, we say that we imagine. We imagine here on the basis of a similar drawing, a presentation in similar traits of the object that is not there. Already we have the notion of something standing for something else, which will be a very important philosophical problem. The image as standing for has a certain kinship with the world of signs, since it's the main characteristic of a sign to stand for, to be put instead of. But that is not all that the image as picture includes. Not only is the picture substituted for something, it stands for it. It makes present what is absent. It therefore gives a mental equivalent of the absent. This is the enigma of the image, to give the thing without giving it, to give it in the presence of its absence. Here we have already a very complex notion.

A second group of images leads from the first, although it can be identified with less coherence. In the second group, the image is the arbitrary evocation of absent things, without the support of a physical photograph, picture, painting, drawing, or diagram. This is what we usually call a mental image, to have the mental image of something. Most of our memories are of that kind. We may say in a loose sense that we have a picture of a past event, but it is not a photograph, since there is no physical support. It is merely mental. This second group is the most controversial, mainly in epistemology and psychology, since it's on the basis of these alleged mental images that the problem of abstraction has been solved in the empiricist tradition. What characterizes the concept of image here is the absence of a thing, the representation without a physical support and only on the basis of a mental image. We then ask whether there is not something in the "mind" that could be like a kind of picture, or is it rather a trick that the word *image* plays on us to transfer the physical picture into a mental picture. Perhaps the mental image is instead a construct; we construct a kind of mental equivalent of a physical picture as if we had in the mind a kind of photograph of things. This is a very difficult problem. And in most cases, and this constitutes the unity of this group, we may evoke these images more or less arbitrarily. That means that if we want, we can evoke them. So the "if we want" is important for the constitution of this group. This is in opposition to the fourth type that I shall present later.

As we turn to a third group, we may say that we are proceeding step by step but with gaps between the examples. The third group is comprised of fictions, and this is a very interesting group for two reasons. First, it's also an evocation of nonactual things, but in the fiction the things evoked are not only absent but nonexisting.[7] For example, the characters of a novel are of this kind. We have to do with nonbeings that have the ontological property of not existing and nevertheless of being objects. The idea of an object that at the same time is a nothing is a very peculiar entity. This group is looser still than the second one. Only the first one has some coherence. I present them in the order of their looseness, of their decreasing coherence. This group is looser since it covers not only literary fictions but such things as dreams. We may speak of a dream as a fiction in the sense that it presents the scene of a mental theater. These images abound in Freud, for example, when he speaks of an infantile scene or the neurotic scene and so on. They are like literary fictions, but they are linked to sleep. This must not be forgotten, because if there is one psychological characteristic of sleep, it's that we don't perceive. In sleep we live in a world that has lost the contrast with reality; the dream occupies the whole. By contrast, when I read a novel, I live in both the fictional and real worlds together. I am caught up in the world of the fictional character, but at the same time I know that I am sitting here. It is an important element of the act of reading to belong to both worlds, while in the realm of dreams the absence of a contrast with reality introduces an important feature that we shall also find in the fourth group: belief. We believe in what we dream. It's an uncritical belief. I am in the world, but I dwell in the world of my dream. In contrast, literary fictions, fictions properly said, imply a sense of the invention of the drama. Consider the definition of the *muthos* by Aristotle in the *Poetics* when he speaks of the tragedy (1450a 80). (He has in mind the Greek dramatic tragedy.) He says that what makes the tragedy is first of all the construction of a plot, of a fable. The possibility of construing plots or fables for artistic purposes is a very important problem in the theory of imagination. But it's difficult to put that under the same title and even the same subtitle as dreams. As we proceed in this survey, we become more and more suspicious of whether we have to do with only one field. In any event, the second significant characteristic of fiction is its contrast with reality, whether that contrast is recognized, as in reading a novel, or not, as in dreams.

The fourth and final group of images is comprised of illusions in general. These include hallucinations in the pathological sense, but there are also illusions without pathology. What is common to pathological and nonpathological illusions is that they are false for somebody else or for us later, according to a subsequent, self-critical reading. What is proper to this group is that the belief in the image's reality obscures the distinction between absence and presence, between reality and unreality. We have our images *as though* they were present. It is the *as though*, the *as if* that constitutes the central kernel of this group. We have an object that others or we ourselves later will deem absent, but we have the deceptive belief that it exists. We may express this as the category of the pseudo, the quasi, the *as if*, the *as though*, the absent as though present, the unreal as though real.

It may be that several other kinds of examples could be provided.

Nevertheless, I would like to try to proceed from this enumeration to a certain construct that would not close the inquiry but would propose at least a certain order of inquiry. And at that point I want to propose a certain mapping. I have only started to do that, but in the form of an enumeration, not a construct. What complicates the difficulty in creating a construct is that we have several pairs of oppositions. I wonder whether we could not place the phenomena that we have surveyed around two axes: an axis of presence versus absence and another axis from belief or fascination to unbelief or critical distance. We shall add more criteria later but start with this double scale of presence and absence and belief and lack of belief. The axis of presence and absence concerns the side of the object, what, in the vocabulary of Husserl, we could call the noematic side, while the axis of belief and lack of belief constitutes the subjective side, what Husserlian language would call the noetic side.

Consider first a horizontal axis from presence to absence. Major philosophies have followed this axis very frequently, putting the image toward one end or the other. What do we have at the first end? We have essentially the idea that the image is the *trace* of a previous perception. This is an important concept in the philosophical tradition, about whether we take this trace as a physiological, perhaps cortical, phenomenon, something that can be stored. Under this view, the trace is therefore in fact a reality but as the shadow of a reality or the residue of a reality. In our reading of Aristotle, we shall see the idea that an image derives from a perception. We cannot have a visual image if we are blind. There is a certain dependence of the imaginative fields on the sensory fields. We have as many kinds of images as we have senses. A certain kinship between the image and the perception is held to be unavoidable. The attempt is to treat the image as just as real as the perception but merely as weaker or less present but nevertheless present. In Aristotle, the *phantasia* is derivative from the perception. Also in David Hume, the image is a weakened impression. And for Benedict Spinoza, there are no nonbeings; everything is actual. Since for him everything is actual in a philosophy of full actuality, it is very difficult to find a place for the image, so the image must be a kind of presence or the residue of a presence. We have forgotten that there was a presence and then we built a world of images. Spinoza's philosophical attempt was to reduce the image to some actual happenings in a completely real world, a world without potentiality, a world with only the dimension of actuality. Aristotle, Hume, and Spinoza are the three main examples in which the image is put as close as possible to the left side of the axis. This first pole defines imagination as mainly reproductive.

Very close to this pole, we may put all residual perceptions, portraits, copies, and diagrams. They are real but of a second order. They derive their content from reality, but it is as if the content of reality is transferred into another sphere, the sphere of absence. It's not the absence that is emphasized here, though, but the fact that it stands for a presence. Memory images are mainly of this kind, at least the less elaborate kinds of memory images, those which burst out. Think of the examples we find in Proust, the sudden explosion of the image as a part of the past which reemerges, a kind of rejuvenation of past experience.

At the opposite end of the axis, the image is emphasized as a function of absence.[8] In our enumeration we met this problem where the image was considered as precisely the counterpart of presence, as if the whole of reality were denied by the image. Suddenly there is something that has no place in the whole of reality. The image here is a kind of threat to reality. In my other lectures where I study utopia, we may say that in the representation of social existence, the function of utopia here comes as this denial of reality as a whole through the possibility of putting beside or outside of reality something else.[9] It is the something else, the something other than real that constitutes the enigma. The more imagination is productive, the more this function of absence is emphasized.

In fact, we could say that this function of absence is emphasized from the beginning on this axis. Even a trace is not an image as long as it is merely the residue of a face of something. For there it is still something, the residue. What makes the trace an image is that it stands for something else. The element of absence is already there. The zero degree of absence cannot be found, because with the zero degree we have no longer an image but a mere physical trace, which is already a something.[10] If we see some footprints in the snow, it is something, but it's only for somebody who interprets it as what has been left by somebody who walked there that it is an image. It is an image only for the one who interprets it as left by or as *re*presenting the presence. But the trace as such is a perceptual thing. It is not an image. We have a scale of negativity from the trace as trace to the fiction at the other end, where the element of presence is reduced to nothing.

We could put along this axis according to the degree of negativity most of the phenomena that we have covered, starting at one end from the trace, then what is the most like a trace in our use of images such as copies, which sometimes we cannot distinguish from the thing itself. A good photocopy is nearly the same as the original. Then come portraits, diagrams, free compositions, and finally fiction. For my part, I should put in the middle of this axis the so-called mental image, because it is in fact a point of balance or equilibrium between trace and fiction. This axis is the axis of reproductive and productive imagination. The reproductive tends toward the trace and the productive tends toward the fiction.

We cannot work, however, only with this one axis. An important factor has been set aside that was so important in the case of illusion and hallucination: the *as though*. If we had only this first axis, we might think that when we proceed from the positive pole to the negative, we proceed also from kept or caught presence to free absence. But that is not true, since we may have a pure absence that has the illusion of presence. We must therefore introduce a second axis, which would be the axis of awareness, awareness of the negative factor, of the phenomenological gap between presence and absence, between real and unreal. This is why I spoke of the subjective, noetic side of the phenomenon in order to speak of the way in which we are involved in the process. We are implicated in it. There are degrees of our implication or commitment in the image. And the degrees of commitment are not necessarily parallel to the degree of negativity of the image.

We may express this second axis according to the degree of consciousness represented. If we put it in a vertical order, at the bottom of the scale we have the image mistaken for reality. We are caught in the world of the image and believe in it, mainly when this belief is not negated by something contradictory. We shall see that this will be the main argument of Spinoza, that as long as an image is not denied by another image, we believe in it. So the first stage on this axis is belief in the image, and it arises especially when there is no critical assessment by a contrary reality, as when we dream. The collapse of perception, the lack of a perceptual counterpart, constitutes the dream as a dream. Some even define dreaming in psychological terms as the collapse of perception. The image occupies the whole place, just as a gas occupies as much room as offered to it.

Many psycho-ethical treatments of imagination rely on this confusion between image and reality, the *as though*. We shall see that this trait has been emphasized particularly by Blaise Pascal in his famous attack on imagination as a master of lie and illusion. Here imagination is considered less as a function than as a power: we are under the power of imagination. We undergo the images. There is a concept of a dynamic function of imagination. In the seventeenth century, at least in the French and German tradition of philosophy from René Descartes to Spinoza through Gottfried Leibniz, the word *imaginatio* covered more or less this field. What was emphasized was not so much presence or absence but confusion or distinction, the belief invested in the imagination. This is why, in the vocabulary of the seventeenth century, *imaginatio* very often covered what we should today call perception as well as imagination. In both cases, we are under the power of the thing. What is emphasized is not presence or absence but the state of bondage. This is why we can speak of a psycho-ethical approach to the problem. We are under the spell of the thing. Even a theological estimation could be mixed in here. The *imaginatio* is the realm of the unredeemed person, the person as sinful. For Pascal there's no doubt that the world of flesh is identified with the image. In Spinoza, the first and lowest degree of knowledge—imagination—is precisely the one in which I am passive and not active, not a part of the universal causality but merely an effect of this causality. In this period the emphasis is not on presence versus absence but on belief versus critical distance.

At the other end of this axis, it is the critical distance to reality that is emphasized. The image itself becomes an instrument of the critique of reality. Many writers have used novels as a kind of social critique. The presentation of another way of life or another mode of existence allows us to see our world from afar. We are transported from one world into another world. It is this exile from reality that constitutes, then, the strategy of imagination. Social imagination in utopia, for example, would be used in that way. Without considering further the social uses of this critical imagination, we may think of some uses of imagination not only in literature but in epistemology, where imagination belongs to this critical approach. I have in mind the concept of imaginative variations in Husserl, when in the First and Second *Logical Investigations* he speaks of the imagination as a tool to explore the yet non-real but potential actualization of a given essence. He speaks a language of essence. The way to disconnect the intuition of essence from mere perception is to add to perception the other possibilities implied in the essence and to explore them by the means of imagination. Imagination then becomes a way for exploring the scope of a concept, of an idea, of an essence, of whatever it may be. What is important here is the capacity of neutralization implied in the image, what I call the denial of reality as such. It is not the denial of this or that reality but a denial of the whole of reality. It is the capacity therefore to emigrate from the real into the irreal. This capacity of emigration is the fundamental trait. We see how it's strange that the same notion can oscillate from what Jean-Paul Sartre sometimes calls, in *The Psychology of Imagination*, magical imagination to, at the other end, a capacity for neutralization. My suggestion is that what we call imagination is in fact a space of variation according to several ranges of possibilities. To order this field could be the first task of the philosopher.

Let me represent the ordering suggested by the two axes in another way and consider not only each line but also the quadrants that the combination of these axes create (fig. 1). (I propose this ordering but do not want to trap us in the figure created. A figure may be helpful or harmful in different cases.) If the horizontal axis moves from presence toward absence and the vertical axis upward from belief toward a neutralizing unbelief, then the side to the left of the vertical axis represents reproductive imagination. In the lower left quadrant we have the trace. It is a form of reproductive imagination that lies below the divide between critical distance and belief on the side of belief and also falls on the side of presence rather than absence. It's twice defective, so to say, since it is lacking both in absence and in critical distance. The most unfortunate theories of imagination proceed from this overemphasis on the problem of the trace, because in the trace we have as little absence as possible and as little power of neutralization as possible.

In the upper left quadrant, I would put the portrait or the picture. It is still reproductive and so falls on the side of presence or actuality, but it has an element of critical distance. If we are not insane, we usually don't confuse a photograph with the real person. That's not always the case, however. In, for example, some advertising or in some movies, the power of the image is so great and the element of belief is so strong that we cannot prevent ourselves from having the same kind of feeling we would have with the real thing. I would put those examples very low in the upper left quadrant that is typi-

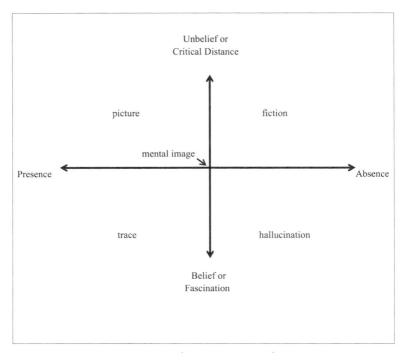

FIGURE 1 Ricoeur's Board Drawing (from editors' notes)

fied as a whole by the picture. The portrait is interesting because it's close to a trace, but it always has a critical distance from the thing being pictured. Critical distance may be reinforced by a trait such as irony, for instance in caricature, where we have a critical distance from the image.

In the lower right quadrant, we could put hallucinations and all the forms of illusions in which the element of belief is strong. I would put in the upper right quadrant fictions. For me fictions have the real function of imagination, since they have the elements of both absence and critical distance. We may therefore say that trace and fiction are absolute opposites. This preference for fictions is of course a choice, but what interests me is a theory of fiction, a theory of fiction as opposed to a theory of trace, a theory of fiction as absolutely and unrelentingly opposed to a theory of portrait and of illusion. Here I want only to invite us to reflect on the spatial variation that constitutes our problem and merely to map this space.

We shall proceed in the following way. In the first part of the lectures, we shall examine some classical texts on imagination, and in the second part, we shall explore some contemporary ones. I shall start from three classical texts. First, Aristotle's *On the Soul* (*De Anima*), Book III, chapter 3. These pages discuss *phantasia*, so it's interesting to see the first attempt to put a certain order to the term *imagination*. In our framework, we could put *phantasia* in the lower left quadrant. Aristotle will himself try to place the image within a scale, but it's a quite different scale, from sensation to concept. The epistemological orientation to the problem taken by Aristotle will last in fact until Kant's third *Critique*, his *Critique of Judgment*. Kant's third *Critique* will be the first attempt to disconnect the problem of imagination from truth, from the evaluation of truth, and then to deliver imagination from the accusation of inadequateness. The concept of inadequate images, inadequate ideas, will come in fact from the problematic of Aristotle.

Then I propose that we read in Spinoza's *Ethics*, the Second Part, Propositions 16 and 17 and the following Note (the Scholium). It's mainly in the Notes that Spinoza speaks in more popular or psychological terms. We shall take Spinoza as a good example of a philosopher who will try to do without negative terms, only with actual actuality, the fullness of actuality. It's very difficult to introduce something negative in this, and the way in which Spinoza does so is very striking. At the same time his is a narrow approach, because it considers only the *as though* of the image. The *as though* is the equivalent of actuality in the inactuality of the image. I shall also propose to read some of Pascal's *Pensées*, where we have the famous declaration of imagination as the master of illusion and so a treatment of imagination in a more or less ethical sense. Aristotle, Spinoza, and Pascal are the three main texts of the classical tradition on image and imagination before Hume and Kant.

We shall then devote some sessions to Hume and Kant. The turning point here will be that Aristotle considers imagination as an intermediary between two poles, an intermediary between intuition and an intellectual grasp in the concept. This intermediary is positioned, however, as a static one. By contrast, first with Hume but mainly with Kant will appear the concept of synthesis. Then we have the concept of a dynamic intermediary or a mediation. Instead of imagination being merely a static intermediary function, it will be a mediating function. This treatment will come more or less to dominate the whole field. With Kant the theory of imagination is divided into two pieces. In Kant's first *Critique*, the *Critique of Pure Reason*, the imagination is a part of the process of knowing. It's swallowed up in the movement toward objectivity; it's a part of the judgment of objectivity. Imagination's function of absence disappears, since it's the function of the judgment about objects that is emphasized. We shall see how in the third *Critique* the concept of free imagination, a free play of imagination, will appear but within a new framework, the framework of the critique of judgment that will be mainly a theory of aesthetic judgment. Here imagination takes on an autonomy from the problem of objective truth, of truth as adequation. The accusation of imagination's inadequateness will be lifted for the first time. At the end of the lectures I shall attempt to enlarge this breach.

Before turning to my own contribution, the second part of the lectures will explore some other contemporary approaches to imagination, such as some new psychological approaches that are very interesting precisely in their attention to the playful use of imagination.[11] The concern here is no longer the problem of hallucination but, on the contrary, an attempt to master reality through play and therefore to consider the concept of taking a role. I shall also use some approaches through language in the theory of metaphors and models and consider how by language we build imaginative constructs in order also to explore reality.

Then I shall reserve some time at the end of the lectures for a more personal contribution to a phenomenology of fiction. At that point these lectures will parallel my other lectures on ideology and utopia, since what I undertake in the other lectures is an inquiry into social imagination, both as deceiving and as exploring, as subversive and, in the case of ideology, as hiding where and who I am. The space of variation that is covered by social imagination from ideology to utopia is exactly similar to the space of variation we examine here. What in fact seems lacking in the sociology of culture is a phenomenological tool to explore these several possibilities of imagination.

PART ONE
Classical Readings

2
Aristotle

In this lecture we shall explore Aristotle's discussion of imagination in Book III, chapter 3 of his treatise *On the Soul* (*De Anima*). This discussion is grounded in a philosophical decision taken at the beginning by Aristotle. Imagination is placed at a certain level in a scale of faculties, a scale ruled finally by the concept of truth. Imagination is caught in a network at the wrong place. The first obstacle, then, to a full recognition of the creative process of imagination lies in philosophy's general trend to link the problem of imagination to that of perception on the one hand and the concept on the other hand. Imagination is treated as a derivation of perceptual experience or as a weak form of conceptual thought. The paradigm of this kind of approach may be found in Aristotle.

Aristotle's philosophical choice is already represented in the choice of a word, the Greek word *phantasia*, which is translated as imagination. The choice of the word says much about the purpose of Aristotle, because in Greek another word was available, which we find in Plato. It was the word *eikon*, which is linked to a quite specific problematics in Plato. *Eikon* is translated either by *image* or, sometimes, as in rhetorical frameworks such as Plato's rhetorical texts, by *simile* or *comparison*. The word *eikon* has the same amplitude as the problematic of imitation in Plato, and that amplitude is nearly without limit, since pictures imitate visible things and visible things imitate paradigms of ideas, and, to a certain extent, all ideas sharing in the supreme Idea of the Good could be said to imitate the Good. Second, the word *eikon* responds to an inquiry about what is really real, *ontos on*. The degrees of iconicity express the degrees of distance from what is really real. We have in Plato a kind of negative scale from the absolutely real, the Good, to that which is less and less real, and the *eikon* appears on this negative scale. In that sense we may speak of images of images, since a statue, for example, is like a human being which in turn is like the Idea of the human, and Ideas in turn owe their actuality to the Idea of the Good. Therefore, the problem in Plato was to approach the Idea through the large, broad concept of imitation according to the ontological degrees of actuality. There is a certain synonymy between *eikon* and shadow. The image is a kind of shadow of reality, something less than. This lack of ontological consistency between the Idea and the image is therefore fundamental.

Aristotle tried to break with this philosophical framework, but we shall see not so far finally to the extent that the term of comparison will be always to something more true than the image. Nevertheless, the choice of the word *phantasia* by Aristotle expresses the will to transfer the problem within a new conceptual framework, that of the treatise *On the Soul*, our first treatise on psychology. The word *psychology* comes precisely from the Greek *psuchē*, which means not only the soul as the living principle of animate beings but also the principle of knowledge and the bearer of emotions and so on. In our text this double task of the treatise is expressed in the first lines of chapter 3: "There are two distinctive peculiarities by reference to which we characterize the soul—(1) local movement and (2) thinking, discriminating, and perceiving" (Aristotle 1966, 586; 427a 16–18).[1] The reference to "local movement" indicates that the soul has the function of animating. It is the *anima*. It is animating a body as an internal principle of local movement. The animal moves, and this is a function of a soul. The soul also discriminates, thinks, and perceives.

The organization of the larger Book III to which this chapter belongs obeys the principle of a hierarchy, a hierarchy of functions. Starting from a discussion of mere sensation in the first chapter of Book III, Aristotle moves ultimately to the *nous*, the spirit, the power of grasping principles. The *nous* is not so much the place of inspiration but the place of the intuition of the principles, of the fundamental rules. It is the philosophical subject within us and also the ethical subject within us, since it's the *nous* that is the bearer of most of the speculative virtues such as wisdom and so on.

What is important for our purposes here is the place of imagination in this hierarchy. Aristotle's important discovery is that the position of imagination is that of an intermediary function. This notion of an intermediary function will play a great role in and have tremendous consequences for the whole history of the concept, both positive and negative. The positive consequence is that characterization of imagination as an intermediary function will establish a certain order among the discouraging diversity of phenomena that I described in the prior lecture. While Aristotle, as we shall see, is not very accurate in his examples and does not attempt to put an order in his examples, he does something else: he identifies the level of reference of all these examples. This is a choice not to define imagination by its phenomenological content—how do images appear, what do they look like—but by the level at which they stand. Instead of looking for specific content, we look at the position on the scale.

This idea of an intermediary position has both a past and a future. It has a past because Plato had already dealt with this problem of the intermediary under the name of the mixed (*metaxu*), what is insufficient and in between. Plato assigned this intermediary position to the function of *doxa*, the opinion. In Plato this concept of *doxa* was embarrassing, because most of the pedagogical paradoxes proceed from *doxa*. For example, consider the question whether we can inquire into something that we don't know. If we don't know it, we shall not recognize whether it is true. And if we already know it, why would we need to learn about it? In *doxa* we know that we don't know. If I dare use the Heideggerian word here, we have a precomprehension of something in *doxa*, and imagination will have more or less this function of precomprehension from Aristotle to G. W. F. Hegel. As we shall see, in our text Aristotle is somewhat embarrassed by the competition between *doxa*—opinion—and *phantasia*—imagination—to occupy the intermediate stage.

The notion of an intermediary also has a future, since Kant will transform the notion of an intermediary position into that of a mediating function. This will constitute important progress in the concept of the intermediary. While the intermediary position has a passive status, a mediating function shares the features of that which precedes it—intuition—and that which follows—the categories. So the idea of a term that has a double allegiance will be the problem of imagination for Kant. The notion of an intermediary function is rich with possibility. An intermediary function also has a negative side, which will prevail as well in Kant, since imagination is squeezed between two strong functions, sensation and thought, both of which have good reputations with regard to truth. Imagination is placed on a scale of cognitive function and will be measured according to its cognitive import, its cognitive bearing.

To that extent Aristotle is not so far from Plato, since cognition in general receives its meaning from its capacity for being, its capacity for truth. Imagination is measured by comparison to two faculties capable of truth, if each in its own way. As to sensation, the claim is that we are not deceived when we see a color. We may be deceived when we say that this is such and such individual who has this color, but we cannot be deceived about the color (589; 428b 22). All of the Greek philosophers will repeat that. We are less sure, because we see that there is a selectivity and therefore a structuration of sensory fields that starts very early. But for the Greeks at least, this passive reception of sense impressions had the surest relation to things. At the other end of the scale, the *nous* is also a kind of supersensation, since it is defined merely by its receptivity to the Forms, to the ideal Forms of beings. Imagination is therefore identified by a system of double comparison with two powers, with two functions that have a truth of their own mainly by their receptivity, their capacity to receive either individual beings or universal being. Between the intuition of the individual and the intuition of the ideal Forms, imagination floats in between. Imagination lacks not only consistency but also reliability in terms of truth. It is in that sense that the path is paved toward a mainly depreciative approach to imagination that we shall examine in Pascal in the next lecture.

Let us now turn more directly to the text. We see that the text presents immediately an argumentative structure, and it is this argumentative structure that will interest me here. The argumentative structure consists mainly in assessing the differences that distinguish imagination from other functions and then subordinating to these differences some similarities suggested either by ordinary language or by common experience. Aristotle often has a good reputation among philosophers of ordinary language, because he proceeds as Austin and sometimes Wittgenstein will do, by not only looking at things but also at what people say about things. The role of common language and common experience converges in the description proposed by Aristotle. The procedure is to add two differences: downward and upward on the scale. Aristotle gives the terms of reference for this approach of contrasts in the opening paragraph of chapter 3. He takes some time there to clearly distinguish the opposite terms *perception* and *thinking* in order to make room for the intermediary term. He wants first to open the space between the two terms. This is not easy because of the weight of contrary opinions. For Aristotle it's always important to consider what people have already said, because we have to choose the best opinion by a kind of philosophical criteriology which does not proceed from nothing but from what has already been said on a subject. Aristotle does not deny the right of poetic expression. He quotes Homer and also the pre-Socratic, Empedocles (586; 427a 21–25). Why does he rely on these opinions? Because there is a function which seems common to the whole field described in Book III, the function of discrimination: to distinguish, to make distinctions. Between perception and reason or thinking there is at least something common: they discriminate.

For us, this argument is still striking, since we have learned not only from the philosophy of ordinary language—I think of J. L. Austin's *Sense and Sensibilia*—but also the modern psychology of perception that perception is a very complex activity of discrimination. In perception we identify and distinguish between forms. At the other end of the scale, thought, whatever it may be, does the same thing at least in its activity of singular identification. When we think of the importance of the problem of reference in modern philosophy from Frege, Bertrand Russell, down to P. F. Strawson, we see that to identify singular entities is an intellectual activity very difficult to distinguish from the discriminating function of perception. Perception and thinking overlap as discriminating.

Before speaking of imagination, therefore, Aristotle develops some arguments to say that perception and thinking are different functions despite their overlapping. He divides this argument into two parts, on practical and speculative thinking. First, while perception is "universal in the animal world," practical thinking is not (586–87; 427b 7–8). This is always an important argument in Aristotle, since the soul is not a thinking principle, as it will be with Descartes, but the animating principle. The soul is common to all animate beings, to animals and to humans. Therefore we need some criterion to differentiate within this function of the soul between what is common to all animals and what is proper to humans. Practical thinking belongs to all humans but not to all animals. Aristotle has the idea that some practical thinking is discernible among higher animals, but it does not belong to all animals. Modern psychology would not deny that.

As concerns speculative thinking, which will culminate in the activity of philosophy, it's different from perception, because it is capable of falsity. As we shall see, this problem of falsity dominates the whole problematics, as it did already in Plato. Recall the problem in Plato of the sophist: how is it possible to mean something that is not. The possibility of the "is not" is always embarrassing for a philosopher who defines knowledge by its capacity to say what is. In Aristotle we have the following argument: "perception of the special objects of sense is always free from error" (587; 427b 11–12). Special objects of sense include colors for sight and so on. They are common objects of sense, such as magnitude and motion, since we may, for example, perceive something in motion by some senses if not by all of them. Aristotle says that perception of the special objects of sense is always free from error. His conviction is that we cannot be deceived when we merely see or hear and so on. He continues that this ability to perceive free from error "is found in all animals, while it is possible to think falsely as well as truly, and thought is found only where there is discourse of reason as well as sensibility" (587; 427b 12–15). The discourse of reason—*dianoia*—means the discursive power of analyzing, synthesizing, and therefore putting under judgment. The distinction between perception and thinking has prepared the ground for the intermediary term.

Then begins Aristotle's direct argument concerning imagination, which is summarized in one sentence, the main sentence of this text: "For imagination is different from either perceiving or discursive thinking, though it is not found without sensation, or judgement without it" (587; 427b 15–17).

This sentence is well balanced. The main emphasis is on the difference: imagination is not this and is not that, is different from either that or that. Yet in the latter part of the sentence Aristotle describes a continuity of functions despite the discontinuity of natures. The four pages constituting chapter 3 do nothing other than provide arguments supporting this sentence's thesis. We have an assertion of a double difference plus a double dependence.

Let us consider the interplay of differences in this differential method. First, imagination versus thinking. For the sake of the argument, Aristotle equates thinking with judging. He takes judging as the touchstone of thinking. "That this activity [of imagination] is not the same kind of thinking as judgement is obvious" (587; 427b 17–18). I say that Aristotle equates thinking with judging for the sake of the argument, because he tries to choose among all the shades of a function the one that is paradigmatic of the difference. Why is judging paradigmatic for thinking? There is an arbitrariness of imagination that is not available in judging. "[I]magining lies within our own power whenever we wish (e.g., we can call up a picture, as in the practice of mnemonics by the use of mental images), but in forming opinions we are not free: we cannot escape the alternative of falsehood or truth" (587; 427b 18–21). Aristotle emphasizes the attitude of the mind when it imagines rather than the nature of the image. As I have said, he's not very accurate with his examples, but here the examples implied seem to be some diagrams—"the practice of mnemonics by the use of mental images"—or pictures—such as portraits or paintings. The portrait here is a mental portrait since we may evoke it freely. In other arguments, other examples will appear that are not very close to this first one, but once more Aristotle's concern is not to place examples in an order but to identify the level of reference. What, then, does Aristotle mean by speaking of the arbitrariness of imagination as opposed to our not being free in forming opinions? The argument seems strange. If judging and opinion are more or less similar, why are we not free to form each of them? The problem for Aristotle is that in judging we are not free: "we cannot escape the alternative of falsehood or truth." The arbitrariness available in imagination is not only the arbitrariness of evoking something but the possibility of not having to choose between truth and error.

This notion will become an argument against imagination, that imagination escapes the alternative of truth and falsehood. That is not a very favorable description if we consider that philosophy puts so strong an emphasis on the capacity for truth. The strange freedom of imagination here will find its expression finally only in the third *Critique* of Kant where the free play of imagination will be for the sake of pleasure or art. It will not be objective in the sense of giving us the object. Imagination's capacity for escaping the alternative of falsehood or truth will find its recognition outside of epistemology and only in aesthetics.

Aristotle brings forward a second argument here that confirms the independence of imagination. He evokes another kind of freedom, the freedom of not being affected by something. In contrast, what is affects us. "[W]hen we think something to be fearful or threatening, emotion is immediately produced, and so too with what is encouraging; but when we merely imagine we remain as unaffected as persons who are looking at a painting of some dreadful or encouraging scene" (587; 427b 22–25). Perhaps he is thinking of the onlooker of the Greek tragedy at the theater. It is the attitude of one who attends a dreadful spectacle but is not affected. What is emphasized is the distance of imagination from passions, emotions. The argument may appear not very coherent, because fear and fright do not seem to belong to thought. But Aristotle is very cautious not to speak of a fearful appearance but of when we *think* something to be fearful. Fear and threat are emotions proceeding from a mental representation, and it's the imagination that keeps us from the pressure of the affections.

Nevertheless, Aristotle does not want to draw a clearer distinction between thinking and imagination, since he says immediately that thinking covers both imagination and judgment. "Thinking is different from perceiving and is held to be in part imagination in part judgement" (587; 427b 29–30). What opposes imagination to sensation on the hierarchical stage of operation brings it close to thought. In that sense, imagination is a kind of thought or judgment. We have to do with overlapping functions. Here the task of the philosopher is to elaborate criteria of distinction in an experience that in fact has a function of continuity. If we have in mind the discussions in Kant's first *Critique* concerning the synthesis of imagination, which is so close to the synthesis of recognition, we understand why Aristotle could say that thinking is held in part in imagination, in part in judgment. Once more the power to discriminate seems to secure a continuity between imagination and judgment. Yet at this point, Aristotle thinks that he has supplied sufficient criteria of distinction between thought and imagination.

Aristotle then turns to the second half of the comparison, the comparison of imagination with sense, and says directly: "imagination is not sense" (587; 428a 5). Ordinary language and common experience provide us with more reliable differentiations between imagination and sense than between imagination, discrimination, judgment, opinion, and so on. Aristotle proceeds by putting his arguments in an order, an approach common to all the Socratic schools, and it seems that here we have as in a course a schema for a discussion. Putting examples in a certain order provides the structure of argument. We may place together the first and the fifth examples. Imagination is not sense since we may dream without sight or seeing. (There is a slight difference between sight and seeing; the first is the faculty of seeing and the second the actual use of this faculty in an activity.) Because Aristotle's examples provide his argument, his choice of examples here once again shows that Aristotle is not accurate in his use of argument. In his first and fifth examples, he speaks of dreams and mental pictures, but, as I said in the last lecture, the problem needing to be raised is whether dreams and mental pictures really belong to the same field. Can we say of dreams what we said of mental pictures, that we produce them at will? Some of Aristotle's examples provide a certain kind of argument while other examples provide another kind of argument. Yet what interests Aristotle is the location of the examples in a hierarchy, and this perhaps obscures or covers over the lack of kinship between them.

Another of Aristotle's arguments here is the second, where he claims that while all perceive, even brutes, not all have imagination (587; 428a 8–11). The distinction is not between animals and humans but between lower animals and superior animals. I wonder how he knows that ants do not and dogs do imagine. Perhaps the idea is that his dog must dream since it appears to jump while asleep.

Aristotle's main argument here is the third, since it has to do with the problematics of truth: "[S]ensations are always true, imaginations are for the most part false" (587; 428a 11–12). This statement is stronger than before, where he said that imagination was neither true nor false, that it did not have to choose between truth and falsehood. Now imagination is for the most part false. We may wonder what he has in mind. Perhaps if by sensation we mean pure impressions without interpretation, such as the pure impression of a color or a sound, then by contrast imagination is susceptible to falsehood because it consists in the interpretation of the sensation, as when we say this shadow is a person approaching in the fog.

What suggests this interpretation is that in Aristotle's fourth argument, he uses imagination precisely not as merely lived but as said, as something expressed in imagination. The fourth argument suggests that falsehood comes with images which are interpretations of inaccurate or failing perception. But these are interpretations in language. This is a warning for us that perhaps imagination belongs more to language than to perception. "[E]ven in ordinary speech, we do not, when sense functions precisely with regard to its object, say that we imagine it to be a man, but rather when there is some failure of accuracy in its exercise" (587; 428a 12–15). The situation considered is that of a sensation that leaves room for different interpretations. There is some failure of accuracy, and then we imagine the object to be a person. This point is very interesting for the phenomenological discussion that we shall have in the second part of the course. The language is intriguing because we say we imagine something to be something. To imagine here has to be construed grammatically as imagining that. We imagine that. And it is not the same when we dream. Then we don't imagine that; we have images. Or perhaps we are images, as Étienne Bonnot de Condillac would say.[2] In Aristotle's example we have a process of interpretation of indiscriminate perception that is, in fact, a way of identifying by guessing: it is a person and not a car or something like that. This idea of guessing in identification will play a great role in literary criticism, in psychology, and in different sciences. To guess what something is is the counterpart of validating a guess as, for example, in a theory of interpretation. The role of guessing confirms the prevailing trait that imagination not only may be false but that it is mostly false, "for the most part false." This argument is shortly repeated: "Neither is imagination any of the things that are never in error: e.g., knowledge or intelligence; for imagination may be false" (588; 428a 17–18).

At that point Aristotle opens a parenthesis because of the statement that imagination may be false. Aristotle renews a discussion that he had closed at the beginning when he said that the intermediary term is not opinion, as Plato thought, but imagination. But to speak of imagination as something that may be false and that is for the most part false is to give it the same role as the *doxa* in Plato. And we shall see that for the classical tradition, there will be a kind of mixture between the *phantasia* of Aristotle and the *doxa* of Plato under the general title of *imaginatio* in Descartes, Spinoza, Leibniz, and so on. *Imaginatio* is more a regime of thought that is not yet cured by the criteria of truth. Therefore it may be both interpretation of a perception and of a fantasy. What will be common across these interpretations by imagination is the epistemological character of its being: it may be neither true nor false and may be false. I don't stay at the level of this discussion, which is rather complicated, because Plato not only put *doxa* in this intermediary position, but he also (in some texts Richard McKeon as editor cites in the footnote on page 588) treated imagination as a kind of compound, an entity of opinion and sensation, whether by addition, mediation, or blending. And Aristotle addresses these issues (588; 428a 26–428 b2), which have to do with the dominant discussion between the Aristotelian school and what would remain of the Platonic school.

For our purposes, the criterion Aristotle raises in this discussion is important, since Aristotle was always very accurate in the choice of his criteria. It's the criterion of belief. This is of interest, since we spoke of imagination not only according to the axis of presence and absence but also according to the axis of the subject's involvement in the process of imagination: between belief and critical distance. Aristotle says belief is always present in opinion, whereas, he goes on, we may have imagination without belief (588; 428a 20–22). This latter argument is closer not to that of the dream but of the free fiction, as with the one who attends a spectacle and who does not believe that it is reality. Aristotle considers as an important criterion the juxtaposition between representation and belief. This juxtaposition is very difficult to preserve if imagination may be assessed simply as false.[3]

At the end of this paragraph, Aristotle provides an example that is interesting since it will return in Spinoza. Aristotle offers as a proof that imagination is not opinion the fact that we may simultaneously imagine that something is such and yet know that it is not such, as is the case with our perception of objects in the heavens. "[W]e imagine the sun to be a foot in diameter though we are convinced that it is larger than the inhabited part of the earth . . ." (588; 428b 3–4). This argument will become even stronger when, after Johannes Kepler and Nicolaus Copernicus, we have to invert the relationship between earth and sun. Yet even in a geocentric representation of the world that will later be formalized by Ptolemy, already we have a discrepancy between what we know about the dimension of the sun and what we imagine it to be. What does it mean that we imagine the sun to be a foot in diameter? It's the same use of imagination that we had when we said we imagine something to be a person. We imagine something to be something. Imagination here involves an interpretation of a perception by an intellectual guess that is not yet submitted to critical knowledge. It is an uncriticized interpretation. We see how inconsistent this example is with that of the dream and with that of reading a picture, because there is literal interpretation in the recognition of somebody in the picture. By contrast, to imagine that or to imagine something being something seems to require a specific treatment under the general title of interpretation as guessing. The lack of consistency does not worry Aristotle, because his concern does not lie there. It is not the consistency of the example that concerns him but the proof that this use of imagination does not interfere with opinion. We may have an opinion about the sun contrary to our imagination of it; we go on spontaneously interpreting the dimension of the sun as being this or that. Imagination escapes the alternative of truth and falsehood. While we are compelled to take a stand concerning truth judgments, we may retain imaginative interpretation in ordinary life. As Spinoza will say, even though after modern astronomy we know the earth rotates, we continue to see the sun rising.[4] Aristotle concludes: "Imagination is therefore neither any one of the states enumerated, nor compounded out of them" (588; 428b 9). The reference to "compounded out of them" is an allusion to Plato's claim, discussed in Aristotle's prior paragraph, that imagination is a mixture of opinion and perception, opinion plus perception, opinion mediated by sensation, and so on (588; 428a 25–26).

At this point Aristotle has completed the first part of his task to elaborate the system of criteria by which he can identify *phantasia* as having a sense. We have a clue to the two-part structure of his argument in the very last sentence of the chapter: "About imagination, *what it is* and *why it exists*, let so much suffice" (589; 429a 9; emphasis added). Up to this stage Aristotle has answered the question what imagination is. He has proceeded from genre to differences, which is typically Aristotelian. But he has still to complete the second task, to address why imagination exists. Here he qualifies imagination's differences on the basis of what they depend upon, their causes. This second step too will have a decisive importance for the history of the problem of imagination. The idea that imagination depends on the sense and judgment depends on imagination, this series of dependences, of derivations, will prevent recognition of the specificity of imagination. If we consider the structure of Aristotle's argument, we see that the problem of the dependence is raised by a change of approach in the argument. We are now inquiring into causes and no longer into what is. In the language of Aristotle, we are no longer examining the formal cause but the efficient cause. What produces images? Causes. When we speak of "why," we speak of causes.

This change in argument is very damaging, because for the recognition of the function, we are putting imagination into a framework—the framework of movement—that may not be appropriate. We understand why Aristotle makes the argument he does. For Aristotle we have to speak of what puts imagination in motion, of what movement it consists, since the treatise *On the Soul* is a part of a great treatise on nature. The soul is a part of nature. We are to treat the problem of imagination according to the main categories of physics, that is, movement and what produces movement. In nature we find both inanimate and animate being; the movement in these things is produced by something. Things are pushed. Beings which have their movement within themselves are the animate bodies. Aristotle's argument here is nonphenomenological, because the intentional relation to an object is obscured by a relation of cause and effect which is naturalistic in essence. Aristotle is very interesting because of this competition in his argument between an effort to describe in terms of difference and to explain in terms of movement. This competition in argument makes his text very dramatic. The main thesis of this second part is summarized in the following sentence: "[I]magination must be a movement resulting from an actual exercise of a power of sense" (589; 429a 1–2). This sentence is quite different from those in the first part where imagination was known on the basis of perceiving, opining, and so on. Now the positive assertion arises in terms of motion.

This change will have dramatic consequences for the history of the problem. Philosophers will be permanently tempted to derive the image from the perception by some process of weakening. The theory is of perception as a trace, as the residue of something. And this theory may miss in imagination the role of, for example, guessing, which is not a trace. My suspicion is that what is completely overlooked in the approach to imagination in terms of motion, causes, and so on is the negative trait of imagination: the absence, the nothingness of imagination that we have in a fiction, the nonbeing. We cannot find negativity in a chain of causes, because we always have to do with actual things generating actual things. We are in the fullness of actuality. We will never find the element of absence, the element of negativity, as will be emphasized in the post-Hegelian approaches to the problem as in Sartre, for example, where the nothingness of the image will constitute its phenomenological character. When imagination is derived from perception, we forget the most interesting example of imagination—to imagine something to be—because it's much more complex than a mere residue of perception.

Aristotle's way of treating imagination on the basis of perception is certainly not without support in experience and in ordinary language. This is why it is so difficult to displace. It's quite true, for example, that if we are blind, we cannot have visual images. Therefore, Aristotle's argument is that surely there is a similarity in content between an image and perception. The image of the sun is similar to a perceived sun, and what has to be shown is what kind of similarity. Aristotle tried to solve the problem by saying it's a similarity in movement, as if our brain or our soul, whatever it may be, had been put in motion in a certain way. When we have a similar image, it is as though a similar movement has been produced in us. The theories of brain traces will say the same thing. A certain cortical center, for example, has been aroused by a stimulus but in the absence of the stimulus, if the same center is aroused once more, then we get an image. It's a similarity in movement. Aristotle's position will find its legitimation in physiological psychology.

Here is Aristotle's argument:

> [S]ince when one thing has been set in motion another thing may be moved by it, and imagination is held to be a movement and to be impossible without sensation, i.e., to occur in beings that are percipient and to have for its content what can be perceived, and since movement may be produced by actual sensation and that movement is necessarily similar in character to the sensation itself . . . (588; 428b 10–14)

The sentence stating that "since when one thing has been set in motion another thing may be moved by it" is a general proposition of physics that covers Aristotle's *Physics* and the treatise *On the Soul*. We are to take for granted a theory of movement developed elsewhere in the Second and the Fourth Books of the *Physics*. The statement is also the first in Aristotle that treats imagination as a movement. That imagination is "impossible without sensation" is an allusion to the fact that a blind person cannot have visual images. The content of imagination is "what can be perceived" and a subject must be percipient of that kind of object. In the succession of the full statement's references to "since," we have a concatenation of a general principle of physics concerning motion with the idea that what may be common between an image and a perception is a similarity in movement. We are moved in the same way when we have a visual image as when we have a visual perception.

Spinoza's theory of imagination will completely derive from that conjunction: we have been affected by something. The affection remains when the object is far off, and then when the same movement is repeated in us, we believe it. What may be explained here is perhaps the dream, but the explanation adds so much besides that is applicable to mythical interpretation, particularly false perception. We understand why imagination is mostly false. We can explain how we may take an image for something else, since it is a similar movement. In Spinoza's terms, an image is something *as though* present or as it is absent. The *as though* present proceeds from the similarity in movement. The *as though* of illusion will be said to derive from this capacity.

Aristotle anticipates Spinoza's demonstration in the following argument, which I summarize very quickly. Aristotle shows there are degrees of truth and falsity already in perception that are repeated in the imagination and increased by the absence of the object. He evokes here three degrees in the use of perception. The first degree, "special objects of sense" (589; 428 b18), is the paradigmatic one. Special objects of sense include objects of sight such as color, objects of hearing such as sound, and so on. The claim is that there is no error of perception here; we cannot be deceived. The second degree includes "the concomitance of the objects concomitant with the sensible qualities" (589; 428b 19–20). Deception is possible here. The perception, says Aristotle, that something is white "cannot be false," but we may be deceived about what the white object is (589; 428b 22–23). When we perceive in a range, we perceive the color, the smell, and so on, and then we may imagine one sensation on the basis of another sensation. Deception is still more possible when we introduce the third example, what Aristotle calls "universal attributes" of perception (589; 428b23). We may speak of universal attributes of perception in the sense that all perceptions have in common magnitude and movement. We may guess magnitude in one sense on the basis of the magnitude in another sense. To the extent that imagination derives from perception, it's not unexpected that it will repeat this hierarchy of truth and error and add its own sources of illusion "when the object of perception is far off": "The motion which is due to the activity of sense in these three modes of its exercise will differ from the activity of sense; (1) the first kind of derived motion is free from error while the sensation is present; (2) and (3) the others may be erroneous whether it is present or absent, especially when the object of perception is far off" (589; 428b 25–30). Then the image will be a kind of deceiving *as though* presence of quasi-presence.

To conclude, let me raise three questions about Aristotle's discussion in this chapter. The first question concerns Aristotle's method of difference, as when he says imagination is neither this nor that. What is the value of a method that locates the function of imagination on a scale and that answers to the question "what is" only by negations? It is not this, and it is not that. It is between. A more satisfactory answer will be given when with Kant we say not only that imagination is between and so neither/nor but that it mediates and therefore is both. There will be a change of approach with Kant when he shall try to say that the mediating term shares both. And perhaps, according to some rare textual allusions in Kant, it could be a common root of both.[5] Heidegger has developed this Kantian allusion that what mediates also in a sense grounds.[6] But we are far from that in Aristotle. He is, on the contrary, accurately saying that imagination is not this or that, and so he is providing not a description but a criteriology.

The second question that could be raised concerns the nature of Aristotle's scale, since it's a scale of truth. Since both sensation and the intellectual intuition are true, is not this way of putting the question disparaging of imagination from the start, because we are obliged to conclude that it may be either true or false and even for the most part false? Here imagination is close to the *doxa* in Plato. Imagination will be recognized in more positive terms when it is no longer placed on a scale of error and truth but approached within another framework, that of aesthetics, in Kant's third *Critique*. Until the third *Critique*, imagination will be always squeezed between two truth functions—sensation and intellectual intuition. I don't mean to say that the problem of imagination has nothing to do with truth but surely not with a certain definition of truth as adequation, as conformity between judgment and reality. It may have another kinship with the problem of truth and then Aristotle would be confirmed but in a different way. For example, in the theory of models, the function of the model is to reopen the field of experience, to redescribe it in fresh terms. The same may be at stake in literary fictions, which can open our eyes to some other dimension of reality. But in these cases we do not have to speak of truth as adequation or verification but perhaps as unconcealment, disclosure, or at least redescription. The relation between imagination and truth is not necessarily closed before Kant's third *Critique*.

A third and final question would concern the last part of the chapter, the notion of a derivation of imagination in terms of motion. This is perhaps the most, if not deceiving, at least obscuring of Aristotle's approaches. To say that imagination derives from perception in terms of motion narrows down the scope of examples to the problem of the trace, the image as trace, and excludes more or less the most interesting examples, those of imaging that, imagination as guessing. Here a problem of method is raised, because can we place the relation between act and object within the physical or naturalistic framework of cause and effect? It's quite possible that precisely the problem of imagination puts in question the limits of this causal approach. We may say that in perception a stimulus is moving our eyes, because there is surely some activity of that kind. An image is also aroused in our brain. But we are missing here what is important, the intentional relation, something that is very strange and constitutes a kind of challenge to the causal approach, when it is a nothing that puts in motion our imagination. The problem of the negativity of the image is what puts in question the physical framework of the problematic. Even if we take the physical in the broad, Aristotelian sense, can we properly speak of imagination as a motion, a kind of movement, similar to the movement of perception? The question is whether the answer to "why" imagination exists does not harm the previous answer to "what is" imagination.

3

Pascal and Spinoza

This lecture continues our discussion of the five or six classical texts that determine our philosophical tradition concerning imagination. Here we examine Pascal's *Pensées* and Spinoza's *Ethics*, both of which have historical fame and, as we shall see, much in common. I am pleased that the text of Pascal includes the original French as well as the English translation, because when we read Pascal—like Dante or Shakespeare—we must have some feeling of the original since a strength lies in its language. It's also a literary text and indeed one of the great literary texts.

We may introduce the specific approach of Pascal on the basis of what we have said about Aristotle. Recall that the fundamental approach of Aristotle was determined by two principles. First, imagination had to be placed on a scale between two strongholds of knowledge: perception or sense on the one hand and on the other intellectual intuition, the intuition of principles, the *intellectus*. Aristotle approached imagination as an intermediary function. Second, and the main implication, if Aristotle considered this scale not only as a scale in knowledge but also as a scale in truth, then imagination is caught and even squeezed between two functions which are by principle true. The suspicion, therefore, was that imagination as an intermediary function was the weak point of human knowledge, since it may be either true or false and is even defined by this indecision concerning truth and error. Consequently, it is quite understandable that in a more moralistic tradition or at least in a theory of knowledge that will be at the same time a theory of passions, a certain merging may appear between an ethics of guilt and an epistemology of imagination. If, then, the first obstacle to recognition of the creative function of imagination owes to linking imagination to perception and the concept, a second obstacle develops from the confusion between two problems: that of fiction and that of illusion or even delusion. This may perhaps arise on the basis of a mixing of the tradition of opinion coming from Plato with the theory of imagination properly said, the theory of mental images.

This is what happens with Pascal. The ethical prejudice against imagination that is expressed in the text of Pascal proceeds to a certain extent from the philosophical decision taken at the beginning by Aristotle. I shall not stay long with the text of Pascal but shall use it more as a kind of ethical introduction to Spinoza, whose text will detain us longer. The main claim of Pascal is that imagination belongs to what he calls the "deceptive powers." He leads into the section of the book on imagination with the following statement: "Begin here the chapter on deceptive powers" (Pascal 1950, 39).[1] This section was part of an apology, in the sense of a defense, of the Christian religion. The attempt was to place oneself on the grounds of the adversary, the alleged unbeliever, and then to show on the basis of these assumptions the misery of human nature in an existence without Christ. The text therefore belongs to a certain strategy of discourse, to a certain rhetoric of persuasion. It is not as in Hume or Kant a treatise on human nature, a kind of scientific approach. It is an apology, and within the framework of an apology the problem is to uncover, to unmask, the deceptive power. The tradition of unmasking does not belong merely to the Christian apology, because we could say that in Freud or in Friedrich Nietzsche the issue will also be to unmask. So the problem of unmasking has both a long tradition and a good reputation in one sense. But Pascal's initial decision to write an apology is very important for his choice of paradigmatic examples.

Recall from the introductory lecture that I said that in imagination we have a loosely connected field of examples. At one end we have dreams, illusions, hallucinations, and so on and at the other end fictions, such as the committed fiction of literature and so on. By Pascal's initial decision to write an apology, the problem of fiction—which will interest me more than any other—will be completely bracketed and obscured, since we start with the deceptive dimension of imagination. We must link at the very beginning the purpose of the apology, which is to denounce, to unmask, to expose the deceptive power, with a certain narrowing of the field of imagination. We will not consider the diversity of the field but on the contrary the paradigmatic case of deception. We will not consider fiction at all.

This way of considering imagination proceeds on the one hand from the Aristotelian treatment of imagination as both true and false. A certain allusion to this tradition appears in the opening lines of Pascal's discussion: Imagination "is man's ruling faculty, queen of lies and error, and all the greater deceiver for that she does not always deceive; for she would be an infallible touchstone of truth if she were a touchstone of falsehood. But being most often false, she leaves no sure mark of her quality, for she sets the same stamp upon truth and falsehood" (39). Imagination is deceptive because it doesn't always deceive. (I think it's a mistake to translate the French *imagination* as *she* rather than as *it*. Imagination has a feminine case in French, but all French words are either masculine or feminine. The translation may also reflect a certain prejudice linked to the idea that what is feminine is sinful, but *imaginatio* was feminine already in Latin before Christianity.)

Yet in Pascal's statement something new also appears that was not emphasized in Aristotle, the notion of imagination as a power. Imagination is a "ruling faculty, queen of lies and error." He writes: "This haughty power, which loves to rule and lord it over reason, her foe, has bestowed upon man a second nature, just to show her great might" (41). This conception of imagination may belong both to the tradition of Plato for which the *doxa* also has power over the person, but mainly it reflects the tradition of original sin, of the initial situation of the human in bondage. The power of imagination is represented as a cleverness: "Men whose cleverness lies in their own imagination are far better pleased with themselves than sensible men can ever reasonably be" (41). The moralistic approach to imagination is more important than an epistemological approach, since imagination is more than error. The problem of error as an epistemological problem is encompassed within the problem of illusion as something that we cannot master merely by a change in judgment. This distinction between illusion and error will play a great role in many other traditions. I have already made an allusion to Freud, but the problem of ideology in the Marxist school also belongs to the same tradition. Deception is a more complex structure of existence than error. We can correct error, something local, by spotting our mistake in reasoning or by changing our methodology, but correction of deception requires a complete process of unmasking the structure of the illusion.

Imagination is finally not only a power but a level of existence, a way of life. "For Reason has had to give way, and at her wisest she takes, as her own, principles which had been recklessly circulated by human imagination" (43). Imagination as a complete regime has to be interpreted in relation to another very important text of Pascal concerning the three orders (321–22). There are three levels of greatness: the greatness of flesh, the greatness of spirit, and finally the greatness of love. Imagination is the key to the first, greatness according to the flesh. I insist on this point because we shall see something similar in Spinoza in a quite different tradition than the specifically Christian, Augustinian tradition of Pascal. The idea is that there are modes of knowledge that are at the same time levels of existence. *Imaginatio* in the tradition of the moralists will represent a mode of knowledge that will be at the same time a level of existence.

What is the most interesting in Pascal's text is the impact of this imagination on human social existence. This approach will not again appear in the classical tradition before Nietzsche, Freud, Marx, and so on. The idea is that the privileged field of deception is social existence; some will call this ideology. A theory of ideology is anticipated in Pascal, since imagination gives an appearance of greatness to what is lacking real greatness. It makes appear great what is not worth unconditional respect. This presentation is linked to the earlier pessimistic evaluation of justice by the sixteenth century tradition of skepticism, English and mainly French, which maintains that human justice is a fake. It's mainly imagination that will offer the appearance of power. I am very much interested in this problem, since in my work on ideology and utopia I try to link one of the functions of ideology to the legitimation of power, of authority, of domination, giving to power a kind of overvalue or surplus value. All the elements of a theory of the surplus value of authority are supported by imagination, as if imagination were there to fill up a credibility gap in the structure of authority. Here is Pascal's text, which when interpreted in the light of some more modern texts, speaks with perhaps more strength: "Who hands out reputations? Who apportions respect and veneration to people, to achievements, to laws, to the great, if not this faculty of imagination? All the wealth of the world would be insufficient without its help" (41). While wealth represents a real value, it's also a kind of fake value. Imagination supports the nothingness in value. All those who bear authority are struck by this unmasking: the magistrate, the advocate, the preacher, the physician, and even the philosopher, since we have this famous allusion: "The greatest philosopher in the world, standing on the brink of a precipice, on an amply wide plank, and convinced by his reason that he was perfectly safe, would be undone by his imagination. Many would be unable even to think of such a thing without breaking into a cold sweat." Pascal writes more generally:

> Would you not say that this magistrate, whose reverend old age makes him respected by a whole nation, is influenced by pure reason. . . . Watch him coming to a religious service, filled with devout zeal, his sound judgment strengthened by his ardent charity. He is ready to listen with exemplary respect. But if the preacher, when he appears, turns out to be endowed with a hoarse voice and an odd sort of face, if his barber has shaved him badly, and if on top of that he looks bedraggled, I will wager that, no matter what great truths he enunciates, our magistrate's gravity will give way. (41)

We think also of judges in the caricatures of modern painting. The social dimension of authority is undermined by this critique of imagination.

What must be retained from this caricature, to a certain extent, is the notion of the make-believe and the power of making believe. As we shall see shortly, this is the main point in Spinoza's analysis, which finally places the problem of imagination not very far from the problem of sophistry as developed in the Platonic tradition. The claim is that there is a kind of natural sophistry, a center of fallacy which is imagination. It is the category of the pseudo, of the quasi. I was thinking of the text in Plato's *Gorgias* where he says that rhetoric is to justice what cookery is to medicine and beautification is to gymnastics (247, 465c 1–2). Each discipline has as its shadow a fake discipline. This doubling by a fake discipline is the sophistry of imagination. The theory of deceptive powers plays the same role in this Christian apologetics as does sophistry in speculative philosophy in the Greek tradition.

I leave Pascal with a final reading that was in fact an introductory text, but it makes sense now when put at the end: "Man apart from grace is but a creature full of error, natural and ineffaceable. Nothing shows him truth" (39). Description of the person as naturally and ineffaceably full of error is a conflation between the Greek tradition on opinion and the Christian, mainly Augustinian, tradition on original sin. If we keep the fake, the deceptive function, as a leading thread, then we better understand the choice in all of the paradigmatic examples concerning imagination, the choice of this segment of the field that we have called the section of the *as if*, the *as though*. This is a powerful tradition within classical philosophy and in rationalistic philosophy, as will be exemplified mainly by Spinoza.

We read in Spinoza's *Ethics* Part Two, Propositions 16 and 17 and the following Note.[2] (The original Latin term for what has been translated as a Note is a "Scholium," which belongs to the vocabulary of geometric order that Spinoza adopts as a model for his logic.) The problem of imagination in Spinoza is approached not from the point of view of a moralist, in the positive sense of that word, but in the tradition that is both one of an epistemology and an ontology. It's first of all as an ontology of imagination that we shall approach the problem. What do I mean by ontology? Part One of the *Ethics* is an attempt to relate all the finite modes of being to the only substantial being, which is called nature or God. (I don't dispute this point.) What is fundamental here is that we have a philosophy of the fullness of being, one that leaves no room for negative existence, for negativity in any sense. It is the least Hegelian approach that we may imagine in philosophy. Everything must be positive, actual, existing, or it has no place.

The challenge is how to make room for something like absence, the representation of not being existing. The problem of imagination is always a challenge for a philosophy that works only with the concept of being and all its derivatives, like attribute, modes, and so on, and so is organized as a hierarchy, a descending hierarchy from the highest being to finite being and so on. The primacy of presence will be reflected in Spinoza's epistemology as the impossibility of giving room to a positive mode of absence and all kinds of absences such as error, the negative. The negative has no place in an ontology that I call here with another commentator on Spinoza, Vladimir Jankélévitch, the fullness of being, an ontology Jankélévitch finds also in Bergson and in some other philosophers who give primacy to the existing as such, to the "absolutely" of the relative existing as such.

What will be the impact of Spinoza's approach on the epistemological level, the approach to imagination in terms of knowledge? We must approach imagination by deriving it from the function that is by principle the mode of presence: perception. Then, as we shall see in the next lecture on Hume, we will have the attempt to derive the image from the perception. There is something similar between Spinoza and Hume not from the point of view of an ontology but from the point of view of a plentitude of presence, which Hume will call the impression. But if we start with the impression, it will be very difficult to make sense of something that is the absence of an impression or the *re*presentation of a presentation. The way in which these philosophers accept the challenge of imagination and try to make sense of it by addressing the problem of the image is for them the touchstone of their philosophy. The problem of imagination is the touchstone for all philosophies of absolute presence, where there is no interval, no gap either in being or in mental presence or whatever may be the function of presence. The image is the challenge to a problematic of presence.

If for these philosophies the first implication concerning imagination is that it must be derived from perception, the second is that it has to be derived not as absence, but as quasi-presence. The choice is to explore images that stand for perceptions. These are the images closest to presence. They are the pseudo-presence, the quasi-presence, the *as if*. This is declared by Spinoza at the beginning of the Note following Proposition 17: "We see, therefore, how it is possible for us to contemplate things which do not exist *as if* they were actually present" (Spinoza 1957, 97, emphasis added). There is a double reduction of the image: first, to a derivative of presence, and second, to the *as if* of presence. This is the weight of an ontology of absolute being on the problem of imagination.

At this stage Spinoza is very close to Pascal, because both meet imagination at the point where it is deceptive. (The reasons for doing so remain quite different due to Pascal's pursuit, as we have discussed, of an apologetics.) They examine imagination not when it is a creative fiction but when it is deceptive, a false presence. The problem of deception is common to them both.

A third obstacle, then, to the full recognition of creative imagination is due to the primacy of presence and the inability to make sense with the power of absence. This primacy is exemplified at its highest degree of consistency by Spinoza's theory of imagination. I chose it not only because it shares with Aristotle the thesis that the image proceeds from a previous perception, and not only because it shares with Pascal the conviction that imagination is deceiving, but because it draws for the sake of imagination all the consequences of a philosophy in which there is no place for the negation, for the void, for the not being, for absence. In a philosophy where everything is actual, there is no place for fiction. There may, though, be a place for illusion, because illusion refers back to presence, to fullness. It is *as if* it were actually present. The whole course of Spinoza's demonstration in Propositions 16 and 17 will be to derive the *as if* from actual presence and therefore to construe the *as if* on the basis of the actuality of presence.

Phenomenologically, we can take as Spinoza's starting point here that the human body is affected by external bodies. This starting point is a consequence of prior decisions earlier in the text. That the body is "affected" by external bodies should be understood not in the narrow, modern, more or less emotional sense—to be affected, for example, by bad news—but in the sense of to receive, to be reached by an action of something, to be passive in relation to something else that is active. Spinoza's second presupposition is that this affection works at two levels at the same time. First, a body affects another body at the level of the body. This can be expressed in modern terms as a cortical movement, for example, the movement of sound waves in hearing. Second, according to Spinoza's principle of the parallelism between soul and body, all that happens at the level of the body is reflected in the mind, since the mind is the form of this matter which is the body. In the first Part of the *Ethics*, Spinoza relates this parallelism to the idea that because in God all attributes are one, the attributes of space and thought are therefore one. God is the unity of space and thought. Distributed in the so-called creatures in the finite mode is a kind of reduplication. It's not by chance that the soul and the body are two things in one, because they are two modes or two different attributes which are one in God. For Spinoza there is no problem at all concerning the relation between mind and body, since it is solved in God as the one who is both.

If we begin with these presuppositions, we have a very strong starting point since when an external body affects my body, then I may say that I have an affection of my mind to which something out there corresponds. This affection of the mind is a perception. The perception is the reflection of this affection of my body by an external body. I feel that I am affected; I have what Hume will call an impression. As we shall see, Hume will solve the problem of the affection or impression in another way, claiming that there is no difference between an idea and existence since the idea is the existence. The idea and existence are indistinguishable. This will create great difficulty in making sense of nonexistent things. It is very interesting to see similar difficulties in Hume and in Spinoza, because both in a sense start from the primacy of the impression, what is called affection in Spinoza and impression in Hume.

Let us read Proposition 16: "The idea of every way in which the human body is affected by external bodies must involve the nature of the human body, and at the same time the nature of the external body" (96). The affection is two-sided, because it involves both the human body and the external body. Spinoza gives a radical account of what Husserl will call the intentional relation between act and object. The relationship between act and object is construed ontologically as the connecting point of an affecting body and an affected body. Note also the language that the affection involves the human body and "at the same time" the external body. We must keep in mind the temporal role, because time will play a role in the construction of the *as if*, of the false presence, of the quasi-presence. The *as if* is an action of time. As we shall discuss later in more detail, it will be after repetition of a certain affection that the trace survives the affection, and so the quasi-presence is what is left afterward. We start, though, from the instance of conjunction between two bodies, one which is my body, and the other which is an external body. This instantaneous conjunction is at the same time the affection. "All ways in which any body is affected follow at the same time from the nature of the affected body and from the nature of the affecting body" (Demonstration; 96). The affecting and the affected are one somewhere. Spinoza's approach is a very traditional way of rendering the problem of perception, since in Aristotle and during the Middle Ages, perception was considered the common operation of the agent and of the recipient. It is a common action, for example, of the color and of my eye. A sensation is the common action of two things, light and the eye.

Corollary 1 of Proposition 16 transfers that relationship into the field of the soul. For Spinoza this is allowed, since all that happens in the body is reflected in the soul. "Hence it follows, in the first place, that the human mind perceives the nature of many bodies together with that of its own body" (96). The word *perceive* belongs to a language game of the mind. Whereas the initial Proposition was written in the language game of ontological modes, we may translate that into either a physiological or mentalistic vocabulary, since the mentalistic vocabulary is founded in the unity of the two attributes in God.

Corollary 2 will play an intermediary role. In the common action of the two bodies, a priority, a privilege, is granted to my body. This belongs to the

Cartesian tradition. When I perceive a color, I miss what is important in the thing, that it has extension, it is a movement. The primary qualities are obscured by the secondary qualities, the qualities properly said. What I call a quality is in fact more the expression of my way of perceiving it than the way in which the thing exists in itself. Therefore, in the conjunction between my body and the external body, my body has primacy. This will explain the ability of my body to retain the trace of an impression and then reconstitute or rebuild the object in the absence of the object. "It follows, secondly, that the ideas we have of external bodies indicate the constitution of our own body rather than the nature of external bodies. This I have explained in the Appendix of the First Part by many examples" (96). As already noted, these examples were typically Cartesian: the colors express more my body than the external body, and so on. We have construed the starting point, the *terminus a quo*, from the Demonstration.

How can we move from this strong theory of perception where there are really things acting on this real thing, my body, to answering how do I get an image, which is something so evasive and even inconsistent? The whole process of the Demonstration in Proposition 17 is to derive the image from the affection. It is interesting to see how Spinoza derives the image in comparison to Hume. In Hume, as we shall see, there is only one way, which is to say that the impression is strong and the image is weak; the image is derived by weakening the strength of the impression. We have only a gradation of strength, which is perhaps more coarse than Spinoza's approach, which is much more complicated and sophisticated.

The key of the solution for Spinoza is the function of time in the process. As we saw, the affection was instantaneous, "at the same time." A human body is affected by an external body at the same time. If we introduce the dimension of time, though, we may introduce an action that survives its cause. This is what we call a trace, so it's a solution by the trace. We may recall that in the first lecture we put the notion of a trace in the left part of the framework on the side precisely of presence, since a trace is also a presence. The affection is something that we may even see, if by chance we have a microscopic approach to some trace in the brain. More generally, it's not impossible to see a trace; think, for example, of seeing a trace in the snow. The trace is something existing. But it's something that exists when its cause no longer does. There is an element of absence in the trace, the absence of the cause. It's an effect surviving its cause, a persisting existence.

If we admit that the idea of the existence of an object is implied in the impression if the impression persists, then we have a durable impression implying the existence of its cause. This will be the *as if*. The *as if*, the *as though* is the temporal effect of a trace. Here is Proposition 17: "If the human body be affected in a way which involves the nature of any external body, the human mind will contemplate that external body *as* actually existing or *as* present, until the human body be affected by a modification which excludes the existence or presence of the external body" (96, emphases added). In the beginning of the Proposition, the "if" repeats what has been stated in Proposition 16, and the attention to the human mind after having spoken of the human body follows from Corollary 1. Phenomenologically, the important word in Proposition 17 is the use of "as." We "contemplate that external body *as* actually existing." We would not say that of perception. When I perceive something, I don't say that I perceive it *as* existing. (Or if I did, it would be a cumbersome form of expression.) The *as* is really the introduction of a new dimension. I have here in mind, of course, the famous section in Ludwig Wittgenstein's *Philosophical Investigations* where there is a long development of *seeing as*. Those who have read this text may remember the example of the ambiguous figure that we may read *as* a rabbit or *as* a duck (p. 194).[3] Or children play with these kinds of ambiguous images to find a hunter in the leaves (p. 196), and so on. We see something *as*. There is an element here of interpretation, since the same drawing can be seen in different ways. Because there is a choice, we can no longer speak simply of perception.

Spinoza's attempt will be to reduce the phenomenological difference between contemplating *as* and merely perceiving. A kind of violence may be done to the experience since we have to level as much as possible the difference between the image and the perception, to reduce the *as* to a mere survival of, a dimension of, the initial perception. This is accomplished by the element of time. The temporal term in the Proposition is the "until": "until the human body be affected by a modification which excludes." (I shall set aside the mention of "excludes" and return to that shortly.) The Corollary develops the *as if*. "The mind is able to contemplate external things by which the human body was *once* affected *as if* they were present, although they are not present and do not exist" (96, emphases added). The temporal element is the "once." And the negative element in fact reappears: "although they are present and do not exist." What has been chased out the door returns through the window. When Spinoza says that in the image the external things "are not present and do not exist," how can we say that they do not exist or are not present? It's only in a future consideration that the thing will not exist. For the present consideration, for the one who contemplates the image, it is an *as if*. We must reserve the not present and nonexistent for a critical view that comes afterward, and, by a kind of reaction or feedback on the image, will reduce its presence. This is the point of exclusion Spinoza notes at the end of Proposition 17: "[u]ntil the human body be affected by a modification which *excludes* the existence or presence of the external body" (emphasis added).

The problem in Spinoza of the negative element is very difficult, and it is reduced to the competition between positive modes. Everything is not compatible, and therefore one thing excludes some other thing. I may have in mind a centaur—this is the seventeenth century, where we're always dreaming of a centaur—but then I see a real horse or a real eagle and so on. These sorts of things exclude the centaur, because I cannot put that into a zoo. There is no place in reality for this image. The rest of reality excludes the image. And yet as such it is a presence. It is a presence but excluded by other presences. If we ask Spinoza how it is possible that there is exclusion in this divine world of presence, he responds by an axiom, the famous axiom of Part Four, that something may exclude something else when it is greater (191). This axiom supports competition, hatred, war, and so on. All that Freud ascribed to a death instinct in *Beyond the Pleasure Principle* has this narrow place of exclusion in the Spinozist system. But as long as reality does not protest against our images, these images are presences. They are merely traces of presence instead of being actual presences.

The role of time in Spinoza also anticipates an important concept in Hume, the concept of custom. Hume relies heavily on the action of time, the repetition of time, and he explains our idea of causation by the repetition of the successive presence of two items. Repetition produces the *as if*.

Following the Corollary, Spinoza provides a Demonstration, the purpose of which is to derive the *as if* of an image from the presence of an affection. The Demonstration relies fundamentally on the role of time.

> When external bodies so determine the fluid parts of the human body that they *often* strike upon the softer parts, the fluid parts change the plane of the soft parts; and *thence* it happens that the fluid parts are reflected from the new planes in a direction different from that in which they used to be reflected, and that also *afterwards*, when they strike against these new planes by their own spontaneous motion, they are reflected in the same way as *when* they were impelled toward those planes by external bodies. Consequently, those fluid bodies produce a modification in the human body while they keep up this reflex motion similar to that produced by the presence of an external body. The mind, therefore, will think as before, that is to say, it will again contemplate the external body as present. This will happen as often as the fluid parts of the human body strikes against those planes by their own spontaneous motion. Therefore, although the external

bodies by which the human body was *once* affected *do not exist*, the mind will perceive them *as if* they were present *so often as* this action is repeated in the body. (96–97, emphases added)

In the initial part of the first sentence, where Spinoza describes external bodies determining the fluid parts of the human body, this we would now characterize by the language of cortical movements. Note also the use again of "often," repetition. The image is explained on the basis of something that happens in the brain. It's a trace theory. Some channels will be instituted by the repetition. Spinoza tries to explain how something that happens only within the brain is similar to something that happens under the action of an external body. The brain may reinstate a process similar to the one produced by the external body. The notion of a similarity between an action from without and an action from within the body plays a decisive role. It is merely in our body. But how we do know the similarity if not by an external similarity? This will be a problem also for Hume. The last sentence summarizes all of Spinoza's answers, which are also each a problem. There is the role of time ("the human body was *once* affected"), the role of repetition ("*so often as* this action is repeated"), the similarity between a repeated action within the brain and an instantaneous impression by a thing, and finally the identity between the image and the *as if* of presence ("*as if* they were present so often as"). The function of a theory of the trace is to derive the image from perception but the image only in the form of a perception of a quasi-presence. Such are the requirements of a philosophy of full being. It cannot give an account of absence as such, but only of derivative implications of presence. More than in any other kind of philosophy, imagination is secondary and perception is primary.

As we have seen, the negative element reappears under the term of exclusion, "a modification which excludes the existence or presence" (Proposition 17, 96). Spinoza's claim here is that we would not be able to differentiate between an image and a perception if the rest of our experience did not exclude the image. This may be challenged because the paradigmatic case that satisfies Spinoza's claim is the dream. When we dream, precisely, we say that we don't perceive, so there is a kind of eclipse of the external world. The image occupies the whole field. But no one knows what is in fact a dream image since we speak of our dreams only when we are awakened. Our account of the dream is for us the equivalent of the dream. Think of the difficulty of dealing in really phenomenological terms with the question of what is a dream, since the consciousness of dreaming is in fact the consciousness of being awakened. And to be awake is to exclude the dream from reality. Then we no longer dream; we perceive. The return of presence when we awaken repels the dream into the darkness of night, but as a kind of memory behind the moment of awakening.

But for Spinoza the larger issue—which, without making comparisons with the Buddha, may perhaps be extended to the whole field of philosophy—is the experience of being awakened. The whole process of philosophy is to awaken, to emerge from a kind of dream. For Descartes and for all the Cartesians the dream is more than a nocturnal accident; it's the paradigm of ordinary life. We are the dreamers. The notion extends back to the pre-Socratics, and we find it also in Plato. In many of the Platonic dialogues, the dream is the ordinary state of the mind not awakened by philosophical reflection. Imagination will cover perception, dreams, and ordinary life; it's considered a mode of being, a level of existence, from which we have to be awakened by philosophical reflection.

The act of excluding in Spinoza is the philosophical act as such which has the function of excluding the illusions, the prejudices, and all the ways of thinking that are natural, that are the first moves of the mind. Again, at stake is more than a mere psychology of the dream image. The concern is for a wisdom of awakened life where the dream becomes the paradigm of all that is inadequate. Therefore, more strongly than in any other rationalistic philosophy, imagination for Spinoza is synonymous with inadequation. The bodily perspective of the affection excludes an adequate perception of things and still more so when we have only the trace of the perception. The question I would raise is whether to give an account of imagination we must start with external bodies, with actualities and externalities, that affect the body. This actuality and this externality are the very presuppositions that a phenomenology of imagination should put into question.

I wanted to keep for the end of our discussion the last lines of the Note, which contain for most critics an unsolved problem. I am interested in these lines, because they preserve the possibility of the fiction as being something more creative than a mere trace. I don't agree with critics' interpretation of this strange qualification. In earlier lines in the Note, Spinoza says that an image does not contain error on its own terms, since it's a presence in the mind as are perceptions. It must be excluded afterward not because it is lacking in itself, but because it is lacking in consideration of the rest of our experience. He continues: "For if the mind, when it imagines non-existent things to be present, could at the same time know that those things did not really exist, it would think its power of imagination to be a virtue of its nature and not a defect, especially if this faculty of imagining depended upon its own nature alone, that is to say (Def. 7, pt. I), if this faculty of the mind were free" (98). It's a very strange text, first, because it speaks of the power of imagination no longer as a residue of a previous affection but on the contrary as a spontaneous act. It is strange, second, because it speaks of this power of imagination as free. In Spinoza's vocabulary, something is free not when it has no causes but when it is its own cause. Therefore, only God is free, because he's determined not by something else but by himself. So imagination is considered as a divine power in a sense, since the definition to which Spinoza sends us back—definition seven from Part I—says that something is free when it is not determined by something else (41). It's the contrary of an affection, because an affection is determined by an external body.

Many interpretations of this passage have been proposed. The most interesting is that Spinoza has here reserved the possibility of a kind of productive imagination, to speak like Kant, that would be the prophetic imagination of the prophets. In Spinoza's *Theologico-Political Treatise*, chapter 2, we indeed have a theory of prophets, and commentators have claimed that this is a theory of free imagination. To whatever extent this claim is true of the *Theologico-Political Treatise*, and I don't know whether it's the only possible interpretation of that text, for two reasons there is no place in the *Ethics* for a prophetic imagination of the prophets. First, there is no place for spiritual inspiration like that of the prophets. Since we have only bodily affections, we would have to say that the prophet is affected both as a body and as a mind. Second, the only way for us to be free in the sense of being determined by our self is to be rational and therefore to proceed from the first mode of knowledge to the second and from the second to the third. It's only in the intuitive intellect, the one that allowed him to write the *Ethics*, that we have this free imagination. We may therefore consider that these lines are something said in parenthesis, which perhaps reserve another possibility that is not exemplified by ordinary life, that does not belong either to ordinary life or to philosophy. It is something beyond philosophy.

If we consider that Spinoza's text is called an *Ethics*, that means that it's a kind of personal transformation from passivity to activity and from activity to intuition. The question is how do we move from one mode of knowledge where we are under the influence of false ideas to a mode of true knowledge. For Spinoza, the pattern is that of a neo-Platonic process, a return to one's fundamental being, a recognition of one's position as a finite mode of God. To recapture this fundamental position in being is the philosophical process. Spinoza's preface in the *Treatise on the Emendation of the Intellect* treats this issue. There he begins, similar to Pascal, with the pitiful state of the person living under passions, and so on. In order for us to rely on a certain instinct for truth in the midst of this unhappiness (*malheur*), we must presuppose that the instinct is not completely lost. It's common both to the Christian and the Jewish traditions that there remains a kind of remnant of the primitive state that allows us to recapture our fundamental existence. Søren Kierkegaard will draw the consequences of this process, saying that there are leaps from one mode to the other. Like the *via*—the modes of being—in Aristotle, each mode constitutes a break in relation to the preceding one. Spinoza, however, does not elaborate the condition of the possibility of his own travel from one mode to another mode of being. Each stage seems an act of philosophical conversion, and there is no answer to how that occurs. Only the one who has gone the path can say that it is the path.

Returning to the last lines of Spinoza's Note, I am tempted to say that they are interesting not only for a possible theory of prophecy but for a theory of fiction. The last paragraph of the Note preserves the place for what Kant will call in the third *Critique*—as he already had in the first *Critique*, although in another framework—productive imagination. What Spinoza has generally provided is a theory of reproductive imagination. Starting from the affection, continuing by the trace, and finishing with the *as if*, we have only covered the field of reproductive imagination. We have not said anything about creative fictions. I consider this final text an acknowledgment of the missing part of a theory of imagination. But perhaps that's to say too much about a text that says so much by itself.

4

Hume

In this lecture I shall present the problem of imagination in Hume in two parts.[1] Hume's approach is interesting, first, as an attempt as radical as that of Spinoza to derive all the features of the image—mainly the absence of its object—from the most actual and most present of all of experience, what he calls the impression. The model is that of a reductive philosophy, the reduction of the image to the impression. I shall try to show the failure of this attempt that we may trace in the work itself. Hume's own examples, which are given more or less at random, don't fit with his initial framework and so put it in question. By means of this failure we explore the difficulty of the problem of imagination and perhaps the impossibility of reducing it to one paradigm.

What is even more noteworthy is, second, the emergence in Hume of a new theme that will completely shift subsequent interest to the following inquiry: analysis of the connecting function of imagination. No longer is the focus on imagination's role in making present the absent but on its role in connecting ideas. The theme will appear in Hume under the title "Of the Connexion or Association of Ideas" (Section IV of Book I, Part I). The theme is quite new. The Kantian approach to imagination as a synthetic power is introduced by Hume.

Hume's *Treatise of Human Nature* contains two main Books, the first on the understanding and the second on the passions. In the Book on the passions there will also be many uses and applications of imagination, but I have chosen what is fundamental concerning our topic and shall concentrate on Book I. Part I of the first Book begins with a section "Of the Origin of our Ideas." The word *origin* shows the intention of the work. It is a genetic approach, not in the sense that a modern psychologist would use the term—following the development of a child from childhood to adulthood—but genetic in the philosophical sense: how we can derive the meaning of something from the meaning of something more fundamental.

This approach raises many questions, such as what is the meaning of *origin* in that sense. But Hume here relies on ordinary experience and ordinary language, on how everyone would understand the term. The claim is that if everyone understands what he is saying, he doesn't need to proceed further in the discussion.

Our first subject of inquiry, the reduction of the image to the impression, proceeds from the initial decision that opens the book.

> All the perceptions of the human mind resolve themselves into two distinct kinds, which I shall call IMPRESSIONS and IDEAS. The difference betwixt these consists in the degree of force and liveliness with which they strike upon the mind, and make their way into our thought or consciousness. Those perceptions, which enter with most force and violence, we may name *impressions*; and under this name I comprehend all our sensations, passions and emotions, as they make their first appearance in the soul. By *ideas* I mean the faint images of these in thinking and reasoning; such as, for instance, are all the perceptions excited by the present discourse, excepting only, those which arise from the sight and touch, and excepting the immediate pleasure or uneasiness it may occasion. (Hume 1965, 1)[2]

In the opening sentence, the word *resolve* is very important and indicates the reductive process; the approach is undertaken by means of a philosophical genealogy of experiences. Note also that the word *images* appears immediately as the kernel of the second category, the idea. Hume's general claim in these lines is that impressions and ideas can be assessed according to only one scale, the scale of force and liveliness. All human experience can be classified on this scale. There are many synonymous expressions for the scale: *force, liveliness, strike, violence,* and *enter.*

We should ask at the very beginning how does Hume *know* these "first appearance[s]" that he calls impressions? The problem here is one later raised, for example, by J. L. Austin in his book *Sense and Sensibilia,* where he argues that this knowledge is in fact a construct of the philosopher, since we must rely on the first appearance of experience. The first appearance of experience is a primitive stage that has to be reconstructed in order to proceed further. Those who have read Hegel's *Phenomenology of Spirit* know that nothing is more abstract than the idea of the impression. It's the construct on the basis of which we may reach ordinary and concrete experience, experience which is immediately more complex, more elaborated. Hume's method is borrowed from the natural sciences: it proceeds from the simple to the complex on the basis of an assumption of what is simple. But the philosophical status of the impression is much in question. We have no access to a pure impression except in some very artificial situations. If, for example, someone projects on a screen a color that has no shape, so that we don't interpret it as being this or that but see a pure patch of color, this might be an impression. Nothing is more rare than a pure impression.

More important for our purposes is the way in which Hume tries to proceed to the image from the impression. He provides many examples that point toward a great diversity of cases. We have already quoted his first example of images that are "excited by the present discourse." Interesting here is that the imagination is close to language, since the images are not merely traces but evocations developed through language. (Later I shall explore this approach starting from how metaphors display images.) Is it not language here, and not the degree of liveliness, that makes the difference between the mere impression and the image? On the next page he evokes another kind of example that appears for him as an exception to his description. On the one hand we ordinarily don't confuse an image and a thing. "The common degrees of these are easily distinguished . . ." (2). Yet the sentence concludes: "tho' it is not impossible but in particular instances they may very nearly approach to each other." And his example is the images that occur in sleep. "Thus in sleep, in a fever, in madness, or in any violent emotions of soul, our ideas may approach to our impressions." The criterion of differentiation between image and impression is immediately defeated. These examples of dreams and hallucinations are examples close to the *as if* present, the *as though* present of Spinoza.

One further difficulty at the start concerns not only the difference between impressions and images but their relation. Hume assumes that there is an irreducible relation between them which is that of resemblance. "The first circumstance, that strikes my eye, is the great resemblance betwixt our impressions and ideas in every other particular, except their degree of force and vivacity. The one seems to be in a manner the reflexion of the other; so that all the perceptions of the mind are double, and appear both as impressions and ideas" (2–3). If the first criterion of impressions and images is their difference in degree of vivacity or force, the second is their relation of resemblance. What is at stake is the basic function of the copy, what is it to copy something. This will play a great role in the future. In phenomenological terms, we could say that the image immediately appears as an image *of* and refers back to something that is similar to it. We could speak here of an attempt to derive the image by the copy, whereas Spinoza tried a derivation by the trace, the trace being a remnant or residue of the experience. In Hume we start from the axiom that every impression may be reduplicated in its own image. We have at the very beginning the representative function reduplicating the function of the impression. This is axiomatic in Hume.

Everything that is an impression may have a copy that reduplicates it. "After the most accurate examination, of which I am capable, I venture to affirm, that the rule here holds without any exception, and that every simple idea has a simple impression, which resembles it; and every simple impression a correspondent idea" (3). This notion of the copy appears on this page several times. It is an axiomatic statement. There is a mutual relation of reflection between an idea and an impression.

What is at stake here is the function of the sign, because immediately we assign to the image a signitive function—the possibility of standing for. Something may always stand for a primitive experience. What is therefore fundamental in human understanding is that I live on two planes. Immediately I have impressions, but these impressions in turn may immediately have their own copy which may signify them. I should say that the word *signify* is too Husserlian and is not Hume's term. Hume uses the concept of representation that is common to the Cartesian and Lockean tradition in which he places himself. Representation here means exactly what the term says. There is not only a presentation but a *re*presentation. The *re-* here is important as the reduplicative function of the image.

This reduplicative function opens the field. If we had only the impression, then we would be caught in the impressional world. But we have a means of escaping the actuality of experience by this action of reduplication. In the distance between the copy and the impression, the complexity of the problem may engulf itself. The distance opens the possibility of having fictions, which are very far from the impressions. We have introduced a kind of principle of dissimilarity under the title of resemblance, since resemblance implies a whole range of degrees of similarity. At one end of the range we have the pure copy, but at the other end we have complex imagination. Hume himself provides these examples: "I can imagine to myself such a city as the New Jerusalem, whose pavement is gold and walls are rubies, tho' I never saw any such. I have seen Paris; but shall I affirm I can form such an idea of that city, as will perfectly represent all its streets and houses in their real and just proportions?" (3). In the first sentence, the phrase "tho' I never saw . . ." indicates that there was no immediate impression. The second sentence suggests that with the copy we have the possibility of an exact copy but also of an independent copy. The question is whether we may put under the same title of copy such opposing examples as images, dreams, the fictions of art, and so on.

But it is typical of Hume's method to be on the one hand very dogmatic, saying there are only two kind of things, and yet to be very flexible in his examples. He's both radical and flexible, but this has to do with the method itself. He claims to establish a general proposition: "[A]ll our simple ideas in their first appearance are deriv'd from simple impressions, which are correspondent to them, and which they exactly represent" (4). This sentence will be the source of great philosophical difficulties. What is the first appearance of an experience? What does it mean to *appear* first? Where do I get simple impressions? What does it mean to *correspond* or to *represent*? What is this relational function introduced within an impression to *represent*?

In section III, Hume turns to the differences between memory and imagination. He was much perplexed by this problem and for one fundamental reason. In both cases I escape the pressure of the existing world. In both memory and imagination, there is the elsewhere of thought. The problem they present is what is the status of nonexisting, not actually existing, objects. This is in fact the fundamental problem: what does imagination add to or subtract from reality? As we shall see, this problem will be raised mainly by aesthetics, where the fictional object is not merely a lack of an object but perhaps the opening of reality by means of fiction.

Historically, authors such as Augustine and others did not so much reflect on imagination as on memory, because the problem of memory was linked to the Platonic tradition of reminiscence. The ontological bearing of memory was more obvious for them, because the claim was that through memory I recover my true being. Memory was not only the dimension of the past in temporal terms but of the fundamental. The subject of memory was both the psychology of memory and the metaphysics of reminiscence, the reminiscence of my fundamental existence, what I "was" and still fundamentally am but have forgotten. The problem of forgetfulness was very important. Memory meets the challenge of the fundamental forgetfulness that constitutes the, let us say, sinful existence, existence in the regime of lost paradise. The question of the fundamental forgetfulness of ordinary life is central. It's more the spiritual problem of recovering my essential being that is at stake. This issue will last very long in the history of thought, since Heidegger also addresses this question of the forgetfulness of ordinary life, the concealment of my true being, and the unconcealment (*a-lētheia*) that constitutes philosophy. (In Greek the etymology of the word for truth, *alētheia*, has to do with *lēthē*, which is oblivion, forgetfulness.) Memory is not merely a psychological problem. It also presents an important philosophical topic, since it raises the question of the nature of time. How is it possible that something that no longer exists once more exists in the form of a memory? The never-more and the once-more are connected. In a sense memory presents a more difficult problem than imagination, since the difference between imagination and memory is that imagination is not linked to the past. It does not have the intention of reenacting a past experience. Imagination is mere absence; it is not temporally bound but free.

It is true that we cannot have productive imagination without some element of reproduction, because I cannot imagine something that would have no connection with past experience. But the examples of imagination taken from the classical period are generally not very good for the purpose of thinking about productive imagination. They speak, as we shall see also in Hume, of centaurs or of monsters made up of parts that belong to actual experience, the wings of an eagle, its beak, and so on. These classical examples skip the problem of creativity, of productive imagination, through invocation instead of the notion of a complex idea. This is indeed Hume's strategy. He substitutes for creativity the question of the complex, a composite or compound image the parts of which have been borrowed from past experience. In that sense, productive imagination interpreted in terms of complex ideas is not distinguishable from memory. Every time in the classical period that the emphasis is put on the trace or even, as in Hume, on the copy, then it is impossible to distinguish between memory images and fictional images. The fictional images are complex ideas derived entirely from past experience.

If we ask, therefore, whether there are two kinds of images, the memory of the past and the free images of imagination such as fiction, Hume's response, typical of a reductionist method, is to put memory and imagination on the same scale, claiming their differences are only in degree. As long as the difference between reproductive and productive imagination is not elaborated as a fundamental feature of imagination, then there is no basic difference between memory and imagination. And this is Hume's claim. They don't represent different experiences, as Husserl would say, arguing that the intention toward the past is not the same as the intention toward the absent. In Hume they are placed on the same scale; some images impose themselves in only a more forcible manner than others. "'Tis evident at first sight, that the ideas of the memory are much more lively and strong than those of the imagination, and that the former faculty paints its objects in more distinct colours, than any which are employ'd by the latter" (9). It is "evident at first sight." Everything is always evident, despite the bundle of problematic difficulties. His differentiation here too has its exception which he shall try to reduce. It's a very honest procedure. First he asserts the axiom, and then he qualifies the claim. He goes on to argue that the difference between imagination and memory lies not only in liveliness but in order. What is important in memory is that I respect the order of experience. He will then proceed to try to solve the difference between memory and imagination by introducing the notion of complex ideas. It's at the level of complexity that the difference occurs.

It's not so much Hume's answer that interests me here as the examples he provides. Memory really becomes a problem when it is developed in a narration, as by historians (9). The art of narration is a very complex act; it's much more than a mere outburst isolated as the return of a past experience. Narration is a construct; it's not merely a return but a construct. What have we then to oppose to the historical narration? A construct in the imagination, fables: "The fables we meet with in poems and romances put this [the ordering role of memory] entirely out of question" (10). Hume speaks of "the liberty of the imagination to transpose and change its ideas" (10). We have gone beyond the impression and mere copying. Hume presents the possibility of creative reconstruction. It is interesting to see that in the extended passage Hume introduces a synonym—*fancy*—that distinguishes what we could now call the creative function of imagination. There is a confluence in this text between imagination and fancy.

> Nature . . . is totally confounded [in the fables], and nothing mentioned but winged horses, fiery dragons and monstrous giants. Nor will this liberty of the *fancy* appear strange, when we consider, that all our ideas are copy'd from our impressions, and that there are not any two impressions which are perfectly inseparable. Not to mention, that this is an evident consequence of the division of ideas into simple and complex. Where-ever the imagination perceives a difference among ideas, it can easily produce a separation. (10, emphasis added)

Hume's examples of the winged horses and so on are perhaps not very illuminating, because he does not raise the issue that what is interesting in a fable is not the particular images but the plot. The real productive imagination occurs in the building of the novel's plot, and the construction of the characters are only partial elements in this general construct. Nevertheless, Hume's statement is enough to raise the question of the liberty of imagination (10). The liberty of imagination is taken as a counterexample to his own notion of the copy, of the idea copied from an impression. He thinks that the notion of ideas as complex is sufficient to meet the challenge of the liberty of imagination. We must balance Hume's first axiom that each impression has its copy with what he calls a "second principle" (10), the liberty in the copying, and all the degrees of independence implied by that. Does this not destroy the notion of the copy? Can we stretch the notion of the copy so far as to cope with the fiction? In future lectures we will discuss this as a phenomenological problem.

For the second part of my discussion of Hume, I turn to his development of imagination's power of connection. As I said at the outset, the notion of connection is the decisive term in Hume's analysis, since it anticipates the

Kantian concept of synthesis that we shall consider in the next lecture. The analysis begins in Section IV: "Of the Connexion or Association of Ideas" (10). The introduction of this new consideration concerning the connecting power of imagination will be of tremendous importance concerning two problems that give to the problem of imagination its philosophical dimension. First, we expect from this analysis the solution of the problem of abstraction. This will be very important in the empiricist tradition. All the following sections of the first Part will be an attempt to derive all the abstract ideas from the complex ideas and the complex ideas from the image. This claim defines the empiricist school. "The idea of a substance as well as that of a mode, is nothing but a collection of simple ideas, that are united by the imagination, and have a particular name assigned them, by which we are able to recall, either to ourselves or others, that collection" (16). Here the connecting power of imagination is more important than its copying power. This is why I insist so much on the two distinct contributions of Hume. The connecting power of imagination is invoked to solve the problem of substance, a problem of considerable weight in classical philosophy from Aristotle to Descartes, John Locke, and so on. The idea is that it's in the imagination that we make a whole of certain impressions and give a name to this collection. While the nominalist convention is that the unity is given by the name, Hume claims that we may put one name to one thing because the imagination has already gathered the piecemeal experiences.

The argument that imagination solves the problem of abstraction is one of the reasons for which, as I said in the first lecture, modern epistemology has so much distrust for the problem of imagination, because the argument may have granted too much to imagination. In Frege and Husserl, the representation (*Vorstellung*) will be excluded from the field of epistemology. For the sake of emphasis on propositional content, modern epistemology will take a quite different starting point, in the proposition rather than in the isolated idea in its representation, in its image. The failure of a philosophy of imagination to solve the problem of abstraction may liberate the philosophy of imagination from this unfortunate and perhaps impossible task and reorient it in the direction opened by Kant's third *Critique*. But this question of abstraction will have to be not only explored but also exhausted before the imagination no longer has the burden of grounding all our abstractions and the categories of substance, mode, and so on.

The second reason the connecting function of imagination will be of a great philosophical import is because of the problem of causality. Hume's discussion of causation occupies Part III of Book I of the *Treatise* in the same way that the problem of abstract ideas occupies most of Part I. The problem of causality is precisely a problem of connecting items: how is the movement of a ball transmitted to the movement of another ball; how is the first movement the cause of the second? Here too it will be the function of imagination to carry the solution of the problem that enters philosophy with Hume as the problem of inference. How do we infer from one event to another event, from one state of the world to another state? The problem of inference is derived from that of connection and that of connection from that of association in imagination. Imagination will carry on its shoulders the two huge problems of abstract ideas and causation. Each presents an issue of connection. An abstract idea is a connection in the form of a collection, a collection then given a name, a concept. The cause/effect relationship of causality is a connection with discrete stages.

In Part I, then, Hume opens two approaches—on abstract ideas and on the connection of causation—and the crucial contribution of section IV lies in its beginning the latter discussion. To introduce this new function of connection we must shift our attention from the problem of resemblance—the resemblance between copy and impression, the reduplication of the same in the different that will represent it—to a problem of movement from one idea to the other. The dynamization of the image becomes the important issue.

> Were ideas entirely loose and unconnected, chance alone wou'd join them; and 'tis impossible the same ideas should form regularly into complex ones . . . without *some bond of union* among them, some associating quality, by which one idea naturally introduces another. This uniting principle among ideas is not to be consider'd as an inseparable connexion; for that has been already excluded from the *imagination*: nor yet are we to conclude, that without it the mind cannot join two ideas; for nothing is more *free* than that faculty: but we are only to regard it as a gentle force, which commonly prevails, and is the cause why, among other things, languages so nearly correspond to each other. (10, emphases added)

The same word *imagination* covers both the function of copying and that of uniting. Note also Hume's emphasis that imagination moves freely from one idea to the other. The end of the argument is strange, because Hume contends that there is sufficient regularity in this free movement of imagination to allow different cultures to make the same connections and collections so that, for example, the names given to collections can be translated from one language to the other.

This argument may reflect that Hume perceives a danger in introducing a kind of wild faculty that would render completely impossible the solution of logical problems such as the identity of an abstract idea and the regularity of the laws of nature. How can the free movement of imagination permit a philosophy worthy of Newton's discoveries? Hume had to introduce a flexible function of connection that yet had enough order both to solve the problem of the creative function of fiction and to support the order of the world in the natural sciences. Imagination is an ambiguous function that is sufficiently interconnecting to support abstract ideas and causation but is also flexible enough to leave room for free fictional creation. It is a principle both of invention and of regularity. Once more we see the ambiguity of imagination which has always two contrary and two opposite functions.

What is imagination's power of connecting ideas? Hume's analysis here is a good piece in the phenomenology of imagination.

> 'Tis plain, that in the course of our thinking, and in the constant revolution of our ideas, our imagination runs easily from one idea to any other that resembles it, and that this quality alone is to the fancy a sufficient bond and association. 'Tis likewise evident, that as the senses, in changing their objects, are necessitated to change them regularly, and take them as they lie contiguous to each other, the imagination must by long custom acquire the same method of thinking, and run along the parts of space and time in conceiving its objects. (11)

It is always plain, evident, obvious. In discussing the "revolution of our ideas," the word *revolution* comes from cosmology and the revolution of the heavenly spheres. Imagination has a running function; it runs "from one idea to any other." Here he calls it "the fancy." Custom will introduce the element of regularity that the running power could destroy.

When we ask of Hume what is this power of connecting ideas, what is this bond, he says that he doesn't know. He doesn't know, and it's not the task of the philosopher to raise questions without answers. It is very interesting to read his honest and modest acknowledgment that this is requisite in an irreducible notion. He presents irreducible notions: an impression may be copied in an image, and two images can be coupled, can be tied together. "These are therefore the principles of union or cohesion among our simple ideas, and in the imagination supply the place of that inseparable connexion, by which they are united in our memory. Here is a kind of attraction, which in the mental world will be found to have as extraordinary effects as in the natural, and to shew itself in as many and as various forms" (12–13). Note the roles played by both imagination and memory. The model is a mechanical one, and that will unfortunately play a negative role in this field. The model transposes a model of attraction of mechanical origin, of balls hitting one another. There is no doubt that it is the model of attraction coming from

Newtonian science and transposed into the mental sphere that paved the way for the discovery of the connecting function of the imagination. The mental world is similar here to the natural world. And Hume says that he doesn't pretend to explain that similarity. "Nothing is more requisite for a true philosopher, than to restrain the intemperate desire of searching into causes..." (13). This is a kind of pre-Kantian statement that the philosopher must restrain oneself to raise questions that have answers. Because we cannot explain the causes of attraction in the mental sphere, we have to say that it is plain, that it is evident. We rely on the surface of experience, and Hume does not claim to go further.

I shall not comment here on the problem of abstract ideas, since I shall take up that topic in later lectures on H. H. Price and Edmund Husserl. I prefer to say something about Hume's solution to the problem of causation, because we find in that discussion some very interesting references to imagination. Recall our earlier quotation of imagination as running, which he relates to fancy (11). Later Hume says: "The fancy runs from one end of the universe to the other in collecting those ideas, which belong to any subject" (24). When imagination runs along, it "runs from one end of the universe to the other." This is the freedom of imagination. While each impression is actual and here and now, imagination runs. How then does imagination, this free capacity of running from one end of the universe to the other, offer connection? This raises the issue of inference. Why does this issue concern imagination? Not only has inference offered connections in the past to experience, but custom is enough to provide a kind of consistency or coherence to this connecting act. What is more important is that we project into the future a connection that holds from the past. This is the enigma of the problem of induction. The problem of induction is that of the repetition of a connection: how may I infer that in the future it will be the same, that the sun will rise tomorrow?

We see that imagination is not only a connecting power but an anticipating function of something as the same. This introduces a new aspect of imagination. Imagination here is quite opposite to memory. Memory puts an order in past experience, but here we put an order in future experience. We have the projection of the constancy of the conjunction from the past to the future. The issue will appear in Alexius Meinong as the problem of the assumption. Hume writes: "[A]s an object similar to one of these is suppos'd to be immediately present in its impression, we thence presume on the existence of one similar to its usual attendant" (90). A bit further: "I wou'd renew my question, why from this experience we form any conclusion *beyond* those past instances, of which we have had experience" (91, emphasis added). The imagination has the capacity to go beyond a past experience and to anticipate future experience on the basis of its model. The productive function of imagination is always there even if without a name.

Hume goes on to say that this productive function is not based on reason. Reason does not tell us why something is the same as what we hold from the past. We don't know the reason it is the same, since we notice only the regularity of the conjunction. We have no idea of how a cause produces its effect. Against Aristotle and others, there is no rationality of production. We have only the regularity in the past that we project into the future. But this projection is an extension. Imagination extends experience.

> Thus not only our reason fails us in the discovery of the ultimate connexion of causes and effects, but even after experience has inform'd us of their constant conjunction, 'tis impossible for us to satisfy ourselves by our reason, why we shou'd *extend* that experience beyond those particular instances, which have fallen under our observation. We suppose, but are never able to prove, that there must be a resemblance betwixt those objects, of which we have had experience, and those which lie beyond the reach of our discovery. (91–92, emphasis added)

Here is the triumph of imagination in Hume, the capacity of projecting a similar experience from the past into the future. Resemblance at this stage is not between a copy and a model but between an experience that we have not had and an experience that we have had. The experience that we have not had is that which is "beyond the reach of our discovery," and this is what we connect to the past. "When the mind, therefore, passes from the idea or impression of one object to the idea of belief of another, it is not determin'd by reason, but by certain principles, which associate together the ideas of these objects, and unite them in the imagination" (92). This is the pre-Kantian text *par excellence*. Imagination has a unifying power that ties past experience to the experience that we have not had, the experience "beyond the reach of our discovery."

Let me conclude by raising the question of the unity of Hume's examples of imagination, since their range is immense, extending from the mere copy of an impression to the projection of a similar state of the world on the basis of a past connection.

5

Kant: Critique of Pure Reason

In this lecture, we shall lose ourselves in Kant's *Critique of Pure Reason.* My introductory remarks will concern the emergence with Kant of a new problematics. We may begin from what we have already said concerning Aristotle, Pascal, Spinoza, and Hume, since in the lineage from Aristotle we have followed one and the same problem: the problem of the intermediary. Imagination was an intermediary between sense and reason. In a way imagination in Kant's work is in this position, too, namely, that of being an intermediary function. Now, though, the problem of the intermediary becomes the problem of the mediating link. Imagination is not only placed at a certain stage in the scale; it connects the extreme ends of the scale.

This connecting function may be linked to a second trait that we may borrow from our study of Hume. Recall that in Hume the problem of the image as a copy, a copy of an impression, was overcome in the treatment of the imagination as a movement from one element to another in a connecting chain. Imagination addressed the problem of the association of ideas, and Hume's approach became classical and then to a certain extent a kind of gimmick in modern philosophy. Kant changes this function as well from within. No longer is association built on the image or metaphor of attraction borrowed from Newtonian physics, the attraction of bodies. The problem of association becomes the problem of synthesis. In relation to both Aristotle and Hume, therefore, there is in Kant a mutation within an issue that is received from a certain tradition but which undergoes a decisive change. Let me link these two changes. If imagination has this mediating role between two extremes, it is because it is connecting. It is mediating because it is connecting. The notion of the synthesis of imagination is hence a kernel issue.

Kant's third decisive step arises in relation to what we said about Pascal and Spinoza. In their two texts, the paradigmatic case of the image was the *as though*, the *as if*, as when we mistake an absent object for a present object. This problem will completely recede in Kant, since thanks to imagination's mediating and connecting role, it will become a constitutive element in the construction of the world, in the constitution of what Kant calls objectivity. The problem of the illusion, the problem of the fiction, will be put aside—and, as we shall see, will return under another mode—for the sake of this constitutive role of imagination. We may link this third change to the difficulties and even the impossibilities of the Humean concept of a copy. In order to have a copy, we must have, as Hume said, a first appearance of something that was not a copy but an absolute given. This was the notion of the impression in Hume. And this notion had difficulties. As we shall see later in E. H. Gombrich and others, the notion of a copy is also problematic. To make a copy of something is a very complicated operation. But for the moment consider what is a copy a copy of? The model of the copy collapsed between Hume and Kant, because it appears that what we call objective reality is already a construct of judgment. The judgment of perception— that this is a tree, that it has such and such characteristics—is an operation of the mind at a high level. If the impression as an absolute given does not disappear, it becomes a limit beyond which we already find ourselves each time that we say that we perceive something. Perception itself appears as a very complicated process within which the imagination is already working.

As mentioned, we could reach this state of reflection on quite another basis than Hume and his issue of the copy of an impression. In *Art and Illusion*, Gombrich's critique of art shows that the simplest drawing of a model—by a child or by anyone—is already ruled by some paradigms, some implicit models. To provide a copy of something is already a construction. Further, if we compare the copy to a photograph we gain nothing, because the photograph too is a certain choice by the one who took the picture. There is a composition of the landscape already in the simple act of directing oneself toward it. The opposition between the copy and the model, the copy and the impression, is a dead end or at least constitutes a problem of its own. Later I shall return to the question of the notion of a portrait with Gombrich.

Because the relation between copy and impression appeared as an impossible problem, Kant replaced it by the question of objectivity and how imagination contributes to objectivity. Objectivity is a work, and imagination is one of the stages of this process in the constitution of the object as an object, as having certain characteristics of universality, of necessity, and so on. The word *object* has a much richer scope than that of the given—data, sense data, and so on.

Due to Kant's choice of the paradigmatic example of the object, the issue of fiction disappears from the forefront of the problematic. That does not mean that the creative function of imagination is overlooked. On the contrary, because of the constitutive role of imagination, we witness the emergence of a distinction between productive and reproductive imagination. But we must not mistake the notion of productive imagination with that of fiction. Imagination is productive within the process of objectifying. What has been given up is the problem of the copy. The notion of reproductive imagination recedes, because the reproductive is the copy. Productive imagination is the synthetical function within perception. This is expressed in Kant's choice of the German word *Einbildungskraft* for imagination's active process of connecting, of mediating. *Bild* means image but thanks to the ambiguity of the German *bilden* it also means forming. It's the way of putting into an image. *Einbildungskraft* means power or faculty. By the choice of the word *Einbildung*, the productive function is emphasized, but it's less the power to generate an image than to generate connecting ties between our capacity to receive and our capacity to order. The connecting link will be between the passivity of the impression and the activity of the judgment of a concept. The undertaking is not a psychological inquiry but rather a transcendental inquiry in the sense that Kant calls a transcendental inquiry any kind of inquiry into the condition of the possibility of something. We are not describing some mental given but a function that is the condition of the possibility of having objects, of having experience and objects of experience. Kant says that the condition of the object and the condition of the experience of the object are one and the same.

Another word Kant uses for imagination is *Phantasie*, what in English too may be called fantasies—illusions, dreams, and so on. There is a split in the field, as I described in the first lecture, and it is expressed by the duplications of the words. *Phantasie* will represent free, wild imagination that is not directed toward this synthetic construction of the objectivity of the world.

The counterpart of the tremendous Kantian advance is that the problem of imagination now is swallowed up by the problem of objectivity. A large part of the field that we displayed in the first lecture is no longer covered. Focus on the role of imagination within the process of objectivity is a choice of a small section of this field. Once more, productive does not mean fictional but the production of objectivity thanks to the imagination's synthetic function. The problem of the creative power of imagination outside of objectivity will be split from the field of the first *Critique* and will reappear within a quite different framework, that of aesthetics. What has been lost for the theory of knowledge is recovered for the theory of aesthetics. All the free expressions of imagination will be reserved for the problem of aesthetics. After Kant we'll have this dichotomy within the problem of imagination between its contribution to the objectification of our experience and its free expression in art and so on. We have a theory of cognitive imagination and a theory of aesthetic imagination. This will be a fundamental trait in the modern problem of imagination.

For my part, I should say that a task after Kant will be to rebuild the unity of the problem of imagination which is split between its cognitive and its aesthetic functions. To a large extent, the opposition between the emotive and the cognitive that is familiar to empiricism is a result of the Kantian dichotomy between the first *Critique* and the third *Critique* concerning imagination despite, as we shall see, that Kant never said that imagination in aesthetics is merely emotive. Kant will link aesthetic imagination to another use of judgment, the judgment of taste. This will no longer be a judgment about objects but about our pleasure and the relation between certain objects and pleasure and pain. Nevertheless, the direction toward an emotive assessment of imagination will be one of the results of the Kantian problematic. Once again, a philosophical problematics is always the choice of a certain paradigmatic case, of a leading thread, and this choice has both its positive and its negative sides.

Turning to the text, our first excerpt belongs to the "Transcendental Deduction" in the first edition. (The volume compiles the two editions of the first *Critique*.) "[A]ll perceptions are grounded a priori in pure intuition (in time, the form of their inner intuition as representations), association in pure synthesis of imagination, and empirical consciousness in pure apperception, that is, in the thorough-going identity of the self in all possible representations" (Kant 1965, 141; A 115–16).[1] The synthesis of imagination is placed as a middle term between two opposite poles, one being called pure intuition—the pure given in space and time such as a patch of color or a sound that merely appears—and a principle of identity that is called here pure apperception, what in Kant expresses the act of the synthesis of making one and the same of a certain experience. With this first quotation, we may identify the place of the problem of imagination. Why does imagination have this place? Because the *Critique* is confronted with a fundamental enigma: the discrepancy between two levels of knowledge, the receptivity of sensible knowledge and the spontaneity of thought. To put it in other language that is equivalent and closer to our text, there is a discrepancy between the manifold—the fact that impressions are scattered—and the one, a difference between the many and the one, to put it in classical terms borrowed from Plato. The receptivity of sensible knowledge is emphasized by the role of space and time, which Kant calls the a priori framework of this manifold, because it is in space and time that we receive all our impressions. The spontaneity of thought is expressed by the structural role of the categories: substance, cause, and so on. Therefore, Kant's problematic is that of a gap, a discontinuity, a discrepancy between two levels.

The operation thanks to which this gap is overcome is the judgment. In Kant the judgment is not merely the logical act of connecting a subject and a predicate but a transcendental act, that of putting an intuition under a concept. When, for example, I say that this is a table, I place a certain impression that I receive from the senses under a label, under a category. In the case of a table it's an empirical concept. If, though, in science I put a certain string of experiences under the category of cause, saying that this is a causal link, then I place it not only under an empirical concept but under a transcendental concept, the concept of cause. Such is the enigmatic experience that allows us to receive and at the same time to determine conceptually an object of knowledge. One of the tasks of imaginations is to make the judgment possible, to make this connection between an impression and a concept, between two things belonging to two different functions. We want, Kant says, a faculty that would be homogeneous to the concept and to the intuition, both sensible and intelligible, intuitive and intellectual. In my opening remarks to the present lecture I called this the heritage of Aristotle: the problem of the intermediary link. But as I also said, imagination is no longer a position on a scale; it's a connecting function between the two poles of opposition. We shall have to retain something from this concept of a function which has both intellectual and sensible features, which is in itself mixed, with a twofold affinity. I shall for myself keep something of this intuition when I shall look at the imagination as a connecting link between the verbal and the visual. The problem of imagination is identified as the problem of the third term, the mediating term, and not only as an intermediary stage on a scale.

In the "Preliminary Remark" (131–40; A 98–A 114) to the "Transcendental Deduction," Kant discusses this synthesis. Kant considered a succession of steps from the mere manifold where an experience is still scattered to its recognition in the unity of a concept. Internal to this analysis Kant will elaborate a theory of reproductive imagination from which he will distinguish productive imagination. We have to do with a series of syntheses, and the imagination is not only the name of synthesis but a certain stage in the synthesis. The first synthesis is the synthesis of apprehension (131; A 98). In order to say that this is a tree or that this is a table, I must not lose the successive aspects or sides of the experience. I must gather them and retain them. "[I]t must first be run through, and held together" (131; A 99). This is an allusion to the expression we read in Hume that the imagination runs along the impressions. For Kant, though, more is at issue than the power of running through and holding together. There is also a possibility of reproducing, of being the same. This is the second synthesis, the synthesis of reproduction in imagination (132; A 100). This is Kant's first kind of approach to imagination in this work. In order to make himself comprehensible, Kant starts with a common experience and from there proceeds to the condition of the possibility of this experience. This common experience is the possibility of evoking a thing on the basis of association despite its absence (the "empirical imagination" [132; A 100]). We make use of the notion of the absence, although not for the sake of a theory of absence as we shall later see with Husserl, Sartre, and the phenomenologists. In Kant here, the problem of absence is incorporated into the problem of association. When I look at an object, I look at it from different sides, and I must not forget the previous sides seen. They must be retained but in the mode of absence, since when I look at one side, I no longer see the other side. In viewing an object, a great part is absent. What I call the object is a presence on one side but an absence on all the other sides. The absent sides are incorporated into the present side. There is an element of absence in the structure of what I call an object, mainly objects in space and solid objects that I cannot see from all sides at once. Apprehension of an object contains the dimension of absence.

The transcendental and no longer psychological approach considers how this association is possible. It is possible, Kant writes, because of "the reproducibility of appearances." Experience, he says, "necessarily presupposes the reproducibility of appearances," the possibility to make present once more what is no longer there, the continuity of experience in contrast to the discontinuity of appearances. The experience of one aspect after the other cannot give us an object if I cannot retain the absent within the present and make a whole of it all.

> When I seek to draw a line in thought, or to think of the time from one noon to another, or even to represent to myself some particular number, obviously the various manifold representations that are involved must be apprehended by me in thought one after the other. But if I were always to drop out of thought the preceding representations (the first part of the line [and so on]), and did not reproduce them while advancing to those that follow, a complete representation would never be obtained ... (133; A 102)

When I draw a line in thought, only one part of the line is present in my act of drawing. All the other parts of the line are outside the present stroke of my thought's pen. A more interesting example than that of the line that I draw is the sentence that I hear. With temporal objects, which are typically linguistic objects, such as a sentence, I hear only one part of the sentence at a time. The meaning of the sentence is a recapitulation of what has been

Kant: Critique of Pure Reason 67

said and also an anticipation of what will be said. I never hear at once an entire sentence. I construct it as if it has meaning as a whole. This is a good example of what Kant calls the reproductive synthesis of the imagination. Kant concludes this section by saying that "the reproductive synthesis of the imagination is to be counted among the transcendental acts of the mind. We shall therefore entitle this faculty the transcendental faculty of imagination" (133; A 102). Kant calls this synthesis reproductive, because there is nothing creative here. We merely prevent aspects of experience from dropping out of the field. This imagination is not at all an alternative to perception but an operation immanent to perception. It's encapsulated within the framework of perception. We have completely given up the opposition between impression and copy. It's a quite different approach.

We now turn to the productive imagination, in the introduction to the "Transcendental Deduction." The productive imagination is Kant's second approach to imagination. We have already quoted Kant's presentation, in the same section, of the "association in pure synthesis of imagination" (141; A 116). That text proceeded from below upward following the stages of a progressive synthesis from the manifold—the pure scattered field—to the unification in one and the same meaning. Now we proceed from above downward. "If, now, we desire to follow up the inner ground of this connection of the representations to the point upon which they have all to converge . . . , we must begin with pure apperception" (141; A 116). Under discussion is no longer the act of gathering the manifold but, on the contrary, the capacity of the central act of saying I am myself, I am the one who in saying myself expands that onto the field of experience. Here the energy of imagination is the power of unity expanding from this center of unity that Kant calls the I. We assume here an original principle of unity that Kant calls the principle of apperception. When I say that I am the one who did this or that, I put the unity of the author behind the multiplicity of acts. Also, when I consider memory, I am able to ascribe to myself some events from the past that I call my childhood and so on. I recognize myself as the one who has these memories. The question of the one who has these and those experiences is for Kant the nuclear kernel of the problem of synthesis. We would not be able to undertake synthesis if we did not have the power of apprehending ourselves as one and the same. It is this power of recognizing ourselves as the one who has these experiences that is expanded and spread over the field of experience.

Therefore, we may reach imagination from both poles, a manifold that is gathered or a one that is expanded. The imagination lies somewhere in between these two poles. This approach has the advantage of placing the question of imagination directly in connection with the problem of the center of unity. "This synthetic unity presupposes or includes a synthesis, and if the former is to be a priori necessary, the synthesis must also be a priori. The transcendental unity of apperception thus relates to the pure synthesis of imagination, as an a priori condition of the possibility of all combination of the manifold in one knowledge" (142; A 118). Then imagination has a productive function. It is productive, because it no longer proceeds from the reproducibility of appearances, but from the power of unifying, which comes from above. The productive is generated by the pole of unity, whereas the reproductive is generated by the affinity of the reproducibility of appearances. Kant even goes so far in this text as to say that we make a shortcut between the unity of our perception and imagination that skips the level of what he terms the understanding (143; A 118–19). In this sense productive imagination precedes the understanding. This assertion is implicitly the greatest revolution, a reversal of priority between understanding and imagination; imagination is the source, the matrix, of understanding. Since "the pure synthesis of imagination" becomes the "a priori condition of the possibility of all combinations of the manifold in one knowledge . . . [o]nly the productive synthesis of the imagination can take place a priori; the reproductive rests upon empirical conditions" (142–43; A 118). We understand why reproductive imagination depends on empirical conditions. It is an empirical fact that an object has several sides, and therefore it's because the several sides are already gathered by reality that we may gather them in our memory. By contrast, the principle of unity is given in Kant with the I, and the I is not deducible from anything else. Hence, we have here the ground of the possibility of all knowledge, especially of experience. "Since this unity of apperception underlies the possibility of all knowledge, the transcendental unity of the synthesis of imagination is the pure form of all possible knowledge" (143; A 118). The imagination is invested with the whole function of producing synthesis. Wherever there is synthesis, there is imagination.

Imagination is no longer a function among others such as seeing an object or having an object in its absence. The latter are local functions. Imagination is a universal function to the extent that it is the connecting function. All syntheses of understanding under the categories will be the work of imagination. "The unity of apperception in relation to the synthesis of imagination is the understanding" (143; A 119). This passage foreshadows Kant's later decisive text on the schematism, which we shall soon discuss. The understanding is generated at the crossing point of this unity of apperception: the I saying I and imagination as synthetic. The categories, which are the pure concepts of understanding, must themselves be generated by this power of connecting, which is imagination.

Post-Kantian philosophy will draw immense consequences from Kant's remark here, which remains within the framework of the problem of objectivity. To say that imagination is the bearer of all productive or creative functions will explode the framework of the *Critique*. Then will arise the Romantic philosophy of imagination, starting with Friedrich Schelling. The problem of objectivity will be overshadowed by the problem of the creative function of the imagination.

In any event, in Kant imagination is a name for the "active faculty for the synthesis of this manifold. To this faculty," he says, "I give the title, imagination" (144; A 120). There would be no application of categories to experience if there were not this faculty of making a whole of our experience. There is a semantic decision to give the name of imagination not to a psychological function close to memory but to a transcendental function, the capacity of synthesis, this "active faculty for the synthesis of this manifold." The problem of the image as a mental appearance of an absent object is subordinated to the problem of the imagination. To have an image of something is a local problem, but to connect experience is a much broader function. Image and imagination are no longer synonymous, as was the case in Hume. Hume spoke of imagination mainly when he had to do with this power of running along ideas, and an image was the copy of an impression. But in Kant the imagination is the power to put into the form of an image. "[I]magination has to bring the manifold of intuition into the form of an image [*ein Bild bringen*]" (144; A 120). As previously mentioned, *Einbildungskraft* means to bring something into the form of an image, where the word *form* reminds us of the German *Bild* and *bilden*, to form. Imagination has a formative function. We may conclude this approach to productive imagination by saying that the function of imagination is to put the stamp of our own unity on the flux of appearances. "According to this principle all appearances, without exception, must so enter the mind or be apprehended, that they conform to the unity of apperception. Without synthetic unity in their connection, this would be impossible; and such synthetic unity is itself, therefore, objectively necessary" (145; A 122).

Nobody before Kant had thought of a function of imagination related to shaping our world of experience. Only the awareness of the gap between understanding and intuition could pave the way for this recognition of the mediating role of imagination. Of course, this role is limited to the constitution of objective knowledge and therefore to the shaping of what we call nature. Nevertheless, the spontaneity of this faculty has been recognized; the imagination is not simply reproductive. Further, imagination's priority and primacy over against understanding opens an immense horizon, which Kant has not explored. We are not very far from the idea that imagination is not only the mediating function between understanding and sensibility but the origin itself of the two functions. The boldness of this insight may be measured when we compare the preceding analysis to the more prudent presentation of the same problem in the second edition of the *Critique* (165–67; B 150–52). There the figurative synthesis is subordinated to the intellectual synthesis. The figurative synthesis follows the tracks of the intellectual synthesis, because it proceeds from the action of the understanding on the sensibility. Nonetheless, the opposition between productive and reproductive imagination is preserved. Only the former is transcendental; the latter is sent back to psychology. In *Kant and the Problem of Metaphysics*, Heidegger will attempt to follow the opening suggestion of the first edition against the restriction of the second edition.

Let me raise some questions here. To what extent does the notion of the manifold retain the impossible concept of an impression? We presuppose that there is something like an impression, that there is first a manifold, and then we gather it. Modern psychology will be more cautious. Where is there a manifold? As soon as we have a first experience—a child, for example, recognizing the face of its mother—we already have patterns. The so-called manifold is beyond our grasp. So to put the problem in terms of starting from a manifold and then gathering it, this initial presupposition does not belong to any kind of experience that we may have. This conclusion is drawn by both the psychology of perception, which shows how much perception is constructed from the very beginning, and the psychology of painting, drawing, etching, and so on. As the latter argues, we may say that painters render what they see, but what do they see? They see, in fact, what they paint. The act of painting is the act of constituting the objects for them. Perhaps what the I does is similar to what the painter does consciously or not so consciously. The question of the manifold is very problematic as also perhaps that of the I which would be the absolute one.

Where, then, do we locate this absolute manifold and this absolute one with which, with Kant, we are to play in between? Perhaps philosophers construct the terms of their problem. They say let us assume that there is a manifold and let us assume that I am the one who says I am myself. Having thus determined the extreme terms of the problem, we proceed by covering the intermediary field, which is in fact the field where something is given, since the manifold is presupposed and the one is posited. There is a self-positing of the one. I am the one who, and then I have the principle of unity. But it is already a post-Kantian rereading of Kant to question his main presuppositions of the manifold, on the one hand, and the one, on the other hand. If we accept his positing of the framework, then we have the problem of connecting the two poles.

Kant's polar framework provides us the clue for the main text in the present lecture, Kant's text on the schematism. This famous and obscure text—which deceives by its shortness of seven pages (180–87; A 137/B 176–A 147/B 187)—is a radicalization of the problem that I've just presented as the paradox of mediating between two heterogeneous principles, a principle of the manifold and a principle of unity. This new and third approach to the problem of imagination is placed in a new framework, the "Transcendental Doctrine of Judgment." The title indicates that Kant no longer considers the product of this synthesis—the categories, that is, the concepts that are the trace of this act—but the act of synthesis itself. When we proceed from the transcendental doctrine of the concept to the transcendental doctrine of judgment, we move from the result to the process. As I mentioned in the introduction to the present lecture, judgment for Kant is itself the complex function of putting an intuition under a rule, under a concept. Kant calls this a process of subsumption—from the Latin *subsumere*, to place under, to grasp under—or of application. We apply a rule to an experience, or we subsume an experience under a rule. In the text the words *application* and *subsumption* are taken for one another: "How, then, is the subsumption of intuitions under pure concepts, the application of a category to appearances, possible?" (180; A 138/B 177). Exactly the same problem is presented in two ways.

This problem is posed in its more radical terms as the search for a homogeneous term, something of the same kind, homo-geneous. We have to look, therefore, for a function that is of the same kind as one pole and of the same kind as the second pole, a term that has a double allegiance, an affinity with both poles.

> Obviously there must be some third thing [*ein Drittes*, a third] which is homogeneous on the one hand with the category [and therefore a structure of the understanding] and on the other hand with the appearance, and which thus makes the application of the former to the latter possible. This mediating representation must be pure, that is, void of all empirical content, and yet at the same time, while it must in one respect be intellectual, it must in another be sensible. Such a representation is the transcendental schema. (181; A 138/B 177)

Kant uses the language of application and no longer that of subsumption, since he starts from above. When he says that the mediating representation must have no empirical content, that means that it is not this or that image, the image of someone or something elsewhere. It's the connecting link as such, not one of the images that I produce by this connection. The change in the vocabulary to the "transcendental schema" underlines the radicalization of the problematic.

Hence the question is what is the difference between a schema and an image, since the imagination is defined by this difference. Kant offers several examples that may provide us a guideline in this discussion. The examples have in common that the schematism is described as a procedure, a rule of synthesis, and even as a method to build images. We are far away from the faculty of representing an object that is not present (as in the B edition, § 24; 164–68, B 150–56). No object is at stake, only the pure possibility of connecting categories and intuitions. We may still speak of imagination, if no longer as the representation of an object but as a method, as a procedure. Let me present a few of Kant's expressions and then support them by his examples. "The *procedure* of understanding in these schemata we shall entitle the schematism of pure understanding" (182; A 140/B 179; emphasis added). The schema is closer to the understanding than to the image, because it's a rule and the concept is a rule. However, it's a rule that is not crystallized or frozen in an intellectual object that we call the concept but a rule that remains in the movement of the procedure. Understanding is a procedure. A few lines further: "This representation of a universal *procedure* of imagination in providing an image for a concept, I entitle the schema of this concept" (182; A 140/B 179–80; emphasis added). And a few lines further: "It is a *rule of synthesis* of the imagination" (182; A 141/B 180; emphases added). We should retain all the expressions that the schema is a procedure, a rule, a rule of synthesis.

Kant's first example is that of the five points:

> If five points [say, five pieces of wood or five pebbles] be set alongside one another, thus, . . . , I have an image of the number five. But if, on the other hand, I think only a number in general, whether it be five or a hundred, this thought is rather the representation of a *method* whereby a multiplicity, for instance a thousand, may be represented in an image in conformity with a certain concept, than the image itself. . . . This representation of a universal *procedure* of imagination in providing an image for a concept, I entitle the schema of this concept." (182; A 140/B 179; emphases added)

We see the difference between the static and dead image of five points, five pebbles, where the image is closed. There are only these points and the method for producing numbers. Whereas the image each time is singular, this or that, the method is indeterminate, since it has a productive capacity. What is important in the schema is that there is both a principle to construct

Kant: Critique of Pure Reason   73

but at the same time a certain dimension of indetermination. It's not a pure indetermination; it's a sphere of possibility that is opened by this structure. This is why he speaks of a "multiplicity," "for instance a thousand." A given number is only an instance of a rule. There is a relation between the rule and an instance, and the possibility of passing from the instance to the rule is the schema. We have to do with a rule for giving determinations that leaves open other possibilities. There is a horizon of possibilities in the schema that we do have not in the image as such, which is reduced to what it is. Sartre will evoke this situation: I try to count in my imagination the columns of the Pantheon in Paris. If I don't know whether there are twelve columns, I may look at the image of the Pantheon in my mind, but I shall not find the number.[2] The image is limited by my knowledge. It's not a schema; it's a mere image. By contrast, the schema contains a sphere of possibilities.

Kant's second example is that of a triangle. All these texts are answers to Hume who claimed, for example, that I cannot have a triangle which is not isosceles or scalene. It must be either one. Kant would say yes at the level of the image but no at the level of the schema. In the example of the triangle, the schema is placed under the condition of geometrical space. When I look at this triangle, it is of one kind. The capacity to see all the possibilities of this triangle is the schema. The schema provides the transition from one actualization to others. It's a capacity to introduce mutation in an image. It's a ruled process of the mutation of patterns. To the structure of the schema belongs a capacity to display itself in images but not to exhaust itself in the image. It merely delineates the sphere of possible images. If we considered only individual triangles "whether right-angled, obtuse-angled, or acute-angled[,] it would always be limited to a part only of this sphere. The schema of the triangle can exist nowhere but in thought. It is a rule of synthesis of the imagination, in respect to pure figures in space" (182; A 141/B 180).

Kant's third example is that of a sensible concept, and he uses the very ordinary example of a dog. "The concept 'dog' signifies a rule according to which my imagination can delineate the figure of a four-footed animal in a general manner" (182–83; A 141/B 180). It would be interesting to compare this example to drawings by children or the way in which painters retain from a landscape what is compatible with their skill and therefore with their capacity of rendering something by a practical means. This is what happens when I consider a familiar object as a type and not only as a singular thing. Children are closer to this when they render by drawing the rule of the object rather than its finite and singular pattern.

Kant's notion of a rule for producing images leads him to a surprising remark, with which we shall conclude: "This schematism of our understanding, in its application to appearances and their mere form, is an art concealed in the depths of the human soul, whose real modes of activity nature is hardly likely ever to allow us to discover, and to have open to our gaze" (183; A 141/B 180–81). This hieratic declaration is very striking coming, as it does, immediately after the trivial example of the dog. It is as if Kant were saying that in the simplest example, a child drawing a dog or a house, we have, in fact, the whole problematic of creativity displayed and at the same time concealed. From now on, the image is sent back to reproductive imagination, and the schema is the kernel of productive imagination. If we keep in mind the notion of the heterogeneity of having rules and having intuitions, the schematism is the solution of the problem. But as soon as we consider the schematism as itself a problem in the sense of asking how can we do that, then we have to do with what Kant calls "an art concealed in the depths of the human soul." This text is an answer to Hume. Hume claims that it is something very simple to connect ideas, and he calls that the "association of ideas." But this is only a name. Under this name we have all the creativity of the mind crystallized in one example. Notice also the strangeness of Kant's text here which seems foreign to the structure and the vocabulary of the *Critique*. He speaks of the soul (*Seele*). He speaks of nature nearly like the pre-Socratics. Recall Heraclitus's statement that nature likes to hide. Kant says that the schematism "is an art concealed in the depths of the human soul, whose real modes of activity nature is hardly likely ever to allow us to discover." The *Critique* gives us only the rules for connecting; the nature of the power of connecting is beyond the *Critique*'s grasp.

The next lecture shall start from the first *Critique*'s application of the schematism in the "Analogies of Experience" in order to oppose it to the same problem in Kant's third *Critique*. The difference will be between the first *Critique*'s tamed imagination in the process of objectivity and the third *Critique*'s free imagination.

6

Kant: Critique of Judgment

This lecture closes our historical survey in classical philosophy with a culminating point, Kant's theory of imagination in the *Critique of Judgment* (the third *Critique*). Succeeding lectures, in Part II of these lectures, will start from this high point and undertake an investigation proceeding in different directions. We shall generally take up as two opposite solutions to the problem of the diversity and inconsistency of the field the skeptical, nominalistic approach of Gilbert Ryle, who says that imagination is merely a word and needs to be dismantled into its separate parts, and Jean-Paul Sartre's attempt to rebuild the whole field around a certain use of negativity. The capacity to retreat from reality creates a break or gap between the real and the unreal, and Sartre tries to reconstruct the field of imagination on the basis of the unreal.

With the third *Critique*, we have an investigation into the notion of the free play of imagination. We shall take this concept as our leading thread. To understand the nuclear function of free play in the third *Critique*, we may start from the contrast between the treatment of imagination in the first and third *Critiques*. The section of the first *Critique* on the "Analogies of Experience," which I shall explore briefly for our purposes, comes in a chapter following the chapter on the schematism. The function of the larger chapter is to explore the way in which the categories are applied. Imagination plays its role between the category and experience. The chapter is entitled "System of All Principles of Pure Understanding," and the word *principle* is taken in its radical sense. The first judgment in principle is the first judgment from which we derive the others. It's the first judgment under which the connection to experience is secured. The main concept of the section on the "Analogies of Experience" is the notion of ruled experience: "to bring the existence of appearances under rules a priori" (Kant 1965, 210; A 179/B 222).[1] It's the process of application, the schema as applied. Understanding is the faculty of rules. Bringing the existence of appearances under rules is opposed to thinking that has merely "played with representations" (193; A 155/B 195). This section is interesting for our purpose because it contains a concept contrary to free play, the connection of experience under rules. We must consider together the roles in Kant of the notions of rule and play. In a certain sense the entire problem of imagination in Kant may be located in this duel, this contest, between rule and play. And the different solutions to the problem constitute the basic figures of their combinatory possibilities. In the first *Critique* we have a total subordination of the power of free play in imagination to the system of rules that is constitutive of the understanding, this network of fundamental rules which are the categories.

In discussing the "analogies" of experience, Kant's usage of the term is odd, but he has in mind the Greek concept of *analogia*, which is proportion. When we say that A is to B what C is to D, then we have a proportion that in Greek was called analogy. The analogy is a way of deriving by calculus the fourth term when we know the other three of them. It's a way of producing a new term. In the case of experience, we cannot proceed mathematically in the sense that we may forecast the missing element; we offer only rules for finding it. The word *analogy* is transformed from mathematics to what Karl Popper would call a logic of discovery.

Causation is the paradigmatic case of the application of the categories through imagination to experience. We are already familiar with this issue, since we previously met it in Hume. Hume has paved the way for Kant's solution, saying that in causation we don't perceive the rationality of a production but merely the connection between two events. But Hume has not solved why we can say that there is a necessity in the connection. Kant's response raises the issue of rules. He argues that causation is a ruled connection; it is a succession according to rules (219; B 234). It's the succession in our representation, not in the object. Succession may occur in two ways, either without order or according to order. Kant explains these different types of succession by invoking two metaphors. They are not merely examples but metaphors, since the examples are empirical but the problem is transcendental. The first metaphor is that of a house (220; A 190–91/B 235–36). When we look at a house, we may proceed from the bottom to the top, from the top to the bottom, from right to left, from left to right, and so on. There is an indifference in the order of how we proceed. We may freely play with the possibility of what modern critical art would call scanning; we may scan the surface, scan the volume in different ways.[2] In contrast, in the second metaphor, that of a boat moving down a river (221; A 192/B 237), an order is imposed; the process has an arrow of sense. On the basis of these two examples we comprehend the notion of a succession indifferent to order and a succession ruled by order. Kant bifurcates the concept of succession in terms of freedom and order.

The free play of imagination corresponds to the first hypothesis, a succession that would not be ruled, that could run along in different ways. In the first *Critique*, the free play of imagination occurs as the possibility that is excluded. Causality is the answer to the challenge of the chaotic succession that is our imagination. Imagination is treated as the chaotic possibility closed by causation, by the order of things:

> Let us suppose that there is nothing antecedent to an event, upon which it must follow according to *rule*. All succession of perception would then be only in the apprehension, that is, would be merely subjective, and would never enable us to determine objectively which perceptions are those that really precede and which are those that follow. We should then have only a *play of representations*, relating to no object; that is to say, it would not be possible through our perception to distinguish one appearance from another as regards relations of time. (222; A 194/B 239; emphases added)

Rule is opposed to the play of representations. The latter would abolish the regular order of time. (The concept of play will later return and play a great role in Nietzsche and in those who have linked Nietzsche to Heidegger.[3] It also will arise in some modern approaches to the problem of imagination—such as Klinger's—that make great use of the play of children, and discuss playing with possibilities, combinatory games, and so on as one function of imagination, a way of trying possibilities.)

In Kant's discussion, imagination as free play is identified finally with what has been translated as *fancy*. The word *fancy* comes more readily when we have to do with free play rather than the master use of imagination.

> In the imagination this sequence [of representation] is not in any way determined in its order, as to what must precede and what must follow, and the series of sequent representations can indifferently be taken either in backward or in forward order. ... *Were it not so*, [were there not this order, regularity, and succession,] were I to posit the antecedent and the event were not to follow necessarily thereupon, I should have to regard the succession as a merely subjective *play* of my *fancy* [*Einbildungen*]; and if I still represented it to myself as something objective, I should have to call it a mere dream. (226–27; A 201/B 246; emphases added)

The dream appears here as a kind of threat to the order of the world, since it's the emancipation from the order of things. We should note that the quotation is presented in hypothetical form. We should have play only if . . . , were it not so. Imagination as free play is only a marginal possibility that has to be kept aside from the purpose of the first *Critique*. A critique of objective knowledge meets this free play as a marginal threat to what we call the order of things.

The function of the third *Critique* will be to shift to the center what was only a marginal possibility. It will make use of free play but for a quite different purpose than knowledge or objectivity; it will use free play for an aesthetic purpose. Due to the point's relevance for discussion in the second part of the course, I must say immediately that the problem of the rule will never be completely excluded but will appear in another way. Rules will no longer be the categories of the understanding but the possibility of giving form, of patterning experience in other ways. We have never to do with a kind of naked creativity. A naked creativity is always something marginal, the raw material of our creation. There is no philosophy of imagination outside an interplay between spontaneity and the capacity of giving form. The third *Critique* is a critique because there is a structure to explore. In the third *Critique* the notion of rule will not disappear but will take the specific form of the structure of the work of art and of the harmony of natural beauty.

Let me say first a few words concerning the philosophical framework within which this analysis is undertaken. The title, the *Critique of Judgment*, is a translation of the German *Kritik der Urteilskraft. Urteilskraft* means the force or the power of judging, which a better translation would reflect. Judgment is at the center of this text. Judgment here does not mean a critique in the sense of literary criticism or in the sense of a critique of art where we judge some productions of art. It's not at all a notion of appreciation or of evaluation. It would be a complete mistake if we looked at this work in that sense. Judgment is instead understood as reflective judgment. This is a cardinal concept in the third *Critique*. To understand the notion of reflective judgment, we must oppose it to what we said about judgment in the first *Critique*, that to judge is to put an intuition under a rule and therefore to apply a rule to a case, a principle to an instance, or to put the instance under the rule, issues of subsumption or application. There, judgment was directed toward the world and, by ordering the appearances, it gave objects their objectivity. In contrast, in the case of reflective judgment, the act of judging is no longer invested in the task of objectivity but in an inner need for order, for purposiveness, which is a requirement of our reason.

The two main examples that will be developed in the third *Critique* are the finality in nature and the kind of inner order that we have in beautiful things, in sublime experience or, in general, in aesthetic experience. So we have two great domains: biology and aesthetics. At first sight, it's very strange to put the two together, since what's common between biology and aesthetics? But precisely what is common is the use of reflective judgment, because we look for a certain purposiveness in nature similar to the kind of purposiveness that there is in the aesthetic experience that satisfies our own need for order. A decisive step is taken here, which Gadamer discusses at length in the first part of his book *Truth and Method*. Gadamer says that Kant is responsible for having completely interiorized the problem of aesthetics, since it's not the things which are beautiful but rather that we judge them beautiful in accordance with our need for order. Purposiveness lies not in the thing, neither in the biological order nor in the aesthetic order, but in a certain accord between particular presentations of phenomena and what we expect in terms of unity, harmony, and so on. In the case of biology that would mean that there is no science of purposiveness; science is simply mechanistic in the sense of Newtonian mechanicism. It's for us that there is an order. There is a complete subjectivity of order in this field. We shall not pursue here whether Kant was right to take as merely subjective this expectation of order in things. It's the role of imagination in relation to this expectation that is our problem here, how the free play of imagination meets the need for order.

The first mention of imagination occurs already in the long "Introduction," which is one of the most difficult philosophical texts. Kant speaks of the "apprehension of forms," which is a common purpose of the philosophy of biology and the philosophy of art.

> For that apprehension of forms in the imagination can never take place without the reflective judgment, though undesignedly, at least comparing them with its faculty of referring intuitions to concepts. If, now, in this comparison the imagination (as the faculty of a priori intuitions) is placed by means of a given representation undesignedly in agreement with the understanding, as the faculty of concepts, and thus a feeling of pleasure is aroused, the object must then be regarded as purposive for the reflective judgment. (Kant 1951, 26; 190)[4]

The key notion here is that when there is an agreement between certain appearances and our expectation of an order, then we have a pleasure of a certain kind that we could call the pleasure of order, and it is this pleasure of order that is the object of a judgment of taste. We speak of taste, then, when we acknowledge the harmony between the appearances and the order. When "a feeling of pleasure is aroused, the object must then be regarded *as* purposive for the reflective judgment." It is regarded *as* it is not. This notion of a quasi-purposiveness in appearances satisfying our need for rational order is not a sensible pleasure but one that Plato would have spoken of as a pure pleasure, since it's the pleasure of the Form. No instinct here is fulfilled, but we meet order in nature. We have an admiration of, satisfaction with, and fulfillment of a wish for order, which is therefore rational in the sense that it is common to all of us and can be universalized. It is communicable by principle. Kant calls this the *sensus communis* (§ 40: 135–38; 293–96), a common sense in the way that we, all of us, expect order and take pleasure when we meet this order.

The kernel of this analysis will be the concordance between the free play of imagination and the apprehension of forms satisfying to the understanding. We shall take some fundamental experiences described by Kant and which may be placed under this concordance between form and free play. Free play is never alone, either in the first *Critique* or in the third. In the first *Critique* it is curbed by the order of the world. Causality represses the chaotic possibilities. But in the third *Critique*, these chaotic possibilities are used for creating order. Instead of being rejected, they are incorporated in the process of presenting a satisfying order.

Section 9 is devoted to the problem of the concordance or the agreement which in the case of the beautiful takes a specific form. The great difference between something that we say is beautiful and something that we say is sublime resides in the way in which concordance is achieved. In the case of the beautiful, concordance is achieved in a peaceful way, whereas in the case of the sublime there are tensions, there are conflicts, and it is more the failure of our imagination to meet with the greatness of the phenomenon that makes the sublime. In the case of the beautiful, then, we obtain order through proportion, while in the sublime, we achieve it through disproportion. Kant provides a very interesting phenomenology of the interplay between imagination and the apprehension of forms. In both cases we have a feeling of order, but in one case it's an order that is peaceful, whereas in the case of the sublime, it's an order that is always threatened and therefore that compels imagination to cope with an impossible task, to join and to catch up with the greatness or the immensity of the spectacle. In the beautiful, agreement is not obtained easily, but it's a kind of miracle of agreement that conceals a very complex procedure. In the sublime, the process is exposed, because there is an element of failure in it that reveals the process. In the beautiful, the process is more hidden because the feeling of peaceful concordance blocks the way of reflective judgment. Reflective judgment is immediately satisfied by this concordance. I shall devote more time to the sublime, because it's more interesting for the dynamics of the imagination.

Kant writes of the beautiful:

The cognitive powers, which are involved by this representation, are here in free play because no definite concept limits them to a definite rule of cognition. Hence the state of mind in this representation must be a feeling of the free play of the representative powers in a given representation with reference to a cognition in general. Now a representation by which an object is given that is to become a cognition in general requires imagination for the gathering together the manifold of intuition, and understanding for the unity of the concept uniting the representations. (52; 217)

The cognitive powers are cognitive in the sense not that they give an object but that they use the same functions as cognition. They involve the presentation of something or "gathering together the manifold of intuition." We recognize here what was described in the first *Critique* as the second synthesis of imagination, between mere apprehension and pure recognition in a concept. It's the same imagination, the same apprehension, and even the same understanding, but it's an understanding that functions not according to concepts but only according to the general principle of giving form, of producing and promoting an order. It's the ordered nature of the understanding, not its specific structure according to the categories, that operates here.

The "General Remark" that ends this part on the beautiful and that precedes the "Analytic of the Sublime" proceeds a step further. The union between the free play of imagination and the need for forms of the understanding is so close that it is as if the activity of imagination were located in this spontaneous harmony with the expectation of our understanding. Kant speaks of imagination as a "free conformity to law": "If we seek the result of the preceding analysis, we find that everything runs up into this concept of taste—that it is a faculty for judging an object in reference to the imagination's free conformity to law" (77; 240). Kant asks us to consider an imagination that instead of shattering any kind of order—instead of producing chaos like the free play so close to the dream in the first *Critique*— would generate and offer to the understanding forms that would satisfy our expectation of order.

There is here a mutual affinity between free play and rule. Free play is in itself a rule. Therefore, with no violence the two faculties meet one another. "Now, if in the judgment of taste the imagination must be considered in its freedom, it is in the first place not regarded as reproductive, as it is subject to the laws of association, but as productive and spontaneous (as the author of *arbitrary* forms of possible intuition)" (77; 240; emphasis added). There is something arbitrary in this imagination. It may create anything.

But it's the grace of imagination that sometimes it produces something that has form. The arbitrariness then is at the same time form, pattern. "And although in the apprehension of a given object of sense it is tied to a definite form of this object and so far has no free play (such as that of poetry), yet it may readily be conceived that the object can furnish it with such a form containing a collection of the manifold as the imagination itself, if it were left free, would project in accordance with the conformity to law of the understanding in general" (77–78; 240–41). This passage may provide an answer to an enigma that we left with Spinoza. At the end of the Note following Proposition 17, Spinoza said that there might be a free imagination not under the determination of external factors but dependent on its own nature. And then he closes this parenthesis. It has no place in the *Ethics* but perhaps elsewhere, in the *Theologico-Political Treatise*. In Kant we see an aesthetic use of this spontaneous order of free play. There is "harmony" (*Übereinstimmung*) and "proportion" in the "accordance of the cognitive powers." "This actually always takes place when a given object by means of sense excites the imagination to collect the manifold, and the imagination in its turn excites the understanding to bring about a unity of this collective process in concepts" (75; 238).

The sublime, then, to which we now arrive, may be defined by contrast to the beautiful by the role of discordance, of disproportion, in the interplay. The process is more obvious and in a sense more open to description because of the tensions that postpone agreement. The beautiful and the sublime differ mainly according to the way in which agreement between imagination and the understanding obtains. In the sublime it is through conflict rather than through harmony. Disproportion takes the place of proportion. Second, the kind of order we are expecting is no longer an order proportionate to the understanding but to reason.

For those not familiar with the vocabulary and the problematics of Kant, the distinction between reason (*Vernunft*) and understanding (*Verstand*) is an important one. They're not on the same level. The understanding is the kind of order we may find or place in nature: causation, substance, unity, plurality, and so on. Reason, by contrast, pertains to a second-order level of rules. Kant here retains something of the Platonic tradition concerning the Ideas. Reason consists of ideas of a higher order, and the concepts of metaphysics—such as freedom, the soul, and God—belong to this order. For Kant, the ideas cannot be treated by the critique of pure reason, because they lead to contradictions, paradoxes, paralogisms, and antinomies and constitute what he calls the dialectic of reason. It is, therefore, a reason that fails or that produces illusions. On the other hand, practical reason may make sense with such concepts as the absolute and the good and so on which make no sense in cognitive terms. They make sense only in practical terms.

This is why the sublime, to the extent that it has to do more with ideas of reason than with the categories of the understanding, has also more to do with ethics than with science. Everyone recognizes that in the feeling of the sublime we have in front of a landscape, in front of a wild ocean disturbed by storm, in front of high mountains or chaotic spectacles. The reason which is evoked is more a moral reason than the reason of natural order. We think here of the superiority of the spiritual world as opposed to the natural world. It is with this evocation of a superior power that the imagination is aroused and put in competition. We have to do with a feeling on the borderline between aesthetics and ethics. The sublimity of a landscape speaks, so to say, of the greatness of justice.

The first descriptive trait of the sublime is that we have to cope with the formless, the lack of boundaries. The beautiful had form in the sense of definite boundaries (*Begrenzung*). The sublime is formless; it lacks boundaries (*Unbegrenztheit*) (82; 244). That does not mean that the sublime is irrational, but the kind of rationality that is implied here resides in the capacity of our imagination to struggle with the ideas of reason through the inadequateness of their presentation. Here Kant has introduced something very important in the philosophy of imagination, the effort of imagination to cope with something impossible. This extension of the imagination (*der Erweiterung der Einbildungskraft*) (87; 249) fights on the borderline between the expressible and the inexpressible. The imagination repels these boundaries and discovers in its failure to cope with the requirement of the idea its extension—both the impossibility of going beyond and the feeling of a beyond that promotes this movement which fails in its attempt to be adequate to the beyond. There is an experience of inadequateness in imagination and through imagination that makes sense only if there is the horizon of an unspeakable and unthinkable order. The imagination is the exploration of this unthinkable by the means of its effort to extend itself.

Kant presents two large categories of the sublime, the mathematically sublime and the dynamically sublime. It's very easy to understand the difference. The mathematically sublime has to do with magnitude, with greatness. Kant offers the important remark that we have to do with greatness when we have to do with greatness without comparison. It's not something as greater than but as great, an absolute sense of greatness (88; 250). When we have to do with greatness without comparison, imagination attempts to enlarge itself, to extend itself, to make itself adequate to this greatness, and then it fails in this effort. "But because there is in our imagination a striving [*ein Bestreben*] toward infinite progress and in our reason a claim for absolute totality, regarded as a real idea, therefore this very inadequateness for that idea in our faculty for estimating the magnitude of things of sense excites in us the feeling of a supersensible faculty" (88; 250). I think that this is the first time in our survey of the classical tradition that we read of imagination as a striving (*Bestreben*), as an effort (*Bestrebung*). This will become a fundamental concept in classical Romanticism, in figures such as Johann Wolfgang von Goethe, Friedrich Schiller, and Johann Gottlieb Fichte. Kant writes shortly thereafter: "We can therefore append to the preceding formulas explaining the sublime this other: the sublime is that, the mere ability to think which shows a faculty of the mind *surpassing* every standard of sense" (89; 250; emphasis added). This "surpassing" belongs to the imagination.

Kant's metaphor is quite different from Hume's metaphor of imagination as running along. Hume's metaphor did imply a certain dynamism of the imagination proceeding from one experience to another. But with Kant we have a difference of level. The imagination is placed in a movement that has a hierarchical dimension. It's aroused by the horizon of rationality to make a whole of our experience, but reaching this whole is defeated. He offers two examples of this movement, experiencing the pyramids (which will play a great role in Hegel's aesthetics) and St. Peter's in Rome. (Kant saw neither of them but relied on stories and reports from travelers he met. He finds the dynamically sublime, such as the greatness of mountains, in books.) After discussing the example of the pyramids, Kant then writes:

> The same thing may sufficiently explain the bewilderment or, as it were, perplexity which it is said seizes the spectator on his first entrance into St. Peter's at Rome. For there is here a feeling of the inadequacy of his imagination for presenting the ideas of a whole, wherein the imagination reaches its maximum, and, in striving to surpass it, sinks back into itself, by which, however, a kind of emotional satisfaction is produced. (91; 252)

This is one of the most wonderful texts on imagination. It explains the feeling of inadequacy but also the idea that there is a maximum in imagination. We shall later discuss that using Gombrich, because Gombrich has seen very well that at any certain time everything is not possible. We experience on the basis of archetypes of taste and acquired skills; there is always a vocabulary by which we read the experience or paint it. It's within the boundaries of this style, with this alphabet of painting or this screen for reading, that the experience occurs. This is the finiteness of imagination. As I said at the beginning of this lecture, imagination is never naked creativity.

A myth of creativity very dangerous for our purpose is that it is a formless power. For creativity always has forms. It fights with its forms but for other forms. It proceeds from form to form. In *The Birth of Tragedy* this has been said by Nietzsche in another vocabulary. The Dionysian becomes mortal if not linked with the Apollonian. We could read the fight of the Dionysian and the Apollonian in the theory of the sublime. The Dionysian is close to breaking the boundaries of the Apollonian, but the Apollonian is here represented by the ideas of the reason and the horizon of totality by which we try to make sense of the whole of experience. I repeat Kant's words: "For there is here a feeling of the inadequacy of his imagination for presenting the ideas of a whole, wherein the imagination reaches its maximum, and, in striving to surpass it, sinks back into itself, by which, however, a kind of emotional satisfaction is produced."

Let me draw attention to an additional word in this passage, the term *presenting* (*darzustellen*), which will have an important destiny in German thought. As I note in my work on ideology, even in Marx we have this idea that if the pure *Darstellung* of practical life were available, then we should have not an ideology but a true science. It's the idea of a pure exposition, pure presentation. Kant's shift in his vocabulary here expresses a shift in the problematics. The term is no longer, as in the first *Critique*, representation (*Vorstellung*) but presentation (*Darstellung*). Imagination is at its height when it presents some superior, intelligible, but not knowable entities.

The key to this analysis is its fight with the concept of boundaries. The beautiful has boundaries and the sublime does not, yet our experience of the sublime has boundaries of another kind. It's our imagination that hits on its boundaries. Reason appears as the horizon of the unbound—what is unbound to the concepts—but it is presented only by the trespassing and the failure to trespass that is imagination at work. In another passage, Kant writes of "the inadequacy of the greatest effort [*Bestrebung*] of our imagination to estimate the magnitude of an object" (94; 255).

Experience of the sublime is also interesting for the sake of a philosophy of pain and pleasure. I remember hearing Elizabeth Anscombe say that what is most needed in philosophy now is a philosophy of pain and pleasure. In fact, there is nearly nothing on this currently except in psychoanalysis, but Plato had seen very well that there are many kinds of pleasures that have not been explored. And here in Kant we find a dialectical identity of pain and pleasure in the experience of the sublime, the pain of inadequacy but the pleasure of trespassing.

> Now the greatest effort [*Bestrebung*] of the imagination in the presentation of the unit for the estimation of magnitude indicates a reference to something absolutely great, and consequently a reference to the law of reason, which bids us take this alone as our highest measure of magnitude. There-

fore the inner perception of the inadequacy of all sensible standards for rational estimation of magnitude indicates a correspondence with rational laws; it involves a pain, which arouses in us the feeling of our supersensible destination, according to which it is purposive and therefore pleasurable to find every standard of sensibility inadequate to the ideas of understanding. (96–97; 258)

We have a complete coincidence between a certain pain and a certain pleasure. Later on the same page, Kant writes: "The transcendent . . . is for the imagination like an abyss in which it fears to lose itself" (97; 258). Imagination and reason come to grips with one another through conflict. Kant even speaks here of the pain of violence: "It is therefore . . . a subjective movement of the imagination, by which it does violence to the internal sense" (98; 259). For Kant, the internal sense is the sense of the inner duration, the sense of the temporality of the flux. This sense of the flux is violated in a more dramatic way than in the image of the house, the scan which may freely be reproduced in different ways. That was merely succession without order. Here it's violence in the successive constitution of the flux. "Thus that very violence [*Gewalt*, not *Macht*, power] which is done to the subject through the imagination is judged as purposive in reference to the whole determination of the mind" (98; 259). The conflict is between the bound and the unbound. Kant writes of "the pain in regard to the necessary extension of the imagination for accordance with that which is unbounded in our faculty of reason" (99; 259–60).

Turning from the mathematically sublime to the dynamically sublime, the latter adds nothing decisive, except that the examples are made more dramatic to the extent that what's at issue is not only the magnitude in a spectacle but the force of nature. Here is one of the points where there might be a bridge to build between Kant and Freud. As long as we had to do merely with greatness, magnitude, we had the spectacle, but when we have to do with the force of nature we have to do with a threat. It is as threat that we deal with the frightful element of nature outside of us or within us. The element of sublimity takes not only a more dramatic form but also has more kinship with the experience of morality. The morality pertains not only to a matter of duty but to the ethical at large. We may think of a case where we are threatened in imagination but not in reality, and yet there is something convincing in the threat despite that it is not real. There is the *as if* of the threat that is fundamental. "Might is that which is superior to great hindrances. . . . Nature, considered in an aesthetical judgment as might that has no dominion over us, is dynamically sublime" (99; 260). The fight is between the threat of nature that could crush us and the feeling that we are superior to this threat. Nature encompasses us by the greatness of its forces, but in this contemplative feeling we feel greater than what is greater than us. There is a dialectics of forces. "[W]e can regard an object as fearful without being afraid of it, viz. if we judge of it in such a way that we merely think a case in which we would wish to resist it and yet in which all resistance would be altogether vain" (100; 260). Sharks might be an example. It's the fearful beyond the threat of, the fear of; it's fearful, and we are not afraid. I have the marginal apprehension of my own destruction by forces greater than me.

The disproportion here is between two kinds of forces, the physical forces that could destroy me and the force that I have in my belonging to an ethical world. The latter makes the experience of the dynamically sublime more ethical than the mathematically sublime and perhaps less aesthetically pure than the preceding one. The language is more of ethical elevation, the elevation of the soul. "[N]ature is here called sublime merely because it elevates the imagination to a presentation of those cases in which the mind can make felt the proper sublimity of its destination, in comparison with nature itself" (101; 262). The comparison is between us, as an ethical being, and us, as a natural being threatened by nature's destructiveness. The assumption of my ethical sublimity is aroused by the threat to my physical being. I must enter into the dialectic of physical weakness and ethical destination. I leave as a question what may be the ethical or quasi-ethical aspect of this kind of sublime.

As for the imagination in the dynamically sublime, it's exactly the same process as in the mathematically sublime of an attempt to cope with a requirement and the failure of this attempt. In a passage incorporating both forms of the sublime, Kant again returns to the interplay between representation and presentation. Representation is retained in images, with boundaries and patterns, but presentation is more a movement than a single image.

> We may describe the sublime thus: it is an object (of nature) the representation of which [for example, in the spectacle] determines the mind to think the unattainability of nature regarded as a presentation of ideas.
>
> Literally taken and logically considered, ideas cannot be presented. But if we extend our empirical representative faculty (mathematically or dynamically) to the intuition of nature, reason infallibly intervenes, as the faculty expressing the independence of absolute totality, and generates the unsuccessful effort of the mind to make the representation of the senses adequate to these [ideas]. This effort—and the feeling of the unattainability of the idea by means of the imagination—is itself a presentation of the sub-

jective purposiveness of our mind in the employment of the imagination for its supersensible destination and forces us, subjectively, to think nature itself in its totality as a presentation of something supersensible. (108; 268)

Here we could have a philosophy of the symbolic structure of reality as symbolizing the ethical order. This will be undertaken in section 59, which I have no time to present here. In the present passage, the idea is that the supersensible cannot be known but can be presented aesthetically. Aesthetic presentation may have an ontological function. Kant cannot go very far in that direction, though, since he starts with the notion of reflective judgment. We must never forget that all that is described happens only in reflection. There may be a certain conflict in the philosophy of Kant himself, since on the one hand everything happens in the judgment—it's for me—but on the other hand it's in the presence of things and not only in the presence of things but of nature presenting the supersensible. Can Kant adjust the notion of a pre-aesthetic presentation of the supersensible with the reflective judgment? This is the kind of problem Gadamer discusses in his aesthetics, arguing that perhaps the ontological element of presentation exceeds the limits of a mere philosophy of reflective judgment.

As that is not our problem here, let me conclude by saying that the freedom of imagination makes sense when the chaotic, wild element of arbitrariness comes into interplay with the rules and ideas of reason. Imagination is the face-to-face interchange between the wild power of imagination and the need for a certain order, for forms. This means that there is nothing like a pure imagination. Imagination always has to do with language, structures, and patterns and never only with naked spontaneity. Perhaps this is what we may retain from Kant. Unfortunately, I had no time to speak of Kant's theory of genius, but I may return to that later. The notion is that it's the genius who is the receptacle of this struggle between the free play and the rule, since the genius is the one through whom nature gives rules to this creative power.

PART TWO

Modern Readings

7

Ryle

In this second part of these lectures, I shall inquire into some modern perspectives on the problem of imagination and try to connect the approaches of Anglo-American analytic philosophy and Continental phenomenology. I shall try to show where they overlap in the attempt both to describe the experience of what occurs in imagination and to describe it in a more proper language. The experiential and linguistic sides of the question will be emphasized together. For reasons that will appear in the course of the study, these two approaches don't cover the whole field of imagination. In particular, when they take language into account, the issue is the problem of the concept, and therefore they relate an isolated word—the dog, for example, or my friend in Berlin—to the isolated image of the dog or friend. Isolated images are related to isolated words. In the third part of the lectures, I shall try to show that more interesting developments appear if we link the process of imagination to large works or pieces of works such as fictions or dramas and therefore start with language as discourse more than as word. The problem word *image* has, I think, imposed itself too much on the approach to the problem of imagination. Hence, the analytic-phenomenological approach will be a stage toward our final one.

In the short introduction to the second part I now offer, I shall try to show how the analytic and phenomenological perspectives may be connected one-to-one at three levels within a common framework. Admittedly, there is always something arbitrary in a distribution of problems. I was led to this one-to-one relationship for didactic reasons; we shall see whether it is more than simply didactic. Let me speak first of the problems to which analytic philosophy, on the one hand, and phenomenology, on the other, address themselves. And then I shall say something about the method used in relation to these specific problems. There is a correlation between these approaches both at the level of the problems they address and at the level of their methods. Three main problems have been emphasized, and they represent three different starting points in this very confused and loose field covered by the words *image, imagination, imaging, imagining, fancying, fantasy*, and so on. As I said in the first lecture, the lack of consistency in the vocabulary is perhaps a sign of a certain inconsistency in the problematic. The choice of a starting point is itself a kind of philosophical decision.

A first problem area, represented by Gilbert Ryle on the one hand and Jean-Paul Sartre on the other, concerns the description of the operation of imagining as such. The problem is posed for its own sake, separately from imagination's incorporation in the process of thought, in the process of perception, or in the construction of larger works of art. The question is therefore what do we experience when we say that we have images. This first question has two sides, typified, as we shall see, by the division in Ryle's chapter on the imagination in his book, *The Concept of Mind*. The first side asks, what do we mean when we say that we see with our mind's eye? What is the mental image? What is the relation of a mental image to what we call a picture in the ordinary sense of the word—for example, a photograph or portrait? As Ryle asks, is the mental image a kind of picture in a paperless material? Is it a particular that exists one way or another in the mind and that we look at and inspect? What, then, is the relation between a mental image and a visible picture? Since a picture exists as does its original, can we use the model of an original and its copy?

Ryle will claim that the mental image does not function as a picture, and so we must give up the original/copy model. What then becomes our starting point? What is the connection between imagination as a kind of seeing and other exercises of imagination that imply some kind of physical or verbal action and therefore are observable? Ryle offers *pretending*. We shall discuss why Ryle chooses this starting point, which covers such things as staging, playing a part, cheating, using irony, and therefore offers all the kinds of make-believe that imply pretending. Ryle's move here exemplifies the second side of the first problem area. We shall see a transfer from the problem of the appearance of the image to the process of imaging or imagining.

We shall compare Ryle's approach to that of Sartre, who will try to return to the problem of the picture. He will place picture and image on the same side, but on the basis of a common structure, that of absence, the capacity of introducing absence into our objects. The notion of an intentional object with absence will be an alternative way of solving the problem. We shall examine two of Sartre's books: *Imagination* and *The Psychology of Imagination*. The first is a critique of tradition, and the second is a positive approach and a phenomenological description. I shall take the latter as the model of a phenomenological description.

A second problem area links the question of imagination to perception but under the condition of a complete reassessment of the issue of perception. As we have seen, the Humean tradition took for granted that there are things such as impressions and then said that an image is the copy or likeness of an impression. But what if there are no impressions? The copy disappears, because the counterpart of the copy has also disappeared. This argument has led to the complete recasting of the problem of perception, not only in modern psychology but in the philosophy of mind. The critique of so-called sense data will be an important condition of the reform of the problem of imagination. We shall consider the sections of Wittgenstein's *Philosophical Investigations* on *seeing as* for this reinterpretation of the problem of perception. There perception itself is an interpretive process. The sections on *seeing as* will relate more closely the problem of having an image to an interpretive act of having an experience. In *seeing as* we have perhaps a clue for rethinking what it means to imagine. I shall compare Wittgenstein's approach to that of Maurice Merleau-Ponty in his works on Paul Cézanne and "Eye and Mind," where the representation of reality in drawing, painting, etching, and so on provides us a good basis for reorienting and restructuring the problem of the relation between image and perception by working on both terms together.[1] Wittgenstein and Merleau-Ponty will each offer a reformulation of the problem of the relationship between impression and copy as raised by Hume.[2]

A third problem area concerns the place and the contribution of images to thinking, where thinking is considered not in its logical structure but as an operation that people exercise either publicly or privately when they solve problems. This question is the rescued survivor of a big shipwreck in the following sense. Recall that in empiricist philosophy, the image solved everything. In the empiricist tradition there are no such entities as universals; we don't see universals somewhere in the intelligible world. If there are no such entities as universals, but there are abstract ideas, from where do we abstract our ideas if not from images? Therefore, as I tried to say in the lecture on Hume, the image was the support of the double field of abstract ideas and causation. (We shall set aside the issue of causation here.) The image bore a notion of likeness. The likeness between experiences and images had to support the whole edifice of thought. Likeness or resemblance was prior to sameness in the sense of identity. We don't see the identity of a notion, but we gather similar cases under a name. What is the cash value of a word if not the capacity for providing either actual facts or images? The image enlarges the field of actual experience and takes on the burden of abstraction.

The question of the contribution of images to thinking is the rescued survivor of a shipwreck because modern epistemology turned its back on this solution. Mainly under the influence of Frege, Meinong, and the young Russell, modern epistemology argued for starting from a different point, from the proposition. The argument was that an approach to thinking by way of the proposition resolved the problem of abstraction, since we have to do with the ideal contents of a proposition and consequently no longer need to bother with the origin of ideas. We start from the fact that the ideal contents make sense within a certain set: the propositional content, the articulation of the sentence with a predicate, and so on. There is a return, if not to the universal of the Middle Ages, then at least to a notion of the ideality of logical objects. These objects have a strange mode of existence. To say that the content of a proposition is ideal is to say that it has neither physical existence nor mental existence. In contrast, according to the traditional approach, the image was an alternative to physical existence; things that don't exist in the real world exist in our minds. There were two kinds of existence; we put them together and then in words have concepts. In modern epistemology, Frege's approach in his famous article, "Sense and Reference," can be taken as representative. Frege disconnects completely the problem of meaning from its representation (*Vorstellung*), which is a private thing. When I speak of a triangle, the problem is what comprises its structure, not how do we represent it, because each of us will draw it differently. The drawings in our mind or the drawings on the blackboard are not the triangle of which we are speaking. The indifference to actualization either in reality or in the mind is a negative trait of the ideality of the object. There is an anti-image movement in the whole field, directed against the excesses of empiricism, which perhaps required too much from the image.

After Frege, Meinong, and Russell, there may be a tendency to require too little from the image by completely expelling it from the field. But if it is expelled from the field of logic, it cannot be expelled from another field that has been always preserved in the Anglo-American tradition and that is the philosophy of mind. The philosophy of mind has never been absorbed by the philosophy of logic. It is one thing to ask what is the truth value of a proposition and another to ask how do we think. The latter raises the issue of the thinker in relation to his or her thinking. It is when we reintroduce the question of the relation between thinking, thought, and thinker that the problem of the image returns. The question of the origin of concepts in images may have been killed but not the use of images to support our concepts, to illustrate them, and so on. We shall see in the third part of the lectures that there is a transition from this ancillary function of the image in thinking and the beginning of another approach that concerns a logic of discovery. The latter will imply a larger string of discourse and no longer merely the concept in its relation to the famous image of the dog or the crocodile. As we shall observe, the image has always been mistakenly limited to the same kind of example, the mental picture of an isolated, persistent object in nature.

I should say for my part that elimination of the issue of the image from logic was a very fortunate turn, because the problem of imagination may be redirected to more interesting purposes than to solving the problem of the concept. When we no longer raise the question, how do concepts proceed from images, then we may raise more interesting questions, such as how are we related to reality through images, how do we work with images when we think, and so on. These are quite different problems that have nothing to do with the cash value of the concept in terms of its truth value but rather with the process of thought. If the image is denied as an origin of the concept, it may be acknowledged as an embodiment of thinking considered as an operation exerted by individual thinkers, whether loudly and publicly or tacitly and inwardly. It is this kind of problem that defines the philosophy of mind over against logic and epistemology. Thinking is a problem for the philosophy of mind, whereas the proposition is a problem for logic. It is important to recognize this decisive distinction between raising a question about propositions and raising a question about thinking. The problem of the image may no longer belong to the first problem, the meaningfulness of propositions, but it may belong to the second problem, how do we proceed to think.

I shall take H. H. Price's book, *Thinking and Experience*, as the model of this approach to thinking on the analytic side. The book is a classic of the post-Fregean approach to the role of image and imagination in thinking. It may be that this work is not well enough known, but it's a very accurate book and perhaps the best book in the philosophy of mind concerning the operation of thinking. We shall discuss chapters 8 and 9, which are devoted to "The Imagist Theory of Thinking" and "Images as General Symbols." We shall see that Price always limits himself to the framework of the concept. As we might say in the vocabulary of Wittgenstein, for Price it's always the language game of naming, of giving names. I shall compare Price's approach with that of Husserl in the *Logical Investigations*, particularly the Second Logical Investigation, which elaborates the status of the image in the process of developing a concept, therefore in the dynamization of the concept mainly as an imaginative variation. I shall try to compare the concept of imaginative variations in Husserl primarily with Price's chapter on images as general symbols. The question is how do we generalize an image.

Let me turn from these problem areas to the methods used to address them. I have already said something about method when I spoke of the philosophy of mind as opposed to the philosophy of logic. But I want to say a few words also about the relation between the philosophy of mind and phenomenology. There is not much difference between them (despite the claim of Ryle, who wrote a very bad article on phenomenology. His criticism seemed mainly about the term and not about the approach). I don't want to claim that their methods are the same but rather that one method implies the other. Their emphases are not at the same place, but each calls for the other, sends one back to the other. In what way? The philosophy of mind claims not to be a psychology, which would add to our knowledge of facts. There are no factual discoveries in the philosophy of mind, but it claims to be analytic in one of the senses of the word *analytic*, which has so many senses. It is analytic not in the sense of a reduction to elements nor in the sense of a reduction to principles (the Kantian and Aristotelian sense) but in the sense of an analysis of our language. When we have reports about what we mean when we say that we have images, the philosophy of mind is essentially a discussion of what is the appropriate language for these reports. It fights against a misconstruction that is linked to an improper language. We shall see one of these claims, for instance, concerning the relation between picture and image. Ryle will try to show that we have been misled by a certain similarity in words between a mental picture and a picture on a table. It's an aspect of the therapeutic function of analytic philosophy to cure philosophical diseases by curing linguistic diseases.

Yet at the same time, if we try to amend our language, it's because we also try to be more accurate in our description. What can amend a language if not the evidence of some facts that either were not taken into account or of which we did not give a good account? The notion of giving a report about what we see, of giving an account of our experience, implies that we try to be more faithful to experience without being distracted from it by empiricist theories or theories of any kind. The linguistic program itself leads to a return to the facts in the Husserlian sense, to the things themselves (*die Sachen selbst*). A movement toward the things themselves is necessarily implied in the process of amending our language. In all three of the analytic authors with whom we'll deal, there is always this emphasis: we are not discussing facts of physiology, of psycho-physiology, and so on, but the conceptual framework. Wittgenstein keeps repeating that this is the concept of seeing, the concept of something else, and so on. But we must appreciate that at issue is the conceptuality of our experience; how do we articulate it in language.

If, by contrast, we start from the other pole, the claim of starting at the intuitive level of our experience, we must acknowledge that this intuitive level is never reached as such. It is always reached according to what is meaningful in it, as it is, in Husserl's terms, noematic, as it is thinkable and discussable in our experience. We cannot speak of an experience that is not discussable, of which we could not make an account. Even in phenomenology, then, I start from the other pole, in the accountability of our experience which makes sense. There is no irrational, mystical experience of anything. On the contrary, the issue is always how our experience can be brought to language.

The movement from experience to language is therefore the counterpart of the movement from amending language toward better observing what we are living. I shall try to show, therefore, how a phenomenology is implied in linguistic analysis and how linguistic structures are always implied in experience. Aside from all consideration of doctrine, this connection could be expected if we consider that human experience is always an experience of a speaking being. Even when we say that we see, we *say* that we see. We don't know what is a completely naked seeing, a seeing deprived of any linguistic articulation of all the objects that we see. This applies both to what we call persistent objects, which are the main objects of our experience, and to events such as an explosion that happens only once; even for that we have words. There is always an exchange between the linguistic layer of our experience and the prelinguistic, purely experiential level.

Our seeing is encompassed in the reports of our seeing, mainly because we have to communicate to others what we see, to say "look" and therefore to call to the other's attention. Even if the communication is only in the form of the cry "rabbit," when the rabbit appears before the hunter. It may be that we no longer have access to a mute perception. Even if for the ordinary person there is perhaps something tacit in experience, the philosopher by definition has to do with reports, with what we say about what we see. We have the same difficulty, for example, with dreams. I have already made several allusions to the paradox that in fact we have access to dreams only when we are awakened and therefore when we give reports of our dream. How the dream is preserved in the report of the dream is a problem in itself.

Let me conclude this introduction by saying a few words about the limit of these thinkers' methodological approach. I already provided a hint when I said that it's too often limited to isolated experience. There's not enough attention paid to the long development of discourse, the long process of imagining such as exploring a hypothesis, and so on. Also, as we shall see, the productive aspect of imagination is not often emphasized. Particularly in analytic linguistic analysis there is a kind of fear of this problem of creative imagination. Consider, for example, the views of Price in *Thinking and Experience*. We shall later see his modesty before a problem, but there is one point where he is not moderate.

As I have said, these are dark and mysterious regions, in which an analytic philosopher may well fear to tread. If we venture into them, we are coming close to what is called the 'creative' activity of mind; we are even on the fringe of dangerous topics like poetic inspiration. Anyone who thinks it is a philosopher's first duty to be clear and talk sense will do well to refrain from discussing generic images. Or are there some subjects so important or at least so intriguing, that it is better to talk nonsense about them than not talk about them at all? (Price 1953, 293–94)

Price's comment reflects a more or less common conviction of all analytic philosophers on this problem. I shall return at length to the issue of creative imagination, including to Kant's discussion of the genius, in the third and final part of these lectures.

In the remainder of this lecture and the beginning of the next, I shall examine the work of Gilbert Ryle on imagination. I start with Ryle because he writes on the problem with which I began the lectures, the problem of the unity of the field of imagination. If we survey the examples given in the classical texts, do they belong to a unique faculty? I shall then turn to Price. This placement of Price disrupts the didactic order I earlier presented, but everything is mixed up in this field, so there is no inherent order, and my didactic order will likely crumble several times, as we shall see.

In Ryle's book, *The Concept of Mind*, I shall concentrate on his chapter on "Imagination." His is the kind of analysis that I want to place in close relationship with what Sartre did on the imagination. The word *describe* is central in this essay and is opposed to all superimposed theories, misconstructions, and misconceptions. The place of these misconceptions is *par excellence* linked to what we say about what we do when we imagine. At several places there is language of this kind: it is "tempting and natural to misdescribe" (Ryle 1949, 253).[3] There is a tendency in our language to miss the target of its own referent. Language about the mind is misconstrued. This is the main topic of the book in general, the mind as the ghost in the machine (15ff.). The book's therapeutic program consists in curing description from misdescription. Nevertheless, there is an optimistic confidence in ordinary language, because finally it will be always some more appropriate expression that will prevail against these ill-formed accounts of how we live. The claim, therefore, is against language but a plea for language at the same time. Otherwise, we should have to do psychology. The book is more a piece of the philosophy of ordinary language brought back to its healthy functioning than a language of psychology. If we do philosophy, then we have to amend language for the sake of language. There is a negative side and a positive side to this approach.

As we shall see, when Ryle says that by correcting our language about the imagination, we let speak the experience itself, this is not enough to oppose Ryle to Sartre. (Ryle's approach is not so far from what Austin calls "linguistic phenomenology."[4]) To my mind, the main differences between Ryle and Sartre are not to be found in their methods—more intuitive in Sartre, more linguistic in Ryle. An initial difference concerns the unity of the field of imagination. Whereas Husserl and Sartre will seem to look for some essence or essential structure of imagination, Ryle's more nominalistic approach denies that there is a paradigmatic case and directs itself against the abusive privilege of imagining in the sense of imagining that we see or hear. His approach is directed against the image as the copy of an actual experience.

A long part of Ryle's chapter is devoted to the fight against a misconstruction of our language concerning imagination and its misconstruction according to the model of the picture. There are pictures in our experience: scores of music, photographs, images in the mirror or in the water, and so on. We speak of images for pictures, and we speak of pictures for images. There is a mixture and confusion between picture language and image language. He takes a long time to dismantle this misconstruction and tries to refer it to some other misconstructions.

The first source of the misconstruction is the division of the mind into cognition, volition, and emotion, the famous tri-partition of the mind as cognitive, practical, and emotional. According to this approach, because imagination has been allocated to cognition, it must necessarily "be excluded from the others" (258). In a sense he's right. Since Aristotle, the scale of functions has been a cognitive scale that has moved from intuition to image to concept. And the empiricists have not at all broken with this tradition. On the contrary, they have reinforced it, since the image has to solve the problem of the concept. The cognitive is overemphasized. Imagination has had to become "the (erratic) Squire of Reason" and "cannot serve the other masters" (258).

The second origin of the mistaken construction of imagination lies in a model at hand that is both enticing and deceiving. We have in question an enigmatic relation: how an image in my mind could resemble a thing out in the world. The enticing but mistaken model suggests that we start from the given likeness between two givens, the given of a portrait and of its model. The picture seems to be a good candidate for providing us a leading thread, a clue in the description of the mental image. Under the heading of picture we may place such things as portraits, photographs, and forged signatures. (The latter will play a great role in Ryle, because it will quickly lead to the topic of pretending [260].) We describe imagination in the idiom of a "paperless picture" (247), a picture that exists in the mind as the picture exists in reality. We transfer something having a physical existence into something having a mental existence and ascribe to both the same ontological status (although Ryle himself does not use the word *ontological* here). The image is said to exist in the mind as the picture exists in the physical world. (This is one of the reasons also for our misconstruction of the concept of mind, which is the main object of the book. The mind is mistakenly viewed as a kind of theater or place where there are inhabitants such as thoughts, images, and so on. We shall see how Sartre fights against the same illusions but with another solution, the concept of intentionality. Ryle does not have this concept.) We say we have pictures in the mind like pictures in reality not only because of the convenience, economy, and elegance of this solution, but also because the visible picture helps us to imagine. It "induces" imagination (253). The picture helps me to seem to see the person in my mind. The likeness of the picture induces the vividness of imagining (254). The importance of the word *induce* will return with Price as applied to thinking and not only to imagining.

A third and final origin of the mistaken construction of imagination derives from the influence of Hume's theory. Hume raised an improper question. The title of the first section of his *Treatise* is "Of the Origin of Our Ideas." Raising the problem of origins, he was not able to see a difference between a picture and a mental image, or at least he had to place any difference within the larger continuity of the process. In Ryle's view, Hume had the absurd idea that there may be something like the copy of an impression (249–50). How is it possible, though, for there to be a sound and then a copy of a sound? Hume tried to say that between the impression and the copy there is only a difference of degree in vividness or intensity. For Ryle, this is again absurd, because I may have a very vivid image of a faint sound (250). To be faint is a characteristic of impressions, but to be vivid is a characteristic of images. We may have a nonvivid image of a strong sound or the contrary. We have two lines here which never intersect.

Therefore, Ryle argues (as will Sartre) that we must start from the break or discontinuity between the image and the impression. Impressions exist, but images do not exist in a fainter way as a diminishing or shadow existence. Ryle's radical answer is that the image exists nowhere, neither in reality nor in the mind. The image does not present a question of existence; it concerns what we do and not what exists. Ryle maintains that we have to denounce the concept of the image as something appearing. The main difference between Sartre and Ryle is that Sartre, having the concept of an intentional object, will try to support the paradox of an object as nonexisting, as an intentional object without existence. Ryle, without the concept of intentionality, has to say that since the image is not a picture in the mind, then we must deny its existence in any way, either physical or mental. What is fancied is not the perceived thing but the perceiving process. People don't see things in their mind; they don't see at all. The question, where does the image exist, is the wrong question. And this wrong question is linked to another wrong question asking about the mind as a place with a location for images. The latter question would obligate us to ask at what distance an image is from another in this shadow theater of the mind.

In a typical text Ryle writes: "Much as stage-murders do not have victims and are not murders, so seeing things in one's mind eye does not involve either the existence of things seen or the occurrence of acts of seeing them. So no asylum is required for them to exist or occur in" (245). The asylum would be the concept of mind that it is the object of the book to refute. The right description of imagining requires amending our language. If there is a likeness in the process of imagining—and the notion of likeness is fundamental in imagination—this likeness lies not between an alleged mental picture, which would be a kind of small thing, and a thing out in the world but in the process of imagining itself. The entire chapter tries to transfer the focus from substantives to verbs. Instead of speaking of images that we should have, we should speak of the imaging (247) that we do. Instead of saying that we see the phantom of a thing, we should say that we are seeming to see (248) a thing. There is only one object—the thing in the world—not two—the second being the image of the thing—but we may engage in two processes, either seeing or seeming to see. It is in the relation between seeing and seeming to see that the likeness of imagining occurs. Ryle's text anticipates the second part of the chapter, on pretending, since the example of stage-murder, of a play and acting a part, is already present. The choice of examples is mixed in with the analysis.

The next issue will be to consider what is the relation between seeming to see and pretending, since pretending is more something visible in space and in motion; it's a behavior. To express the relation between seeing and seeming to see, Ryle will write of the latter as "seeing," in quotation marks (for example, 246). This bracketing may have something to do with the bracketing (*epochē*) discussed by Husserl. There is perhaps a kind of *epochē* that is not elaborated as such here. In the theory of pretending we shall see that the bracketing has to do with a certain use of language. When we mention something without assuming it, we put it within quotation marks. The theory of quotation, which is very familiar and very well developed in linguistic analysis, observes that we may have two uses of the same proposition, asserting it or quoting it. We transfer into the problem of imagination an important distinction in language itself between direct language and language in quotation marks, what has been called in traditional rhetoric oblique discourse (*obliqua oratio* or *obliqua sermo*) (259). An oblique discourse is here already implied. Later we shall see how the same problem of bracketing is treated by Husserl as a certain element of nothingness. Husserl and Sartre will have no difficulty saying that there is an appearance, but it's an appearance that is bracketed. I don't know why Ryle goes so far as to say that there is no appearance in an image. I think that this is not good phenomenology. Price will not follow Ryle on this point. He will say that surely something appears when I have an image. But because Ryle does not have the idea of objective inexistence, then he has to say that the absence of existence must be total. Consequently, he displaces the problem from the appearance of the image to the operation of imagining. Yet, as we shall later discuss, if we have a correlation between act and object in an intentionality, then if in imagination there is bracketing of the act, there must be some bracketing somewhere of the object.

The positive side of the description of imagining is already anticipated, since the difference between seeing directly and seeming to see is pretending. The second part of the chapter is devoted to this paradigmatic example. The immediate advantage of shifting the description from mental image to pretending is that the latter involves a behavior. In Ryle there is a behavioristic trend that is linked to his fight against the concept of mind as the ghost in the machine. There is something both linguistic and behaviorist in the concept of mind that is expressed in the following way:

> There are hosts of widely different sorts of behaviour in the conduct of which we should ordinarily and correctly be described as imaginative. The mendacious witness in the witness-box, the inventor thinking out a new machine, the constructor of a romance, the child playing bears, and [the British actor] Henry Irving are all exercising their imaginations; but so, too, are the judge listening to the lies of the witness, the colleague giving his opinions on the new invention, the novel reader, the nurse who refrains from admonishing the [children acting as] "bears" for their subhuman noises, the dramatic critic and the theatre-goers. (256)

All these examples should be treated at the level of long strings of discourses. The constructor of a romance, the inventor of a new machine, and so on will disappear from the analysis, which will be always related to isolated, consistent objects such as a picture, the image of a smell, and so on. We need to reopen and redisplay Ryle's examples themselves.

Ryle pleads against the reduction of imagination to mental imaging. In so doing, he denies the unity of the problem of imagination and assumes a nominalistic position: "There is no special Faculty of Imagination, occupying itself single-mindedly in fancied viewings and hearings. On the contrary, 'seeing' things is one exercise of imagination, growling somewhat like a bear is another; smelling things in the mind's nose is an uncommon act of fancy; malingering is a very common one, and so forth" (257–58). A little earlier he writes: "Just as ploughing is one farming job and tree-spraying is another farming job, so inventing a new machine is one way of being imaginative and playing bears is another. No one thinks that there exists a nuclear farming operation by the execution of which alone a man is entitled to be called 'a farmer'" (256–57). This is very close to Wittgenstein's notion of language games. There are several imagination games. Yet in my earlier introduction of Ryle, I may have too much emphasized Ryle's attitude against the unity of the field. If he wants to reopen the field, which has been closed too much by the classical problem of the mental image, he is in fact restructuring it around a paradigmatic phenomenon despite his claim that there is no such a thing as a faculty of imagination. Pretending offers a new nuclear experience, since Ryle's examples of imagination have in common the make-believe. Other examples, for instance, include: "[a]ssuming, supposing, entertaining, [and] toying with ideas" (263). Pretending also covers the whole spectrum from the deliberate to the involuntary, from simulating to dissimulating, with or without knowing. It includes all degrees of skepticism and credulity. For Ryle, therefore, there is a centrality of the phenomenon of pretending.

What Ryle wants to undertake is a logical analysis of pretending through amending language and putting it in the right place. "To describe someone as pretending," he says, "is to say that he is playing a part . . ." (259). And he goes on to discuss what it means to play a part. He wants to describe the logical ingredients of pretending. As previously noted, the decisive comparison comes in paralleling playing a part with quoting in discourse (259). The comparison is introduced to show that pretending is a much more complicated operation than direct action, just as quoting is a more complex operation than making an assertion. We must first know how to do the direct action in order to pretend it. Talking obliquely is the inner structure of pretending (259). We have completely turned our back on the notions of copy or trace. They are too simple, because a copy is a material reduplication or a trace of something that is left by the action of an agent. We must forget the image of the photocopier that produces a copy of the original but in fact produces a duplicate. With pretending we have to do with "a performance with a certain sort of complex description" (260). This complexity is expressed by the quotation marks used to describe the pretended "seeing" and "hearing" (for example, see 246), since a "[d]eliberate verisimilitude" (260) is a part of the activity. (Many kinds of copying are actually complex, too. As we shall discuss in a later lecture, in painting or drawing, copying what we see is a very complex operation.)

We may also describe pretending in other language similar to that of quoting. We can say that we do a performance in a hypothetical manner (263). Here we apply another model from language which is not that of quoting but of assuming: let us assume that, let us suppose that. We display our thought without committing ourselves in it (263–64). Two aspects are at work: what we say plus the assuming or noncommitment that is added to it. All these expressions—"seeing," quoting, assuming, and pretending— have in common a duality in the description of the one and the same action. We describe the same action as both actually performed and as pretended. The difference lies, Ryle says, in the subordinate clause (261). When I say, "he seemingly fights," I say first that "he fights"—main clause—and second, "seemingly"—subordinate clause. The structure of pretending is a "dualism between the direct and the oblique" (261).

I must say that I am not quite satisfied with Ryle's position, because the difficulty has been displaced. There are at least two complexities that would require a phenomenological analysis. First is the noncommitment and therefore the negative. The negative always is haunting the field of imagination. Ryle has expelled it from the side of the object, but it returns on the side of pretending as an operation. He offers, for instance, the example of the sparring boxer, where there is "a series of calculated omissions to fight" (261). There is the omission as opposed to the commitment. There is a noncommitment, and therefore the negative is reintroduced on the side of the boxer's involvement. The bracketing has been merely displaced.

Second, there is an element of likeness that is also complex. No longer is likeness between things, such as an object and a picture, but it is not easier to describe when it is between operations, between seeing and seeming to see. It is not easier to understand this likeness than the rejected likeness at stake in seeing an appearance or image of something. We may say that seeing an appearance of something is an absurdity, but the operation of appearing to see or seeming to see is perhaps something much more difficult to describe. We have given only the linguistic trace of the phenomenon when we say that seeming to see happens as a quotation, that it occurs because there is oblique discourse, because we may take distance and imitate. So in question are the descriptions of the dual relation between not doing and as if doing and the correlation between the not and the *as if*. Perhaps we have reduced the difficulty to something nuclear, but the difficulty is all the more dense in that it is concentrated on one point, on the *as if*.

There is one more reason to be hesitant about Ryle's analysis, and that is because the "dualism between the direct and the oblique" (261) is not specific to the examples of pretending. As Ryle sometimes acknowledges (261), in his chapter there are many other examples of oblique discourse than that of pretending. For instance, I cannot describe an act of someone complying with a rule (261–62) without giving two descriptions, first, what is the person doing and, second, what is the rule being obeyed. Or consider the act of repenting (263). I do something now as an act of repenting but by reference to something else, keeping a resolution. There is my action now, and the prior promise I made. More generally, when I say, as in repenting and other examples, that what I do in the application is a lower order of something that has a higher task (263), then I describe the application for itself, but I also describe it as a lower order task related to a high order task. The dual description of the direct and the oblique is not very specific. As I have suggested, what is specific is the combination of the *as if* doing with the nonperformance, the omission.

There is one point where Ryle is very close to Husserl and Sartre, and that is when he says: "We have to learn to give verdicts before we can learn to operate with suspended judgments" (264). A suspended judgment presupposes that we are acquainted with giving verdicts; the categorical assertion is suspended in the form of the hypothetical. Perhaps here we are circling around the difficulty of the *epochē* both in the appearance and in the act. But I understand that this chapter is more directed against logicians and epistemologists who assume that an assumption is something simpler than an affirmation. And I think he is completely right on this point. Sometimes we say that first we have a hypothesis, then we add evidence, and then we have an affirmation. But to have a hypothesis, we must first have the notion of direct assertion. Then we suspend the assertion to put it into play as a hypothesis. As Ryle says, "The concept of make-believe is of a higher order than that of belief" (264). Similarly, Husserl will place imagination among those terms that he calls modification by suspension. We must have first a kind of direct belief in something and then suspend it in order to make an imaginative process.

The next lecture begins with the last part of Ryle's chapter, where he attempts to combine the first part of his analysis with the second, the seeming to see and the pretending to do. Here the unity of the field will become stronger despite the claim that it is more scattered than the notion of a faculty of imagination would imply. Ryle will use the concept of *imaging* (247, 252, 264) to distinguish between "fancied perception" (264) and pretended behavior. The lecture will then continue with analysis of Price.

8

Ryle (2) and Price

This lecture finishes the discussion of Gilbert Ryle and then examines H. H. Price's *Thinking and Experience*.

Recall that we have examined two tasks that Ryle undertakes in his chapter on imagination. First, he tries to demolish the so-called classical theory of image identified with a picture, if we take the word *picture* in its ordinary sense, as a physical object that has a likeness to something else. (We shall see that in Price the notion of picture returns as a replica, which is a good synonym, a replica of something that exists elsewhere.) Ryle says that it's false that the image is a kind of paperless mental picture, something without a physical support. Rather, it is something else. It's something else in the sense that it's not something appearing, since it does not exist at all. And if it does not exist at all, we have to shift the emphasis from the image as something before our mind's eye to imaging or imagining as a verb. With this verb we may say that we don't see something that seems to exist, but we *seem* to see something. Seeming to see is a fancied perception.

Second, Ryle sets aside fancied perception to consider handier examples that can be ordered under the notion of pretending. When people pretend, they do something. It's a behavior that can be described: the play of children, the part played by an actor in a play, and so on. The first advantage, therefore, of attention to pretending is that we typically see something; it's a behavior that generally has some external marks. But it is also more appropriate for a conceptual analysis, because there is a kinship between pretending and certain uses of language that can be considered as oblique or indirect, such as quoting or mentioning something without assuming it. In this sense, Ryle says, even if they don't offer external marks, supposing, entertaining, and toying with ideas are varieties of pretending since they "are all ways of pretending to adopt schemes or theories" (Ryle 1949, 263).[1] We discover that pretending is a very complex act, because we must have first the notion of the performance and then the qualification that the performance receives by being merely pretended. Applying to the notion of pretending that of quoting, we see that the description of it implies two clauses, a main clause describing the action itself and a subordinate clause qualifying the action by "seemingly."

In the latter part of his chapter, which we shall now consider, Ryle asks how we can restructure the notion that we have put aside—the fancied perception, when we seem to see—according to the paradigm of pretending. He proposes to speak of *imaging* to cover the type of make-believe that includes imagining and fancying (264). What are the differences between the two sets of examples, between *playing at*, pretending as an actor, child, or liar would do, and *fancying that*, as having an image? There are two minor differences and a major difference (264). The first minor difference is that when we speak of *playing at*, it's more what spectators say that somebody is doing, whereas *fancying that* is what individual actors say, because they alone know they have an image. But these roles may be exchanged. Second, *playing at* is more often deliberate, whereas *fancying that* is sometimes very casual and even involuntary, if not compulsory. The third difference is more important, since *playing at* is obviously a kind of action. As Ryle says, it's a mock action (264). If in a play there is a murder, nobody is killed, so it's a mock murder (245). On the other hand, if we may use the word *mock* for fancy, it's a mock perception.

But then the whole problem returns: what really is the difference between a mock action and a fancied perception? The distinctiveness, linked to the part played by action or motion in pretending, tends to shrink and even to disappear if we get rid of the illusion discarded at the beginning and accept that the image is not a mental spectacle to be seen in one's mind. If we describe correctly the problem and the experience, then the parallelism is greater between *playing at* and *fancying that*, in the sense that in both we have two verbs. We have the unity of two verbs, a verb of action in pretending but also a verb of something like an action and even an action in fancying. To see is a kind of action. This is a very important and positive contribution of Ryle's, which I think no one can deny. As I have previously emphasized, seeing is not well described in the theory of imagination. We take for granted that we know what seeing is, and then we say that imagining is a kind of seeing. But to see is not merely to have a passive impression; it's a way of observing. What is fancied in the imagination is precisely this active part of the perception, not the passive impression. Ryle keeps repeating that he doesn't know what could be the trace of an impression or the echo of a sound impression (see, for example, 249–50). If we get rid of this idea of a shadow sensation, then we have to look at the activity implied in recognizing something. He takes as an example following a tune running in our head (265 ff.) and discusses the similarity of this example with actually following a tune in the concert hall. A very complex operation is implied that puts perceiving very close to thinking, or, at least, as he says, to one of the uses of the word *thinking*. "Imaging, therefore, is not a function of pure sentience; and a creature which had sensations, but could not learn, could not 'see,' or picture, things any more than it could spell" (266). Imaging is a way of using one's knowledge of how the tune goes. Here the parallelism between pretending and fancying begins to reemerge. When a person pictures Helvellyn, "[t]here is nothing akin to sensations. Realising, in this way, how Helvellyn would look, is *doing something* which stands in the same relation to seeing Helvellyn as sophisticated performances stand to those more naive performances, whose mention is obliquely contained in the description of the higher order performances" (266, emphasis added). The reference to an oblique mention alludes to Ryle's prior discussion that we examined in the last lecture. The difference between perceiving and doing is less striking if perceiving is also a kind of doing.

We may more or less merge the two descriptions of fancying and pretending on the basis of the idea that there is something active in following a tune. What we do in following a tune is to expect and be prepared to hear some sounds that would fit with the idea that we have already of the kind of music. This analysis will be undertaken more accurately by Husserl and Merleau-Ponty. The notion is that in perception we have anticipation, what they call protentions; perceiving is a way of assuming what the object will be, how it will appear. Merleau-Ponty very often uses the notion of assumption; assumption not in a linguistic sense but in the sense that I am always in advance of and prepared for.[2] This expectation may be mistaken, deceived, disappointed, or surprised; we expect something and something else appears. There is an interplay therefore between expectation and the real appearance. To listen for the notes to be heard is the act of being silent in expectation of the sound. Listening for what is due to come "is already to suppose, fancy or imagine" (Ryle 1949, 268). Ryle distinguishes his approach from the traditional one:

> Going through a tune in one's head is like following a heard tune and is, indeed, a sort of rehearsal of it. But what makes the imaginative operation similar to the other is not, as is often supposed, that it incorporates the hearing of ghosts of notes similar in all but loudness to the heard notes of the real tune [as in Hume], but the fact that both are utilisations of knowledge of how the tune goes. (269)

To listen is to know how the music will go on. It is the incorporation of this phase of knowing how that may be fancied. The element of fancy is put in this active phase of perceiving.

The real difference between pretending and fancying is not, therefore, between mock action and mock perception but more largely between the performance and the *as if* performance. Even if listening as a part of the musical performance is not the same as a fancied performance, we may shift from this anticipation that is already a way of fancying to the hypothetical manner of following a tune. To fancy a tune, Ryle says, is to follow the tune in "a hypothetical manner" (269). The language of following in a hypothetical manner reconstitutes the complete parallelism between both forms of following a tune. "[T]he purely imaginative exercise is more sophisticated than that of following the tune, when heard, or than that of humming it; since it involves the thought of following or producing the tune" hypothetically (269).

As my own commentary here, let me say that from this analysis emerges what I should call the fundamental problem of imagination: the conjunction between the *not* doing and the *like* doing, the *as if* doing. The remainder of our discussion of imagination will address this conjunction between the not doing—what Ryle calls the "abstentions from producing" (269)—and the *as if* doing. In the case of the sparring boxer, for example, he is omitting to hit his adversary, so there is an omission of doing in the *as if* doing. We may spot in Ryle's text the alternance of the *as if* and the abstention.

> We might say that imagining oneself talking or humming is a series of *abstentions* from producing the noises which would be the due words or notes to produce, *if* one were talking or humming aloud. That is why such operations are impenetrably secret; not that the words or notes are being produced in a hermetic cell, but that the operations consist of *abstentions* from producing them. That, too, is why learning to fancy one is talking or humming comes later than learning to talk or hum. Silent soliloquy is a flow of pregnant *non-sayings*. (269, emphases added)

It's the conjunction of omission and seemingly doing that raises the problem. But in linguistic analysis, we cannot go further. We are only observing that if we have an exact report of what happens in imagination, then we must have these two expressions somewhere: negative expressions in terms of omission and hypothetical modes in terms of having. What, though, is the condition of the possibility of joining the negative of abstention and the positive of *as if*? It will be the task of phenomenology to address this question and to try to go beyond the mere amending of our language to the root of experience that supports this combined use of the *as if* and the not.

What is convincing in Ryle is the parallelism established between fancying and pretending as combining the *as if* of the hypothetical mode and the abstention of the performance. But I see two difficulties that will be better handled by Price. The first difficulty is Ryle's suppression of the element of appearance in the image. For my part, I am not at all convinced by this radical disconnection between picture and image. Here we are going too far against ordinary use precisely in a philosophy that claims to return to ordinary use. There must be some reasons in the imaginative experience itself that we speak of an image as a picture and therefore as something appearing. I don't know why our author has separated completely the element of the quasi from the appearance of an image to concentrate the quasi on the operation of imaging. If there may be quasi-listening, as to a tune in one's head, why can there not be quasi-existence? Perhaps this is the real problem of the image. The unavoidable kinship between image and picture relies on the paradox of the image that is alluded to here, that it is a kind of nonexistent object. We must then have some conceptual framework within which we can think this notion of nonexisting objects. To my mind, this will be the advantage of a phenomenological approach. With the concept of intention, we may have an intentional act with nothing in front of it, but this nothing is a part of what appears. The nothingness in the appearance and also the likeness in the appearance both have an important part. So my main problem in Ryle is whether we can get rid of the quasi-presence of the image.

My second difficulty, although I raise it as a more hesitant question, is whether in Ryle we are not substituting the report about imagination for imagination itself. What I have in mind is the operation that we are doing when we say we "fancy that . . ." This is a way of writing the experience that takes advantage of introducing a parallelism with "I think that." In modern Anglo-American philosophy of logic, the latter phrase is an important part of the discussion concerning intensional logic that started with Peter Geach's book, *Mental Acts*. Modal logic and discussion of "I think that" was based on the possibility of having a proposition in thought that has an operator. Imagining is then treated by Ryle as a logical operator. The parallelism with modal logic comes with the notion in imagining of the hypothetical. Imagining is a way of saying P—the proposition—hypothetically. Is it the same thing, though, to think that—to have images in one's mind—and to fancy that? If so, then we have elaborated our experience at a higher level of discourse, the level of discourse where we have propositions. We have placed imagination at the propositional level in order to have the "that." I was interested to see the shift in Ryle's chapter itself where the word *fancy* is followed not by an object—I fancy something—but suddenly by a proposition—I fancy that I see (see, for example, 248). Is it true, though, that when I have an image of something, I am fancying that? We have here a rewriting of the experience or of reformulating it in terms that are more manageable for a propositional logic that would introduce operators such as the hypothetical. My question is raised to this kind of linguistic analysis where the linguistic element is perhaps stronger than the phenomenological element. The phenomenological basis has been overwhelmed by the logical apparatus. This may be typical of the approach of linguistic analysis as compared to phenomenology. Fancying is reconstructed as pretending on the basis of a propositional reformulation.

I assume it's very difficult to overcome the paradox that if we claim to give a report of an experience, we have to give a linguistic structure to the report and then by necessity the way in which we structure the report is decisive. The case with "fancying that" is typical, but I wonder whether the language here does not do violence to the experience itself by compelling it to enter into a kind of Procrustean bed. "Fancying that" must have the same formulation as the hypothetical proposition, so it becomes a hypothetical proposition. Then the nonverbal element of the image is swallowed up by its own verbal expression. But this may be my bias, as I have not been raised in this tradition. I am more struck by the fact that the logical apparatus is stronger than the phenomenological basis despite the discussion of pretending being a good piece of phenomenology. I am not sure that the discussion of pretending solves the problem of the mental image. We shall see how Price solves the issue.

Let me proceed to say something about H. H. Price in his work, *Thinking and Experience*, particularly chapters 8 and 9. Recall why I have chosen Price. I have proposed to put the discussion in the second part of the lectures under three headings. First, what is the act of imaging or imagining? We addressed this in Ryle and will return to the topic in Sartre. Second, how is imaging or imagining incorporated into thinking? This is the contribution of Price. Third, how does imagination work in relation to perception? We shall discuss this through Wittgenstein's treatment of *seeing as*. As I have previously mentioned, Price's issue of how imaging or imagination is incorporated into thinking is a residual problem of a classical topic, since the bulk of the theory of imagination in the seventeenth and eighteenth centuries— let us say from Locke to Kant through Descartes and so on—asked how do images provide us with concepts. The question of the relationship between image and concept was the central problem in the whole discussion. And in its excess, the imagist theory, to call it as Price does (see, for example,

Price 1953, 234), claimed that the image is the origin of abstract ideas and that therefore we can get rid of the medieval universals.[3] Further, in the connection of the image to imagination, we have the clue to the question of causation. The imagination was the solution of everything. There was an inflation of the role of the image mainly in the empiricist tradition. Everything proceeded from images. Subsequently, there was a deflation of image's role with the emergence of movements in logic led by Frege, Husserl, Meinong, and Russell, who argued that we should forget the problem of the image and start from the proposition. The theory of the proposition and its inner structure had nothing to do with what we think or feel or what kind of images we may have. If we speak of the properties of a triangle, we don't rely on the drawing of a triangle on the blackboard or on a mental blackboard. There are no longer blackboards but only the object. The ideal structure of the object was completely severed from the psychological. The image was sent back to psychology, whereas the proposition was retained for logic and epistemology.

Price's work is an attempt to introduce a better balance between what he calls the verbalistic theory of thinking (237) and the imagist theory of thinking. Consistent with modern epistemology, Price assumes that the imagist theory is wrong in its claim to be a substitute for thinking in logical terms, that is, thinking in words. Nevertheless, he says, there is a more modest role for the image if we consider thinking as an operation done by a thinker. We must be aware of Price's title: it's not *Thought and Experience* but *Thinking and Experience*. It concerns what we do when we think. The ground on which we stand here is not that of the logic of the proposition but of the operation of the mind. This subject belongs to the philosophy of the mind. If we assume this starting point, the first question is what is it to think *with* images, to think *in* images. The prepositions are very important. We have no longer a claim that thinking proceeds from the image, but rather that if there is something like thinking, we can analyze the role of images in it. This is, for Price, the moderate and then legitimate claim of what he calls the imagist theory of thinking over the opposite excesses of the verbalistic theory of thought, according to which our words as defined in the dictionary and the grammar of our language will bear the whole burden of thinking.

At a first level, the role of imagination is to support the grasping of identities on the basis of resemblances. (This is discussed in the first chapters of Price's book, which I consider only briefly.) Price describes the permanent fight between two traditions, what he calls the philosophy of resemblances against the philosophy of sameness ("universals"). Some say that in order to perceive a resemblance I must have the idea of the common kernel between two things. Others ask how we know that two things have the same meaning unless on the basis of their resemblance. Under this view, we assimilate; we find a resemblance. At the very least there is in this dialectic between resemblance and sameness an important part played by *perceiving* resemblances. For my part, I cannot forget that in the *Poetics* Aristotle says that to metaphorize is precisely to perceive resemblances (Aristotle 1973, 703, 1459a 5–8). Perceiving resemblances has to do with imagination but in a more complex way than having an image of something. Words would not work without the support of a faculty or function of grasping similarity, grasping resemblances.

As Price comments in chapter 8, we cannot say that the study of imaging is a subject of "mere psychology" (Price 1953, 235). If we take a complex case such as problem solving, we see that we cannot problem solve without trying new hypotheses on the basis of drawings, using diagrams, and also mental images. We try the solution in our thought. This is what in ordinary language we call to imagine. In some extreme cases, there is a kind of sudden appearance of the solution, a kind of outburst of the solution. "With a visual image, one can quite often 'see at a glance' what the solution is . . ." (236). Even if we don't rely too heavily on this exceptional if real example of people who discover a solution to a problem in dreaming and so on, it's only a more dramatic formulation of something very ordinary: that we try our ideas in images. Even in ordinary thinking, to understand a sentence or a word is to know "what it would be like for the sentence to be true" (236). We frequently test through images the capacity for verification or falsification of a sentence's idea. It is in this way that Price introduces the problem of thinking with or in images, with modest claims as opposed to the extreme claims of the pure imagist theory of the empiricist tradition.

In fact, it's very unusual for us not to use such images in thinking. We would not use images, Price says, only in the case of "primary recognition" (238). When I look out through the window, I see that there is a tree. I make no use of an image, the claim goes, because there is an immediate adherence between the word and the instance. There is no intermediary step between perception and recognition. This example is not convincing, though, because we know that we perceive through typical schemas. I return very often to the cases quoted by Gombrich in his book on *Art and Illusion* where he shows, for instance, the painting of an English landscape by a Chinese artist. The trees are depicted in a Chinese style. The artist sees the trees on the basis of a typically Chinese schema of trees (Gombrich 1969, 83–84). Between the instance and the word there are some intermediary schemas, types, or typical perceptions that help us precisely to recognize, not only to cognize. It's quite possible that primary recognition does not exist at all.

In most cases, we want to test our concepts with some objects of thought that are precisely both absent and like possible examples. The combination between *not* and *like*—the element of absence and the element of likeness—is immediately introduced into the discussion. Price speaks of "non-instantiative particulars" (239), which is rather awkward but very efficient for his purpose. The expression implies the identity of the picture and the image. What does the term mean? Words that name a class, such as "dog," are not particulars but universals. To cash in—Price's phrase (for example, see 239)—the meaning of the word of a class, I give either an instance of the class by showing one of its members or by producing a drawing or a mental image. I may rely either on real, present instances of the class—this is Fido, a dog, which may be all that we can offer the first time that we have to give a name to something—or, more usually, I introduce a particular that is a member of the class but that is not an instance, in the sense of an actual, present example. Drawings and mental images fall into the latter group of non-instantiative particulars (254). (As we shall see, Price will go on to modify his characterization and describe drawings and mental images as quasi-instantiative particulars [256].) What was wrong, therefore, with the imagist theory was not the claim that there are images in thinking but the claim that these non-instantiative particulars are the only content of thought, and hence that so-called concepts are merely substitutes for these images. We may completely set aside the claim, which seems no longer assumable in a modern theory of knowledge, that concepts are merely substitutes for images, but even if images are not the origin of the concepts, at least they support the operation of cashing the meaning of concepts by the means of particular, absent cases, by means of non-instantiative particulars.

Among the non-instantiative or quasi-instantiative particulars, the exemplars that are not instances, what is an image? Price writes very strongly in support of the claim that images must be like entities in order to satisfy this role. These pages seem directed against Ryle, although his name does not occur. Remember that Ryle wanted to discard the notion of the image as entity-like and to promote imaging as a process or operation. For Price, by contrast, it's very important that if the function of an image is to cash a meaning, it must give us a quasi-instance of the example. It must work like a real entity that is perceived and must have the same function. For example, if I want to speak about Japan but have never been there, how may I cash the meaning of this word? I may travel there and actually see the country, or I may read travelers' reports. To make sense of the word, the travelers' reports play exactly the same role as my going there. Because of the reports, the word will not remain empty. The reports must have the same function of presenting the meaning as my going there, but in absence. The notion of a presentation in absence is very fundamental here (Price

1953, 255). Price's scruple is exactly similar to mine, or the contrary, I should say that my scruple is the same as his: that what he calls entity language (248) in fact must be well-founded in our experience. We cannot say that to have an image is seeming to see or fancying that we see, because something in a sense appears, but with the feature of not being there. Price does not go further, but he assumes that this is good phenomenology. He uses the word *phenomenology* (248) to assume that there are these kinds of strange appearances. In contrast, for those people who say that these images exist nowhere, there is no appearance of the images. Why don't these people like the language of images as appearing? "It is simply because they are not at all interested in the phenomenology of imaging, whereas they are passionately interested in the phenomenology of talking" (248). This is exactly my objection. In fact, I wrote my objection before reading that passage, so I was reinforced on seeing it. The phenomenology of talking—even talking about imagination—must not kill the phenomenology of imaging. And so he makes a plea for entity language.

We speak of images as appearing "*as if* they were things" (248, emphasis added). Nobody is misled by that talk except people who have hallucinations, but precisely we say that they are mentally ill. If we are not mentally ill, when we say that we have images before our mind's eye, we never say that it is a hallucination.

> [I]n imaging we seem to be confronted with something, to have something over against us or presented to us. . . . [W]e are aware of an entity . . . because we are experiencing *something which behaves in an entity-like way.* It shows a certain independence of us, a certain obstinacy or recalcitrance, almost as if it had a will of its own. . . . What behaves in this way is naturally described as an entity, a particular. (248–49, emphases added)

Therefore, Price maintains that we have no interest in shifting from noun language, which is convenient for this entity language, to a verb language, to saying that there is no image but that we are imaging. If we say that we are imaging, we are imaging *something*. In the phenomenological correlation between act and object that I shall later discuss, the *as if* of the act is also the *as if* of the object, and we cannot have one without the other.

The importance of Price's contribution is that we are allowed to say that images *are* pictures. It's not a linguistic mistake to say this, as Ryle would insist, arguing as he does that while the picture exists somewhere, the image exists nowhere, and therefore images are not pictures. In fact, ordinary language is more reliable than philosophers' theories. Once more, it's interesting to say that against Ryle, since he claims that it's always the philosophers who distort experience. Perhaps he did the same here. (It is, in fact, very difficult to be a phenomenologist. We cannot undertake phenomenological analysis without talking about what we see, but what are the criteria for a faithful report of a phenomenological experience?) Price's point is quite explicit: "[T]his something, the visual image, does have a good deal in common with a picture" (249). What the visual image has a good deal in common with the picture is, I think, the function of cashing meanings. The parallelism between pictures (drawings, photographs, and so on) and mental images lies in our ability to accomplish both. We may draw a triangle if we are in a course on geometry, or we may think of the triangle. There is a mutual substitutability between the physical picture and the mental picture. They are substitutable for one another. This substitutability is a good criterion not only of their common role but of their common constitution.

Ryle might respond to Price by claiming that Price is raising a different problem than his own. Ryle asks what it is to imagine, while Price raises the question what do we do when we think in images. Presenting the problem in terms of thinking in images perhaps implies that we have to do with noninstantiative particulars, and the difference between image and picture is de-emphasized because of the nature of the problem. We must be always aware in a philosophical discussion of what is the general framework of the discussion and to what extent does the framework determine its answers. Nevertheless, I think that Price's arguments are independent from the initial framework of discussion. Consider again his arguments for the mutual substitutability of picture and image. Images are pictures, first, because they impose themselves. As has often been contended, images have an independent career. It's a mental career but still an independent career like photographs, which may fade, be destroyed, or be burned, in the same way as we may lose a memory.

Price's second and perhaps decisive argument is that images have a space of their own. This claim is very important for a phenomenology of the image. Price's argument is that Ryle made a mistake of language in saying that images don't exist because they are nowhere. When we say that images are nowhere, we suppose that there is only one place for them, namely, physical space. It's true that images have no place in physical space. Yet they may have a somewhere of their own which is precisely the paradox of the image. Price's answer to the question of where are images is that "they are where they are" (250). That's a good phenomenological answer. The false assumption is that "if an entity is somewhere it must be somewhere in physical space." But a visual image "is spatially extended. . . . And as a whole it is nowhere; or, if you prefer, it is its own 'where.' It is a spatial world of its own, though a very poverty-stricken and short-lived one" (250). (That the image is "nowhere" opens up the possibility of the utopia.) To those, says Price, who claim the image is in my head, I would have to say that I have an image "two and a half inches from my left ear, or some other number of inches," which is absurd (251).

> We must just take the phenomenological facts as we find them, and we cannot settle the matter off-hand by the mere dogma that all extended entities must be somewhere in the space of the physical world. I repeat what was said before. Images are where they are, and have such spatial relationships . . . to other extended entities as they are empirically found to have. (251)

Price dares to use the word *phenomenological*, because he doesn't fear words with more than two syllables, as in his writing the impossible expression *non-instantiative*. In a sense Price says let us be more empirical, more phenomenological, and then we will hit on paradoxes. There is a paradox of the image, and Ryle reduces this paradox by equating "I fancy that" with "I do hypothetically." There all the difficulty has been dissipated.

I am aware that scientists claim that images are associated with activity in the brain. This activity is, then, located somewhere. But this activity is not an experience. It's for the scientist, not for me. The image is not there. We must not mix what the scientists know and what we experience phenomenologically. There are two levels. There is the level of scientific explanation and the level of phenomenological description. For example, where, descriptively, is Hamlet? He's not in history. Are there as many Hamlets as there are brains? In a way, but in another way, there is only one, who is in Shakespeare's play. The play is the place where Hamlet is. Where is that place when the play is not being performed? Phenomenologically, we cannot reduce the absence of the image to the presence of something in my brain. This reduction diminishes the paradox of the image appearing nowhere.

Let us now reflect on the main function of images, the function of cashing in absence. Image-cashing, says Price, "is something which we do in the *absence* of the object or situation" (253, emphasis in original). How can images cash? They can do that because the concept is not something immutable in our thought but is itself a capacity to recognize and to extend our experience. Therefore, we must speak of concepts in the language of capacities. If we define thinking in dispositional terms (253), then we may consider the act of testing to be very fundamental. Thinking is not only putting an instance under a concept that is already dead, but it's a capacity that we exercise by trying it. To think "is a capacity for recognizing [old and new] situations which would render the sentence true and for distinguishing them from situations which would render it false." If I am unsure about what may make a sentence true, then I may "try to cash the sentence by means of images. I shall try to 'envisage,' to 'picture to myself' what it would be for the sentence to be true" (253). The cognition in absence, which is the fundamental trait here, is linked to the conditional, to what it would be for the sentence to be true. The conditional of the "would be" is linked to the absence of the image.

All quasi-instances may play the same role as images. I may proceed with "replicas" (257), that is, "[m]odels, diagrams, or pictures known publicly" (256). They have "the same quasi-instantiative function as images have" (256). This common quasi-instantiative function provides us an important reason us to think they are quasi-presences; like mental images, they too "may cash our words in absence, or approximate to cashing them" (256). They are connected with the same recognitional capacity.

Let me close analysis of Price with a few remarks on his discussion about the differences between words and images. The role of the word is to introduce a function of distinction. In a dictionary a word is differentiated from another word, and structuralists have emphasized that the role of the word is to introduce a diacritical function, to introduce discontinuity in our articulation. By contrast, there is a tendency of images to overlap. In an awful example, Price says that in our language cheese and soaps are different words, but "[c]heese often looks like soap, feels like soap to the touch, and even tastes like soap" (270–71). I should say that only an Englishman could have written that, and no Frenchman would have introduced this example! In France we have no cheese that we can mistake for soap. Price claims that if these two words were ever indistinguishable, they have become differentiated as a "kind of Natural Selection among speech-habits" (271), while I would say that for us it would be a natural selection among *cooking* habits. The larger point is that even if the capacity of images is harmful for the process of distinction, it's not harmful but positive for the process of extending meaning. For my part, I should say that the theory of metaphor would explore that better in metaphor's use of strange predicates and the odd combination of words.

The limit of Price's analysis is that it speaks of separate words. There are very few examples of sentences; the focus is always on a word, the dog and so on. As long as we remain within this framework of word and image, we are in a framework that is too narrow. Nevertheless, within this narrow framework, the image has a fundamental function when it is not only a local, instantaneous image but what Hume spoke of as "'presence in power'" (Price 1953, 284, 296; Hume 1965, 20). It is not only "'presence in fact'" (Price 1953, 285) but presents a capacity for development (296). Surely the image provides this capacity for extension thanks to its overlapping character. "If the 'ambiguity' of physical replicas does not in practice mislead us, why should the 'ambiguity' of mental images mislead us either? In actual fact it does not" (272). It is this ambiguity itself that is helpful. Image thinking implies that "we have the capacity to produce other suitable images at need" (272–73). We are very close here to Kant's use of the schema (Price 1953, 292, 296–97). Recall Kant's definition of the schema, when he said the schema is a rule for giving images for concepts. This capacity of extending the field of instances is perhaps the productive function of the image. In other words, to give a quasi-instance is not merely to give something like a unique instance but a series of instances. The dispositional character of imagination corresponds to the dispositional character of thinking itself (296).

In concluding our appraisal of Price, I want to insist on the phenomenological quality of this piece of work, which prepares us for discussion concerning the conjunction of the element of absence and the element of likeness in the quasi. What is a quasi-experience? How is it possible that there are things that are like an experience but not an experience?

To anticipate my contention in the third part of the lectures, the relationship between *as if* doing and not doing will be more addressable when we no longer discuss isolated images—such as the image of a dog, as in Price—but larger pieces of imagination, such as works of art. If there is something like imagination, it is perhaps a way of perceiving. But in imagination we have an object that has its own consistency; it is not reduced to a mere local appearance of one image. The same holds true of examples that Ryle and others have not treated but only alluded to, such as assuming, in terms of an argument. There we have a string of thoughts and words. Assuming is not merely having one image right now. Further, the example of following a tune is not equivalent to following a complete opera or a complete work. There is more to see in a complex work such as a museum picture than in a mental picture. It's within the museum picture itself that the interplay between the presence and absence of likeness works. Here perhaps language is less obtrusive; it does less harm to the aesthetic. We remember from Kant that the work of art pleases without concepts.[4] Recognition of the pleasure without concepts is a very important part of the analysis. Knowledge of the operation of how pleasure occurs seems less cogent in this case. The aesthetic use of imagination is less affected by the report on the work; the latter is the work of the critic. Critics write about works of art, but that's a marginal activity in comparison to the activity undertaken when we look at the picture in the exhibition. We may be critics when we do so, but it's not the most important part of the pleasure that we experience. The relationship between imagination and pleasure so much emphasized by Kant in the third *Critique* should return.

In the next lecture we shall turn to Ludwig Wittgenstein. We shall see that it is impossible to build the framework of a regular lecture because of his very Socratic type of thinking. It will be a question of discussing some of his examples and his way of treating examples and of putting the examples in a certain order.

9

Wittgenstein

Let me recall the framework in which we are placing the present lecture's reading of Wittgenstein on *seeing as*. I have proposed to consider three different examples of the "linguistic," mainly Anglo-American, philosophical approach to imagination. The first was on imagining as having images, and we took Ryle's concept of pretending as a leading thread. Second, we looked at Price's analysis of how we think in images. There images were treated not for their own sake, as in Ryle, but for the purpose of checking our concepts, as offering quasi-instances of what is meant by concepts. Third is the present lecture's discussion of *seeing as*, of describing an aspect. Here we have moved closer to the problem of perception.

In a sense we could say that Wittgenstein's text on *seeing as* is not about imagination. If we remember, though, the image has always been treated by way of opposition to the impression, the perception. Therefore, all reforms occurring within the problem of perception have, in fact, their counterpart in the theory of imagination. We can no longer oppose imaging or imagining to seeing, if seeing is itself a way of imagining, interpreting, or thinking. We must reformulate the opposite terms in the perceiving/imagining pair, since they have to be recast together. In the third part of the lectures we shall see the same need for reformulation when we speak of some uses of imagination within a broader framework than that of the single image, for example, in building models in science, in pictures of art, and in metaphoric and poetic language. In all of these cases, we shall see moving together the aspect of the world and the aspect of imagination. There is a simultaneous reshaping of both problems—of seeing the world and of having fictions about it—such that we see the world in different ways. Discussion of *seeing as* may be a good transition to this extension of the problem of imagination beyond the extreme and boundary case of the mental image as a separate, isolated experience.

The text on which we shall concentrate, from Part II of Wittgenstein's

Philosophical Investigations, is very difficult to read, because it's both substantive and at the same time an exercise in philosophical method. It's impossible to speak of this section without saying something about its philosophical method, and I shall do that fairly quickly so that we can move to discussion of Wittgenstein's examples themselves. Let us start from Wittgenstein's statement earlier in the book about the puzzling features of language for philosophy, which could be put as a subtitle here: "The results of philosophy are the uncovering of one or another piece of plain nonsense and of bumps that the understanding has got by running its head up against the limits of language. These bumps make us see the value of the discovery" (Wittgenstein 1958, 119).[1] This statement can be taken as a warning at the beginning. Since I am more trained in the phenomenological tradition, I come to Wittgenstein with great precaution, surprise, and puzzlement, but if I rightly understand his interest in his odd discussion and its examples, it is that we are running our heads up against the limits of language. What is assumed here is that we run up against the limits of our language when we speak of the mind, mental processes, mental events, and so on. Why does Wittgenstein take so much time to discuss all these examples and reports about toothaches (665; p. 208) and having a pain in the hand (478) if not because our language is for the most part an object language? All the distinctions in language have been made in order to manipulate objects. The linguistic system on which we rely is well adapted to the distinctions available for dealing with objects but not with the mind. The mind is at the limit of language, or if we could use here the language of Wittgenstein's *Tractatus*, it's where we can longer speak and have the choice between keeping silent or showing (Wittgenstein 1961, 4.1212; 7).[2] Dealing with the mind involves a constant play at the limit of the possibility of our language.

We have to do here with unavoidable puzzlements that are typical of this realm of experience put under the title of the mind but also with unnecessary puzzlements that arise from our tendency to construe mental events in general—and mental processes and mental images in particular—as the weaker brother of something external. I borrow this expression from a book by Alastair Hannay, *Mental Images: A Defence*, that includes a chapter on Wittgenstein. Hannay says we tend to construe mental images as the weaker brother of an outer picture, because in the latter we have something to rely upon, for example, a photograph that is the likeness of something (Hannay 1971, 175). We previously saw this argument in Ryle, that picture language is both useful and deceiving, because we tend to construe the mental image as a kind of inner picture. Because all the vocabulary of the inner picture is merely transferred from the outer picture, we get into trouble, as Wittgenstein will show with his examples. We have paved the way for behaviorism by introducing an unobservable thing in the mind as a kind of box within which there are stored images. As we cannot find those images, then the behaviorist's argument is strong that we should simply describe behavior, external movements done by people.[3] Wittgenstein's argument is that this wrong grammar concerning mental experience has paved the way for behaviorism, which is the punishment for a false grammar in the use of our language about mental images.

Given the difficulties posed by relating mental images to external pictures, it's easy to read Wittgenstein's text either as radical skepticism or as something yielding to behaviorism. I don't think, however, that this is the general trend in Wittgenstein. Instead, it seems he is contending that we have always to fight for a better language. There is no capitulation to language but rather an attempt to work at the limit of language to cope with what is required. This seems the function of his examples. Wittgenstein would say that the one mistake of the philosopher is not to be careful enough in the choice of examples. Here there is a very good warning that philosophizing is an art of producing new examples. The logicians know this since they proceed by counterexamples or by paradoxes. All of Anglo-American logic since Bertrand Russell has relied on the solution of paradoxes, knots. There are knots; we must untie them. But usually the examples of the philosopher are so poor: the triangle, the piece of chalk, the cube. There is an art of renewing the examples to produce boundary examples that constitute a puzzle for description. We must put our language—or at least the usual frameworks of thinking—in a desperate situation that has to collapse in order to provide a way to new understanding. My conviction is that the problem of imagination is so difficult precisely because it's typically paradoxical from the beginning to the end. The *is not* is conjoined with the *like*, and the absent with the present. The problem of imagination is a test case for any kind of coherent conceptual framework. It's one of the reasons why philosophers are not as at ease with this problem as with concepts, statements, and propositions, which have to do with something more homogeneous and manageable.

Wittgenstein wants to multiply examples to provide new experiences that require something from our language and ask us to speak in a better way, to give accounts that should take care of what is experienced. He takes the word *impression* (*Eindruck*) (see, for example, Wittgenstein 1958, pp. 199–202, 204, 207, 212) not in Hume's sense as a pure impression but as something that needs linguistic expression. It is that about which we are now speaking that I have some impression—when I see some face smiling—and then the question is what do I say about this impression. I read these pages as a kind of indefinite struggle between language and experience, experience

always providing new cases—boundary cases, strange cases, and so on—
that shatter the customary uses of language and therefore prevent us from
relying on the usual descriptions of usual accounts or reports. For Wittgenstein, understanding the mind requires us to be watchful of distinctions in
experience and to amend our reports with infinite patience.

Wittgenstein considers that the philosopher is responsible for one thing:
the honor of language. While scientists study facts and add new facts, the
only thing that the philosopher can do in a scientific time is not to extend
our knowledge of facts but to improve our language. This is quite opposed
to a Heideggerian position, which says that we have to reenact the ontological background of the scientific experience. Yet although Heidegger has a
different approach, his may be connected with Wittgenstein's in the sense
that we cannot recover a pure relation to the world before it's obscured by
manipulable objects without refining our language, and Heidegger tried
to do that. Like Wittgenstein, then, Heidegger also fights with language,
because this language has been shaped by its use in relation to manipulable
objects. What seems, in a Wittgensteinian sense, merely linguistic, has, in a
Heideggerian sense, an ontological import. Many scholars are now trying to
connect Heidegger and Wittgenstein, and at first sight that seems a strange
enterprise.[4] But it is not if we see that there is a common fight against the
misuse of language. When we start to talk, language has been already mis-
used, so there is a therapeutic task. The aim of Wittgenstein's philosophy, he
says, is "[t]o shew the fly the way out of the fly-bottle" (309). Elaboration
of the concept of mind is one of philosophy's desperate tasks, because, as
I have already suggested, Wittgenstein is not at all a behaviorist. He would
never assume, for example, as do some monists, that we have to cancel from
our vocabulary all mental terms. Instead, we have to fight against the misuse
of mental terms, where misuse is predominant.

Before turning to our principal text on *seeing as* (pp. 193–214), let me present a general statement by Wittgenstein once more about the philosophical
task but that is already addressed to our problem. "One ought to ask, not
what images are or what happens when one imagines anything but how
the word 'imagination' [*Vorstellung*] is used." At first glance, the question
appears to be only an exercise in language, but this exercise in language is
ruled by *what* it is that has to be said. "But that does not mean that I want to
talk only about words. For the question as to the nature of the imagination
is as much about the word 'imagination' as my question is." As I said in the
introduction to this second part of the lectures, comparing phenomenology
and linguistic analysis, we cannot improve experience without improving
our language about experience. There is something circular between the
progress of experience and the improvement of language.

And I am only saying that this question is not to be decided—neither for the person who does the imagining, nor for anyone else—by pointing; nor yet by a description of any process [e.g., the process by which we make a physical model]. The first question also asks for a word to be explained; but it makes us expect a wrong kind of answer. (370)

We have to fight against a wrong kind of answer but also a wrong kind of question. I propose that we read the section about *seeing as* as a conflict between what is seen and what is said. Everything happens between what is seen and what is said.

Let us start from what is said, since what is seen may be provided by the examples. Wittgenstein keeps repeating that he's not looking for causal explanations in the sense of physiological or psychological experience. He has several expressions such as the following, here describing a particular experience: "Its causes are of interest to psychologists" (p. 193). In contrast, Wittgenstein goes on, "We are interested in the concept and its place among the concepts of experience" (p. 193). The issue is therefore not how we explain, but how we make sense of an experience in the nature of giving a report about it—reporting it, describing it. The task is descriptive. In question is whether we describe what we see when we say such and such. In this sense, Wittgenstein is very close to Husserl, Merleau-Ponty, and Sartre. In terminology more typical of Anglo-American philosophy, the problem is that because our language is ruled by use, all our words have already been used prior to this experience. There is a discrepancy between what we say and what we see, because what we say has already been fixed by previous uses, and mainly uses in relation to outer pictures of things in general. We have to amend the rules imposed by use in such a way that it can accommodate the new case. But to do that requires taking a narrow path between two pitfalls, either superimposing a previous grammar (the rule of use) imported from external experience or giving up the task of speaking. (I think that Wittgenstein takes *grammar* and *use* as synonymous. This is at least the interpretation of Hannay and some others. The grammar is the rule of use.) We are on the edge between making use of fixed language or merely giving up the task of speaking. Each time that Wittgenstein says no, this is not a good way of saying that accurately, he repeats that he is looking for better concepts. He is seeking a conceptual justification of what we say. Again let me resort to some texts outside the section on *seeing as* to clarify Wittgenstein's inquiry.

How does the philosophical problem about mental processes and states and about behaviourism arise?—The first step is the one that altogether

escapes notice. We talk of processes and states and leave their nature un-
decided. Sometime perhaps we shall know more about them—we think.
But that is just what commits us to a particular way of looking at the matter.
For we have a definite concept of what it means to learn to know a process
better. (308)

The temptation merely to keep silent is raised, because the claim that we can
learn to know a process better is in itself deceiving. Consider also a second
text, on telling.

> "But when I imagine something, something certainly happens!" Well,
> something happens—and then I make a noise. What for? Presumably in
> order to tell what happens.—But how is *telling* done? When are we said to
> *tell* anything?—What is the language-game of telling?
>
> I should like to say: you regard it much too much as a matter of course
> that one can tell anything to anyone. That is to say: we are so much ac-
> customed to communication through language, in conversation, that it
> looks to us as if the whole point of communication lay in this: someone
> else grasps the sense of my words—which is something mental: he as it
> were takes it into his own mind. If he then does something further with it
> as well, that is no part of the immediate purpose of language.
>
> One would like to say "Telling brings it about that he knows that I am
> in pain." . . . Mental processes just are queer. (363)

The question, "[w]hat is the language-game of telling," is an important in-
terrogation. Like many of our authors, Wittgenstein recognizes that there
is something paradoxical about images: they are like pictures but are not
pictures. To preserve the paradox is a task of telling an experience and telling always in a more appropriate way. At issue is the appropriateness of a
language that was not prepared to tell that new experience. The fact that we
cannot escape language despite its inappropriateness and inadequacy may
be summarized in this last quotation before we return to the text on *seeing
as*: "The mental picture is the picture which is described when someone
describes what he imagines" (367). There is something circular between
the description and the experience, and in another way it's the experience
that opens its way through language. Wittgenstein's is an odd philosophy
about odd experience through odd reports. I imagine Wittgenstein as a kind
of Socratic figure, always disquieting both the answers and the questions of
his interlocutors. An indefinite exercise is opened; we could go on and on
with the inquiry.

I have read Wittgenstein's pages on *seeing as* by making three columns. In one column I put all of his examples, in a second I put his reports, and in a third I tried to put his general statements, which are very rare, about eight or so. There is a movement in the text from the constant renewal of examples to an attempt to fix them in an appropriate report and then to an attempt to generalize the report, but the generalization has to be refueled by the examples, and then the process goes on and on. Let me speak first of the examples, some of which can be divided into families, then turn to the descriptions—the reports—and then to the generalizations. I was struck first by the role of drawings in these examples. There are very few examples of perceptions of actual objects. Most examples are a perception but of something that is not actual. Consider the famous example of the duck-rabbit (p. 194). A line drawing of a duck with an open-mouthed bill becomes at a second glance the drawing of a rabbit with ears (or vice versa). There is nothing like a duck-rabbit in nature; it's in the drawing. We are not in the ordinary situation of perceiving something, and what interests Wittgenstein is that nevertheless we say that we see something. He assumes as a valid question here, "What do you see?" There is always an interplay of questions and answer:—"What do you see?"—"I see that I see a rabbit." We have to do with a drawing that has a certain ambiguity. This ambiguity has to be decided by providing an answer to a question that requires the exclusion of ambiguity. The question, what do you see, provides the clue for making a decision in language in front of an ambiguous picture (*Bild*). The *Bild* is accompanied by the question, what is it, what do you see. The drawing is put in a linguistic situation. The duck-rabbit image is a pun in drawing. This ambiguous image comes from a very specific situation. Wittgenstein notes the prior use of the image by Jastrow (p. 194). In the same family of puzzle-pictures (p. 196) is the image of the hunter in the branches (p. 196), which we have to discern.

Just as the concept of meaning has families of use in Wittgenstein, here we have families of use of the term *to see*. Close to the family of puzzle-pictures is the drawing of three-dimensional objects, such as a cube (pp. 196, 202). No one sees more than three sides at once of a three-dimensional object. There is a side that only someone else sees. When I try to find out what this person sees, I do so by different means, such as making a drawing or building a model, and these themselves have to be interpreted. Next in a progressive ordering, still among drawings, would be an illustration in a book, where the same drawing appears in relation to diverse topics. A parallelogram, for example, might sometimes represent a box, sometimes a stair, and so on. The context supplies an interpretation of the same drawing that is potentially different each time. Here it's not the picture—the parallelogram—that is ambiguous, but the requirement of the context that asks for an interpretation (p. 193).

A different perspective is offered by perceptions that have physiognomic value. Wittgenstein presents many examples here. We might start with some unfamiliar shapes that appear suddenly, and at first there is a lack of recognition (p. 197). We're unable to say what they are. We get stuck in our report. The act of recognition of the unfamiliar shape takes time. It is in this period of time that we say that we recognize. A similar case is recognizing someone whom we have not seen for several years (p. 197). The person is older and looks older. Before recognizing the old friend in the new figure, we have to reconnect the new image with our memory. That reconnection is a part of recognition. So in these two cases we use the term *recognition* in two different senses: first, of an unfamiliar, that we have to put it in a certain class of familiar things, and second, of something that is the same in many ways—same name, same social role, same person, and so on—and yet has become unfamiliar.

The inverted image also plays a major role in Wittgenstein's discussion. If a face is drawn upside down, for example, we may recognize that it is smiling but have more difficulty identifying what kind of smile it is than with a face drawn in its ordinary orientation (p. 198). We as well have a greater difficulty identifying geometrical figures when they are inverted (p. 198). Wittgenstein also raises the example of reading in reverse, as in a mirror, a word written in cursive form, where it seems that the shape of the word is more confused than in its regular order (p. 198). A number of matters are involved here. Reading requires a learned form of seeing. Further, in the case of the word in reverse, while we may have learned how to read, our learning is now being applied outside its categories of use. When we are put in front of that unfamiliar shape, it's unfamiliar not because we cannot put it in an ordinary framework, but because what we have learned cannot be used to decipher it.

To search for a figure in another figure (pp. 203–5) is a variation on the duck-rabbit, but the duck-rabbit is an ambiguous figure against a neutral background. When we see two hexagons with a conjoined boundary line, do see we two hexagons or a drawing of a step (pp. 203–4)? Another set of examples involves completing a figure, such as an animal "transfixed by an arrow" (p. 203). When we see lines extending from either side of the animal, do we see them as an arrow or merely know that they are supposed to represent parts of the arrow?

It's difficult to group Wittgenstein's examples, but perhaps we could put in the group having physiognomic values the example of our impression that a museum picture is living (p. 205). The museum guide says that the picture looks at us no matter where we stand. The eyes in the portrait look in our direction, and I'm sure that I see the look directed toward me. Here, though, I think we are closer to the ordinary uses of imagination, and that is less *seeing as* than a way of completing pictures, as in some games. It's a way of playing the game: "It could be this too" (p. 206). For example, children see a chest as a house. And when they play a different game, the chest could be something else (p. 206). For the first time in this part of his analysis, Wittgenstein here uses a word that has been translated as *fancy*. He says, "A piece of fancy is worked into [the game]" (p. 206). The German says *Erfindung*, which is more discovery or invention, but *fancy* is a good translation also.

In the "double cross," a white cross on a black background can also appear as a black cross on a white background (p. 207). The double cross is not that different from the duck-rabbit, since both are ambiguous figures, but Wittgenstein observes that the double cross is different to the extent that sometimes we see one color as the gestalt and the other as the background. The alternation between gestalt and background is not the case in the duck-rabbit. When I see the duck, I no longer see the rabbit. Wittgenstein adds:

> It is possible to take the duck-rabbit simply for the picture of a rabbit, the double cross simply for the picture of a black cross, but not to take the bare triangular figure for the picture of an object that has fallen over. To see this aspect of the triangle demands *imagination*. (p. 207)

This is the only place where Wittgenstein uses the word *imagination* as a distinct act. It is strange that in this book Wittgenstein never uses *Einbildung* for imagination but usually *Vorstellung*. I don't know why. Perhaps he has reserved *Einbildung* for another use in art or painting. With imagination as *Vorstellung* comes "the possibility of illusion" (*Täuschung*) (p. 208). Deception has a more distortive effect on seeing than the types of seeing represented in prior examples. I cannot say that I am deceived when I see either the black cross or the white cross or the rabbit or the duck. They are ways of looking at the thing. With this example, we proceed at the limit of the field of *seeing as* toward purely imagining something absent.

What is common to all of Wittgenstein's examples is negatively that we never have to do with really absent objects. We are not speaking, for example, of a character in a novel or in a play. The ontological status of the absent object is not his topic. Instead, he raises a series of cases in which with good reason we use the term *to see* but with qualifications. These qualifications that we have to add to our reports on seeing constitute the topic of Wittgenstein's descriptions.

If we consider the reports themselves, they all constitute a struggle with words. Using available language, some reports have failed. The task is therefore to rework these reports into more appropriate reports. I have tried to make a list of the qualifications of the term *to see* that are put under the general title of *seeing as*. First, Wittgenstein discusses noticing an aspect: "I contemplate a face, and then suddenly notice its likeness to another. I *see* that it has not changed; and yet I see it differently. I call this experience 'noticing an aspect'" (p. 193). "Noticing an aspect" seems to survive Wittgenstein's criticism of language. An aspect (see, for examples, pp. 194–97, 199, 203, 204, 206–8, 212) functions as belonging to the field of seeing since it is an aspect of the thing seen. But it's because we notice the aspect that it is emphasized.

Second, we have the notion of interpretation in a perceptual context. A drawing may appear in several contexts, and the function of interpretation is to supply the context and to connect the drawing with the context. Wittgenstein insists, though, that the notion of interpretation here must not be taken as a kind of reasoning, a complex phenomenon; it's not an indirect description (pp. 193–94). I may observe that each time that I have this visual experience, then I have such and such interpretation. There is an immediateness of interpretation, something that is close to noticing an aspect.

Third, in cases such as "picture-faces" (pp. 194, 204), the notion of *seeing as* comes to the forefront. But the term *seeing as* is more a source of puzzlement than a solution. It provides a verbal framework within which we are now speaking, because *seeing as* is a part of our language. We say that we see *as*; the *as* is a grammatical term. We try to have the *as* of our language cope with the appearance. The *as* may be interpreted in terms of praxis, since Wittgenstein speaks of children who talk to their dolls, who treat them *as* dolls (p. 194). This case is very close to Ryle's notion of pretending.

Fourth, *seeing as* is also a decision, as it is compelled by a question posed. *Seeing as* is part of a question and answer situation. The question is what do we see. *Seeing as* appears at first as an exclamation: "rabbit" (p. 195). The exclamation precedes the comparison and the justification. Wittgenstein studied in several places the language game of exclamation, because the exclamation comes before the description in an articulate way. Wittgenstein says that the exclamation is close to a cry. It is "forced from us.—It is related to the experience as a cry is to pain" (p. 197). It's a use of language that is extracted from our heart and our voice.

Fifth, Wittgenstein tries to interpret the *as* of *seeing as* by means of the concept of "organization" (pp. 196, 208). He always puts this term within quotation marks, because he does not assume for himself this notion which comes, I suppose, from gestalt psychology. There is no doubt that for Wittgenstein the notion of "organization" is more an escape than a solution, because we don't know where to locate this organization. If it is part of the thing seen, then we should be able to put it "on a level with colours and shapes" (p. 196). That does not work, however, because I don't see the thing's organization, I see colors and shapes. On the other hand, if I locate the organization outside of the colors and shape and say it's not a part of perception but only a subjective interpretation within me, then I fall into the pitfall of the inner picture. I can no longer reconcile the organization with the perception (pp. 196–97). Hence we find one of Wittgenstein's very scarce general statements: "'Seeing as . . .' is not a part of perception. And for that reason it is like seeing and again not like" (p. 197). The statement means that if we are very cautious in our description or report, we may see that we have always to do with paradoxes where language is put on the brink of failure. This seems a main lesson of Wittgenstein. It's very difficult to know where to locate the notion of organization, because it is already a violence done to experience.

The sixth qualification of the term *to see* concerns the case of recognition. When I recognize that we have something like a sudden discovery, a vision of the solution of the puzzle, the report is also a cry of recognition (p. 198). It is so and so suddenly when we recognize something. Here Wittgenstein introduces a new concept to treat this issue of recognition: the *Darstellung* of what is seen. "The concept of a representation [*Darstellung*] of what is seen, like that of a copy, is very elastic, and so together with it is the concept of what is seen" (p. 198). I interpret this sentence in the following way. We want to give a good depiction (*Darstellung*) of what is seen, and we try to say that there is first an impression and second a concept. That does not work, though, because it is rather the case that there is a complete unity between what we call the concept of what we see and what is seen. "What is the criterion of the visual experience?—The criterion? What do you suppose?" Answer: "The representation [*Darstellung*] of 'what is seen'" (p. 198).

In these two passages, I was surprised to see that *Darstellung* has been translated by *representation*. In German *Darstellung* means a report that is not an interpretation but the presentation of what is seen. What confirms my belief that *Darstellung* should be translated in these passages by *depiction* is that the word later returns and is there translated by *depicted*: "Perhaps the following expression would have been better: we regard [*betrachten*] the photograph, the picture on our wall, as the object itself . . . depicted [*dargestellt*] there" (p. 205). There is a depiction that is in search of its own language. This language should be a report, but this report relies on available distinctions such as to see and to give a name through a concept. The act of recognition lies beyond this dichotomy between thinking and seeing, since it's a process of thinking in seeing or seeing through thinking.

Similar to recognition in the case of physiognomic figures is to see a likeness between two faces, to say that two people resemble one another (p. 193). The resemblance appears at the level of the expression but the expression of the face. We don't superimpose on the face a mental image. As Ryle says, when a girl sees her doll as smiling, there is not a doll that does not smile to which is added a smile. How could we put the smile on the doll? These very simple things are paradoxical to an extent that we have a great difficulty grasping. There is a role here of what Wittgenstein calls a surmise (*Vermutung*) (p. 198), where we try on an interpretation.

Finally, Wittgenstein discusses *trying* to see as, such as: "'I am trying to see it as a . . .'" (p. 206). He distinguishes this from the example of seeing a picture of a lion (p. 206). When I see the picture, I don't try to see it as a lion; rather, I cannot do otherwise. There is a range of possibilities from *trying* to see as to *being compelled* to see as. In the latter, there is no *Erfindung*, no discovery.

After having discussed Wittgenstein's examples of *seeing as* and then his reports or descriptions of *seeing as*, let me conclude our investigation of the text by discussing its few general statements. First, as previously noted, we are not doing psychology but testing our conceptual framework: "Its causes are of interest to psychologists. We are interested in the concept and its place among the concepts of experience" (p. 193). This is a very important statement. We must not place Wittgenstein among the nominalists or skeptics. We might draw an impression that we can no longer speak after these struggles with words. He says no, we have to improve our speaking.

A second general statement is: "The concept of the 'inner picture' is misleading, for this concept uses the 'outer picture' as a model; and yet the uses of the words for these concepts are no more like one another than the uses of 'numeral' and 'number'" (p. 196). A general obstacle in our language is our ordinary use of the word *picture* in the sense of an outer picture. There is a mere homonymy, in a sense. But why? It's very strange that we nevertheless keep speaking of mental pictures. As Price said, in fact the two kinds of picture play the same role at least in thinking, because I may proceed either by a drawing or by a mental image. They are substitutable in certain circumstances. Perhaps because they are substitutable, we apply to them the same description, saying of a mental image that it's a picture, not an outer picture but an inner one. We may think that we have only to change the adjective—from outer to inner—whereas, and here we rejoin Wittgenstein, we have to give a quite different description. There is a snare of language in which we fall. As Wittgenstein says in a general statement previously quoted: "'Seeing as . . .' is not part of perception. . . . [I]t is like seeing and again not like" (p. 197).

Another of Wittgenstein's general statements is: "[T]he flashing of an aspect on us seems half visual experience, half thought" (p. 197). This notion of the half visual, half thought is surely one of the keys to Wittgenstein's analysis. On the one hand, our language relies on differences. As linguists have emphasized, the system of words is diacritical; one word is defined on the basis of its difference from other words. Experiences, on the other hand, have to do with shadings. Language is not well equipped to give an account of this merging or blurring of edges. The concept of what is seen and the visual representation of what is seen are interrelated, but they are not alike; there is a togetherness without a similarity. It is an obstacle for language to give an account of what comes together but is not alike.

Perhaps Wittgenstein's most important general statement is: "What we have rather to do is to accept the everyday language-game, and to note false accounts of the matter as false" (p. 200). The statement appears contradictory. We are first told "to accept the everyday language-game," but this everyday language game has already been infected by, for example, theoretical terms coming from popular psychology. Think, for example, how much the language of psychoanalysis has become a popular language; we may say that now it's a part of our everyday language. Everybody speaks of repression, of sublimation, and so on, so it's very difficult to see what is the everyday language game. The everyday language game is a kind of deposit; in the language of Merleau-Ponty we should have to speak of it as a very sedimented language.[5] There is no innocent language. The second part of the sentence—"to note false accounts of the matter as false"—cancels or at least qualifies to a great extent the first part. On the one hand, we have to rely on the everyday language game against constructs of behaviorism, mentalism, and so on, which are in fact imposed by bad philosophizing under the cover of psychology. The everyday language game is a good tool against that. On the other hand, to the extent that this everyday language game is itself infected, we have to amend it. How do we amend it but by confronting it with a renewed example of seeing? Once more I return to this fight between seeing and telling and speaking.

Let me mention only briefly three last general statements. First: "Do not try to analyse your own inner experience" (p. 204). This is an invitation to think about the examples and not to retreat into a secondary, inner world. Always stick to the examples. This is most important. Second: "Here it is difficult to see that what is at issue is the fixing of concepts" (p. 204). I relate this general statement to the idea that we must not capitulate but must always fight for better concepts. Third: "We talk, we utter words, and only *later* get a picture of their life" (p. 209, emphasis in original). This *later* is the sedimentation that provides the everyday language game.

In closing, we might regain a broader perspective on Wittgenstein by comparing him to a figure such as Kant. Wittgenstein surely would say that Kant has constructed two ghosts, the intuition as a pure manifold and the understanding as a system of categories, and then he fights desperately for a middle term. Kant starts from the ends and then looks for the middle term, the *Dritte* as he calls it, the third. To construct it, he has to think of something that has a double allegiance, that is homogeneous with both. He creates a specific problem of the double homogeneity of something that has an affinity both with the understanding and with appearances. Kant struggles to find the third term and must face all its difficulties, including the schematism and so on. In contrast, Wittgenstein says let us start from the experience where we *are*, at the level of the third term: *seeing as*, interpreting a drawing, etc. Then the task is to discern what is required by these intermediary situations where we are both thinking and seeing. This conjunction of thinking and seeing does connect Wittgenstein back to the double homogeneity in Kant. Wittgenstein is more linked to Kant than to someone like Hume.

In Europe today many speak of the death of philosophy.[6] I always ask whether it is necessary that so many people attend the burial! Perhaps there is a philosophical death, if one speaks of the death of philosophy, and the task is to do it properly. But this death is not my conviction, and it is not the conviction of Wittgenstein. Wittgenstein is the contrary of a skeptic. He's someone who perplexes, just as Socrates is compared to a fish that stuns.[7] First we must discover the poverty of our analysis.

In the next lecture, I shall provide an introduction to the phenomenological approach to the same problems that we discussed in linguistic analysis. I shall then proceed to discuss mainly the First and the Second of Husserl's *Logical Investigations*. In the succeeding lecture I shall discuss the neutralization of presence in Husserl's *Ideas*, and subsequently I shall turn to Sartre's discussion of the element of negativity.

10

Husserl: Logical Investigations

After our three readings in linguistic philosophy, we now undertake three readings in the phenomenological tradition with Edmund Husserl, Jean-Paul Sartre, and Maurice Merleau-Ponty.[1] Let me start with a few words about the relationship between the phenomenological and analytic approaches. I previously addressed this relationship when I introduced the three Anglo-American authors at the beginning of lecture 7, and I shall improve this comparison on the basis of what we have since discussed.

The parallelism and even to a certain extent the overlapping between the two traditions is grounded in the connection between the two tasks that are common to both but taken in a reverse order. The two tasks are, first, to describe what occurs and, second, to amend our language as it is used in the reports and the accounts of our experience. As we saw in the readings of Ryle, Price, and Wittgenstein, linguistic analysis lays the stress on language because it starts from statements, from what we say. Its argument is that philosophy is not responsible for extending the domain of facts but for criticizing our language. As we saw with our three authors, though, it is always under the pressure of experience and sometimes as guided by a very complex strategy of fresh examples that language can be amended. In the last lecture I spoke of a confrontation between what we say and what we see as the dynamic principle of the whole process of description. Phenomenology, in turn, is said to start from *lived experience*. This catchphrase has contributed perhaps more harm than help to the understanding of phenomenology. The use and the abuse of the term *lived experience* has too often led to a sterile opposition between the description of the "lived" and the analysis of "statements." It is the gap between this initial opposition that I want to bridge. I want to consider what may be the conditions of a phenomenology of lived experience. I shall try to show that these conditions have, by necessity, linguistic implications and presuppositions that are akin to those of linguistic analysis, particularly in the ordinary language tradition.

In raising the question of the possibility of describing the lived experience, we may present three or four themes that will lead us step by step to the borderline with linguistic analysis. First, phenomenology is a *discourse* on the "lived." Phenomeno*logy*, the logos of the phenomena, is a discourse and therefore cannot be a reduplication of the experience as such. We live once, and that's all. To live is to live, and to speak is something else, sometimes something more, sometimes something less. Phenomenology is at least a kind of investigation, inquiry, or whatever may be the term. Husserl describes his own work as logical investigations (*logische Untersuchungen*). (Perhaps by chance, the word *investigation* is common to Wittgenstein and Husserl.) As an investigation, phenomenology's first presupposition is precisely that experience can be said, that there is not in experience whatever it may be—emotional, practical, ethical, religious—something so opaque that its articulation in language is impossible. Phenomenology's most radical presupposition, then, is that there is no absolute gap between *bios* and *logos*, between what is lived and the possibility of articulating what is lived in a discourse. There is a fundamental speakability of experience. Experience is not unspeakable.

Of course I am aware that many phenomenologists have insisted on an intuitive approach. The word *intuition* linked with the lived seems to insinuate that there is a kind of mystical site in experience. But we must never forget that the word *intuition* in Husserl is always linked to the context of the essence of experience. It's the intuition of what is essential in an experience. This *Wesen*, this essence, is the real object of the investigation. The investigation concerns the essential features of the lived, so the object is not the lived as such but the lived to the extent that it offers essential features capable of being described. In the next lecture, we shall see that imagination is already implied in this transition from the lived to the essential features under the form of imaginative variations.[2] What we explored in Wittgenstein was a kind of imaginative variation. We explored his variation of examples. (As appropriate, the translator even translates Wittgenstein's term *denken* as *imagine* that [for example, Wittgenstein 1958, p. 193]. *Denken* here means let us think of this or that.) This way of changing the examples provides a permanent transition from the lived to the essential through imaginative variation. This is implied in what I call the first presupposition of a phenomenology, that experience is not completely mute, is not foreign to language, because it has essential structures that are available to some reports.

The second presupposition for a linguistic treatment of the lived is linked to the role of reduction, if not in Husserl's early work, *Logical Investigations*, which I shall consider in the present lecture, then at least in the classical works of his starting from the *Ideas* to the *Cartesian Meditations* and *The*

Crisis of the European Sciences. I shall not develop for its own sake this concept of *epochē*, the suspension of judgment, the reduction. I use it only for the purpose of the concept of description: How is it possible to describe something in lived experience? For that purpose I shall insist on two aspects of this famous reduction: reduction *of what* and reduction *to what*. When Husserl introduces the concept of reduction, it's always directed against the pseudo-evidence of the given, of the what, of something that is merely there: there are things, there are tables, and so on. Unfortunately, he will tend more and more to interpret this suspension as an abstention concerning the ontological preexistence of things. And this will be very foreign to the realism of English and American philosophy of language, which starts always with G. E. Moore's stance that there are things, and then let us speak of them. Many phenomenologists, Roman Ingarden and I among them, regret this idealist trend in Husserl, but it has at least the advantage of introducing from the very beginning a critical distance.[3] We are not gaping in front of experience but taking a kind of distance from it. This element of distanciation, which I use in another context in relation to hermeneutics, has its root in the *epochē* of Husserl.[4] We do not merely live what we live, but we consider it; we consider it from the distance of the observer. We become the observer of what we live. This critical distance makes language, once more, possible. In language itself we have this critical distance, since language relies on a system of signs, and a sign is not the thing. We have this negative element in any kind of sign. If a sign stands for something, it is because it is not a part, an element, an aspect of the thing but something other than. This element of otherness is a condition of use of any system of signs, not just linguistic signs. A semiotics of experience is possible on the basis of this fundamental distance between what is meant through a system of signs and what is lived or seen or experienced in general.

The word *epochē* comes from the Greek and in particular the Stoic tradition that implied that we may always suspend our judgment. For the Stoic this was an ethical principle, since to be able to suspend our judgment is to be able to not be involved either in pain or in any kind of emotion. The goal was to reach *ataraxia*, the way of not being affected, an absolute serenity. Distancing ourselves from our emotions and experience therefore has a long tradition in philosophy. If Husserl did not retain the ethical and sometimes religious coining of this *epochē* in the Stoic tradition, he retained the notion of suspending one's judgment, and he applied it to the that is, the what is. This is the reduction *of what*.

We take a step further when we ask reduction *to what*. The reduction reduces experience to the meaning of experience for a consciousness. For our purposes, what needs attention is not what we lose in this reduction:

the density of experience, the ontological presence that Heidegger will re-emphasize. Instead, I prefer to insist on what we win by this reduction, its positive aspect: a field of meaning for experience instead of self-contained realities existing in themselves. We have the *for us* of experience. The emphasis is on this *for us* of meaning. Meaningful for whom? For a consciousness that is the center of its own experience, the one that has the experience or for which the experience is. This notion also has been perhaps expressed too much in idealist language in the classical work of Husserl as being not only *for* a consciousness but *in* the consciousness.[5] There is said to be an immanence of meaning, and consciousness is the source out of which meaning arises. Here a critique of ideology should prevail and reduce this claim of consciousness to be the origin of meanings. But we may retain apart from this idealistic coining the idea that it's among meanings that phenomenology moves: meanings of perceived objects, the experience of the will, practical or emotional experience. Therefore, phenomenology is an inquiry not into the lived but into the meaning of the lived. This is the shift that constitutes, I think, phenomenology as such. We don't repeat the lived, but we emphasize the meaning of the lived. The notion of meaning is the leading thread of this analysis.

What I think preserves the difference here between linguistic analysis and phenomenology is that for phenomenology the concept of meaning is not related first to statements but precisely to the experience, since meaning is already an element of perception. I perceive an object as being the same despite that I see it from different sides. There is an element of sameness in the meaning of the object even in perception, below the level of language. But if the level of meaning is prior to that of statements, statements are possible because these meanings present a fundamental articulation. Even if there is meaning before or below language, the articulated character of experience implies a fundamental speakability of this experience. Husserl uses the word *structure* very often. There is a structure of meaningful experience.

A third theme will lead us a step closer to an encounter with linguistic analysis, namely, the central position in phenomenology of intentionality. Here too I want to emphasize the linguistic implications of the concept of intentionality, and in two ways. First, in general terms, the concept of intentionality has a kind of triviality, since it means that all consciousness is consciousness *of* something. It is always possible to describe any experience as a correlation between the *what* and the *how* of the experience. The *what* is called the object. Yet, importantly, we shall see that an image is an object, even if it is a nonexistent object. An intentional correlate is implied in the notion of intentionality. Second, we may speak of an act not necessarily as active or spontaneous but as a movement toward. The correlation between an aiming at and an appearance of something constitutes the fundamental correlation of intentionality. The claim of phenomenology is that we may apply this correlation between aiming at and the appearance of, this act/object correlation, in all dimensions of experience. For example, in his book on the emotions Sartre will try to show that even an emotion is intentional in the sense that it is not something that I simply undergo. When I am in fear, things appear in a certain way as frightful. The relation between the frightful and fear is itself an intentional correlation. The classical opposition in linguistic analysis between the cognitive and the emotional is denied by the concept of intentionality, which is inclusive of both.

The claim that it is always possible to apply this correlation in all domains provides, too, the possibility for language, because our language is the language of the correlation. This is shown by ordinary language, which always provides us a substitutability between verbs and substantives. I may speak, for example, of perceiving a memory or of the perceived, remembering and the remembered, forgetting and the forgotten, and so on. The intentional correlation has its linguistic expression in this functioning of verbs and substantives, particularly the verbs of mental acts. The British author who has come the closest to this is Peter Geach in his book on *Mental Acts*. Some other linguistic analysts too have stressed the functioning of verbs in our accounts of mental facts. We shall see how it's possible to get rid of false entities such as an image in the mind if we replace this notion by an aspect of intentionality. Many paradoxes of the image will be if not solved at least approached in less paradoxical terms by means of this correlation between intention and the correlate of intention.

It is not only this correlation that gives room for language. As Husserl emphasizes, a specific aspect of intentionality is that we can speak of an object only when there is an assumed unity of a multiplicity of partial intentions. To be an object of is to be the assumed or presumed unity of a singular intention converging in one and the same. This is the strong sense of intentionality: a convergence in a unity of meaning. There is always a synthetic act in all intention. We may recognize here a Kantian tradition concerning the synthesis of imagination, the synthesis of experience. Throughout Husserl's work, the phenomenology of perception will support this claim. An object is always a certain identity of sense, an identity of meaning, a unit of meaning involving and embracing an infinity of perspectives. This integration of perspectives is a fundamental trait of intentionality. With this concept of intentionality, it is less trivial to say consciousness is consciousness of. More important, however, the aimed point is a point of convergence of several lines.

In concluding this introduction, I insist that phenomenology is not at all a plea for the irrational. On the contrary, it's a plea for the fundamental structures of experience. This is reflected in the vocabulary that will prevail after the *Logical Investigations*, mainly at the time of the *Ideas*, when Husserl speaks not of psychic experience but of noesis and noema, of the noetic and the noematic. It is a language of the *nous* and not a language of the psyche. The language of the psyche is the language of psychology, of a natural science, a natural science that has not yet been submitted to the *epoché*. In contrast, the word *nous* comes from the Greek tradition dating back even to the pre-Socratics, but it's mainly a distinction introduced by Aristotle in his work *On the Soul*. As we saw in an earlier lecture, the third part of the book is about the *nous*. The *nous* is the capacity for receiving and articulating an experience in general. The vocabulary about noema and noesis, which conveys the correlation between intentions and their objects, expresses the fundamental presupposition that experience is not ultimately opaque even if it is never completely transparent. It's always possible to bring experience to language. If it is true that the structure of experience makes discourse possible, it's also true that it is only in discourse that we take hold of these structures.

I would present the possible overlapping between phenomenology and linguistic analysis in the following way. The referent of statements for linguistic analysis is what phenomenology will call the lived experience. In turn, the noetic/noematic structures are what make possible the articulation of the statement itself. Because of this overlapping, I thought that it was not absurd to try to correlate, even in great detail, as we shall see, the Husserlian tradition with Anglo-American linguistic analysis. I shall try to articulate the presentation of the phenomenology of imagination along the same lines I did with linguistic analysis. The parallelism with linguistic analysis is verified by the fruitfulness of a division of problems similar to the one we observed in the Anglo-American linguistic approach. On the one hand, thinking with (or in) images is situated in correlation with a harsh critique of the "imagist" tradition of empiricism. Because the image is not the origin of conceptual thought, it plays another role, which is implied in the carrying out of conceptual thought itself (something similar to cashing words by quasi-instances). On the other hand, the image is considered as a mode of givenness of objects as absent or not existing. At first sight there is no transition from one problem to the other, at least in linguistic analysis. There is a mere polysemy if not homonymy between *imaging* and *imagining*. Perhaps the phenomenological approach may provide the transition that is lacking at the level of linguistic analysis.

In the remaining part of this lecture, I shall start from Husserl's first approach in the *Logical Investigations*, Investigations 1 and 2. We shall see important similarities with Price's *Thinking and Experience*. In this first approach, the problem of the image is not dealt with as such but in relation to the claim of empiricism that we draw concepts and conceptual thought from images. Both Price and Husserl deny empiricism's claim. The image is not the origin of language, it is not the origin of concepts, and so on. But elimination of the image's role as origin allows recognition of its specific role. For Husserl, the theory of knowledge always returns to the image in the latter's function of illustration. I shall try to compare this function with Price's notion of cashing the meaning of words in non-instantiative or quasi-instantiative images, and we shall discover some very interesting correlations.

In subsequent lectures, we'll see a more positive and more independent treatment of the mode of givenness, the kind of givenness of portraits, pictures, mental images, and so on. We'll examine this first in Husserl's *Ideas*, mainly *Ideas* I, sections 99 and 111, but I shall use that text only as an introduction to the work of Sartre, who will offer a development and dimension to this analysis only suggested in Husserl. Husserl's *Ideas* and Sartre's theory of imagination will provide us a parallelism with Ryle on pretending and the question of the unity between fancied experience and pretended actions. We shall see whether in Sartre we have an answer to the paradox of the similarity and nonsimilarity between, for example, pretending in play and the fancied image found in some more contemplative uses of images. It is mainly within this framework that I shall discuss the elements of absence and likeness, how the image is not the unreal but the like-real. This connection between *like* and *not* will be the center of the analysis.

At a third stage, in which Wittgenstein's concept of *seeing as* could be considered the leading thread, I shall refer mainly to Merleau-Ponty in his essays on painting, since the notion of drawing was so important in Wittgenstein's examples. The issue here is to what extent is imagination not only the possibility of having absent objects but the possibility of remaking or structuring reality in an active way.

What I expect also from this phenomenological description across these three stages is to see more clearly the transition from one problem to the other, since in the lectures on linguistic analysis I presented the three approaches in a scattered way. They were scattered because it is perhaps not at the level of language that the correlation and continuity of the problem may be located but in the underlying structures of the experience itself. Perhaps by necessity there are no transitions possible in linguistic analysis between the three main uses of the word *image*—between pretending, thinking in image, and *seeing as*. It may be that a certain unity of the problematic is provided by the underlying intentional experience common to all three. But I may promise more than I can bring forth.

Turning to Husserl's *Logical Investigations*, we may consider it a work of the beginning of the twentieth century, when it first appeared, and therefore contemporaneous with Frege, Meinong, and the first works of Russell. Common to all these thinkers is a general anti-psychological approach to logical problems. It's within this anti-psychological stand that the problem of the image is approached. What is emphasized is the inadequation of all theories of the image to solve the problem of abstraction, of universal thinking, and so on. The writings are directed against the image, but in Husserl we shall decipher between the lines a certain recognition, with reluctance, of a functioning of thinking in image or with image that gives to the imagist theory, to name it as Price does, a certain right despite its fundamental failure. It is the disentanglement of what remains true in a theory of image beyond the collapse of its fundamental claim to solve the problem of abstraction, of universal ideas, of universals in general, that will interest us.

Husserl's work is called *Logical Investigations*. In my introduction I discussed the term *investigation*. But why *logical* investigations? In this early work, Husserl is concerned about the problem of the foundation of logic. This is a common purpose of all the thinkers I named. But Husserl is the only one to link this problem to a phenomenology. The volume's "Prolegomena" discards and rejects psychologism. The "Prolegomena" is a long text that is a struggle with ghosts who are no longer around. But psychologism was very prevalent, particularly in Germany, at the end of the nineteenth century after the complete decay of Hegelianism and the shift of neo-Kantianism toward a philosophy of introspection, of mental operations. Logic had become a branch of psychology, the psychology of logical operation. For example, the problem of number was solved by an investigation into what we do when we calculate. The principle of identity $(a = a)$ was treated as the *feeling* of sameness between two objects. There was a reduction of logic to psychology. Therefore, for authors such as Husserl, the first task was to sever completely all links between logic and psychology, even at the price of a certain Platonism. There is a certain Platonic overtone among all these authors. What is decisive about Husserl is that he was not satisfied by the separation of logic from psychology. This was for him only prolegomena. The "Prolegomena" to the *Logical Investigations* are more or less on a level with Frege, Meinong, and Russell. The six investigations that follow try to build the autonomy of logic on the basis of a theory of meaning, and this is specific to Husserl. It is in the logical structure of what we call a meaning—the meaning of a proposition, of a statement, of an experience in general—that the independence of logic is possible, because the principle of independence is a structural trait of the meaning.

We shall discuss the first two of Husserl's logical investigations. As its title indicates, the First Logical Investigation concerns meaning and expression. Expression here is not taken in the sense of a physiognomic expression but in the mathematical use of the term, an algebraic expression in the sense of a formula. We must not be deceived by the title's conjunction between meaning and expression; the topic is the meaning of a logical expression. *Expression* in fact should be translated into modern English by *statement*. What gives logic a basis in the constitution of meaning? The fact that a meaning implies a kernel of identity, of sameness. When I draw a triangle, it's not the individuality of my drawing, it's not the singularity of my experience of this figure that constitutes the meaning, but something identical which is not a part of the experience of any of the thinkers who are now thinking this triangle. The entire First Logical Investigation pertains to this principle of sameness.

Where does the problem of imagination occur? It occurs when we raise the question of the nature of "the acts which confer meaning [*der bedeutungverleihenden Akte*]" (Husserl 1970, 299).[6] To my mind, this is exactly the problem of thinking. Recall Price saying that he is not writing about thought as the condition of possibility of, say, a system of categories, but rather he is writing about thinking, about what people do when they think. We have to do with acts that confer meaning. My presumption, as a way of rereading Husserl's book, is to look at the function of image as illustrative, exactly similar to the instantiative function of the image in Price. Consider, for example, that the title of §17 is "*Illustrative* Mental Pictures as Putative [that is, assumed] Meanings" (299, emphasis added). (It is also interesting to observe in this section that the vocabulary is still very uncertain. Husserl speaks indifferently of *Phantasie*, which would be closer to *fancy, Phantasiebild*, translated here as *mental picture* or *image*, and *Phantasievorstellung*, translated as *image*. Elsewhere, as in §18, he sometimes uses the term *imaginieren*. As we have seen, it's a general feature of the problem of imagination that there is a competition between several words.)

The issue, therefore, is what is the function of an image when we understand an expression in the sense of a logical formula? The contention is that all the characteristics of the image prevent it from providing support for the claim that the image is the origin of universals. An image's viability is developed only sometimes: sometimes it is clear, sometimes obscure. An image can be elusive, as when we say, for example, that we have virtually no image of something or that we have no time to have an image, because we are running along with the words. It's only when we dwell on a description that we develop images. The image is hence sometimes not even possible. Images can also be vague. What image can we provide for notions such as culture, calculus, or algebraic roots? What images are available for proper names? When we say Mr. so and so, we do not necessarily have an image to support recognition of the name. Sometimes it is impossible to have an image, as when we have an absurd meaning. (The notion of absurd meaning played a great role at this time, since all these thinkers thought about absurdity in order to evaluate the notion that there may be sense without reference.) If I speak of a round square, I say something which is not, as if I pile up a heap of syllables. I say something, but I cannot precisely cash the meaning. Nevertheless, there is a meaning.

Thus, an image is properly invoked only in terms of exemplification, of partial illustration. For this purpose Husserl has many expressions that are close to those of Price. I was interested in Husserl's vocabulary, because it betrays something that he does not develop. The notion of *illustration*, for example, is in itself worth attention. In German the term is *Verbildlichung* (§18), and that means to put something into an image. I have to put something into an image despite that the image does not make the meaning; it supports it. We find also the notion of *Anhalt* (§18), which has been translated by *foothold*, to provide a foothold. It aids. There is an ancillary function of the image that cannot be completely dissolved in the anti-psychological stand.

In the Second Logical Investigation, we proceed a step further. The Second Logical Investigation develops the plea against images along a slightly different line, that of empiricist theories of abstraction. Here the function of the image will be greater, since Husserl raises the problem not only of the identity of a notion, its sameness, but of universality (what Husserl calls Species).[7] The question is the applicability of a concept to a certain number of members of the class. We would call that today the extensional function of the concept. An image will play a greater role in the process precisely of displaying the concept and distributing the concept among a range of individuals. Perhaps the image is precisely this act of displaying the meaning. It applies the meaning in the Kantian sense of the term *to apply* (*Anwendung*), since to apply is at the same time to explicate, to display. The imagination will be the milieu of this display. As Kant has already seen with his theory of schematism, we want an intermediary milieu between the universal and the individual. The milieu in which this plurality in application proceeds comes from the kernel of the identity of a notion.

In this inquiry, the image provides four positive abilities. First, it offers the function of likeness. We speak of images when we say that something is like something else. We cannot diffuse the identity of a concept without relying on the likeness of the individuals that present this identity. This discussion in chapter 1 of the second investigation about similarity is very close to the discussion early in Price's book that I alluded to only briefly. The chapter is about sameness and resemblance. Husserl observes that there are two great traditions in the philosophy of the concept. On the one hand, there are those who would argue that we first perceive likeness and then abstract sameness on the basis of likeness. On the other hand are those who reply, but how could we say that two things are alike if we don't know in which respect they are like; the right respect in which they are alike is their sameness. There is a circularity between sameness and likeness or identity and resemblance that may be constitutive of the problem itself. If it is true that there must always be the unity of a rule to construct a set of similar of cases, the similarity is connected by a certain rule of identity, but we check this identity on the basis of the similarity. Therefore, the first contribution of the image to this problem of the universal is its support of likeness to check the sameness of the concepts.

In chapter 2 appears the image's second positive function: the function of providing instances. Why is this function important? A meaning as such is ideal. Husserl uses the same language as Frege and Meinong, saying that a meaning is ideal in the sense that it has no place in reality. It exists nowhere. The question, "Where is the triangle?," makes no sense, because the triangle is not in nature, and it is also not in the mind as if the mind were a place to store entities. The triangle has no place in reality, either physical or mental; it is merely ideal. The way for us to take hold of the ideal is to use the possibility of the unreal. Here we see the important function of the image, because the element of absence that is fundamental in the image is for us our ordinary access to the ideality of a meaning. Most of our examples are precisely imaginative examples: let us imagine that. It is always through an exercise of imagination that I grasp the ideality of meaning. Despite the particularity of the image, which is not continuous with the universality of the concept, the image provides unreal instances that fuel the ideality of the meaning. The chapter concerns a discussion between reality, unreality, and ideality.

A third function of the image, discussed in chapter 3, is linked to the use of attention. The problem of attention is no longer highly visible, but it was very popular in Germany at the end of the nineteenth century. People said that an abstract idea is something that we abstract by attention. We consider and isolate an aspect. In the experience of visual attention, we may abstract by focusing on only part of a spectacle, and we may enlarge our attention by narrowing down its scope. In a psychological treatment of logic, this capacity of extension and concentration played a great role. In a less pretentious way, we may say that seeing an aspect also paved the way for grasping the independence of a notion. An aspect is of course dependent on the thing. But the capacity of isolating an aspect is a step on the way to grasping the independence of a meaning. This notion of seeing an aspect has some parallels in Wittgenstein's notion of noticing an aspect.

The fourth and most interesting function of the image, though, relies on its substitutive function, a subject of chapter 4. This had been already emphasized by John Locke and George Berkeley. An image may represent something out in the world, but it may also represent another image. This is a consequence of the play of similarity, because what is similar may replace something else that is similar. There is a fundamental substitutability of images. An image is not something that is static before our mind's eye. It is not something that does not move, for the imaginary world is a world of permanent substitution. This will be developed by psychoanalysis. It's a basis of the psychoanalytical approach to the image that the image of the mother may be replaced by so and so. An image may conceal something, because it may be a substitution. The substitutability of the image is a fundamental trait. This notion has been used and abused in the empiricist tradition. In the French tradition of Étienne Bonnot de Condillac and the British tradition of Berkeley, there was an attempt to identify the notion of the image with that of the sign. The claim was that a sign represents something just as an image represents something.[8] In chapter 4 of the Second Logical Investigation, Husserl quotes favorably Locke, with whom he was very much impressed on the topic of substitutability:

> "Words are general . . . when used for signs of general ideas, and so are applicable indifferently to many particular things: and ideas are general when they are set up as the representatives of many particular things. . . . their general nature being nothing but the capacity they are put into by the understanding, of signifying or representing particulars. . . ." (Husserl 1970, 394)[9]

There is an exchange between signifying and representing. Husserl uses two words for this signifying or representing function. *Stellvertretung* is the vicarious function; we speak of the Pope as the *Stellvertretung* of Christ. As the English translation of this section indicates, to represent is to do duty for. Husserl also uses the word *Repräsentation*. This term is unfortunate, because it belongs to too many semantic fields at the same time. It was coined in fact to translate Locke's term *representation*. But the signifying or representing function is exactly this vicarious function of doing duty for.

The notion of doing duty for may be the best argument for an imagist theory, because if we did not have the capacity to substitute things, we would have no money, no exchange, and no signs. It may seem strange to speak of money and signs at the same time, but we saw the capitalist vocabulary of Price when he spoke of the notion of cashing words by images. A Marxist would say that it is precisely the ideology of the bourgeoisie to put even a theory of language in market terms. It is, in fact, a language of the market. (In turn, the language employed by the market is also a language of signs, since we speak, for example, of monetary signs.) The vocabulary of economy is very important for our discussion of images, because we spare ourselves intellectual labor by using signs instead of needing to manipulate them. The notion of sparing intellectual labor and therefore of making an economy of thought by substitutive signs is the basis of many fields: think of algebra (which is an economy of calculus), cybernetics, the economy in logical procedures, and so on. This economy is surely based in the primitive substitutive function of the image.

For Husserl the substitutive function of the image is too psychological to solve the logical problem of the universal, because substitution occurs at the same level; we substitute a particular for a particular (Husserl 1970, § 31). But if substitution does not solve the problem of the universal, at least it gives a greater density to the notion of illustration, thanks to the kind of effacement of content linked to the substitution process. An illustration is not only a shadow of our concepts, it is a process. An illustration is the process of substituting something for something. There is a process of generalization. The universality of a notion is supported by this process, the possibility of going from one image to another image, of not only placing an image but replacing it.

Why does Husserl engage in this endless fight against an imagist theory of meaning? Is the intuitive grasping of ideal meanings possible without images? The same problem is addressed in Price's thinking in images. But what is declared by Price is, if not concealed, merely conceded by Husserl. The equivalent of cashing the meaning with quasi-instances takes various forms in Husserl. We may conclude that the image is entrenched in the theory of knowledge in a way that perhaps explains the permanent return (even if now not very popular) of an imagist theory of knowledge. When we think that Husserl spent thousands of pages to get rid of the image, that suggests there is something that resists the reduction.

Let me add a personal suggestion on the basis of the notion of *clarification*. When we try to clarify an idea, this metaphor says a great deal, because it is a metaphor of light and of space. To clarify is on the one hand to put something in the light, and on the other it is to expand and to extend and therefore to provide a sense of the thing's exterior relationships. The relations that are implicated are explicated in a logical space, using an expression of Wittgenstein in the *Tractatus* (for example, 1961, 3.42). A visualization of relations will play a great role in the third part of the lectures when we consider the function of models in epistemology, which will provide this visualization of new relationships. Since in the present part we work only with isolated images, it's not easy to see this function, which will appear only when we have the larger framework of works, works of thought, aesthetic works, and so on.

To say the same thing in other words, the process of clarifying, of giving clarity and distinction to ideas, has much to do with other operations that are described by Price, such as recognizing and grasping. When the recognition is immediate—this animal sitting in front of me is a dog—this process is not very interesting, but the process is interesting when recognition is not immediate and we recognize something that is not identical to the type familiar to us. The latter is a very complex operation in which we have to interpret the details to organize the perception in such a way that it may be coherent or compatible with the type. We have an adjustment between the concepts and the experience which is an interpretation (*Deutung*). In section 23 of Husserl's First Logical Investigation, this relation between clarification and interpretation appears under the general title of grasping (*Auffassung*). Grasping is an interesting metaphor because it is not only a physical gesture but also a mental gesture, to take things together. Grasping is the counterpart of expanding. These two notions have to do with mental gestures in relation to abstraction.

Perhaps the most irreducible role of the imagination concerns interpretation of what in the First Logical Investigation Husserl called occasional or fluctuating meanings (Husserl 1970, §§ 26–27), which are the usual meanings of ordinary language. They are "occasional" in the sense that completion of their meaning depends on consideration of their circumstances. One type of these fluctuating expressions that is not accidental but essentially fluctuating is the personal pronoun. *I* can each time mean someone else. It depends on who says it whether *I* means me or you. The meaning of *I* is essentially realized on the basis of one's own I-presentations. We rely on the logical function of signs, which has been called *indicative* in the First Logical Investigation and which corresponds to ostensive signs in the Anglo-American tradition. This demonstrative function is not reducible to the personal pronouns but includes our entire system of demonstratives, which includes terms such as *these* and *that* and adverbs of time and space such as *now, then, here,* and *there.* The demonstratives also include such typical expressions of language as when a German says *the Kaiser,* he or she means our German Kaiser. *The* is an ostensive word here. When I say *the lamp* and mean the lamp in my study, the *the* is a demonstrative. We cannot complete the meaning of our words without connecting them to a circumstance, to an occasion, and therefore without trying the meaning in an image, in the imagination. This may explain why Husserl does not break the ties between meaning and representation and keeps speaking of universal representation and singular representation, as if thinking needed always the support of *displaying before* (*vorstellen*), in the form of quasi-instances which "fulfill" the intellectual intention. We could speak of quasi-fulfillment in order to clarify, to grasp and recognize, or to complete meanings. The capacity of extending the meaning of our words to occasions, to circumstances, is not a matter of merely intellectual looking; it requires a process of laboring with the meaning. Perhaps this is what is implied in the German *Vor-stellung* (to place before), but this is Heideggerian more than Husserlian. (Heidegger has reflected on this German *Vor-stellung*.[10]) Placing before is an important act of thinking. I cannot think without placing a notion before my mind's eye and therefore displaying it.

This kind of reflection leads us once more into the vicinity of Price, when Price speaks of the quasi-instantiative function of the image to provide quasi-examples. The corresponding notion in Husserl is that of a quasi-fulfillment. I give a content to, I fulfill the empty notion, but in the modality of the quasi. In the following lectures on Husserl's *Ideas I* and on Sartre's theory of imagination, this topic will be the object of a direct inquiry: what do we mean by the quasi; what is the absence and the quasi-presence of the image; what is the status of the quasi?

The reading I proposed in this lecture emphasized the negative side of Husserl's text. Husserl was always engaged in a denial of the image, but at the same time he said something about the image by denying the role given to it by the tradition of empiricism.

In the next lecture, on Husserl's *Ideas*, I shall discuss mainly sections 99 and 111, on the notion of the neutralization of reality as the central function of imagination.

11

Husserl: Ideas

In the present lecture I want to say something more about Husserl as an introduction to the treatment of imagination by Sartre. My treatment of Husserl's *Ideas I* relies in part on Sartre's reading of that text in his book *Imagination: A Psychological Critique*, a work that I shall discuss more directly in a subsequent lecture.[1]

Let me begin with an introductory remark connected to the previous lecture. Recall that in the *Logical Investigations*, we saw Husserl's first approach to the problem of imagination. There the issue was not the problem of the image as representing something but as an illustration of thought. We compared this approach to Price's in *Thinking and Experience* where the issue similarly was not the problem of what is it to imagine something but of what is it to think in images. These two problems are always overlapping in the philosophy of imagination. It is very difficult to disentangle them because, as we shall see in the third part, it's mainly because images are part of something—as thought or painting and so on—that the problem of the image takes on its philosophical bearing.

In this lecture we shall isolate the second problem: what is it to imagine something or to have an image of something? We shall use the *Ideas I*, published in 1913, since it's the work of reference for Sartre. Let me make a few comments concerning the method of the *Ideas*. We said already something about this method when we compared phenomenology with linguistic analysis. First, the *Ideas* is ruled by the famous notion of reduction, *epochē*, which comes from the Stoic tradition. In the *epochē*, we suspend our judgment. About what? We suspend our judgment mainly about existence as absolute. We take no stand concerning ontological statements in order to make statements concerning only the meaning of our experience. The *epochē* is a reduction of the absolute status of things in order to move among appearances for us. This problem of the *epochē* is in itself a very complex one, and I shall not discuss its bearing on perception, which is surely an important topic.

That question would be: how can we reduce the being of things and have a philosophy of perception, since perhaps in perception we are involved in being, as Heidegger and Merleau-Ponty will say.[2]

My second methodological remark is that in the *Ideas* phenomenology doesn't stay at the level of singular experiences of psychic events but claims to grasp the essential meaning of this experience. The notion of essential grasping is, in the language of Husserl, *eidetic*. An eidetic insight is a fundamental one. We don't stay at the level of the experience, but we try to find its types. The eidetic method seeks to establish a typology of experience. If we combine the transcendental reduction of the *epochē* with the eidetic reduction, we see that we move among essences of our experience.

A third methodological remark, this essential grasping is supported by examples, but the relation between an essence and an example is of a specific kind and is not reducible to the relation between a fact and an inductive law. This is also a difficult issue, but it marks a great difference between psychology as a science and a phenomenological psychology. In psychology, we collect facts and we try to find regularities, but in phenomenology we grasp immediately the essence of something and we support that by examples. This may seem antiscientific, but for Husserl the psychologist presupposes the delineation of the psychological domain. If we don't know the difference between a perception and an image, we shall never be able to start a psychological inquiry. The delineation of the domain is an essential delineation and not an inductive delineation. Any kind of inductive inquiry presupposes recognition of the main structures of the domain being studied. This will be very important in the case of the difference between imagination and perception, because that difference is not something that we learn step by step. We have always understood what the difference means, because it has to do with an essential difference in our experience. This is a point very important for the epistemological discussion with linguistic analysis. Husserl would say that we cannot undertake an examination on the basis of linguistic statements if we don't start with this preunderstanding, this presupposition, that, as we shall see, we are looking at quite different essences when we inquire about images and perception.

Let me close these remarks on the method of the *Ideas* with a final point concerning the use of examples. Husserl says that examples may be taken from fictional works as well as from ordinary life. This is important because imagination is implied for the first time in this way. We may support an essential description, a description of essences, with fictional examples. Sartre refers to Husserl's text when he says that phenomenology moves among fictions, that the exemplification of an essential grasping may be pure fiction (Sartre 1962, 128). Sartre quotes the following passage from the *Ideas*:

"'Hence anyone fond of paradoxes may say in strictest truth, provided that he understands the ambiguity attaching to the term, that "fiction" is the vital element of phenomenology as of all eidetic science, the source from which knowledge of "eternal truths" draws its nourishment'" (128, quoting Husserl 1962, § 70, p. 184).[3] Whereas psychologists always start from the data of experience, Husserl claims that for an essential insight we may imagine an example. We may remember that Wittgenstein also proceeded by the way of fictional examples (think of this or that). In that sense he was himself engaged in essential analysis where the facts exemplify essences but do not support inductive generalization. Here there seems more than a coincidence between Wittgenstein and Husserl. Typical of Husserl's method, then, is fictional exemplification of eidetic insight.

Let us now consider the major issue discussed in Husserl's text. The kernel thesis is that there is no transition but a logical gap or rather an eidetic difference between two modes of givenness for anything: to be given in the original or to be given in an image. The claim is that we may understand that difference on the basis of one well-chosen example only. For instance, to perceive the book I am holding is not the same thing as to imagine it in my library. One example only suffices. The method operates not on the basis of a generalization of similar cases but by an instantaneous insight into an eidetic difference. We shall see that Sartre never changed his mind despite all the countering facts we shall discuss. Apparent confusions—such as when I see something in a fog and think it's a person but it's a tree—seem to be a perception mixed with an image. All these cases will have to be treated according to the essential difference between perception and image to show that in fact at issue is a perception wrongly interpreted, not an image. Against the starting point of Hume that an impression may produce a copy of itself in an idea, this notion of the copy of an impression is denied on the basis that everyone knows from the beginning that there is a gap between these two fundamental structures of experience. Sartre will try to relate this difference between modes of givenness to an ontology, claiming that on the one hand we have being and on the other hand we have the nothingness of our freedom. This will be quite different from Husserl. With Husserl we remain at the level of modes of givenness; we are describing modes of givenness.

Husserl wants to say something first about the mode of givenness of perception, because it provides the contrast to the mode of givenness of the image. Already in the *Ideas* are the main traits of the phenomenology of perception that Merleau-Ponty will develop to its perfection. I shall insist on three main traits of the intentionality of perception, because all three will have their importance by way of contrast to the phenomenology of the image. First, in perception there is a specific transcendence of the perceived.

The perceived is out there in such a way that it refers to nothing else than itself. This is very fundamental. To perceive is not to have an image of the thing but the thing itself. We cannot say that what we see is the image of something else, because the something of which it would be an image would instead itself be perceived rather than by means of an image of it. At first sight this seems a very simple statement, but it must be preserved against all opposite suggestions. The main objections against which we have to fight are those learned from modern sciences: that what we see—colors, sound, and so on—are not what we call the real thing. The real thing, we say, is made of atoms, electrons, and so on. We are therefore tempted to say that what we see are mere images. The confusion between perception and image arises not only from the fact that we treat images as some kind of givenness, a given of the same nature as the perceived, but that we already treat perception as images of something else. The Cartesian tradition is very tempting here, because it says that we perceive only the image of real things; the real things are not themselves perceived. In that case, the perceived loses its status of being the ultimate given of reality. As Husserl discusses in §§ 40–43 of the *Ideas*, we must fight against this false construction of the perception as the sign of, the image of, or the portrait of. Husserl argues that we should construe reality in the reverse way. It is first because we have a perceived world that then we may construe its physical predicates. The physical predicates are a scientific commentary on perception and not the perception; these predicates provide a portrait of the physical reality. When the scientist speaks of the structure of the atom, that's a system of predicates that refer ultimately to the visible world. The visible world is the bearer of existence. It is on the basis of a first assumption of the existence of the visible that I may construe the physical world. The latter is a second order system of predicates that refers to the first order predicates of the perceived object.

Phenomenology here reverses the apparent order that we have in Descartes and the rationalist tradition. That tradition speaks of primary qualities and secondary qualities. Only that which can be measured is real and a primary quality. What has only visible or auditory qualities and so on are called secondary qualities. What can be measured has a primary existence, and what is only qualitative is dependent on what is quantitative. The qualitative is relegated to a secondary existence. If, however, as phenomenology argues, we bracket presuppositions, theories, and constructions and return to what is given, what is given is that the perceived is not the sign of anything else. We cannot treat what we see as the sign of what we don't see. This is what is implied in the notion of the originary in Husserl (1962, § 19). Husserl sometimes uses the metaphor of seeing something in "flesh and blood" (for example, § 111, p. 287). He also sometimes says we see things "in person" (for example, § 43).[4] We see things themselves. There is nothing mediated. In the perception is the im-mediate. If something is given it's the perceptual world. We may determine (*bestimmen*, § 40) it further, and this we determine by means of physics. But we add nothing by the use of physics to what we already know concerning existence. We learn what existence means by looking at things. What we learn in physics is something else, a determination but not givenness.

The second trait of perception may also possibly be confused with the image. Despite the full givenness of something, we must say that in fact what is given is each time only a side of the thing. The thing is not given all at once. The thing is given, of course, since if anything is given, it is in perception, but what we call a thing is more than what is given at each point in time. Consider the famous image of the cube, an example found among all phenomenologists. No one can ever see a cube from all its sides at once. We see at most three sides, but nevertheless we speak of the cube. What we call an object is more than what is purely perceived despite that it is construed on the basis of the perceived. We have to take into account the perspectival structure of perception. This applies mainly to solid objects in space but also to some kinds of nonpersistent objects such as temporal objects, in melodies and so on. Something similar to the perspectival constitution of the thing may also be at work in the latter case, since we may hear the same symphony at different places in the auditorium. There's a similarity here to the object perceived from one side. The unity of the perceived object is presumed. It's a presumption, since, in seeing only a limited number of sides at once, what we call the object is the synthesis of only one phase that is actually intended with the retention of the previously perceived sides and the expectation or, as Husserl says, the protention of the coming phases. This synthesis is particularly evident in temporal objects such as, for example, a sentence that we hear. To understand a sentence is to gather the previous phases that have just been heard with those that we expect. In German, for instance, we may expect the positioning of the verb at a sentence's end, so sometimes the meaning of the sentence is in suspense until the whole sentence has been displayed. We see that with a temporal object we live only one phase at a time and that what we call the sentence is the synthesis.

We are tempted once more to say that this synthesis is an act of imagination. This is a second occasion where there may seem to be a mixing of the image and the perception. The first occasion was treating secondary qualities as images of primary qualities; this second is treating the non-actually perceived phases of an object as images. Can we not say that the nonperceived sides of the cube or book that we see are images and that the cube or book is the unity of all its sides? Husserl's reply is that we must not confuse the image of something that does not belong to perception with the phases of the same object perceived. If only part of a rug is perceived because another part is hidden by the table, the hidden part is not an image. It's either a retention or a protention, and those are part of the perception. A perception is not actual in all its phases. For Husserl, the retention and the protention are the inactual parts of perception but nevertheless perception. They make sense in relation to an actual phase that is actually perceived. If I speak of the other side of the object, it's because I am now perceiving one side. The object is actually perceived from one side, but the other, non-actually perceived sides are part of the perceived object. A perceived object does not have all its phases in actuality, but the potentially perceivable sides are also parts of perception. As we can see, how to classify the non-actually perceived side of a perceived object is a very delicate issue.

It is not only a matter of vocabulary to say that something is or is not an image. That determination rules the way in which we draw the line between the imaginary and the real. The nonperceived side may be placed on the same side of the line as the perceived side, because they can be gathered under the same unity of meaning. It's the presumed unity of meaning, what we call the object, that determines that something belongs to perception and not to imagination. A very complex problem is introduced by the notions of perspectives, profiles, and adumbrations.

A basic reason not to classify the nonperceived sides of an object as an image but as part of perception is that this nonperceived side has a role in a fundamental phenomenon that is obviously a phenomenon of perception, what we call observation. We shall see that for Sartre it is a basic point that we don't observe an image, whereas we do observe a thing. To observe is to complete the actual phases of an object by means of the potential phases of the object. In other words, to observe a book is to turn it from one side to the other and therefore to present successively all its phases; we learn from observation. In observing an object, what is inactual and potential in the horizon of perceptibility of the object comes to the forefront. This variation between potentialities and actualities concerning the same object constitutes observation. Sartre will draw heavily on this phenomenon, showing that in fact our sense of reality proceeds from the awareness that there is something inexhaustible in the perceived world. What we call an object is not only what is actually perceived but what is potentially perceivable. The concept of perceptibility, of perceivability, is a fundamental structure of reality. Each object has still other sides, other phases. To observe is to call to actuality what is only potential in the field of perception.

This interrelation in perception between potentiality and actuality is linked to another phenomenon, that of attention, which is more or less synonymous with observation. To pay attention to something is to emphasize an aspect at the expense of other aspects. Our visual attention may focus on a very particular aspect or it may expand; there is a movement of concentration or expansion of attention. The fact that we may move our attention shifts it. This is connected to the physiological structure of optic perception—we may move our head and eyes—and so perception is an action that we undertake with things. It's in relation to some actions that we can undertake with our body that differences in appearance occur in the spectacle of the world. Attention is the active side of observation, something that we can do. The power of our body is implied. Merleau-Ponty will develop this aspect extensively, the body as the sum of my powers, of what I can do.[5] In perception I can do something—see or not see, shut my eyes, move my glance, and so on. In correlation with these moves of attention, there are shifts in the appearances of objects, and this is what we call observation. These shifts in appearances will provide an important criterion of the image, because if we seem to observe, it's at best a quasi-observation. We shall discuss that with Sartre. Husserl does not develop this aspect.

A third trait of the phenomenology of perception that will be of importance for its contrast with the image concerns the status of the nonintentional element in perception. I'm not at ease with this aspect of Husserl and perhaps not with that of Sartre as well, since he will rely heavily on Husserl's analysis. Husserl wanted to give a specific status to mere presentations that have no intentional status. He says, when I perceive a red object, I have an impression of red. But this impression is merely undergone, it's a passive element animated by an intention aiming at the object. When I see the red of the object, I have an impression of red, but it is not experienced as my impression but is related to the object. Husserl, though, analyzes perception as having two components, including an impressional content *through which* we perceive (§ 85). He has this metaphor of the *through*. We don't stay in the impression, but it is through the impression that we see. I have wondered about Husserl's analysis here very often. When I translated the *Ideas I* into French, I put some notes on this in the translation that are at the same time question marks.[6] Why does Husserl preserve this impressional, nonintentional content in a theory that is typically intentional? I see several reasons that are perhaps not conclusive. First, because psychologists speak of the impression, for example, a patch of color or a sudden sound that is not yet related to something. There is therefore a persistent tradition concerning impressions not only in Hume and British empiricists but in psychology. It is the distinction between pure sensation and perception. Is Husserl's analysis then a concession to a tradition that has always made meaningless the distinction between the sensation and the mere impression? Is his analysis also a way to preserve the psychophysiology of perception, which implies an impressional element before the interpretation, before the process of gathering impressions? I don't know. Is the analysis also a suggestion of our language? Whatever Husserl's reasoning, though, his analysis leads to a duplication of qualities. We have to say that the red as an impression of red is an analogue to the red of the object. Then we are reduplicating everything; we have the red as a predicate of the object and the red as an impression in my body. With the latter we are once more reintroducing something like an image. Husserl calls this a presentation (*Darstellung*) (§ 85). If we have a presentation and a perception, there is a duplication.

Husserl expresses this differentiation in a classical, Aristotelian vocabulary, distinguishing between matter (*hylē*) and form (*morphē*) (§ 85). For Husserl, the hyletic is a presentation (*Darstellung*). We can ask why does Husserl speak of the hyletic element since he will speak separately of the image. But the hyletic element will be the central element in Sartre's theory of the image, because the family of images—portrait, pictures, mental images—will rely on a common hyletic element that will be animated in different ways. The second part of Sartre's book, *The Psychology of Imagination*, on the probable, concerns the role of this analogue.

I wonder for my part whether reference to an impressional element is not the residue of a dead tradition. If I am right, the psychology of perception has now more or less dropped this notion of impressions. Perception is more and more treated as a kind of scanning of reality and then as a permanent interpretation, a behavior in relation to the object. Is there such a thing as an impressional stage? This issue has also been discussed in linguistic analysis in Austin's *Sense and Sensibilia* when he tries to prove that the impressional stage is a misconstruction due to a bad grammar. My suggestion, then, is that there is an attempt to get rid of the pure sensation as a component of the real perception, as this stage may be canceled either on psychological or linguistic grounds.

We could add perhaps a fourth trait to the problem of perception, but this is more marginal because it has to do with the judgment of perception. Nevertheless, it is very significant since we *speak* of our perception. It's important to see how the world of perception is achieved by human language. It's mainly by the modalities of judgment that our perceptual world is spoken. We speak of our perceptions according to the modalities of judgment: as real, possible, necessary. The fundamental component of perception is this belief in reality which is linked to our use of the verb *to be*. We use in a very assertive way the verb *to be* to describe what we see. All the tenses of our grammar relating to the indicative present are connected to perception. We shall note, by contrast, how the image will be linked to another language game, more that of the conditional, the *as if*. Merleau-Ponty will develop this aspect when he speaks of the primordial belief that accompanies perception.[7] For him this will be a very strong argument against a phenomenological reduction, because in perception we do the contrary of a reduction. We are taken by the presence of things. It is very difficult to understand how Husserl could at the same time say let us reduce being to appearance and then say that it's in perception that we have the density of appearance that we call the real. How is it possible to connect the modality of the real with the suspension of ontological belief? For myself, I don't rely so much on the tradition of reduction that both Heidegger and Merleau-Ponty have questioned.[8]

We are now prepared to turn from the intentionality of perception to speak of the intentionality of imagination. Husserl's fundamental thesis is that image and perception, or better the imagined and the perceived, don't belong to the same category, to the same mode of givenness. The only thing that we can do is to provide examples that support this eidetic distinction and discuss apparent counterfactuals that seem to provide intermediary cases that have to be referred either to the image or to perception. Three examples are treated by Husserl. The first example is the classical example of a chimera, the flute-playing centaur. The example is a fiction. I insist on that because Sartre will always start from another example, my friend Peter who exists elsewhere and of whom I have an image instead of a perception. In Sartre's example, we have the same referent for an image and a perception, and this referent exists elsewhere. As we shall see, the choice of this paradigmatic case has advantages and disadvantages. The advantage is that it's on the basis of the same referent that we have two modes of givenness. Since the referent is the same, the example offers a good approach to the pure difference in givenness. The disadvantage is that the example is not a pure image, since it is a portrait of something existent. I may travel to meet my friend Peter in Berlin. By contrast, if we start from a fiction, the fiction has nothing in common with a perceived object, since it cannot be perceived in other circumstances. In Sartre's example, there is an element of perceptibility that remains in the case of the absent object while with the inexistent object we have a pure case.

Husserl treats the case of the inexistent object in § 23 of the *Ideas*, which is entitled "Spontaneity of Ideation, Essence, and Fiction."

> [S]o far as the flute-playing centaur is concerned, it is a presentation in the sense in which that which is presented is called presentation, but not in the sense in which presentation stands verbally for a mental experiencing. Naturally the centaur itself is not mental, it exists neither in the soul, nor

in consciousness, nor anywhere else, it is in fact "nothing," mere "imagination"; or, to be more precise, the living experience of imagination is the imagining *of* a centaur. (82)

We have a very fundamental case here of something that is in front of, that is an ob-ject. I am not only speaking of a centaur, but in a sense I am quasi-seeing a centaur. We can give the centaur all the characteristics of an object, since it confronts me, it's in front of me, it's before me, but precisely as nothing. Here's a decisive case that immediately introduces the radical difference between perception and imagination. The fiction is the paradigmatic case, because it implies the difference between existence and inexistence. The problem of inexistent objects has also been treated elsewhere under the issue of absurd meaning. For example, a round square is not merely a heap of sounds, since I mean something, but I mean something that is impossible. There is a logic of inexistent objects. This is an important part of logic, because the problem of truth value starts from there. I may have meanings without a referent, and a meaning without a referent is nevertheless a meaning. It's merely an empty meaning. In the language of Husserl, to confer meaning is an act that is first empty and that can be fulfilled, either by perception or by images. But we could say that the pure case of meaning occurs when it cannot be fulfilled. The unfulfilled meaning is the meaning. We have this null fulfillment with the centaur. Perhaps the linguistic approach, through meanings without reference, and the inexistent object of Husserl intersect here.

Husserl's second example is given in § 99 in order to introduce after the concept of objective inexistence the notion of the modification of existence. This notion is related less to the problem of empty meanings than to the problem of the modalities of belief. In this section he considers a series of modifications by which we qualify step by step the initial belief in the presence of things. We have a kind of progressive reduction of presence that proceeds in three steps. He offers the example of an "appearing tree." First is the tree that I have just perceived but that is still adjacent to my perception. Second is the tree no longer adjacent to my perception, no longer a retention, but a mere representation. Third is the tree as an imaginative representation.

> We are made aware of this identical element [the appearing tree] at one time in a "primordial" way, at another "through memory," then again "imaginatively," and so forth. But what are thereby indicated are characters in the "appearing tree as such," discoverable when the glance is directed to the noematic correlate [that is, to the noema common to the three stages,

that we call each stage a tree], and not to experience and its real states of being [an allusion to the hyletic element]. (268)

In the three steps a series of modifications occurs in which the element of credence or belief is progressively reduced. The example here is quite different from that of the flute-playing centaur, because the centaur was never a perception. In that example there was no identical element between a perception and an image, whereas here it's the same perceivable that passes through the different stages, which he calls modifications. But the modification is a way of approaching the essential difference. It's a way of giving account of the essential difference.

Husserl continues: "More accurate analysis shows us that the characters mentioned above by way of illustration do not belong to a single series." Husserl's argument is that there is a break or leap in the series; it's not a continuous modification. "On the one hand we have the plain reproductive modification, the plain representation, and this, remarkably enough, figures in its own essential nature as the modification of something other than itself" (268). We have a modified perception but one that belongs to the same series as the perception. Having perceived something is part of the meaning of now evoking it. The "plain representation" still has a foot in perception. The grammar expresses this using a verb of perception but of the past. We speak of a past perception to describe what we call a memory. Having perceived something is part of the meaning of now representing it. We may modify a perception as far as we can by reducing it along the series of modalities—real, putative, probable, inexisting, impossible, and so on. But the reductions are still within the same series, the series of having perceived something.

"On the other hand," Husserl says,

> the imaginative modification belongs to another series of modifications. It represents "in" the form of an "image." But the image can appear in a primordial form, e.g., the "painted" picture (not indeed the picture as a thing, of which we say, for instance, that it hangs on the wall) which we grasp in and through perception. But the image can be also something that appears as reproduced, as when we have presentations of imagery in memory or free fancy. (268–69)

We have here in a nucleus the whole of what Sartre will call the image family, starting from the painted picture to the free fancy. They constitute a family without any common element with the family of perception, which we may follow from something being perceived or perceivable, to its having been perceived, and so on. Between the two families, there is no common element.

We have only an allusion to the subject of the portrait or picture in the paragraph quoted, when Husserl said that the "image can appear in a primordial form." The canvas appears first as a perception, but we don't perceive it with a belief in its existence, since we are directed through this perceived object toward the imagined object. It is here that the notion of neutrality-modification appears. What is specific to the portrait is that perceptive support is neutralized. We don't posit the picture-object's existence. The issue is treated more extensively in § 111, which is called "Neutrality-Modification and Fancy [*Phantasie*]." Husserl returns to the problem of the series of modifications that remain within the cycle of positing an object as real. (Recall that Merleau-Ponty will develop analysis of the concept of belief that accompanies perception.) Husserl says: "We can satisfy ourselves [for the moment] with the help of an illustration that the neutrality-modification of the normal perception which posits its object with unmodified certainty is the neutral consciousness of the picture-object, which we find as a component in our ordinary observation of a depicted situation perceptively presented" (286). This is a very complex case. Husserl discusses it after the example of the centaur, because in the example of the centaur there is nothing in common between the fiction and a perception. They are two different worlds, a fictional world and the world of perceptibility, whereas here we have the support of something belonging to the world of perception that enables the perceived image. The characters of the painting are depicted. (Again we have this question of what does depiction mean.) We could say that there is something common to perception and imagining an image here since we have the canvas, the colors, and so on. But, in fact, we have no perception at all since, as we said, the fourth component of perception is belief in the existence of the perceived object. Here, though, we neutralize our belief in the existence of the canvas. When we enter a gallery, we come with the intention not to perceive but, on the basis of neutralized perception, to imagine. We enter into a world of imagination through a neutralization of the belief in the existence of what we see. Let me reiterate the opening of the quotation and then extend it.

> We can satisfy ourselves with the help of an illustration that the neutrality-modification of the normal perception which posits its object with unmodified certainty is the neutral consciousness of the picture-object, which we find as a component in our ordinary observation of a depicted situation perceptively presented. Let us try to make this clear, and let us suppose that we are observing Dürer's engraving, "The Knight, Death, and the Devil."

We distinguish here in the first place the normal perception of which the correlate is the "engraved print" as a thing, this print in the portfolio.

We distinguish in the second place the perceptive consciousness within which in the black lines of the picture there appear to us the small colourless figures, "knight on horseback," "death," and "devil." In aesthetic observation we do not consider these as the objects; we have our attention fixed on what is portrayed "in the picture," more precisely, on the "depicted" realities, the knight of flesh and blood, and so forth.

That which makes the depicting possible and mediates it, namely, the consciousness of the "picture" (of the small grey figurettes in which through the derived noeses something other, through similarity, "presents itself as depicted"), is now an example for the neutrality-modification of the perception. This depicting picture-object stands before us neither as being nor as non-being, nor in any other positional modality; or rather, we are aware of it as having its being, though only a quasi-being, in the neutrality-modification of Being. (286–87)

There are three phases. First, we see the engraved print with black lines and so on. Second, we identify the characters: that's a knight, that's death, that's the devil. There is a phase of observation in the sense that we recognize something. We don't only receive impressions from traits, lines, and so forth, but we identify something by recognizing the object that sometimes receives a name at the bottom of the picture. Yet, third, instead of positing these singular entities in the physical world, in the spatio-temporal world of existence, we take them as standing for something that has no place in reality.

It's interesting to see that of the three characters—knight, death, and the devil—the knight could be perceived in exactly the same way as Sartre's example of my friend Peter, but death and the devil could not, at least in the sense of meeting them on the street corner as real persons. The identification of the characters is not the same. The knight may also be subject to a commentary in the sense of a sociology of culture: the institution of nobility in the Middle Ages and so on. There too we are speaking of reality. Something real is depicted. But the knight is expelled from reality thanks to his encountering of death and the devil. Or, if we were to speak of reality, it's no longer reality in the sense of perceptual reality but an existential experience with what Karl Jaspers would call two boundary limits of existence: death at the end of life and the devil as the radical possibility of evil in our existence.[9] All three characters are depicted in the sense that their meaning is presented to us through a quasi-perception that is neutralized as perception in order to function as depiction. "In aesthetic observation we do not consider these as the objects. . . ." In other words, it's not about them that we are speaking and describing what we see. "[W]e have our attention fixed on what is portrayed 'in the picture' . . ." (287).

The word *picture* is very deceptive because it means two things. It means both the picture that is hanging on the wall and what we see. The latter we don't see as on the wall. We see a hole in the perceived world, since this picture is a window, whose frame is very important, since the act of imagination is itself framed by it. There must be a dividing line between the picture and its support, the wall, and so on. There is no transition at all between the two but a leap from one to the other. This leap is itself portrayed by the frame. Then the black lines of the picture function as the hyletic element. Instead of functioning as the object of perception, they became the matter of the image of the imagination. Sartre will rely on this concept of a hyletic element, because through the neutralization of the perception, the perceptual support now functions as the matter by means of which we address ourselves beyond the perceived traits toward a depicted that is not there and that then belongs to the inexistent world at least in terms of ordinary perception. (Think again of the comparison with the flute-playing centaur, which I hope not to have pushed too far.) The neutralization of perception is here a component and a condition for this leap into the inexistent which is imagination itself.

Let me end with Husserl's elaboration of the third and final phase, which appears in the following paragraph, which concludes §111 of the *Ideas*:

> But it is just the same with the object depicted, if we take up a purely aesthetic attitude, and view the same again as "mere picture," without imparting to it the stamp of Being or non-Being, of possible Being or probable Being, and the like. But, as can clearly can be seen, that does not mean any privation, but a modification, that of neutralization. Only we should not represent it as a transforming operation carried out on a previous position. (287)

The object depicted is the knight, death, and the devil not as in the engraving but as intended imaginatively on the basis of the engraving. The object depicted is not given the stamp of Being or non-Being and so on, because those are a series of modifications that belong to the series of modalities of the judgment of perception. I finish with this gap between positing and neutralizing that underlies the lack of transition between the two modes of givenness. One implies the positing of its object and the other implies the neutralization of its object, at least in the case of the picture or portrait. In the latter mode, something is perceived as neutralized in order to be imagined. There is not a combination of a perception and the imagination but a neutralized perception and its support of the imagination.

The next lectures turn to Sartre. We shall discuss Sartre's phenomenological approach and offer a comparison with Ryle's theory of pretending. I want to compare the analytic and phenomenological approaches through the choice of examples in both schools of the role of language and the concept of neutralization.

12
Sartre (1)

In this and the following lectures on Sartre we shall end this section on the image and its ontological and epistemological status. We shall then turn to consider the function of the image in larger frameworks, such as the epistemological function in models, the poetic function in metaphor, and the aesthetic function in painting and in nonlinguistic art. So what we are analyzing now is a *statics* of the image, the image considered in its isolation, apart from its function. It may be that this abstraction is responsible for some of the failures or ambiguities that the statics cannot overcome. That is the case with Sartre's approach to the problem of imagination. At the end of his main work on imagination, *The Psychology of Imagination*, he shows that there is an imaginary life. Before reaching this level of the imaginary life, we have been working within a very abstract framework. It is within this abstract framework that the statics of the image is elaborated and construed. For most of our discussion of Sartre we shall remain within this narrow framework. Then we shall prepare the transition to the third part of the lectures by consideration of the imaginary life, something that we not only call an image in the sense of an image of, but that encompasses what it means to live in the mode of imagination.

Sartre's contribution to the problem of imagination is twofold. First, he attempts to elaborate the status of the isolated image as a particular mode of intentionality. As we shall see, this analysis will be based on the choice of a paradigmatic example, the image of the absent object. Second, Sartre attempts to rebuild the image family along the lines of this model. We may recall that there are two difficulties in the analysis of imagination. First, what is the paradigmatic case and how shall I analyze it? Ryle says the paradigmatic case is pretending. Sartre says that it's the image of the absent. Starting from this paradigmatic case, the second question is then how to rebuild the whole field and overcome the apparent lack of consistency in our vocabulary concerning the image: imaging, imagining, fancying, and so on. Sartre is therefore confronted with the twofold problem of undertaking a phenomenological analysis of a paradigmatic case and then rebuilding the whole field according to this paradigmatic case. In this lecture we shall consider Sartre's paradigmatic case and his analysis of it. In succeeding lectures, we shall discuss his reconstruction of the field by means of the image family and then the transition to the imaginary life.

Sartre's choice of an initial example is decisive. In his two volumes devoted to imagination, *Imagination: A Psychological Critique* and *The Psychology of Imagination*, the same example keeps returning: I have an image of my friend Peter who is now absent. Why is the choice of this example decisive? Because we have to do with someone who exists elsewhere and therefore provides us the contrast of absence. The choice is deliberate in order to put ourselves immediately in connection with the negative element of the image, the absent. We shall see later to what extent the inexistence of the fiction may be built on the basis of the absent. Sartre's choice is deliberate also for the sake of the intentional element of the image. We are drawn by the force of the example outside of the mind in order to make the image not something that would be in our minds as a kind of small miniature of the thing but as a relation to, as this intentional element. This transcendence of the object is preserved by the fact that the absent object could be perceived or has been perceived. It's the same object, the same person whom I previously met and about whom I am now thinking. The problem of the object is raised by the possibility of perceiving it. It is the same object that is perceived onetime—present onetime—and another time is absent. Therefore, the problem is shifted from introspection addressed to a mental entity toward a mode of the givenness of existence. Sartre says in the introduction to *Imagination: A Psychological Critique* that we are constrained by the choice of example to describe the difference in givenness of the same object that can be present in flesh and blood or in image (Sartre 1962, 3) (*en image*).[1] Even if it's odd to translate *en image* as *in image*, I shall translate literally because the literal translation makes the best sense. The existing translation writes of the image *as* image (3). The *as* may be problematic and should be questioned, since it does not retain the intentional quality of *en image*. There is a difference in the mode of being given, givenness in image as opposed to givenness in flesh and blood. This contrast is provided by the fact that in both we have the same essence, the same person whom I imagine or perceive.

Using the language of linguistic analysis, we could say that we have to do with the same particular or the same reference. Phenomenological and linguistic analyses converge. When Sartre thinks of the different modes of existence, we could speak here in the language of linguistic analysis of the sameness of reference but with two different qualifications: I imagine that or I perceive that. It is in the operator that the difference will appear. A phenomenological approach, in turn, relies on an essential analysis. We are supposed to understand immediately on the basis of one well-chosen example the split, the logical gap, between these two modes of givenness. We have already understood what it is to be present in flesh and blood and to be present in image.

As we saw previously with Husserl, what is fundamental for perception is that the perception does not depend on my spontaneity. It has what Sartre calls inertness (1962, 2). Sartre does not use the word *inertness* in the sense of physics, where inertia means that a physical body is not moved or shifted in its trajectory; it goes on with the same speed and the same direction. Rather, inertness means that something escapes my spontaneity. The thing is a limit to my spontaneity; it affects whether I may give myself an image (1–2). We shall return to this problem later in our discussion of Sartre's chapter in *The Psychology of Imagination* on "The Imaginary Life," because to a certain extent this spontaneity is obscured by other phenomena that Sartre will call fascination, the magical relation to the thing (1948/1966, 177/159).[2] I claim to be under the spell of my images; it happens to my perception. Yet, as Sartre keeps repeating, fatality is a dimension of consciousness, not of things, since things may be determined, but fatality is a failure of freedom (245/220ff.). Fatality is an attribute of freedom, whereas determinism is an attribute of causality. So even if we shall find in the imaginary life an element of fascination, of the magic of the image, as Sartre will say, this has to be related in a way to the spontaneity of the image. It's a complexification of spontaneity. Fascination does not happen to things; it happens only to spontaneity.

If we start with the sameness of the individual who can be reidentified as the same but who is given in two different ways, the difference in status concerns a mode of givenness. We shall provisorily define the image as a mode of being, "an existence in the form of an image" (1962, 3). In his first volume on imagination, *Imagination: A Psychological Critique*, Sartre paves the way for a direct description that is given in the first part of the second volume by a critique of what he calls in the later volume the illusion of immanence (1948/1966, 5/5), which prevents us from seeing this essential constitution. The problem of imagination is plagued by an illusion. We also have to explain the illusion that we are tempted to say that the image is something in the mind. In the two volumes Sartre keeps fighting against the temptation to confuse the two modes of being by putting in the mind an equivalent of the thing that would have the mode of existence of the thing but within an inner rather than outer space. We may draw a comparison here with Ryle's notion of the mind as the ghost in the machine, the idea that we consider the mind a place where there are these little things that we call images. In the next lecture we shall see that there is perhaps something in the image which, without justifying this illusion, induces it. There is a certain material element in the image through which we are directed imaginatively toward something. This is the problem of the hyletic, of which I spoke in discussing Husserl. It's through a certain mental content that I am directed toward the absent. For the present, though, we don't introduce this element in order to address ourselves to the main illusion against which we have to fight to pave our way toward the direct description. The problem is how to think about the image without forming this illusion of immanence, the illusion that there exists something like an entity in the mind. It's the type of illusion that we have in Hume when he says that an impression is equal to a thing. The copy that is the impression is a kind of weaker thing.

What is more problematic is that this is not only the illusion of some philosophers but is the naive ontology of the "man in the street" (1962, 4). "[A] naively conceived theory" is superimposed on "spontaneous experience" (4). It's not enough to return from theory to ordinary language, because ordinary language too is infected by the illusion. This is an important difference between phenomenology and linguistic analysis to the extent that linguistic analysis tries to rely on what people say and then analyzes their reports of their experiences. These reports may be questioned to the extent that they are themselves infected by the illusion of immanence. As Sartre says, I may speak of the sheet of paper at which I am now looking and then shut my eyes and think of the same sheet of paper. Are there two sheets of paper, one real and now a second one in the mind? Do I have a duplicate reality, first as physical then as mental (3)? The notion of absence will be very important here, because it's really the absent with which I have to deal and not an internalized, weakened presence. In ordinary language, when we speak of the image we see instead of the "same sheet of paper on two levels of being, . . . two sheets of paper exactly alike and existing on the same plane" (4). Sartre sees a model in the philosophy of Epicurus: the *eidōlon* (the *simulacrum* in Latin) travels in that space; it is somewhere in our brain or in our mind (4). The image turns into a thing that we see within our mind. It's "a lesser thing, possessed of its own existence, given to consciousness like any other thing, and maintaining external relations with the thing of which it is an image" (5).

Sartre discusses this illusion of immanence within different philosophical systems and schools of psychology which I shall not summarize. Most of the latter are dead or unknown, as they pertained to French psychology in the first part of the twentieth century. I shall consider only the structure of his argument and the contribution of the critique to the positive description. Sartre's main objection against the reduplication of reality within the mind is that we transfer to the image the main characteristics of the thing, including, most fundamentally, the thing's passivity. Thus, for example, in a long chapter Sartre criticizes Henri Bergson's concept of the image, because he says that Bergson tries only to make the image more fluid by replacing the notion of a solid thing with the image of a stream (63), as in William James's idea of the stream of consciousness.[3] But it's not by making something more fluid that it is less thingly. Sartre undertakes to show that all modern psychology attempts to give more fluidity to the image without putting in question the status of its existence. A fluid existence is no less a thingly existence. "Imagination, along with the sensory, remained the realm of bodily passivity" (76). "[T]he image remains in the guise of an inert element" (77) even when subjected to the laws of the flux. The image is always treated the same way; it's the rebirth of an inert sensory content.

To dissolve this illusion, Sartre proceeds, as do some British philosophers, by means of counterfactuals and by showing some fundamental paradoxes. I focus on his eighth chapter, which is called "The Contradictory Consequences of the Classical Postulate." The fundamental argument is that the classical postulate implies two incompatible facts. First, we preserve the metaphysical identity between image and perception—they're from the same stuff, so to speak—and nevertheless, we maintain a distinction between them (85). In the next lecture we shall see that phenomenologists put themselves in front of an opposite task: having assumed that there is a logical gap between the image and reality, how is it possible to have something like the make-believe and the confusions of realms? Phenomenologist thinks that they are in a better position to give an account of the confusion than their opponents, who are at a great loss when they have to provide a difference that is not basic and so have to posit a difference on the basis of a fundamental identity. Most philosophers and psychologists start from the idea that an image is a kind of perception but internal and weaker, and they usually rely on external criteria to assess the image. Those extrinsic criteria don't belong to the experience itself of having an image or a perception, such as the inconsistency of the image with the rest of our experience. Hume has already used this argument, namely, that I try to find some clues, some criteria, external to the nature of the image. This appearance is supposedly confirmed by an experience very often introduced at this stage, but Sartre, like Husserl, will claim that in fact the example does not concern an image. For instance, I go for a walk in the fog, and I take a tree trunk for a man (87). This is a classical example of a confusion. We say that we did not know whether what we saw was an image or a perception. Then we use some other criteria to resolve the confusion. There was, for example, movement, or he did not answer when I called out to him. I want more information to choose between the image and the perception.

But is it the case here that I have a hesitation between an image and a perception? No, says Sartre: "[T]his is no confusion of image and perception. It's a false interpretation of an actual perception" (87). I really perceive something that I cannot recognize. It's the problem of identifying a confused perception. Consider when I first say of the object in the fog that it's a man and then discover that it was only a tree. When I said that it was a man, I did not speak about an image. I was trying to give a name to my perception and therefore to relate this indistinct form to a known type of perceived object. Price offers a better analysis of this reaction in terms of the process of recognizing. The problem belongs more to recognizing an object than to choosing between an image and a perception. With the concept of observation in Husserl and Sartre we have the parallel conception to what is called recognition in Price. They are more or less the same phenomenon and process. The example is not an exception to the radical difference between image and perception. "[I]f images and perceptions do not differ in quality in the first place, it is hopeless to attempt to distinguish them subsequently in terms of quantity" (88). Quantity here means a quantity of further information. If we assume that we first confuse images and perception and then distinguish them by contrast and opposition, we become caught in an infinite regress that never equals the intrinsic difference between being present and being absent. "[T]he differentiating judgment will never be anything but probable" (95). For Sartre, by contrast, we have to do with a kind of certainty here concerning the distinction between two essences (96). The difference between essences can never be recuperated by the process that is always a probable approximation of a difference. The process of recognizing—of identifying—a perception may be an indefinite and endless process, but confirming an expectation about real things is something quite different from recognizing the difference between two modes of givenness. With the latter we no longer have to do with an inductive process always requiring new arguments. It's immediate; it occurs at the beginning or never.

Sartre also offers the example of the dream. We may sometimes hesitate in deciding whether we are dreaming or perceiving, but to be awake is precisely to make the difference. Perception should not be seen as "at every moment a victory over dreams. . . . Such a world, where one never stops connecting appearances [as either images or perceptions], where every perception is a judgment and a victory, bears not the slightest resemblance to the world around us" (100). The world Sartre rejects is one in which we would always have to choose between an image and a perception. The mixing of image and perception is for Sartre a distortion of the most primitive experience concerning our relation to the world. "No image ever mixes in with real things" (101).

> The starting point, instead, is the following unimpeachable given: I cannot possibly form an image without at the same time knowing that I am forming an image; and the immediate knowledge I have of the image as such may become the basis for judgments of existence (of the type of "I have an image of X," "This is an image," etc.), but it is itself prepredicative evidence. (101)

Before being able to express the judgment that something is an image in a definite fashion, I must live in the movement of having an image and knowing that it's an image and not a perception. No neutral entity is available that allows me to orient myself toward the real or the imaginary. The distinction between them cannot be rendered at a secondary level if it is not already primary. What induced the error was the presupposition of an impressional matter, of a sensory content identical with that of perception, received in the mind, and given in that sense.

Since I want to stay longer with Sartre's principal book on the imagination, *The Psychology of Imagination*, let me conclude our discussion of the present book by insisting on the role of spontaneity in the argument. This is more specific of Sartre than of Husserl. Husserl makes an analysis mainly in terms of noematic analysis—how do things appear—but for Sartre the nothingness of the image is the counterpart of my spontaneity. This is typically Sartrean, because precisely in *Being and Nothingness* he will define freedom as nothingness, as a kind of absence in the texture of reality. It's a kind of lack that I fill in by my action. Therefore it's important to see that in the present book the concept of spontaneity is always connected with that of nothingness: nothingness comes from the side of what appears and spontaneity from my side. We recognize the language of *Being and Nothingness* that permeates the last part of the eighth chapter.

> That exists spontaneously which determines its own existence. In other words, to exist spontaneously is to exist for oneself and through oneself [*exister pour soi et par soi*]. One reality alone deserves to be called "spontaneous": consciousness. To exist and to be conscious of existing are one and the same for consciousness. Otherwise stated, the supreme ontological law of consciousness is as follows: for a consciousness the only way of existing is to be conscious that it exists. It is therefore evident that consciousness can determine itself to exist, but that it cannot act on anything but itself. A

sensory content may be the occasion for our forming a consciousness, but we cannot act by means of consciousness on the sensory content, dragging it from nowhere (or from the unconscious), or sending it back. If images are consciousness, they are pure spontaneities. (Sartre 1962, 115; French citation appears in original)

According to Sartre, any theory of imagination is obligated to satisfy two requirements. It needs to account for the spontaneous discrimination between image and perception and explain the role of images in thought (117). The classical conception fails twice. To endow an image with a sensory content is to make it a thing obeying the laws of things and not the law of consciousness. And thus, there is no way to conceive the relations of these things to thought. But Sartre's philosophical theory of self-transparency obscures the issue. Once more! Why link the difference between image and perception to spontaneity, transparency, and freedom? Because a *thing* in consciousness would deny consciousness? Why not start instead from the givenness of the image as an *appearing*? The appearance of the image does not entail the spontaneity of consciousness. Sartre substitutes the alternative between thing and consciousness for the difference between appearing as there and appearing as absent.

Sartre's argument on spontaneity will also be somewhat difficult to articulate in relation to some important aspects of the imaginary life that, on the contrary, preserve many aspects of compulsion and coercion. We shall have to construe the concept of inner fatality as a counterpart of spontaneity. It's only within the realm of spontaneity that there can be something like fatality. We shall reserve this problem for further discussion. We leave this book with a final quotation. Sartre says: "An image is an undoubted psychic reality. An image can in no way be reduced to a sensory content, or be constituted on the ground of a sensory content" (125).

After having cleared the way for a direct description of having an image in his first book on the imagination, Sartre tries to elaborate in his second book, *The Psychology of Imagination*, the distinctive feature of having an image on the basis of the paradigmatic example of the spontaneous production of the image of an absent person or absent thing. This example represents two choices in one by Sartre: the choice of the absent as the paradigm of the image is also a choice of the image as production. We discard the example where I am overwhelmed by the flux of images. Instead, I produce the image. Sartre will later qualify this concept of production in the chapter on the imaginary life. For the sake of analysis, Sartre chooses the simplest case of being the master of the image and having the image as the representative of something that exists elsewhere, the absent. The problem of the object is solved at the beginning, since the object is my friend Peter out there. We shall not speak of the image in terms of being an object, since the image is an image of an object. It's not an object in the mind, since there is an object elsewhere. To what extent the object elsewhere is paradigmatic also for inexistent objects is perhaps one of the main difficulties of this theory. Is it possible to build the concept of inexistence on that of absence, because in absence there is existence? There is an existent but elsewhere, whereas in fiction what will be the object? We shall preserve this discussion for the next lecture, when we shall discuss the image family.

In the case of the absent, we have at least the simple situation where something existing appears not as such. That is, it is perceived but in the form of an image, because we may say that when I produce the image, I am directed toward the absent and not toward the image. It is only by a secondary act of reflection that I say it is given as an image. I shift the emphasis from the intended object which is out there to the mode of givenness, and then I treat the mode of givenness as a new object for reflection. Perhaps we have here the source of the illusion of immanence (Sartre 1948/1966, 5/5). The illusion of immanence may appear only in a moment of reflection, when I am no longer thinking of my friend out there but of the image as distinct from his presence. I reflect on the absence instead of reflecting on what is absent. By an act of the second degree, I shift from the object to the manner in which the object is given. Then I may produce the judgment that I have an image. I now speak of a little something that is the image. I transform the mode of givenness into a mental phantom. Since all descriptions of an image occur by means of a reflective mode, the problem will be to preserve the status that the image has in the direct act, the intentional act. We must not destroy the meaning of the intentional movement of the image in reflection. We must not fall into the illusion of immanence, which proceeds as an interiorization of the object in the mind.

Sartre builds his analysis of images on the basis of what he calls their four distinctive characteristics. The first is in continuity with the critique of the illusion of immanence. The second, third, and fourth introduce new positive elements. First, the image is *a* consciousness (4/4). (Here we have to do with a use of the German word *Bewusstsein* in a specific sense [see the book's preface]). Usually we don't speak of consciousness as something singular, as each time *a* consciousness of something. (I don't know whether it makes sense in English or French to say that an image is *a* consciousness. Already in German it was strange when Husserl spoke of *Bewusstsein* as each time the act of.) Sartre speaks of *a* consciousness for the sake of saying that consciousness is always a relation; it's a relation and not a thing (8/7). We are so accustomed to dealing with objects in space—mainly with solid objects and sometimes with fluid objects—that we have a kind of invincible difficulty to form the idea of a mode of givenness without treating it as a kind of new object. To have a picture of Peter is not to have a second Peter in miniature. This illusion of doubling is induced by ordinary language, which speaks of the image in the language of a picture, the way we put a kind of portrait in our mind. This is the argument that perhaps owes more to Sartre than to Husserl. If we are to preserve the character of the spontaneity of consciousness, we cannot put a thing into this realm of spontaneity. A material portrait in the mind would destroy the synthetic structure of consciousness and break its continuity. "Consciousness would cease being transparent to itself; its unity would be broken in every direction by unassimilable, opaque screens" (6/6). The evidence for this argument is provided by the same kind of example as in the first volume. The same object as first perceived, then as an image, exists only once. In both cases the object does not enter into consciousness. We can see the advantage of this strategy. (As I shall develop further in the next lecture, this example has many disadvantages, too.) The choice of an absent object compels us always to put the referent outside the mind. If an image and a perception have the same referent, then it's the referent of the perception that provides a referent to the image. We cannot reach the thing that is the referent and put this thing in the mind as that would entail having two things and therefore two referents. We have only one referent.

My problem here is whether we are not in fact dealing already with an account, because everything happens finally in language. When we say that we have perceived or that we have an image, we must rely on the capacity of sentences to have not only a sense but a reference. Are we speaking of the referent of our discourse about the image or the referent of our image? I shall discuss this further in a subsequent lecture also. In any event, Sartre says that in order not to reduplicate the referent, the word *image* means only "a certain manner in which the object makes its appearance to consciousness" or "a certain way in which consciousness presents an object to itself" (8/7). It's very difficult to maintain the relational character of the image and not immediately substitute for the relationship a kind of entity, because the image is also something that appears. We have to give an account of the fact that the image is a relationship, it's a manner of being related to, but it's also a manner of appearing. Not only does Sartre not attempt to elude this, but he deals with this in his expression of "a certain manner in which the object makes its appearance to consciousness" (8/7). The fight against entities *in* consciousness does not rule out entities of a certain kind *for* consciousness.

We may recall our discussion of Ryle and Price on this issue. Ryle said let us get rid of all entity language in our invocation of the image. We should no longer speak of the image appearing but of ourselves *seeming* to see. We displace on the side of the verb what has been given to a certain kind of appearing object. But Price said that we cannot do that, because there is something in the appearance itself that resists, the fact that we see our images. Something appears, even if it's not an object that appears. Price's argument was to say that there is an alternative to our assumption that if the image is an entity, it must be a thing. The image is an appearance without being a thing. This is the crucial difficulty with the problem of the image. We cannot get rid of entity language, the language using substantives—I see an image—because this entity language is supported by an aspect of the experience, that something appears. Or we say that there are not two Peters but rather that there is one Peter who appears in the image. We must give an account of the fact that the mode of givenness is for us a kind of appearance. This is the crucial difficulty of the problem of the image, the ontological problem, that we have to do with a manner of being related to but a manner that takes the form of an appearance, an appearance that is not a thing.

In order to deal with this difficulty, Sartre introduces the second characteristic of the image, what he calls "quasi-observation" (13/12). This preserves on the one hand the characteristic that the image is an observation—we observe certain appearances—but on the other hand that we are merely quasi-observing. This is an intermediary way between Price and Ryle. Sartre is saying with Price that we observe something but with Ryle that it is *as though* we are observing. The quasi qualifies the observation. We take away with one hand what we have given with the other. The concept of quasi-observation is paradoxical enough, but it gives a good account of the strange situation of the image. There is something of a kind of an observation, but elements fundamental to observation are lacking, which compels us to speak of quasi-observation.

What does it mean to observe? To observe may be defined by two main traits. The first is the perspectival character of observation. Consider again the famous example of the cube. I see only a series of profiles, and therefore I have to learn the object by making a synthesis of appearances (9/9). I may be deceived if someone playing a game puts a false object—fake fruit, for example—in a cup. I follow the usual order of appearances and I am deceived, because my expectation of the next step of perception may be fulfilled by the next appearance. This is one aspect of observation, the step by step process through a series of profiles. Second, to observe is also to relate, to give to an object an indefinite number of relations in all directions in order to connect it to the rest of the perceptual field. I may either concentrate my attention or diffuse it over the perceptual field. We could summarize this character of observation by the experience that there is always more to see

(11/10). This is what is important: I am overwhelmed by a surplus of reality that is never exhausted by observation. This is very fundamental. I have the impression of borrowing from a treasure that is never exhausted. To learn is only to borrow something from this surplus of appearances.

Sartre claims that in the image as opposed to the object of perception we have knowledge first; there is no step by step process (10/10). I am not quite convinced by Sartre's argument on this point. There is, he says, no progression in learning; the image is complete at the moment of its appearance. If I try to imagine a monument and then try to count its columns, if I don't know how many columns the monument has, I cannot look to my image of the monument to provide greater accuracy. The image is immediately complete; it has or has not three or four columns. I cannot imagine more than I know. My previous knowledge is embodied in an image, but the image does not go further than what I already know (127/114). I am not sure that that this is true; it's surely not true of fiction. Perhaps too much is linked here to the problem of absence. In the case of absence I cannot put into my image what is not already in the thing. If I don't know something about the thing, I cannot fill in the gaps. In contrast, I can develop a fiction indefinitely, because fiction is not ruled by reality, by a reality existing elsewhere. This for me is the questionable aspect of Sartre's analysis; it is too much tied to the situation of absence where the object existent elsewhere finally rules the image. Therefore it's not a good example of spontaneity. I should have preferred to start from the fiction, where my spontaneity is more obvious. The image of the absent is ruled by the properties of the existent, because absence is finally a characteristic of reality. It's the same reality either present or absent. The properties of the real thing do not depend on whether it's present or absent.

Sartre's argument that the image is immediately complete may also be the product of the claim that the image is poor (11/10–11). I don't know whether this claim is linked to another situation that is not as paradigmatic as Sartre claims. When I read a book, I sometimes stop reading and try to imagine a situation—for example, the crime being depicted. The fact that I stop reading perhaps imposes a certain stability on the image and its lack of development. I wonder whether it's not the fact that in stopping my reading, I dwell on an image, and then the interruption by the dynamism of thought is reflected in the poverty of the image. What is, I think, true in this analysis is that we are never sure when we discuss an example whether we can conclude something about images in general. Wittgenstein has warned us against the claim to master the field. Perhaps we have to remain with examples. Sartre, though, like Husserl, is more systematic. He thinks that since we have to do with essences, there is something paradigmatic, something that permits essential descriptions. We have to deal with essential traits, not universal ones. It is true, though, that in comparison to observation or perception, we do not have this feeling in images of the overflow of the aspects of perception. It's also true that if we rely only on the context of the absent that there is an essential poverty of the image. Sartre uses this point as an argument against the confusion between image and perception. "[T]he objects of the world of images can in no way exist in the world of perception. . . . [T]he object of the image is never more than the consciousness one has . . ." (12/11). This is why we must speak not of observation but of quasi-observation (13/12), because we are observing a certain appearance. Sartre himself speaks of images and therefore uses substantives. The use of substantives is imposed on us by the fact that there is "something" to observe. It's not a thing, but nevertheless it's not nothing; it's something. To be present in an image is a mode of appearing. This is why we speak of observation. Ryle also dealt with this problem, when he put the "seeing" in quotation marks. I see something, but I "see" my image. The same verbs keep recurring—to see, to hear—and with the verb comes the substantive correlate. I have an image of sound, so I have sound appearing. I have colors and shapes appearing. Sartre ends this section by acknowledging that there is something paradoxical in the expression quasi-observation, because while there is something quasi-external in the image, because we observe it, it's also internal in the sense that we determine the image by what we know (13/12). It's only what I know about the object, my friend Peter, the information that I have not forgotten, that allows me to produce an image. In a sense there is nothing else in the image than my knowledge put in the form of an image. I nourish my image with my knowledge. What I know about my friend appears to me in the form of this shadow presence.

The third and ultimately main trait of the image concerns the status of the object when appearing in image, the object's nothingness (14/13). It may be that the fundamental contribution of phenomenology is to have made of nothingness a phenomenological feature of the imaginary. "All consciousness is consciousness of . . ." (14/13), but when we become conscious of the image, it is in the reflective act that we read the trait of absence in the image. To introduce this notion of nothingness, we have to introduce something that has not been already considered, the element of belief, because being and nothingness are not characteristics of the thing. We cannot say that we have to add the thing's being to its color, its weight, and so on. It's an aspect of what Sartre calls the positional act, the way in which we posit the thing (15–16/14–15). This vocabulary of the positional act is not so far from the vocabulary of belief coming from Hume. When we speak of something as existing, it's a way of positing it as existing. Therefore, there are not only modes of givenness—for example, the givenness of something as an image—but within these modes of givenness there is a certain dimension, a dimension of belief (16/15), that has to be expressed in terms of the modes of positing, in terms of the characteristics of positional acts. What does it mean to posit a tree *in image* (*"en image"*) (15/14)? It is not to posit it first in the world, then to exclude it afterward according to external criteria. The image must contain in its very nature an element of basic distinction. Reflective investigation shows that this element lies in the positional act of imaginative consciousness. When we introduce this notion of the positional act, we may already start to display the image family, because there are several modes of nothingness. Sartre has a kind of intuitive insight into the problem but one that is not developed very accurately. Anglo-American logicians would treat the problem more accurately in terms of a logic of modality. The conjunction between the logic of modality and Sartre's phenomenology of being and nothingness could be fruitful.

Sartre considers four modes of nothingness: the nonexistent, the absent, the existing elsewhere, and what he calls neutralized existence, that is, suspension of belief (16/15). He says there are only four modes, so it's more or less a philosophical insight. Unfortunately, he does not provide examples of these four cases, but I shall try to do so on the basis of the context and the examples that will appear in the following part of the book. First, there is no doubt that *nonexistence* is the case of fiction, for example, the Dürer engraving, "The Knight, Death, and the Devil." The classical examples are the centaur and the chimera. All through the literature on the subject we have these fantastic objects that have no place, that are neither present nor absent but nonexisting.

I have some difficulty with the difference between Sartre's second and third modes, since *absence* and *existence elsewhere* seem to be the same thing. But these are not the same phenomenological experiences. Our sense of absence arises when I enter a room looking for somebody but don't find him. I say he is absent, because I was expecting his presence, and I am disappointed. The element of expectation plus disappointment is fundamental to absence. With the *existing elsewhere*, there is not this disappointed expectation. I am directly related to something existing elsewhere. The negation is implicit, because to exist elsewhere is not to be present here and now. The here and now is implicitly negated. (According to Sartre's terminology, then, the example of the "absent" Peter that we have considered to this point is not exactly a case of absence.) If we want to distinguish the absent from existence elsewhere, the former is a stronger case of existing elsewhere. Perhaps the difference is only that in the first case the negation is explicit and in the second case it's merely implicit.

The fourth mode, the *neutralized positing*, the *suspension of belief*, concerns the case of the status of the picture—the portrait, the painting—as perceived object, in which I suspend the positing of existence in order to address myself to the depicted thing. When I am in a gallery of paintings, I perceive them but in a neutralized way, since I don't posit the existence of the canvas. I go through the canvas toward the depicted object which may be *existent elsewhere* (if it is the portrait of somebody), *absent* (if, for example, dead), or *nonexistent* (if something that does not exist). If I am right in my interpretation of Sartre's rather cryptic presentation of these four modes of nothingness, the painting must begin as the fourth case in order to be furthermore one of the three other cases. But Sartre's presentation is something offered very quickly.

I shall try to show in the next lecture that there is less parallelism than Sartre claims between the nonexistence of the fiction and the absence of my friend Peter, because the problem of the object is quite different in each case. I may speak of the sameness of Peter as the sameness of the referent of a perception and the referent of an image. But this is not the case for the chimera. Sartre solved the problem in a footnote, saying that the chimera exists nowhere, neither in the mind nor in an object (8, n. 1/8, n. 5). We must treat nonexistence as a kind of radical absence, the absence that could not be compensated for by a possible perception. This therefore preserves the objective dimension of nonexistence. But Sartre's book is not about fiction, although there is something about it in the chapter, "The Imaginary Life." I wonder whether the whole work does not suffer from the tyranny of its example. It is the example finally not so much of absence but of existing elsewhere. That example can be justified by the general strategy of the work: to break with the illusion of immanence. The case of absence is the most favorable for fighting against this illusion, because the absent living object definitely exists elsewhere, so we cannot put it in the mind. In contrast, if we start with the chimera, we would always be tempted to put the chimera in our mind as a little thing that dwells there. We cannot do that with the absent object, because it has its own existence elsewhere. But can we construct the case of the chimera along the lines of the analysis provided by the description of my absent friend? There I have some doubts, as I shall develop in the next lecture.

Sartre contends that there are only four possible cases of nothingness, but he does so without providing the rules of the construction. I don't claim that there are only four possible cases. Yet we may say at least that there is something common to the four he did describe: the "privative, negative character of the positional acts of the image" (17/15). What makes it difficult to recognize this negative character is that it is placed on something intuitive. Here once more we have to acknowledge that the image is not only relational, as Sartre says, but an appearance. Because what is negated here? On what is the emphasis of negation put? On the appearance. This is said very clearly: "In the image, belief posits the intuition but not Peter" (18/16). Sartre also says that Peter is "'intuitive-absent,' given to intuition as absent" (18/16). The term *intuitive-absent* is one of the best expressions in the book; it is the most striking and surely the most convincing. The status of the image is intuitive-absent. We rely on the quasi-observation or the intuitive. We have discussed how Sartre develops the nature of observation, and the quasi is interpreted by means of the absent. Peter is "given to intuition as absent." We see once more the paradoxical character that Price also emphasized when he said that phenomenology must describe what is. If we ask where is the image, it is where it is. The image imposes its own character even if it defeats our language. Our language is defeated in the sense that in the image there is a kind of assertion but also the destruction of an assertion. The image asserts itself and destroys itself to the extent that it presents its object as not being.

Once more we have to say something about what is bracketed in this analysis and which will reemerge in Sartre's chapter on the imaginary life: all the magic of the image, its fascination. The possibility of being fascinated by the image relies not on its character of absence but rather on its character as intuitive, on the fact that there are appearances. We may become fascinated by the appearances and forget the element of absence. Sartre will say that the fascination is not about the image but about the reaction to the image. He will be obliged to isolate the image from our reactions to it in order to have the pure appearance. He says that he provides here only the statics of the image (19/17).[4]

In the next lecture, lecture 13, I shall speak of the image family, namely, Sartre's attempt to rebuild the whole field on the basis of my friend Peter who lives in Berlin. I shall treat Sartre's discussion of the fourth characteristic of the image, its spontaneity. In lecture 14 I shall examine Sartre's discussion of the imaginary life. This lecture will provide a transition to what I shall undertake in the third part of the course, a kind of functional approach to the image: what we do with our images in order to do something other than only to have an image. Perhaps Sartre accurately describes that he analyzes only the statics of the image.

13
Sartre (2)

In this lecture I want to discuss mainly the second of three topics in Sartre's phenomenology of the image. Let me recall the general framework of his book *The Psychology of Imagination*. First, he wants to analyze the essential structure of the image and the paradigmatic case of an absent person. (When we discuss the role of desire and the quasi-presence in the third theme in Sartre, we shall see that it is important that the absence is an absence of a person, not only of a lost object or something like that.) The first issue, then, is to isolate a paradigmatic case and treat it according it to the method of essential description. Second, Sartre wants to rebuild the general field of imagination along the line of this first inquiry. This is the topic of his chapter titled "The Image Family." Third, we shall see how the imaginary life introduces new dimensions related to belief, desire, and all of the environment surrounding an image, since Sartre had proceeded thus far by way of the abstraction that I have or produce an image. The existential background of the production of the image was bracketed. So the three steps are, first, the theory of absence; second, the image family; and then, third, the imaginary life.

In lecture 12, we had nearly finished the first part of this inquiry. There was only a last distinctive character that had not been treated, and it will provide us with a transition to the second part. In discussing the first part, we said initially that for Sartre an image is a relation to something. This point was set over against the illusion of the image's immanence, an illusion against which Sartre's first book on the imagination, *Imagination: A Psychological Critique*, was written. We qualified Sartre's argument, though, as follows. Despite that the image exists in relation to, that it is a way of being directed toward, an absent object and is not a thing in the mind, we have to say that something nevertheless appears. This is the paradox of the image; it has its referent outside of the mind. In the case of absence, there is only one referent, the referent of both the image and the perception. Nevertheless, something appears before the mind. The second trait of the first part was precisely this character of quasi-observation, since something appears, although it is not the thing itself but the thing in image. It had most of the characteristics of an observation, but if observation involves the inexhaustibility of the real over there, then Sartre had insisted in that respect on the poverty of the image. Perhaps that poorness is typical of the image of absence and not, for example, of the fiction. I shall return to that subject in the next lecture. The third point was that the ontological character of the appearance is nothingness. To introduce this notion of nothingness, Sartre had to introduce at the same time the positing act. We posit the real as existing, whereas we posit the image as nonexisting. The dimension of belief is here at stake; we believe in the image as nonexisting. To bring together the second and the third traits, Sartre says that the image is intuitive-absent.

The fourth trait, which we had not described, concerns the spontaneity of consciousness in the imagination (Sartre 1948/1966, 18/17).[1] This characteristic is difficult to grasp for two reasons. First, it does not belong to the intentional act as such, which is directed toward the thing as absent. It pertains to what Husserl and Sartre call the reflective dimension, the fact that at the same time that consciousness is consciousness of something, it is also consciousness of itself (15/14). If it were unconscious, then we would have the paradox of a consciousness of something that is not itself a consciousness. We want therefore to introduce here what Sartre calls a nonthetic consciousness (234–35/209–10), that is to say, an aspect of consciousness that does not posit anything but which is conscious of another aspect of consciousness positing something. This is described at length in *Being and Nothingness* where Sartre writes of "consciousness (of)."[2] It's not a consciousness of something but a consciousness that I am now having an image. It's a transversal consciousness (18/17) that has to do with the structure of time. The issue of the nonthetic consciousness in Sartre is a very difficult problem, since it is the possibility of reflection before reflection. When I look at something, I know in a sense that I am looking, but it's not a thematic consciousness of now being looking. There is a dormant or inchoative self-consciousness accompanying consciousness. It is for this inchoative self-consciousness that is not thetic, that does not posit something, not even itself, that we may speak of a passivity or activity. The opposition between being passive or being active belongs to this nonthetic consciousness. As I shall proceed to elaborate, both activity and passivity are part of the spontaneity of consciousness. The fundamental character of the image is spontaneity, as opposed to receptivity in perception.

Here arises the second difficulty in grasping the concept of the spontaneity of consciousness. It's very difficult to describe the concept of spontaneity correctly, because we tend to identify it with the will. For us, the conscious form of being spontaneous is to will, to act by decision. But we must acknowledge that this creative aspect of the image (18/17)—the claim that we put something into the image, if only what we already know—may appear to us either as free or as fascinated—as captured or bound by the image—as we shall see in the next lecture. It is always an aspect of spontaneity that it may be bound or be free. Nevertheless, it's spontaneity. We must disentangle the concept of spontaneity from that of the will and the voluntary and be prepared to speak of a spontaneity that is involuntary in the sense that it is not at our disposal in a positive way (24/23). At issue is the notion of an act. We are acting but not necessarily as a willing agent. This difficulty was already addressed in Husserl and is present also in analytic philosophy, although it's never treated as such.[3] When John Searle, for example, speaks of a speech act, what does he mean by speech *act*? We must have a concept of spontaneity and therefore consider all the possibilities that this spontaneity may be bound or unbound. I am not sure that Searle and other linguistic analysts have reflected on the possibility of speaking of an act in general that does not require introducing a philosophy of will. The concept of spontaneity is linked to the notion of a positional act, and it does not imply a psychology of the will. On the contrary, we shall see that in most cases of imaginary life, at least those that Sartre describes, our spontaneity appears to us in the form of boundness. We must be prepared to admit that involuntariness does not exclude spontaneity but rather presupposes spontaneity. Sartre will say in a later part of *The Psychology of Imagination*, as we shall see in the next lecture, that we must not confuse fatality and determinism. Determinism is an aspect of things, while fatality is something that may happen only to a consciousness. Only a consciousness may be free or fascinated, because these are accidents of spontaneity. It's within the dimension of spontaneity that we may speak either of freedom or of fatality. In the present part of the book Sartre brackets the alternative of freedom or fascination/fatality to speak only in terms of spontaneity. He examines the abstract example, I produce an image of Peter, and considers whether I produce it freely or by coercion. He brackets alternatives to emphasize only that I produce, which is an act of spontaneity. The section on spontaneity is very short (18–19/17), because the concept is very abstract. It's only the condition for discussing freedom or the lack of freedom. It concerns only the relationship of the image to its object, the fact that I posit the object as nothingness. Because of the abstractness of the example, Sartre remarks that "the relationship between the image and its object is still very obscure" (21/19).

What Sartre has undertaken in this first part of his text is analysis of what he calls the "statics of the image" (21/20), whereas when he speaks of the imaginary life, he shall proceed from the statics to a functional approach, how the image functions in life. In the present part he raises the question, how do images appear? Outside of any context he has framed the question of appearance as nothingness. The analysis is decontextualized. This is a good way to proceed in an essential inquiry.

When we turn to the second issue in Sartre's text, the image family, the topic is particularly interesting for us if we keep in mind the same difficulty as discussed in Ryle. Recall that Ryle had addressed the problem: does the notion of a picture belong to the same category in the philosophy of the mind as a mental image or as playing, pretending? And he had tried to reconstruct the whole field on the basis of pretending. Pretending in a game— for example, the girl who pretends that her doll is smiling—was for him the model. Ryle then tried to claim that when we have a mental image, in fact we pretend to see. Sartre will take the opposite path and construct the whole field of the image on the basis of the portrait. For him the portrait— the picture of—will be the starting point. Why? As a first survey of this difficult, cumbersome chapter, for Sartre the solution of the problem of the unity of the field does not rely on the intention to produce the presence of something absent but on the role of what he calls the *matter* of the image. The matter functions as an analogue, "as an equivalent, of the perception" (23/22). The term in the original French text is *analogon* and comes from Husserl.[4]

At issue is the famous problem of the hyletic, which is the most controversial part of the theory of perception. I have already spoken of this notion in our discussion of Husserl. Husserl claimed that when I perceive this red thing, the red of the object is not in my mind but belongs to the thing, the intentional object. It is transcendent. But in order to have a transcendent red of the object, I must animate (23/22) a red that is an impression I undergo; I am, so to say, the red. It's through a nonintentional impression that I aim at an impression. As we have discussed, this implies a very difficult situation, because I have two reds. On the one hand, I have the red of the object, or in the preferable terms of linguistic analysis, the red is a predicate in language only. It's predicated of the object. On the other hand, I have an impressional red, the psychophysiological sensation corresponding to a change in brain processes whatever it may be, a cortical impression. Sartre's genial idea is to say that what does not work in a theory of perception—to have an impression animated by an intention and directed toward the homonym, so to say, of the impression—works quite well with the image. What Husserl had done when he was speaking of an impressional matter (*hylē*) was in fact a theory of the image, because in the image we have an analogue of the thing. This is precisely what we call a portrait. Sartre thinks, therefore, that if we could show how the analogue works in the case of the portrait—of the drawing of the face on the picture as the analogue of the real face, of the face as it could be perceived—then we would have a good model for the mental image (27–34/26–31). The claim is that it's quite possible that there is an analogue in the mental image although one more hidden, more concealed, because it has no physical basis but only a kind of mental existence. As we shall discuss shortly, Sartre will try, in the part of the book called "The Probable," to isolate this analogue as perhaps some ocular movements or some changes in my feelings that would provide the equivalent of the analogue in the portrait. The theory is a powerful one, starting from a material analogue in the portrait and then progressively decreasing the thickness of the analogue to a point where it is quite invisible and must be derived only on the basis of some hints and clues provided by inductive psychology. Sartre's move to discussion of the matter of the image explains a strange shift in the paradigmatic examples in his book. He started with the mental image, my friend Peter in Berlin, and four characteristics were derived from the description of the mental image. Then suddenly he shifts to the portrait, because it's the portrait that provides us with the solution of the material or matter (*hylē*) of the image. The vocabulary is Aristotelian with its opposition between matter and form. Husserl had preserved this vocabulary, speaking of *hylē* (matter) and *morphē* (form). There is the hyletic and morphemic of perception.

Let us see how Sartre's approach here works. I must say that I am very much impressed by this analysis, because I don't see how we can put within the same framework a photograph and a mental image if there is not in common some equivalent, some representative of the real object that is overcome, that serves as a basis for a leap besides and beyond the material support. To put it in more metaphorical terms, there must be a material support for the leap toward the unreal. According to Sartre's thesis, what is common to all the cases is this movement toward the unreal. The differentiation within the class of attitudes toward the unreal is the role of the material support for this movement toward the unreal. A good clue for approaching this problem is the possibility of substituting one material support for the other and therefore showing that they play the same role. Let us say that I try to recall the face of my friend. I have three means at my disposal that I may use successively or in a parallel way. I may try to recall my friend's face, I may bring out a photograph from my drawer, or I may use a caricature (22/21). We have then three stages of the same process, three moments of a unique act, which is to aim at or envision the absent (23/22). For one intention I have three different material bases intended to make present for myself the absent object. As I cannot make my friend present directly as a perception, I have recourse to a certain material that acts as an analogue, as an equivalent of perception. The strategy of making present the absent object gives a kind of unity to these discordant analogues. Wanting "'to make him present' to me" (23/22), I may change the analogue that will support this attempt. (Our problem will be whether this analysis is confined only to the question of the absent and whether the fiction, that is to say, the relation to the inexisting object, will be the same. I reserve that discussion for the next lecture.) Therefore, at least in these three cases—a portrait, a caricature, and a mental image—I have the same intention, and in the external element of the photograph or caricature the analogue can be shown. It's the physical support of the image.

Hence the problem is raised: is there not a kind of concealed analogue in the mental image that could be reached by presenting a series of examples in which the material basis is progressively canceled, abolished? The difficulty of the enterprise is whether we are not reintroducing the illusion of immanence by putting something in the mind. The answer to this objection will be to say that this immanent material is meaningless so long as it is not animated by an intention (23/22). The status of this material as such is that of paintings in a gallery when the gallery is closed. They are then only canvases on the wall; they are only material objects. It's only when someone is animating the painting with his or her glance and then seeing somebody depicted in it that it is an image. Absent that, the painting is only a physical object, something that may be stolen, may be burned, and so on. The physical object when it is not animated is not an image. Therefore, if we say that there is some material in the mind, whatever the "in" may mean here, it's not the image that was put in the mind in the tradition of Hume, since this material is not at all an image. It's only a material for producing an image. There is something in the mind, but it's not an image even if we place the material of the image in the mind. It's the equivalent or the representative of the absent object. The image properly said is really absent to the mind just as it is absent to the photograph. So Sartre shall try to construe the matter of the mental image according to the model of the material of the physical analogue of the portrait. This is why for this kind of inquiry the portrait, and no longer the mental image, is taken as the paradigmatic case. The portrait is the paradigmatic case, because it provides us with the independent presence of the material.

The strategy of this chapter is to proceed from the physical density of the analogical representative (26/24) in the portrait and move in the direction of the problematic mental status of this analogue in the mental image. I shall not describe in detail Sartre's intermediary cases. Here Sartre displays the

talent of the novelist with an abundance of detail. There is not only cleverness in these examples, but some are very striking. For example, he develops
the case of an actor's onstage imitation of another well-known actor. The
bodily movements of the onstage actor provide the likeness of the absent
original actor (34–40/32–38). When we attend such a spectacle, we retain
only a few clues that allow us to create for ourselves the absent image of the
other actor. The spectator constitutes the analogue by oneself, extracting
from the display only the clues necessary to embody the absent image. The
spectator uses only some of the features as analogues plus some emotional
values embodied in the gesture and the face, what we call their expressive-
ness (40/37). They become expressive of something else. We constitute
the analogue by ourselves. We abstract the analogue for the representation.

When Sartre moves from the case of imitation to that of schematic drawing (40–46/38–43), the intuitive element that plays the role of the analogue
is still further reduced, and the activity of consciousness building for itself
the analogue is increased. Sometimes the real similarity with the model is
very fragile and reduced to a few abstract features. (The example of schematic drawing is very close to what Max Black, in *Models and Metaphors*,
calls an analogue model, as we shall discuss in a subsequent lecture.) When
I draw in very schematic traits a person who is running (41/38), I intend
an absent running person, but I do so on the basis only of some structural
relationships between dots and strokes of the pen. The schematic drawing provides a guideline for organizing the picture in such a way that it
represents a running person. It's the movement of my body that enacts a
pantomime of the drawing. We have a "knowledge which enacts a symbolic pantomime and a pantomime which is hypostatized, projected into
the object" (44/41). From the portrait to the imitation to the schematic
drawing, there is a decrease in the physical analogue that is itself constituted
by some movement of my body and some feelings that gather scattered impressions. The role of the body and the movement of the body that draws
the drawing will be key in the production of the mental image, since here
it is only eye movements and some feelings related to the absent thing that
carry the movement toward the unreal (47–48/44). By contrast, in perception, the movements of the eyes when I look at a drawing are ruled by the
object. With schematic drawings, it's my knowledge and the intending of
the object as aimed at abstractly that rule the movements. They are ruled
by a knowledge and no longer by the presence of the thing, and they are
felt as spontaneous (47/44). I may say that in the schematic drawing I see
a person running, but I see the person in an image because I know that I
produce the pattern (41/38). We are close to getting the key to the problem

of the mental image, since already in the case of the schematic drawing we may observe the embodiment of a knowledge. An abstract type of a person running through some movements gives a body to the intention.

We may proceed a step further with examples where we bring the analogue within the picture. We constitute not only the image but the analogue. Think of when we see some faces in the fire, some figures on the wall, motifs in a tapestry, and so on (49–52/45–48). The movement of our eyes and the general movement of our body shape the forms; they interpret some meaningless spots as forms. The *matter* is not the spot or the movement of the flame but our way of looking at it and drawing the figures in the smoke or in the clouds or in the fire. The figure is both absent and present, since I put in the flame the analogue that I see. It's an analogue of a figure or of a face that I don't see but that I imagine.

The example that is the closest to the mental image is provided by the hypnagogic, the kind of images that we have when we are close to sleep (52–71/48–65). They provide an interesting link toward the pure mental image, because it's mainly some phosphenes in the eyes (57/52) that provide a physical, bodily basis for projecting the image. What is interesting in this case is not only that the thinness of the analogue is mainly provided merely by some movement of the eyes (and perhaps some light inside the eyes [64–65/59]) but that we have entered the state of fascination and have a conviction that what appears in the image exists (63/57–58). This issue introduces for the first time the problem of fascination that will be dealt with in the final part of the book under the title of "The Imaginary Life." In the state of fascination, the control of the real has collapsed. This state is in contrast with the real, which, by its collapse, leaves room for belief in the existence of what appears. This consequence does not mean that there is no boundary line between the unreal and the real. But when the real disappears as the background for the unreal, and when I am bound by the presence of the image, then this fatalism in the play of images becomes a kind of equivalent of reality. Fatalism has no place in the physical world and determinism no place in consciousness. In captive consciousness the representation of the real and of the possible is lacking (67/61–62). This argument will be central to the final part of Sartre's text. The image occupies the whole place. This does not mean that the image is mistaken for the real, but there is no real to provide a contrast. Thanks to the lack of contrast with the real and the state of fascination of the mind, the unreal seems to imitate the real.

The mental image, then, may be introduced at the end of this analysis (74–77/68–70). It was at the beginning in the first chapter, but it's at the end in the second chapter, because now we have no direct access through the analogous representative that was provided by physical things in all the preceding examples, even in the case of the hypnagogic. The physical representative had been increasingly impoverished (73/66), and then there is a boundary case where the material has to be reconstructed inductively. Here phenomenology yields to an inductive psychology (77/70). The only claim of phenomenology at this juncture is that there is a material basis to the mental image. What kind of right does Sartre's argument have, though, if not by means of an argument by analogy? I am not sure how we know that this analogy between, let us say, a portrait and a mental picture relies on an essential structure. I was struck by the boldness of Sartre, who keeps repeating that there is no doubt that the mental image has a material. There is no doubt, because he thinks that this relation between a matter and an animating intention is a phenomenological given. Even if we don't know what the matter is, we must assume it, because it's an essential structure of consciousness to build its intention on a matter. What the matter is will be the object of certain conjectures, for example, that it is constituted by movements, by feeling, and so on. This is conjectural, but what is not conjectural according to Sartre is that there is a matter for the mental image that will play the same role as the physical analogue in the case of the portrait. The portrait has displayed its material contents, and then we construct the material for the mental image on the basis of this analogy.

> It would now seem that all we need do is to describe this analogical content just as we described the material contents of the consciousness of the portrait, or of the impersonation [the imitation of one artist by another]. But here we meet with a great deal of difficulty: in the cases we have previously described, when the truly imaginative consciousness wanes, there remain a sensible residue which is describable; namely the painted canvas or the spot on the wall. In repeating certain movements or in permitting the lines and the colors of the painting to act upon us, we could at least reconstruct "the analogue" without too much trouble, from this sensible residue, and do so without actually forming the imaginative consciousness over again. The material of my imaginative consciousness of the portrait was obviously this painted canvas. It must be admitted that reflective description does not tell us directly anything concerning the representative material of the mental image. This is due to the fact that when the imaginative consciousness is destroyed its transcendental content is destroyed with it; no describable residue remains, we are confronted by another synthetic consciousness which has nothing in common with the first. We cannot therefore hope to get at this content by introspection. We must choose: either we form the image, and get to know the content only by its function as analogue (whether we form a non-reflective or reflective conscious-

ness), we apprehend on it the qualities of the envisioned object; or we do not form the image, in which case we no longer have the content, nothing remains of it. In a word, we know—since this is an *essential* necessity—that in the mental image there is a psychic factor which functions as analogue but when we wish to ascertain more clearly the nature and components of this factor we are reduced to conjectures. (76–77/69–70, emphasis added)

There is, according to Sartre, an essential necessity that there is such a material animated by the intention toward nothingness, toward the unreal existence of the image. But it's by conjecture that I may say what it is. That it is is evident, but what it is is a subject of conjecture.

We must, therefore, leave the sure ground of phenomenological description and turn to experimental psychology. That is, form hypotheses and seek evidences in observations and experiment, just as is done in the experimental sciences. Such evidences never permit us to go beyond the domain of the probable. (77/70)

The reason why the second part of Sartre's text, to which his book now turns, is called "The Probable: The Nature of the Analogue in the Mental Image," is because we have no direct access to the image's material. The material dies with the image. When we have a mental image, we are beyond the material, and if we try to isolate the material, then the image dies. We can approach the nature of the material of the mental image only by conjecture.

But how do I know that there is such a material or what is its nature? Sartre's presupposition is that a picture (or a portrait) and a mental image belong to the same function. The identity of the intention justifies my looking for a material in both cases. The sameness of intention allows me to look for a sameness in material. This is the fundamental argument here, that there is a sameness in attitude that calls for a sameness in the material supporting this attitude. As I have already begun to suggest, though, I wonder to what extent the intention is the same. Before drawing all the consequences for the material of the similarity in intention, we must be sure that we have only one kind of intention. This similarity of intention may be true to the extent that all the examples have to do with absence. There may be an image family of absence. But I am not sure that this image family includes inexisting objects and for one fundamental reason. We may speak of an analogue in the case of the absent because there is an original. We have a rule for using the word *analogue*: something is an analogue to something else that can be shown. In all the cases that can be related to absence, the analogue stands for a real thing. But what about the fiction? I cannot say that in the case of the fiction. This will be my subject in following lectures, where I shall deal mainly with fictions. So I was wondering whether the problem of fiction is already included in Sartre's analysis. Sartre insists that when I recall the image of my friend Peter, what I want to do is to make him appear in image. As we shall see, this will be the basis of fascination, because I want to possess something in absence. But can we say that my intention in the case of a fiction is to make something appear in an image, that I want to possess it in absence? I wonder whether here the portrait is still paradigmatic. Only one class of images, I think, falls under this general description.

To put this in terms of logic, I am tempted to say that there is not a symmetry in Sartre's classifications. Recall that Sartre divides perception and the image, and he says that the image depicts negation. In the image there are four categories of negation: absence, presence elsewhere, nonexistence, and suspended existence. (To exist elsewhere and to be absent are more or less the same.) If, however, we draw the dividing line instead between the real and the unreal, presence and absence are subclasses of the real. Is there not a radical difference between two dividing lines, Sartre's division between presence and absence and a division between the real and unreal? For Sartre, negation is a form of nothingness. But is the nothingness of absence of the same nature as the nothingness of the unreal, because the unreal is not only absent, but opposed to possible reality? I wonder, then, whether there is not more continuity between presence and absence than between the real and the unreal. The proof is that between the absent and the present we may have the same referent. This was an important argument in Sartre, that the same Peter may be seen and may be imagined in absence. In a statement about particulars, to put it in the language of P. F. Strawson, there is one part of the nothingness that is in common with presence: the same referent. We have the same process of identification of particulars. The absent is a case of reality, whereas the fiction is not only absent but does not belong to the real. To put that in other terms, I should say that presence and absence are distinctions relative to reality, while fiction has to do with the unreal. There is a lack of consistency in Sartre's vocabulary. He shifts constantly from the unreal to the absent, and they are not equivalent terms. In the final chapter, for example, he speaks of the absent as a relation to the unreal (177–78/159–60). The notion of nothingness is a cloudy term that covers several inconsistent cases.

Even if we don't want to emphasize the logical difficulties here, the phenomenological difficulties are enormous, because the notion of an original can no longer provide us with a leading thread for speaking of the analogue in the case of fiction. I wonder whether the fiction is based on an analogue and therefore whether the theory of the analogue still works here. In fiction, the correlative term of the original cannot be shown, cannot be identified as the same. I shall return to this question in the next lecture's discussion of the problem of the imaginary life, because the theory of imaginary life is an extension of the theory of absence and the latter, to my mind, does not cover the theory of fiction.

Let me close with a few comments about Sartre's treatment of the analogue in the mental image as discussed in the part on "The Probable." Sartre claims that we can construe this conjectural analogue in the mental image in three ways. On the one hand, we have in the mental image a knowledge. (In French, the term for knowledge here is not *connaissance* but *savoir*, meaning that we know something about.) It's a knowledge about, what I know about my friend Peter. This knowledge is not presented as conceptual knowledge but as a debased form of knowledge (83/75). Sartre forges the concept of *savoir imageant*, which I would translate not as imaginative knowledge (for example, 89/80) but as imaging knowledge. Knowledge here presents more or less the same problem as the schema in Kant (87/78). The schema is a rule for producing a certain number of images, but this rule is not known as such, since if it were, then it would become a concept. There is, then, a conceptual structure but one that emerges in the image. There is a conversion of conceptual knowledge in the image. Knowledge transforms itself by a kind of degradation or debasement in the image. It becomes intuitive; it becomes an expectation of an image. "If we begin with knowledge, the image will arise as a result of thought trying to make contact with the presences" (96/86). We have a conversion to intuitivity in knowledge itself. Sartre relies here mainly on the Würzburg psychological school (89/80) and its experiments on what people feel when they have a notion in mind. There is a conversion to concretion of conceptual thought. This is the first step toward the construction of a mental analogue of the absent thing.

The second component is feeling (96–104/87–94). Here too we must qualify the theory of feeling usually available, because feelings are too often treated as merely subjective states, as closed on themselves (97/87). There is a traditional consensus concerning the solipsism of affectivity. We must correct this phenomenology of feeling and assume that feelings too are intentional, that hatred is hatred of, that love is love of, that when we feel fear, the world appears as fearful (98/88). The intentionality of feeling contributes to an elaboration of a substitute for an absent thing. We may have an emotional description, an emotional equivalent of the thing. We have the emotional texture of a face, of the way in which somebody appears in his or her general way of behaving. I have an affective image of the other.

Applying that to the notion of desire—of desire of—we have in our need, in our lacking, a negative presence of the other.

> In a word, desire is a blind effort to possess on the level of representation what I already possess on the affective level; through the affective synthesis it envisions a "beyond" which it pursues without being able to know it; it directs itself upon the affective "something" which is now given to it and apprehends it as the representative of the desired thing. (102/91–92)

We may speak with some caution, in a very conjectural way, of an emotional representative of the absent thing.

This analysis confirms more and more that it is appropriate to absence and to a certain kind of absence, the absence of someone. I am related emotionally to the absent by desire—by love and hatred and so on—and desire may pertain only to a category of absence. It pertains not to absence in general but only to a category of absence because the desire to possess in absence concerns people to whom we are related by emotions. We must have an emotional tie that we nourish by images. Here the image is a stage in the desire, and it's a way of staging the desire and playing its presence. Again, as I shall try to show in the next lecture, I don't think that fiction functions in that way. Fiction is not a substitute for presence but rather shapes the world in a new way. That is quite different from trying to possess something that exists already but from which we are separated by distance. It is not the main function of fiction to create the illusion of presence or to attempt to fill up the gap of absence. As soon as we introduce this emotional representative of the absent, we are within a narrow group of imaginative processes, and we no longer cover the whole field.

The same may be said, if in perhaps a less striking way, of the third component of a conjectural analogue, kinesthetic movements (104–19/94–107). If the first kind of equivalent of an analogue lay in a cognitive schema of the absent and the second in an emotional schema, the third is a kinesthetic equivalent. If we try to imagine an absent thing, such as a person, in effect we draw the shape of the absent face. It has been shown by psychological experiments that in drawing this image, we have movements of our eyes (106/95–96). If we prevent these movements of the eye, we cannot produce the image. If we block the eyes, then we cannot draw the portrait mentally (116/104). There is a kinesthetic portrait that plays the role of the photograph or of the physical portrait. Sartre relies mainly on studies where kinesthetic movement substituted for perception. We may, for example, replace a visual figure by a drawing that we undertake. A muscular structure may represent a visual form. Sartre's claim is that if this role of kinesthetic movement is true for visual shapes that can be seen, it is also true for absent shapes. If visual shapes may be substituted through a kinesthetic structure, then by extension a kinesthetic structure may become the representative of an absent thing (117/105).

To conclude, we have two kinds of analogical *matter*, kinesthetic impressions and emotional schemas (117/105). There is no concurrence between the two kinds of explanations, since the kinesthetic equivalent brings out mainly the spatial features of the absent object, whereas the emotional schema describes its qualitative aspects. In a human face, for example, we have these two elements, the structure in terms of the spatial distribution of features but also the global appearance, the facial expression, which has more emotional characteristics than geometrical conditions. The kinesthetic and the emotional merge here in the constitution of an analogical matter. This is the way in which the "object, when absent, presents itself through a presence" (124/111) that is an affective and kinesthetic analogue. According to Sartre, the presence of the analogue explains why we continue to speak of images as seen and heard and nevertheless are nowhere (124/111). There is really a presence, but it is a presence that is overcome by the absence. It is through this tiny presence of the analogue that we envision the absent thing. This contradiction seems to belong to the nature of the image. How? A first belief aims at the object itself in images. A second, reflective consciousness is a belief in the existence of the image. Then I say that I see the image of the Pantheon (127/114). The contradiction proceeds from the belief transposed in reflection. Then a "something" intervenes, which is the analogon, with an affective and a kinesthetic presence. The illusion of immanence starts when we ascribe to the analogon the feature of the absent. But there is no consciousness of this analogon. Thanks to its affective quality, the image escapes the law of individuation as well as that of identity. In that way, we may claim that an image is an intention toward but embodied in an affective-kinesthetic presence that gives to the image a stable appearance. Far from being a "reborn sensation," the image is "an essential structure of consciousness" (134/120).

As we see, all theories of the image have to make sense of this strange way of speaking of it in the vocabulary of entities, in Price's term, despite that it's an operation without an object. But there is a something that justifies our vocabulary of entities despite that the image is an intention of which we should speak with verbs. We should only say that we imagine, not that we have images. But this is not only a mistake in our vocabulary. It is not only because we deal with images as though they were things, but because there is a something in a sense that is the support of this act of imagining. We imagine through a certain analogue which, without being a thing, is nevertheless a something. This is convincing to the extent that it is a theory of absence.

In lecture 14 I address the problem of the inadequacy of this theory in discussing Sartre's treatment of the imaginary life. In lecture 15, I shall start with Gaston Bachelard and introduce my own approach to the problem through metaphor, how a certain use of language develops a certain kind of image, the poetic image. I shall present two or three lectures on the poetic image, the image as a stage in the poetic process. This discussion will offer a complement to what Sartre describes as imaginary life, less in terms of fascination than in terms of creative fiction.

14
Sartre (3)

I want to close this section on the phenomenology of imagination with a summary and a discussion of the last part of Sartre's *The Psychology of Imagination*, which is entitled "The Imaginary Life." Here Sartre lifts some of the brackets placed at the beginning of his work when he decided to isolate the image. In the present part he reconstructs the framework and the background against which this "statics of the image" (Sartre 1948/1966, 21/20) was constituted.[1] Whereas in the section on the statics of the image the emphasis was on spontaneity, the present part is mainly a study of *fascination*, the state of mind of fascination created by the imaginary life. To my thinking, this focus is a second limitation Sartre imposes on the theory of imagination, but it's a limitation coherent with the first one—restricting imagination to the example of absent objects—since it's mainly with absent objects that we are caught in this attempt to make them present and possess them despite their absence. I wonder, then, whether this study of the so-called imaginary life identified with fascination is not more or less parasitic on a theory of absence and less appropriate for fiction. This study adds a second kind of limitation to the subject matter since there may be several other reactions to absence than fascination.

Sartre's choice has a specific motivation, because it will provide us with counterfactuals, since in the state of fascination we seem to mistake images for reality. Sartre orients his study of the imaginary life—on hallucinations, dreams, and these kinds of fascinations—by the image of desire. It is within the framework of desire that his analysis makes sense. The analysis offers further proof that between the image and reality, between the unreal and the real, there is a logical gap. Therefore, Sartre must deal with the apparent counterfactuals provided by fascination. He chooses these examples because they initially provide arguments to those who claim that images are weaker impressions and that we have to separate the image from reality by using secondary criteria extrinsic to the image. Sartre must show that there is here a further factor at work in these counterfactuals that belongs to the world of *belief* and not to the structure of the image. He must introduce the *belief* in the *as though*. When our images are mistaken for reality, it's not a consequence of the image as such but of what we add to the image, of what Sartre calls our reaction to the unreal (195/175). Mistaking the image for reality does not belong to the inner conceptual constitution of the image, to the unreal as such. Sartre first had to speak, in the earlier parts of the book, of the inner constitution of the image, and then he reintroduces a supplementary factor that adds a further complication and tends to blur the distinction that belonged to the image as such. This is one explanation that I would offer of Sartre's strange choice to reduce all of the analysis to fascination. The choice belongs to the strategy of the book, which is directed always against the claim that there are transitions between the real and the unreal. He must prove this argument by responding to less favorable cases.

Another reason for Sartre's attention to fascination may be found in the discussions in his book on the emotions where there is a very pessimistic approach to the world of emotions as inducing magical attitudes toward the real and therefore belonging to the inauthentic way of life. The theory of inauthenticity also plays a great role in *Being and Nothingness,* where the relations of love and hatred and so on are plagued by inauthentic relations when we want to possess the object. The theory of the possessive character of human feelings is reflected as well in the book. We see that in the first lines of the part on "The Imaginary Life."

> We have seen that the act of imagination is a *magical* one. It is an incantation destined to produce the object of one's thought, the thing one desires, in a manner that one can take possession of it. In that act there is always something of the imperious and the infantile, a refusal to take distance or difficulties into account. Thus, the very young child acts upon the world from his bed by orders and entreaties. The objects obey these orders of consciousness: they appear. But they have a very unique existence which we shall attempt to describe. (177/159; emphasis added)

The part begins with a sudden reduction of imagination to a magical relation to the world that is claimed to make sense within the framework of desire. There is a decided reduction, since we have to do with childish attitudes. All the mature uses of imagination in fiction or in models cannot appear within this framework. Imagination is an incantation to obtain things, "to reproduce their integral existence" (177/159) in their absence.

Here the imagination is an attitude that enters into conflict with action, with a responsible way of dealing with things. It is an escape from the task of dealing with things in action, in praxis. By a strange detour, we return to the deceptive (178/160) power of the imagination that we saw in Pascal. Imagination appears less the contrary of perception than the contrary of praxis. Perhaps I push this interpretation too far, but I don't think I am unfair in saying that this is the main line of his argument. Sartre keeps returning to the fact that we are "unrealizing" ourselves when we project on the unreal (for example, see 178/160, 188/169). The more Sartre emphasizes the "unreality" of imaginary objects, the more he emphasizes the depth of self-unrealizing.

> Consciousness is thus constantly surrounded by a retinue of phantom objects. These objects, although at first sight possessing a sensible aspect, are not the same as those of perception. Of course, they can be plants or animals, but this consists of qualities, of species, of relations. Soon as we try to observe one of them we find ourselves confronted with strange creatures beyond the laws of the world of realities. They always occur as indivisible wholes, as absolutes. At once ambiguous, impoverished, and dry, appearing and disappearing in a disjointed manner, they invariably occur as a perpetual "elsewhere," as a perpetual *evasion*. But the evasion to which they invite is not only of the sort which is an escape from actuality, from our preoccupations, our boredoms, they offer us an escape from all worldly constraints, they seem to present themselves as a negation of the condition of being in the world as an *anti-world*. (193–94/173–74; emphases added)

The notion of an "anti-world" is very important and is perhaps the key word of this part of the book. We must join a phenomenology of desire with a phenomenology of absence to obtain the analysis in this last part. The image becomes a stage in the magic attitudes of desire. Two negative elements merge. The lack of something—the negative aspect of need, of lacking what we want—and the absence of the image are superimposed. The quasi-observation of the image plays the role of a fantastic or ghostly presence of the thing. When Sartre speaks of the magic of the image (for example, 177/159), the image is a kind of trick aiming at reviving or recovering our feelings. "[T]he object is reproduced for no other purpose than to arouse the feeling" (203/182). A few pages later he writes of "a dance before the unreal, in the manner that a corps de ballet dances around a statue" (205/183), the statue of the absent. We have imaginary feelings about something absent, but these are feelings in which we believe, because an imaginary feeling is nevertheless a feeling, it's something present. A reading of Proust (209/187) invades this analysis, because Proust keeps returning to this—the side of Swann, the relation with Odette—where the imaginary is a tactic to provide a false presence and disappointment. The image functions as both deceptive and disappointing. There is a preference for the imaginary, which is a way of escaping the difficult nature of the absence. The imaginary offers a deceiving therapy regarding the absence. To prefer the imaginary is then to prefer imaginary feelings and behaviors, because the real surprises and requires adjustment to unforeseeable situations. The essential poverty of the imaginary becomes an escape from the difficult law of action.

It is not by chance that immediately after having developed this fanciful behavior concerning the unreal, Sartre shifts to the pathology of imagination (213/190). He was already on the borderline of a pathological use of imagination, since he addressed a childish way of dealing with absence, the pathology of absence. The dance before the unreal was already on the way toward this pathology. The three cases of the imaginary life treated in this part are: hallucinations—mainly among psychotics but also the dreams of neurosis—dream images, and then, as we have seen, some forms of aesthetic experience in which the magic of quasi-presence works. The problem raised is not at all lacking in interest, since hallucinations and dreams have always provided arguments for the thesis of the fundamental identity between impressions and images. The problem is also important for the purpose of the book, which is to preserve the dividing line between the two in all cases, so it's fundamental that we cope with these apparent counterexamples. Therefore, the question has to be reformulated not as how do we distinguish between images and perceptions, since there is an absolute difference, but how can we sometimes mix images and perceptions. Sartre's answer is that the mixing of the two is not the real problem. The real problem is not that we mistake an image for a perception but that we *believe* in the reality of our image. A more precise reformulation of the problem, then, is "how can the patient believe in the reality of an image which occurs in essence as unreal" (218/195). In essence it is unreal, but in a practical sense it is mistaken for something real. We have to find in the structure of the belief the motives for this apparent confusion.

To say that it is a problem of belief is to say that it's something that happens to the positional act (218/195). This act is recovered, no longer identified by the subject as positional. The reactions to the unreal simulates relations to the real. The solution has to be located in the direction of a phenomenology of fatality (245/220). There is a fatality that conceals the nature of the belief as positing something absent. This happens at the level of what Sartre calls the nonthetic consciousness, not at the level of the thetic, the positional, act (245/220). It's in the relation of the subject to its positional act that something has been distorted. In the nonthetic, nonpositional relationship of consciousness as spontaneous, this spontaneity is no longer acknowledged and recognized by the subject. It's when I am no longer aware of positing the unreal that I mistake it for the real. Something happens at the level of the belief, not at the level of the appearance.

The problem of the dream raises the same question, because it's too often assumed that the dreamer confuses the real and the unreal. This argument is very famous among the French, at least those who keep reading Descartes as the Anglo-American reads Hume. (Descartes is our Hume. We always start from Descartes, but to say that he was wrong, exactly as the Anglo-American uses Hume.) Sartre quotes Descartes's "First Meditation," which is an argument for doubting.

> "I must always consider that I am a man and that consequently I am in the habit of sleeping and representing in my dreams the same things, or very similar things, which I experience when awake. How often have I thought during the night of being in that place, that I was dressed, that I was close to the fire, whereas I was lying naked in my bed. It now seems obvious that it is not with sleeping eyes that I am looking at this paper, that this head I am shaking is not drowsy; that it is deliberately and purposefully that I stretch this hand and that I feel it: what happens in sleep is not at all as clear, as distinct as all this. But in thinking of it carefully, I recall being often deceived during sleep by similar illusions, and, in pausing at that thought, I see very clearly that there are no certain indications by which it is possible to distinguish clearly the wakeful from the sleeping state, that I am completely astonished by it; and my astonishment is such as to almost persuade me that I am asleep." (231/207)[2]

Sartre's argument here, which is very convincing, begins by asking who speaks in this passage. It's not the dreamer; the dreamer does not develop a theory of the dream. By definition the speaker must be awake and therefore must perceive in order to develop the theory of the dream. When I perceive, though, how is it possible for me not to be convinced that I am perceiving, that I am not separating dreams from reality, since it is under the presupposition that I am awake that I raise the question. Only a perceiving consciousness may evoke in memory a dreaming consciousness for which the criteria of reality are lacking. It is from within a consciousness that knows the criteria distinguishing reality and dream that the problem can arise of the dream's ignoring or not knowing these criteria. To dream is precisely not to be awake but to be asleep. What is lacking in sleep is the criterion of reality. The state of sleep is the collapse of reality. Phenomenologically, there is no other definition of sleep than that I am no longer perceiving. The contrast between the real and the unreal allows me to raise the question of what is the dream. If I did not know the difference by being awake, I could not raise the question about what is sleep, what is the dream. If there is something in the dream itself which afterward for the wakeful consciousness appears as a confusion between the real and the unreal, it is at the level of the belief, since sleep does not provide the criteria for making the distinction (236/211). The confusion arises not at the level of the image but at the level of belief. What is decisive in dreaming is that because I have no relation to the real world by means of perception, I am the prisoner of the image. I am caught in the image. I am in the state of dwelling among my images as a kind of prisoner of the image. In that sense we may say that there is an imaginary life but not an imaginary world (242/217). There is no world for the dreamer; the dreamer is without a world. There is a world only when we can have clues for observing, describing, and relating things. Even if the dream is sometimes a consistent spectacle, it's related to nothing. It's floating absolutely; it is not related to anything else.

There is a fundamental similarity between the three cases examined in this part: image as a stage of desire—an attempt to play or stage the presence—the hallucinatory image, and the dream image. In all of these cases, we are building the imaginary life on the ruins of the real world. We escape reality, because the difficult nature of reality is too great to support, as Freud has described in the process of mourning.[3] In the first, we treat the absent as present, so we deceive ourselves, and the process of self-deception has its equivalent in the state of hallucination and in the dream image. We have here a phenomenology of fascination that seems to bridge the gap between the unreal and the real but that alters not the status of the unreal but the status of our belief. Sartre speaks of the "'spell-binding' fiction" of the dream (255/228). The dream is a story that we believe, a spell-binding fiction. This is one of the only places in the book where he speaks of fiction, but I wonder whether it's a good use of the term.

> It is primarily a story and our strong interest in it is of the same sort as that of the naive reader in a novel. It is lived as a fiction and it is only in considering it as a fiction which happens as such that we can understand the sort of reaction it arouses in the sleeper. Only it is a "spell-binding" fiction: consciousness—as we have shown in the chapter on the hypnagogic image—has become knotted. And what it lives, at the same time as the fiction apprehended as a fiction is the impossibility of emerging out of the fiction. . . . [There is] the fatal nature of the dream. It is the seizure of this fatality as such which has often been confused with an apprehension of the dreamed world as reality. In fact, what constitutes the nature of the dream is that reality eludes altogether the consciousness which desires to recapture it; all the effort of consciousness turns in spite of itself to

produce the imaginary. The dream is not fiction taken for reality, it is the odyssey of a consciousness dedicated by itself, and in spite of itself, to build only an unreal world. The dream is a privileged experience which can help us to conceive what a consciousness would be which would have lost its "being-in-the-world" and which would be by the same token, deprived of the category of the real. (255/228–29)

The realm of the real leaves open the room for this captivity which occupies the whole place.

Sartre's description of fascination is quite convincing, but it confirms our initial doubt concerning the paradigmatic character of the absent object and of the reaction to absence motivated by a desire to make present (fascination, fatality). Sartre's whole description is absorbed by the magic of quasi-presence. We understand why Sartre chose this strategy of description. On the one hand, the absent object existing elsewhere cannot be held to be a thing in the mind. On the other hand, fascination provides the occasion to deal with the counterfactual aspects of confusion and to complete the thesis on nothingness and spontaneity by an argument on spellbound spontaneity, on fatality. Sartre's two paradigms may be questioned, however. Is fiction similar to an image of something absent but real? Is fascination the paradigm of response to the imaginary?

In the lengthy "Conclusion" to his book, Sartre draws two kinds of conclusions. There are some general conclusions which are very sound, if only partial, concerning the unreal. And there are some more limited conclusions concerning absence as a particular case. I think we must distinguish between what is said about a theory of absence—and about imagination as a relation to absence—and what is said concerning nothingness in general. The weak point in the book is that absence is taken as paradigmatic for nothingness. As for Sartre's general conclusions about the unreal, nothing stronger has been said than by Sartre concerning the function of the unreal in general. In the final pages of the text, Sartre offers a very strong argument about the alternance between the real and the unreal as constitutive of consciousness as such. He raises the question: what are the characteristics that can be attributed to consciousness from the fact that it is capable of imagining (260/234)? Asking this question is a contribution of phenomenology that has no parallel in linguistic analysis because it's a question concerning the condition of the possibility of having images. This question is broader than the question about absence, and it is narrowed down by the question about absence. The larger question is phenomenological and no longer linguistic, because it's not about what we say, what we report, but it's a transcendental question concerning the condition of possibility of having images. His question asks: is it contingent for consciousness to have images? Is it a mere fact that we have images, or is it required by the concept of consciousness that we have images (260/233–34)? This is a very fundamental question. The question makes sense only if images are not kinds of *things* (260–61/234). If they were, then a theory of the relation between consciousness and things would be enough. We should have only to qualify our notion of things to have external things and internal things. But if the image is no-thing, then we must construe the concept of consciousness in such a way that it implies this relation to what is no-thing. The question asks about the kind of positional acts of which consciousness is capable. What must consciousness be to be able to posit successively real objects and unreal objects? We must have a consciousness capable of positing nothingness. The question includes both absence and inexistence. To cover the whole area, we must have not only a phenomenology of absence but an ontology of nothingness.

> We now can see what the essential requisite is in order that a consciousness may be able to imagine; it must have the possibility of positing an hypothesis of unreality. . . . To posit an image is to construct an object on the fringe of the whole of reality, which means therefore to hold the real at a distance, to free oneself from it, in a word, to deny it. (265–66/238–39)

Sartre's question goes much further than the theory of imaginary life about fascination, which was too specific a case.

His question has two sides. On the one hand, how must our relation to the world be that it provides room for the unreal, and second, how must consciousness be in relation to itself to be able to deny reality as a whole? As concerns the first question, Sartre is less Sartrean than Heideggerian. It's not by chance that Heidegger is cited several times (267–71/240–43), because Sartre tries to show that it's an implication of the concept of being-in-the-world that nothingness is implied. "What Is Metaphysics?" is an essay by Heidegger precisely on nothingness where he shows that it's only against the background of nothingness that I may posit things. How? Heidegger tries to show, in a very convincing way, that to be in the world means something very specific, because it's the way in which a consciousness rather than a thing is in the world. A thing is located in the midst of the world, it's among other things, whereas to be in the world is to be able to take a distance to my own experience, to make a whole of my experience, to make a synthetic totality, and therefore to surpass experience and to be free in relation to it. Only a free consciousness may be in the world. A thing is a part of the world, but I am in the world in such a way that I can take a distance from my experience. It's in this difference between being in the midst of the world, among things, and being in the world as a consciousness that the moment of nothingness appears. Sartre has some very important expressions here. "Thus the thesis of unreality has yielded us the possibility of negation as its condition. Now, the latter is possible only by the 'negation' of the world as a whole, and this negation has revealed itself to us as being the reverse of the very freedom of consciousness" (267/240). Only a free consciousness may project the unreal, because the unreal is the correlate of its freedom. I must be absent to reality in order to have appearances as absent. There is a regression in analysis from the fact that I have images, a regression from absence to unreality, from unreality to nothingness, and from nothingness to freedom. Freedom is the condition of the possibility of nothingness which is the condition of possibility of unreality which is the condition of the possibility of absence.

> Thus, if consciousness is free, the noematic correlative of its freedom should be the world which carries in itself its possibility of negation, at each moment and from each point of view, by means of an image, even while the image must as yet be construed by a particular intention of consciousness. But, reciprocally, an image, being a negation of the world from a particular point of view, can never appear excepting on the foundation of the world and in connection with the foundation. . . .
>
> Thus the critical analysis of the conditions that made all imagination possible has led us to the following discoveries: in order to imagine, consciousness must be free from all specific reality and this freedom must be able to define itself by a "being-in-the-world" which is at once the constitution and the negation of the world; the concrete situation of the consciousness in the world must at each moment serve as the singular motivation for the constitution of the unreal. (269–70/242)

This covers a broader field than all the conduct relating to nothingness as denial. Implied in this theory is the theory of utopia as the possibility of the *nowhere* in relation to my social condition. I am interested in the connection between a theory of utopia and a theory of imagination, because the nowhere is included in this relation to situations. In fact I am not a pebble in the universal determinism; rather, I am a consciousness, because I am able always to deny what is by what is not.

The second side of Sartre's thesis is that this nothingness which I in a sense am, I cannot know as such. I have no intuition of it. It's only through the intentionality of an unreal world, it's only the image as unreal that presents to myself my freedom. This second aspect of Sartre's thesis is important. I cannot have a world without being able to deny it in order that it be a world in which I am. Further, my freedom is not an object for me. This makes sense through the notion of a nonthetic consciousness. I don't posit myself as nothing, but I grasp my nothingness by seeing it in the unreality of some object. Imagination presents my own freedom to myself. I read my freedom in the nothingness of the image. Therefore, we have first to introduce this nothingness in the structure of being-in-the-world, and second, to connect this freedom by a theory of nonthetic consciousness to the capacity of imagining.

Here the argument to which Sartre responds comes no longer from Heidegger but from Henri Bergson. Bergson has several essays arguing that the concept of nothingness is secondary to being.[4] Absence is always something else, another presence. There is a strong critique of the concept of nothingness in Bergson that derives from Spinoza: it's always the plenitude of what is that can be conceived. The answer to Bergson is to say, yes, there is no intuition of nothingness, but I have an indirect relation to nothingness through the unreality of the image. After having said that being-in-the-world implies this moment of nothingness in order that it be a relation to a situation and not merely a physical determinism, Sartre says,

> But, in its turn, the imagination, which has become a psychological and empirical function, is the necessary condition for the freedom of empirical man in the midst of the world. For, if the negating function belonging to consciousness—which Heidegger called surpassing—is what makes the act of imagination possible, it must be added on the other hand that this function can manifest itself only in an imaginative act. (271/243–44)

I have no direct glance into nothingness. I cannot see nothingness. That would be absurd. I have no intuition of nothingness. "There can be no intuition of nothingness just because nothingness is nothing and because all consciousness intuitive or not is consciousness of something" (271/244). The only way to preserve the intentionality of consciousness is to say that I am intentionally related to this nonintentional nothingness by putting the nothingness in something which appears with this character of nothingness.

> Nothingness can present itself only as an infra-structure of something. The experience of nothingness is not, strictly speaking, an indirect one, it is an experience which is in principle given "with" and "in." The analyses of Bergson are pertinent in this connection: any attempt to directly conceive death or the nothingness of existence is by nature bound to fail. (271/244)

To posit something that is not is the only way to deal with the problem of nothingness in the absence of an intuition of nothingness. This is what I retain from this analysis.

I wonder, therefore, whether the theory of absence does not reduce the scope of this theory of nothingness. In the case of absence, we have an original that exists elsewhere; it's an imperfect nothingness. I ask whether it's not in the theory of fiction that we have the full expression of the theory of nothingness, or to put it in Kantian language, when we don't want to reproduce what is but to produce new entities. After having seen the broad scope of a theory of nothingness, Sartre strangely enough reduces it to a theory of absence. He has some good reasons for this reduction, but they narrow the scope of his analysis. First, he wanted to place the object of the image outside of consciousness. To preserve the intentionality of the image, he had to start from the absence of the object. The object is out there, and therefore I cannot put it within me. The theory of absence had a didactic function and a polemical function: to get rid of the illusion of immanence. In contrast, with a fiction I am always in danger of placing the fiction within me as if the image of a horse would be a miniature horse in my mind (120/108). With a fiction I attempt to put a miniature horse in my mind when I have the image of a horse. Sartre's approach belongs to the strategy of a polemic.

Sartre's second reason for his reduction of the theory of nothingness was to deal with the counterexamples linked to the states of fascination where it's my spontaneity that is bound. He wanted to dissolve the objections arising from examples such as hallucinations, dreams, and so on. At the same time, though, he himself became the prisoner of some particular states of mind that concern our bound spontaneity. I wonder here whether the theory of fiction could not open other possibilities than the mere attempt to possess something absent and therefore connect the unreal with the real in a quite different way, not to possess it magically, but to reshape it intentionally. Sartre stops the analysis of imagination at the point when it is a retreat from the real, and he has to do that in order to dissolve the fascination offered by the absent. But when we have to do with fiction, we are no longer in danger of mistaking fiction for the real. Then we may use fiction as an instrument for looking at things in another way. In other words, the stage of nothingness would be only a provisional stage, a first stage as the negative condition for remaking reality. We shall see that this is the function of models and of poetic fictions. As long as we deal with reproductive imagination—the portrait, the mental image—we have to disentangle the image from reality, and we have to fight against these magical attitudes toward the unreal. With free fiction, by contrast, we may consider perhaps a return from the image to the real in the sense that Nelson Goodman offers when, in *Languages of*

Art, he discusses reality as remade. This capacity to remake reality could be the positive counterpart of the denial of the real.

If I am right, Sartre has been prevented from considering this positive counterpart, because, first, he deals with reproductive imagination and not with productive imagination. There is already something real. The image cannot contribute to the real, since the original precedes the portrait. Here is the great difference between absence and inexistence, since with inexistence fiction may contribute to reality. Second, Sartre's polemic against the illusion of immanence condemned him to follow only one argument, that images are unreal even when we seem to mistake them. He must always preserve the unreality of the image from any confusion with quasi-reality. Third, perhaps the case of absence also led him to the narrow problematic of desire and fascination, of magical presence, which does not plague in the same way the problematic of fiction. Sartre misses the most interesting case: the fiction not tied to fascination, the fiction where we make no attempt to deal with its objects *as though* they are real, because these objects are inexistent and not merely absent. These fictional objects may work as guidelines for redescribing reality.

There is a kind of denial of reality in the image. Here the Sartrean approach is not only unavoidable but the only basis for any kind of theory of imagination. Perhaps, though, the negative side is only the important side in the case of reproductive imagination, because as we have already an original, what we have in the image is only the element of absence. Here the image provides only a negative dimension because it is reproductive. When it is productive, however, it produces a world of its own that enlarges our world. I shall later use some of the modern theories of painting, which show that painting in fact adds to reality. It's not merely a denial, but it enhances reality. I borrow from a French critic, François Dagognet, the notion of iconic augmentation.[5] Also, Gadamer's theory of image—of picture, *Bild*—develops the fact that the image increases reality for us, because it directs us toward unnoticed aspects of reality. I would not say that a painting produces reality, but it produces a new way of looking at things as they are. When I have seen, for example, a painting by Paul Cézanne, I'm related to reality as a landscape. Now, for the first time, I see the country. There is a restitution of aspects of reality that are overshadowed by ordinary dealing with manipulable objects. The denial of reality is only a component of enlarging reality.

Sartre is right to say that when I look at the portrait of Charles VIII, I see the canvas and I see lights on the canvas, but also I imagine the absent on the basis of this representative of an absent (274/246). What, though, if the portrait is not of somebody who has existed? Sartre would be correct to maintain that the portrait is also of someone absent. And yet now it's of an unreal as inexistent that is not in the painting. I am directed toward something even if nobody is depicted, even if I cannot identify that this is a person, a horse, and so on. Even if I have only lines and colors in what is called nonfigurative painting, on the basis of what I perceive, I am directed toward things that I shall never see, that are completely unreal. Even if we have only spots or patches of colors, it's the analogue of something that does not exist. Perhaps I should extend then the notion of an analogue to an analogue of the unreal. When I have seen nonfigurative painting, I have lived among the unreal, but it's an unreal that has no name, that I cannot identify, because the referent has no grounding in perception. I return to reality when I leave the museum. Perhaps I have the real fiction when the referent is itself nothing. It's not only the kind of presence that is affected by absence, but there is no reference that can be shown. In the situation where I wait for my friend Peter at the station, he is absent, but he also has a referent that belongs to the perception of the other. By contrast, when I have to do with a fiction, I have a real unreal, a genuine unreal. I am drawn beyond the painting not elsewhere but to the absolutely nowhere.

In the final section of his "Conclusion," Sartre offers a kind of appendix about the work of art, where he tries to say that it's not a feeling that is realized in a painting, but it's a painting that is unrealized (275/247). He is right to say that, because the realities—the canvas, the colors, and so on—are de-realized by the very act of painting, by treating the work not as a thing but as a painting. It's always a painting *of*, even if it is not a painting of something that has a name that I could express. I would say that the painting is completely unreal when it is nonfigurative, because there is no reference that could be shown to be similar to what is painted. We are directed toward the feelings of the painter but to the extent that they have been externalized, first, in a real thing which is the canvas and the colors, and second, in an unreal thing, in what is meant by the painting. The painter has de-realized himself or herself. We are connected with the feelings of the painter, but as they have been externalized in the analogue and de-realized through the act of treating the canvas as the support of something unreal. It is in this unreal world that we have to meet a Beethoven. Sartre discusses the example of the Seventh Symphony (278–80/250–52), saying that the performance plays the role of an analogue. The same symphony as an unreal is performed several times, but it's the same Seventh Symphony and has exactly the same status as Charles VIII, as re-presented. Charles VIII has his analogue in a painting. The only difference is that in music the performance is a temporal object and therefore has no subsistence whereas in painting there is a permanent spatial object. But the status of the temporal object and the spatial object are the same; each is an analogue for an unreal (280/252) to which I am directed. I cannot reach the author, the painter, or a Beethoven elsewhere than in the analogue of the unreal object that he proposes to me.

I should add only that then I'm led to return to reality with new models for perhaps reshaping it. Here the imagination would have a function not only of evasion (193–94/173–74) but of reorientation. This is similar to the utopia, because the utopia will redirect action in new ways; it's not only a kind of escape. The nowhere is a starting point toward a new position in reality. My claim is that this positive counterpart of the image can be seen only with fictions. Fictions may produce a new reality, because they don't reproduce a previous reality. They are not bound by an original that precedes them. Perhaps, though, it's always easier to offer a theory of reproductive imagination than of the productive imagination, because the latter presents difficulties of its own. I am convinced that Sartre has solved some of the difficulties of a theory of productive imagination by providing a general theory of the unreal on the basis of a limited phenomenology of the absent.

I will stop here, as I don't want to anticipate further what I want to say about the potentiality of fiction to open a new reality. My permanent problem is that fiction has a referential dimension, precisely because it's not the repetition of something already real. With the theory of absence, we are caught in the referent that is already there in the original. When the image has no original, then fiction provides an original of its own.

In the next lecture I shall discuss the concept of redescription, which I borrow from the theory of models. A model may provide a redescription of reality, because it's not reproductive but is productive of a new reality. I shall also speak of the poetic image and of the relation of the image to certain uses of language. How does the particular strategy of language in metaphorical discourse and in general in the poetic use of language display an image? The analysis will examine the relationship between language and the image, between the verbal and the visual.

PART THREE

Imagination as Fiction

15
Fiction (1): Introduction

The third part of these lectures will be devoted to the problem of imagination as fiction. This lecture proposes some introductory remarks concerning the transition from the study of the theory of image in linguistic analysis and phenomenology to this new stage. My claim is that until this point we have discussed only reproductive imagination and not yet productive imagination. I want to develop this contention by a survey of what we have analyzed thus far.

The main problem we have discussed is the following one: what is it to have an image? All of our authors discussed this problem. For example, we think, like Sartre, of our absent friend Peter who is now in Berlin. We have an image, and the question is whether this image is a kind of picture like a material picture transposed into the mind. Ryle in turn says that to have an image is not to see something but to pretend to see. We don't see an image, but we *fancy* seeing an image. Whatever the solution to the problem of the appearance of an image in the mind's eye, we were always dealing with an image that was more or less the picture of something that already existed. There was always somewhere an original for the picture. Our problem is to consider whether we have exhausted all the possibilities of the issue by construing the question in these terms—what is it to have an image of.

I shall elaborate the shortcomings of this approach in the following three stages. First, in terms of the referent. I shall take Ryle and Sartre as two representatives of the question what is it to have or to produce an image. For both Ryle and Sartre, the image has a referent that already exists. This is the trait common to pretending to see in Ryle and to producing the image of in Sartre. In both cases, having an image and producing an image presupposes an original. We see this in the details of the analyses. As a linguistic analyst, Ryle proceeds by way of a construction of statements or reports about images. He emphasizes the grammar of pretending. He writes that I fancy that I have an image. His claim is that the grammar of pretending—as in the case of the child pretending to be a bear—is more complex than that of saying or doing. He compares this grammar to the logic of the *obliqua oratio*, the logic of quotation. First we produce a direct statement, and then we quote the statement. Therefore, we must know first what it is to say something direct before knowing what it is to pretend and to quote. The logic of the *obliqua oratio*, the logic of quotation, imposes the primacy of the referent of direct speech onto the referent of indirect speech. There is a priority of the grammar of direct speech over that of indirect speech.

It's the same with the phenomenology of absence that we developed in Sartre. We can also express this phenomenology in terms of linguistic analysis. The same Peter can be seen or can be imagined. What is important is that we have the same referent. The difference between perception and image is only a difference in the givenness of the same referent. The sameness in the referent compels us to place the distinction between image and perception not in the referent but in the mode of givenness. If we say that in the image the object is absent, that does not change anything in the fundamental situation. For Sartre the reference to the real Peter is not abolished by the description of the image as nothingness. It's only in reflection that the image becomes a kind of secondary object. When I imagine, I am directed to my friend Peter who is actually out there. It's the image in or for reflection that becomes a quasi-object, not far finally from the pretended object of Ryle. The quasi-object seems to be different from the real Peter. The nothingness of absence seems to be a species of the unreal, of nothingness, along with the inexistence of the fictional object.

The phenomenology of Sartre suffers from a lack of accuracy in linguistic analysis, because he builds his notion of nothingness as a general category with the subcategories of nonexistence, absence, existence elsewhere, and neutralized presence. But this series is in fact not homogeneous, because while presence and absence are two modes of givenness of the real, the genuine unreal is the nonexistent and that entails the nonexistence of the referent. In the case of the absent, we have the same reference as in that of the present. The distinction between present and absent lies only in the mode of givenness. With fiction we have something quite different. There is no referent or, as I shall argue, the fiction builds its own referent and therefore opens new ontological possibilities that were blocked by the already existing, by the previous existence of the reference in the case of absence. What I shall try to show in a later lecture is that with fiction we have a quite different situation where nothingness, if we keep the vocabulary of Sartre, is a trait of the referent. We are directed toward this nothingness, not only in reflection as with absence but as a fundamental trait of the object. It's the inaccuracy in the construction of the concept of nothingness as encompass-

Fiction (1): Introduction 219

ing the nonexistent, the absent, the existing elsewhere, and the neutralized presence that allows us to shift from the case of absence to the case of fiction. There is a discontinuity in the phenomenology of both Ryle and Sartre. That is why I claim that in both Ryle and Sartre we have only a theory of reproductive imagination, to repeat the distinction of Kant. The phenomenology of fiction remains to be done.

My second argument follows from the first one. Because both authors have focused on the simulation of reality, they miss a quite different relation to reality apart from providing a replica of reality in the image. The new possibility that we shall explore I propose to call provisionally a productive reference, the capacity of fiction to open up to new insights into reality. This dimension of productive reference—I don't hold to the term, it's a problem for which I offer a name—could not be acknowledged, since the image already has a reference that is not its own reference but the reference of a perception, a possible perception of the same, what we call the original of the copy, the original of the photograph, even the original of a painting. (But we shall see that in painting we have more than a copy; we have a certain creation of its own original.) Whatever this original may be—an action in Ryle's behavioristic terms—it's a doing, which is first pretended, before "seeing." In the case of Sartre the real Peter is not affected at all by the attempt to possess him in an image. This was the main function of imagination for Sartre: to possess the absent in image and therefore to fancy its presence. There was a self-delusion in what Sartre called imaginary life precisely because there was an impotence of the image as regards reality. The image was not able to shape reality, since reality was already given to the image or before the image. The reproductive imagination raised issues only in and for reflection, since it is a problem only of sense and not of reference, if I dare use the vocabulary of Frege in this case.

We could also discuss the relation between likeness and negation, since the image is like but is not the original. There is a dialectics of similarity and negation. We may recall Ryle's example of mock fighting. It is like fighting, but it involves an abstention from hitting. This abstention is a fundamental trait of mock behavior. When Sartre speaks of quasi-observation, the quasi is like Ryle's mock action. It's *as if*. We could reformulate the quasi-observation in Sartre in terms of mock observation. In looking at a photograph, we could speak of a mock observation but with also an abstention in positing the material photograph as existent. When I look at a photograph, I no longer posit the existence of the photograph. I neutralize this positing in order to direct myself to the absent object that exists elsewhere. To look at a picture with a kind of mock observation preserves both the likeness and the nothingness. But this interplay between likeness and nothingness has no influence on the object as such. It is only for reflection that the appearance raises a problem of its own. This appearance is marginal in relation to the real object.

Therefore, the paradox I shall try to deal with here is that it's only when we start from the fiction, which seems to be nonreferential in the sense that it has no object, that a new kind of reference may be opened thanks to the absence of an original. Whereas reproductive images are marginal as regards reality, it's the genius of productive imagination—of the fictional—to open and change reality. Productive imagination may enlarge and even create new worldviews, new ways of looking at things, and, finally, may change even our way of being in the world. This is excluded in reproductive imagination, which appears spontaneous only in reflection. It is a kind of reflective spontaneity and not a creative spontaneity. As we saw in Sartre, the spontaneity of reproductive imagination exhausts itself in producing what he calls, in one of his most extreme expressions, an entire anti-world, a counter world as we speak of a counterculture, an interplay between likeness and absence but for the sake of absence. My task will be to show how the interplay between likeness and negation will cooperate, will work, in the sense of remaking reality, to anticipate an expression of Nelson Goodman in *Languages of Art*. I shall use his expression of "reality remade" (Goodman 1968, 3) or Mary Hesse's expression, in *Models and Analogies in Science*, of "redescription" (for example, see Hesse 1966, 157, 170–71) through heuristic fiction. The problem of the connection between heuristic fiction and the redescription of reality will be central to this second part of my argument.

A word I was tempted to use is the notion of *mimesis* in Aristotle, when he says in the *Poetics* that the function of poetry is mimesis (Aristotle 1973, 670, 1447a 15). Since the term is misunderstood, it would have to be amended at the same time that we used it. For most readers, mimesis means imitation, and imitation sends us back to reproduction. If, however, we read Aristotle's *Poetics* accurately, we see that poetry is mimetic to the extent that it is creative. Because the poet has construed a *muthos*, a plot, a fable, a tragedy, the poet then provides a mimesis of reality that is not a description of what is, but a depth inquiry into the essence of human life and human action. As Aristotle says also, poetry is more true than history (682, 1451b 5), because history, at least for his time, remained at the level of anecdotes and therefore at the level of the contingency of events. By contrast, we grasp the essence of human action in tragedy precisely because it is fictionally construed. The construed fiction speaks the truth. This is what I call productive reference, which I put together with the mimetic function, the notion of the mimetic as productive, as productive reference.

I'm less sure of the connection between my third argument and the sec-

Fiction (1): Introduction 221

ond, just discussed, but I think that there is a link. If not a real derivation, there is at least a certain connection. We have spoken to this point of sense and reference. In all of the examples discussed thus far, the image was always isolated: I have an image of my friend and so on. In those examples, the image is taken in isolation. I wonder whether there is some relation between this situation and the previous shortcomings of which I spoke. I wonder whether in order to be mimetic the image must belong to a broader framework, the framework of some enterprise of thought, of discourse, an action, in which the image is only a phase, a component, a moment. There was something very abstract in the previous treatment of the image as a picture that is a manipulable object that can be placed in a drawer, hung on the wall, or looked at outside of any framework of reference. For fictions to have reference, I think they must have a *framework* of reference. Fictions seem to be components or stages in some strategy of discourse, thought, or action that provides a framework for the mimetic function. As we shall see, whatever that framework may be—writing a poem, for example—it's within the poem that the poet provides images. A painting must be a work with a frame; storytelling is a kind of language game that has its own dimensions; we construe a hypothesis within a scientific model; we elaborate a strategy of action in order to make a decision; we try this or that possibility in imagination. There must always be some broad project encompassing the production of imagination. Later in this lecture I shall use Gaston Bachelard's writings to introduce the problem.

I should like to use the word *work* in a broad sense to characterize the issue. It's always within a certain work that imagination is productive. On the one hand, I use the word *work* as it is invoked commonly, as when we speak of a work of art. But I should also like to speak of a *work* of discourse, because the word *work* introduces into the field the productive dimension. The word is borrowed from the field of action, of *technē*, in the sense that work is applied to some material; the material is shaped by our action. Work is a category that belongs in the large sense to a *technē*, but it's only when images are worked, in one way or another, that imagination is productive. The theory of fiction will be largely the theory of the works within which imagination becomes productive.

To introduce this concept of work, we may use as a contrast Sartre's notion of the imaginary life. We shall see immediately in what sense that is not a work. There is therefore a certain coherence in the fact that reproductive imagination is, first, already his referent, second, spontaneous only for reflection, and third, is not a work. Recall that in the last part of his *Psychology of Imagination*, Sartre escapes the narrowness of the mere statics of the image and proceeds to a functional approach to imagination. But what is the functional in what he calls the imaginary life? For the most part what he calls the imaginary life is the least productive kind of attitude, since it is an attempt to possess, in a magical way, the absent object. I want to oppose magic to work. It's in the play of desire or want that Sartre tries to fill the absence of the object of desire by a quasi-presence. This is what he calls fascination by the image, which is a magical act of making something present without doing anything, without doing any work. What is characteristic of magic precisely is that it acts on some forces without technically dealing with them. The self-deception of desire by the magic of quasi-presence constitutes the paradigm of the imaginary life. This is why his examples are always taken from childhood, hallucinations, or dreams. In dreams we fundamentally don't work. Bachelard says in *The Poetics of Reverie* that even reverie is what we do when we are awake and not when we sleep (Bachelard 1971, 14). Sartre's imaginary life blurs the distinction between the real and the unreal by the magic of fascination. The reproductive imagination fulfills its own absence by the *as though* of presence. This is a very powerful phenomenology of fascination. We have a phenomenology of fascination that takes the place of what I should like to call a phenomenology of the work in fiction. The imaginary life is parasitic on absence, because magic is the opposite of work. The magic of quasi-presence makes the imaginary life the opposite of the fictional work.

It is true that in the previous section of these lectures we had some hints of work with images. Authors such as Price, in *Thinking and Experience*, and Husserl, in the *Logical Investigations*, linked the image to thought. Price is very cautious not to speak of thought as a kind of abstract capacity but of thinking as an activity. We have already an activity, an activity of thinking, and therefore we may be prepared to meet more productive imagination. But because this thought activity is not elaborated in terms of a work, we are unable to go much further than examples borrowed from recognition, the recognition of an object. And the relation between concept and instance is in fact the least productive way of thinking. Here thinking is not a work, since we apply a concept that already exists to instances. Recall that the vocabulary of Price is very interesting at this point since he speaks of imagination as producing quasi-instances. He says that through imagination we may quasi-instantiate our concepts.

I was directed toward this critique by my reading of Donald Schon's *Displacement of Concepts*. Schon says that when we relate a concept to an instance, we have no displacement of concepts but only application of concepts (Schon 1963, 28). We apply it to examples. The relation between concept and instance does not displace our concepts but only enlarges the scope of their extension. Let us evoke the examples given by Price in terms of this warning that the relation between concept and instance is not really productive. Price's vocabulary is in a sense a capitalist vocabulary, since he speaks of cashing the value of a notion. (I think that the expression of the cash value of a concept came from John Dewey, but I am not sure. I am not familiar with Dewey.[1]) How do I cash the value of, for example, the meaning of the word *dog*? I may show a dog, make a drawing of a dog, look at an illustration in a dictionary, or have a mental image. We have a range of instances, but all of these instances have the same function, which is merely to cash the value. If I am right, there is not a great difference between the notion, in this pragmatic language, of cashing the value and the Husserlian notion of fulfilling an empty intention. There is a fulfilling, which is not at all to displace and to enlarge or extend.

It is not by chance that we choose as examples of cashing the value of a concept the quasi-instantiation of isolated names. I keep returning to the problem of the isolation of the image in all these descriptions, which has its counterpart in the notion of giving an instance, because the instance is the instance of a name. I cannot forget the beginning of the *Philosophical Investigations* when Wittgenstein says that the greater part of our theory of language is about the language game of giving names (Wittgenstein 1958, 7). As I said in my own study of metaphor, I fight against this reduction of the problem of language to the changing of a name, to give another name, to shift names. Because we have this narrow framework of a dog and giving the image of a dog, we have nothing creative. What we call thought is only giving names, and what we call an image is giving an instance, a quasi-instance of an isolated name.

All that is being done here is a phenomenology—a description—of recognition. We recognize what we mean by this or that. To speak of recognition, to speak of application, to speak of instantiation implies no genuine displacement of concepts as will happen when we build a model of something that will change our reading of reality. Even the term *quasi-instance* shows that it is still an instance, and an instance belongs to the procedure of recognition, not the procedure of discovery. We want a phenomenology of discovery, but discovery is a long procedure in which the image is only a stage, whereas recognition is a short event of thought. Even if we have some initial hesitation in recognizing a friend whom we have not seen for a long time—the friend has changed and we have changed—the mutual adjustment is not really a process of discovery. On the contrary, we have to reidentify the old in the new without changing the old. In recognition finally the old prevails over the new. When we have to reshape old concepts in order to deal with new situations, then there will be complex procedures in which imagination will itself have to be more creative.

My claim is that in Husserl, at least in the *Logical Investigations*, we do not go far beyond this mere recognition of a concept in imaginative instances. Recall that the paradigmatic case in the First Logical Investigation is the notion of illustration: how do we illustrate a concept? The notion of illustration is itself borrowed from the techniques of the picture. A dictionary gives an illustration of a definition by providing a typical image, as of a dog. We are always within this narrow framework of instantiation. In truth, Husserl goes a step further than mere recognition when he considers that illustration concerns something complex. It is an active procedure when it provides a clarification that a direct, intellectual insight could not. We explicate, we unfold the structure of the concept as though the imagination were a kind of space in which we analyze, in the proper sense of the word, the structure of an object, because we express the logical relations in terms of spatial relations. We have a spatialization of connections, and that is already something productive.

Husserl takes an additional step when he speaks of the very important categories of concepts that have a fluctuating meaning. In the First Logical Investigation, he calls them occasionally fluctuating meanings because they are related to occasions (Husserl 1970, § 26). For example, one type of this concept are personal pronouns such as *I* or *thou. I* means anybody, but to know who is saying *I* we must consider the situation. And we have plenty of concepts intermediary between personal pronouns and logical concepts that are only prescriptions for building certain descriptions in certain situations. The imagination has not only a function of giving an instance but of building the framework of reference to connect the potential meanings of the word with the actual givenness of the situation. Then, Husserl says, we determine the notion, which is more than fulfilling a concept already formed. There is in ordinary language—and this is not far from what linguistic analysis says about ordinary language—a kind of flexibility. Whereas logical words have their meaning by definition, most ordinary words have an open-ended meaningfulness that is actualized each time according to the situation of discourse. Our words in ordinary language are built for that use. They have a polysemy of their own; they mean several things. To choose among all the potential meanings what is appropriate implies a certain apperception of the fitness of one meaning among others to the situation. We have to envision the situation in order to extend the word to the situation.

Several times Husserl even further extends this more creative role of imagination by what he calls imaginative variations.[2] In order to test the identity of a concept, we provide a great spectrum of examples, of cases, that helps us to disentangle the concept from its typification in its usual situations. We must break the framework of habit and custom by imaginative variations, and then we have to test and check the essential kernel of the word. There is already something creative in the sense that we provide unusual cases that allow us to separate a concept from its usual context. Schon offers the example that the concept of a wave was applied not only to liquids but to sound and then to light (Schon 1963, 18, 71). An imaginative variation on the word *wave* separated it from its ordinary framework as the action of some liquid on the sides of a vase. We first retain only a certain style of movement between a wave in water and sound in air, and the parallelism between water and air provides a kind of similarity of the material bearer. But we have to go a step more with light, because we can no longer draw on the parallelism between water and air. More than intellectual insight arises on the basis of the imaginative variation. There is a real displacement of concepts.

I shall try to show that the imaginative variation is a productive, creative function when it is not only a way of checking a concept but really of creating new concepts. The relation between the old and the new will be fundamental. By contrast, the analysis in the *Logical Investigations* could not go so far as to speak of creative imagination because a certain identity of the concept is presumed. For Husserl the imaginative variation is a procedure to test the sameness that is supposed to be given in a kind of Platonic world. As long as we presume this kind of sameness, this fixity of the identity of concepts, we don't really get out from the narrow framework of instantiation.

We may wonder whether this incapacity to grasp productive imagination is not linked to the incapacity to apprehend thought itself in its creative process. My suggestion is that we must forget these examples of instantiating a name, which perhaps are the reason for this narrowness. With naming we have too narrow a framework. We shall have to consider sentences and a certain way not only of giving names but of giving predicates. I shall develop this topic in a subsequent lecture on metaphor. Metaphor is not part of a game of giving names but of giving up predicates. There is a movement in our thought. Concepts are displaced. We have processes of discovery that go further than merely a strategy of tacking by naming. The isolation of the image has its guarantee and also its limit in the isolation of names, in the short relation between concept and instance.

For the remainder of this lecture and then the ones following, I shall proceed in the following way. I shall start from poetic imagination and poetic images, that is to say, from images in a poem. The important point is the framework of a *work* of discourse, as in the poem. I do not claim that only poetry deals with the productive imagination, but I shall use the example as a kind of breakthrough. I shall then try to show that there is also an epistemological imagination, which is no less productive. I don't agree with the opposition that we have, even in Susanne Langer's *Philosophy in a*

New Key, between poetry and science, as though creativity were poetic only, were monopolized by poetic activity (for example, Langer 1948, 116). There is in scientific thought a situation parallel to poetry that belongs to the logic of discovery. As we shall see, the theory of models and analogies in science bears witness to the role of imagination in scientific thought. The kinship between metaphor and model will provide us with and will preserve the continuity between the two uses of imagination.

If I start with poetic imagination, it's for two reasons. First, it's the best way of showing that images blossom when aroused by certain specific uses of language. In a sense we return to a situation perfectly grasped by Price and Husserl, that imagination alone is nothing. Imagination is productive only in conjunction with a certain use of language. The verbal and the visual must be placed in a dialectical situation. It's only when language is creative that imagination is creative. There is a mutual promotion of the creativity of language and the creativity of imagination. I shall support this first claim by using Bachelard's description of poetic imagination, that is to say, imagination aroused by poetic diction, if I may employ Owen Barfield's wonderful expression (1964). It is when there is poetic diction that there are poetic visions. Diction and vision come together and move together.

The danger to avoid is the assumption that the poetic sinks us into the irrationality of creativity, creation, and so on. Recall by comparison Price's warning that he can say something about images when they are quasi-instances, but when people speak of creativity, he must say to them good-bye and good luck. I do not follow him. The second step in my argument, then, will be that the creative use of language can be described and analyzed. There is nothing absolutely mysterious here. Even if, as we shall see, there are no rules for writing good poetry, at least there are rules of reading. A theory of reading may, to a certain extent, fill the gap. Schon claims that we are caught between two pitfalls, either to say that there is nothing new and therefore to show that all newness proceeds from the old by merely new combinations, mechanical changes, and so on, or to say that there is something new but we can say nothing about it (Schon 1963, 3). Like Schon, my argument is that between the illusion of newness and the reductive explanation there is a narrow path. I will use the contemporary theory of metaphor to support this second claim, that we may analyze to a certain extent the creative procedures of language. I will take this opportunity to draw consequences for the theory of imagination from my own interpretation of metaphor. I have not done that in my work on metaphor. What would be the next step for a theory of interpretation? How is imagination implied in this process that I have described only as the use of odd predicates? What are their images when there are odd predicates? This will be the problem.

Fiction (1): Introduction   227

This interplay between productive language and productive imagination will provide us with the transition to a theory of epistemological imagination. At this point I shall shift from the theory of metaphor to the theory of models. (We could have taken the reverse course and started from the theory of model and then applied it to metaphor. It's only for the pedagogical reasons that I developed that I did not proceed in that way.) I shall use some material different from what I used with David Tracy last year in a seminar on analogy in theological discourse.[3] It's not analogy as an argument that I shall analyze but analogy as displaying an imaginative element. Just as I shall develop the imaginative side of metaphor, I shall also develop the imaginative side of the model and the analogy. This will be the program for the last section of the lectures.

I shall use Bachelard's Introductions to *The Poetics of Space* and *The Poetics of Reverie*. I am somewhat hesitant to start with him, as he does not speak of the strategy of language as metaphor and even indicates some reluctance to do that. I use Bachelard only for my first argument, namely, that it's when language is poetic that imagination is creative. Bachelard tends to define the imagination as a dimension of language and not as a trace of perception. There is a shift in the treatment of the image. In the Humean tradition, as we have seen, we start from the impression and then we try to move from the impression to the trace, the echo, of perception. In Bachelard, by contrast, if the image is an echo—he will use the expression of *reverberation*—it's an echo of language, not an echo of perception. This is a decisive alteration in approach.

The first emphasis in Bachelard's two Introductions is on the concept of newness, the birth of something. These Introductions speak poetically of poetry, which is why I use him as an introduction to a more analytical approach. In *The Poetics of Reverie*, he says that he undertakes a phenomenology of newness (Bachelard 1971, 3), a phenomenology of the birth of something.[4] We never spoke of newness when we discussed having an image of something that exists already. Bachelard's shift to newness is distinctive. He calls his approach a phenomenology, and we see why. "[T]he goal of all phenomenology is to situate awareness in the present, in a moment of extreme tension" (4).[5] He speaks of an increasing awareness. "[A]ny awareness is an increment to consciousness, an added light, a reinforcement of psychic coherence" (5), an increase of being as well as an increase of consciousness. He takes up first the etymology of poetry, *poiēsis*, as a creation. We are confronted with a creation.

The same attention to novelty is asserted in the earlier *The Poetics of Space*:

The poetic image is a sudden salience on the surface of the psyche, the lesser psychological causes of which have not been sufficiently investigated. Nor can anything general and co-ordinated serve as a basis for a philosophy of poetry. The idea of principle or "basis" in this case would be disastrous, for it would interfere with the essential psychic actuality, the essential novelty of the poem. (Bachelard 1969, xi)[6]

Note the emphasis on the actuality of novelty, newness, the emergence of something new. There is something unique here offered in language. We are far from the relation between concept and instance. The poetic image is not an instantiation of something already there but the emergence of something new. If we may speak of the relation of the poetic image to types and even archetypes—a kinship with Jung—the relation is not a causal one (1969, xii). The poetic image is not an echo of the past. These two works of Bachelard break with what remained typological in his early work, since he wrote several volumes on imagination that were ruled by the four material elements of water, fire, earth, and air, what he called "the four principles of the intuitive cosmogonies" (xiv). Here he dealt with a material imagination (xiv). We shall return to the cosmogonic theme when discussing the ontological implications of imagination, namely, that imagination saves the world, saves what is fundamentally. At this first stage of his new writings, though, Bachelard says that we must turn our backs on the too prudent approach in his prior work to the imagination. "The 'prudent' attitude itself is a refusal to obey the immediate dynamics of the image" (xiv). For him, there was a split in his own thinking, a crisis which "contains the entire paradox of a phenomenology of the imagination" (xiv). The paradox of imagination involves "a study of the phenomenon of the poetic image when it emerges into the consciousness as a direct product of the heart, soul and being of man, apprehended in his actuality" (xiv). Note again the emphasis on emergence and on the action of actuality. The novelty of the image constitutes the paradox of a phenomenology.

> [H]ow can an image, at times very unusual, appear to be a concentration of the entire psyche? How—with no preparation—can this singular, short-lived event constituted by the appearance of an unusual poetic image, react on other minds and in other hearts, despite all the barriers of common sense, all the disciplined schools of thought, content in their immobility? (xiv–xv)

The breakthrough of the new is the paradox. "Only phenomenology— that is to say, consideration of the onset of the image in an individual consciousness—can help us to restore the subjectivity of images . . ."

Fiction (1): Introduction 229

(xv). Even the archetypes are accessible only through the newness of the emergences.

The decisive step in this phenomenology of a birth is that this birth is in language and through language. The image is a transposition of the archetypal image by the poetic text. There is less derivation of the image from a Humean impression, which would be here the first qualities of the archetypal elements, than its belonging to a world of language. The derivation from the elements has given way to a metaphorical use of language. The images are in the position of metaphor. The place where the lived act of consciousness can be acknowledged is language. This is why we have to say that the image is not an appendix to perception, even as pretending, but a dimension of language, "a new being in language" (Bachelard 1971, 3). This new being is not the breakthrough of an antecedent reality but a "positive conquest of the word" (3). When Bachelard speaks of "poetic images" (3), he means the images given by the poem. We must understand the expression in that sense. This is a decisive step, because while we are unable to write directly the phenomenology of the poet, we can write the phenomenology of the poem, as it is the poet who gives us our image. The examples that we try to draw from ourselves—I have an image of—are so poor. The psychology of the image consists in giving us this order: to have images. But we are poor at doing this; we have empty hands. But we receive plenty of images from the poet; it's the poet's gift. Because the poet has spoken, then we have images as a reader. The gift of the image to the reader of the poem is the center of the new being. A psychology of inspiration is always too poor. A meditation on the poem as giving us images is the center.

In the Introduction to *The Poetics of Space*, Bachelard says something more precise when he questions how does language give us images. He answers with a metaphor but a metaphor that says much. He speaks of the "reverberation" of words in images (1969, xii, xviii–xx). Reverberation is a metaphor, but it's a translation of the French *retentissement*. *Retentir* is the phenomenon of the *echo*; it's echoing. When we hit a sealed vase, there is a multiplication of sonority. This is what Bachelard calls *retentissement*. It's an auditive metaphor; a space is filled with sonority. He cites a French psychiatrist, Eugène Minkowski, who dealt with the destruction of the perception of space and time in psychosis (xii). Minkowski speaks of the metaphor of how the "hunting horn, reverberating everywhere through its echo, made the tiniest leaf . . . shudder" (Bachelard 1969, xii n.1, editor's note).[7] Reverberation is the dynamism of sonorous life. It's the capacity of awakening by a kind of chain reaction. The creativity in language produces a kind of chain reaction in all the spheres of perception. The image is a residue of perception that is reenacted. What is important is that this reenactment, this retrieval of perceptual traces, is the echo of the birth of new entities of language. It is because language has produced new linguistic beings that this newness of language is echoed in all the spheres of perception. (Bachelard is very difficult to quote, because his text offers semipoetic, semiphilosophical language about poetry. This is why I shall try to proceed in another way.) "By its novelty, a poetic image sets in motion the entire linguistic mechanism. The poetic image places us at the origin of the speaking being" (xix). If we put this in the framework of reading, we may understand better, because it's what happens to the reader.

> Through this reverberation, by going immediately beyond all psychology or psychoanalysis [a point that Bachelard goes on to develop here], we feel a poetic power rising naively within us. After the original reverberation, we are able to experience resonances, sentimental repercussions, reminders of our past. But the image has touched the depths before it stirs the surface. And this is also true of a simple experience of reading. The image offered us by reading the poem now becomes really our own. It takes root in us. *It has been given us by another*, but we begin to have the impression that we could have created it, that we should have created it. It becomes a new being in our language, expressing us by making us what it expresses; in other words, it is at once a becoming of expression, and a becoming of our being. Here expression creates being. (xix; emphasis added)

We have an anticipation of what I shall try to develop in another vocabulary as productive reference.

We must stick to Bachelard's statement that the image belongs to language, not to perception. "[T]he poetic image ... stems from the logos" (xix). It is first newness in language before being a renewal of perceptual residues. "I always come then to the same conclusion: the essential newness of the poetic image poses the problem of the speaking being's creativeness" (xx). If we perceive the quality of an origin somewhere, it's in language. "[P]oetry puts language in a state of emergence, in which life becomes manifest through its vivacity" (xxiii). There are many comparable quotations.

In the next lecture I shall return to Bachelard mainly to insist on the ontological bearing of newness. We are not caught in the nothingness of the image and the anti-world. On the contrary, we are redirected toward reality. I also want to speak more technically of the strategy of language in metaphor to support this general claim of Bachelard, which remains a poetic description of poetry and therefore not very satisfying philosophically, at least for me. I shall reference my own work on metaphor.

16

Fiction (2): Metaphor

To introduce these lectures on fiction, I am using the work of Gaston Bachelard to make essentially two points. First, as previously discussed, it's in and through language that imagination may become creative. It's to the extent that the process of imagination is involved in a creative process of thought and language that imagination itself is productive. The poem is used by Bachelard as the strategy of language in and through which this process evolved. I offered several quotations from the Introductions to *The Poetics of Reverie* and *The Poetics of Space* to insist principally on the novelty of the poetic image and on the novelty being given to us, because someone else speaks, because I receive an image from the poet. The second point I want to emphasize, before considering more technically the language game that provides us such images, is the ontological dimension of fiction. This is my main argument: when we start from reproductive imagination, there is already an original, and therefore the main thrust of the analysis is on the negative side. I retreat from the original; all the spontaneity of imagination is exhausted in producing this nothingness alongside reality, in the margin of reality. The imaginary life is more or less described as a flight, as an escape. By contrast, if we start with an image without an original, then we may discover a kind of second ontology that is not the ontology of the original but the ontology displayed by the image itself, because it has no original.

This thesis is stated very strongly by Bachelard in his Introductions to his two works. I shall rely mainly on *The Poetics of Reverie*, because this cosmic element of the image is emphasized forcefully there. In the Introduction to that work, he begins by saying that poetic reverie is the hypothesis of another life (1971, 8), and I shall use this kind of description for utopia, too.[1] It's a kind of cosmic utopia (13). He keeps repeating that a world emerges (for example, 8). He has this expression of a "dream world" (8, 12). The reverie is not a derivation from dreams, however. To dream is to be asleep. Reverie is awareness. The phenomenology of reverie does not proceed from the psychoanalysis of dreams. "The night dreamer cannot articulate a cogito. The night dream is a dream without a dreamer" (22). By contrast, the reverie has a subject, who is a poet—the poetic cogito. In reverie we address ourselves to an aspect of the world that is not describable in terms of an object but of a situation, a situation of being, as when he speaks of the "repose for a being" (12). The concern is with our being in the world, from the side of our own being as well as the being of the world. Concerning our own being, Bachelard returns to the language of the soul to say precisely that it's not the psyche discussed by the psychologist but this emerging existence responding to an emerging world. Psychology is not useful here. The question is not that a poet is a person but that a person becomes a poet, despite the experience of ordinary life. Bachelard speaks of the "the world of a soul" (15). Why? Because both on the side of the ego and on the side of the world, something is suspended. There is an *epochē*, mainly an *epochē* of care and desire. For Bachelard, a psychoanalysis, at least of the Freudian kind, must fail, because by principle and constitution such a psychoanalysis deals with the adventures of desire, in sublimation and so on, but it's always desire. According to Bachelard, though, poetry is more than sublimation, because it's not merely a transformation of desire working in another way. It's a real *epochē*, a detachment from care. We could find in Heidegger's work on serenity (*Gelassenheit*) surely some important parallelism.[2]

That this imagination is cosmic is secured by its conjunction and complicity with some fundamental structures of reality (Bachelard 1971, 13). We spoke previously of Bachelard's discussion of the four elements, which are more than physical or chemical structures but dimensions of existence. To be related to the world as fire, water, wind, or stone involves more than dealing with manipulable objects; it's to be related to some fundamental physiognomy of the universe. The metamorphoses of these elements through language constitute the root images of poetry. The situation is not so much an anti-world as a metamorphosis of the appearances of the world, and this is the ontology of imagination. There is something also very Jungian in this approach, the fact that I mirror these fundamental structures in my own psychic structure according to the correspondence between macrocosm and microcosm that comes down from the Middle Ages and the Renaissance. Some of Bachelard's expressions remind us as well of Merleau-Ponty, particularly his most cryptic expressions in *The Visible and the Invisible* when he says that the world looks at me. There is an exchange between the seen and the seer (Merleau-Ponty 1968, 139, 202, 274). Bachelard writes similarly, "[E]verything I look at looks at me" (1971, 185). It's by describing in poetic terms some aspect of the universe that I receive the meaning of my own existence, exactly as the Greeks spoke of the correspondence between the sun and the eye. When we speak of the rays of the sun as the gaze of the eye, there is a poetic exchange between the two poetic predicates. Let me conclude these quotations of *The Poetics of Reverie* where Bachelard speaks of these "images of high cosmicity" (190). I wanted to end with this semi-poetic suggestion offered in a philosophical language.

Similar statements appear in *The Poetics of Space*. Here they are linked to the theme of reverberation presented in the last lecture. Because language is creative, it is echoed in all the deep layers of my existence by a kind of infiltration step by step of all the layers of psychic life. To these layers of depth correspond new kinds of relation to the world. "The poet speaks on the threshold of being" (1969, xii).[3] Here expression creates being. Speaking of a new being in our language, this new being, Bachelard says, "express[es] us by making us what it expresses" (xix). To the extent that there is an ontology of the I, of the ego, this ontology is connected to a similar ontology of reality. I finish with the following striking quotation, which provides an answer to the mere nothingness of Sartre. "Thus, contemporary painters no longer consider the image as a simple substitute for a perceptible reality. Proust said already of roses painted by Elstir that they were 'a new variety with which this painter, like some clever horticulturist, had enriched the Rose family'" (xxix). There is a paradox, but there is an expansion of reality. I shall develop this theme in the next lecture with some examples borrowed from painting. Through the image we may have an augmentation of reality and not merely a shadow within ourselves. To the extent that the image is not the copy of something exterior, and so without an original, then it adds to reality. I shall use the expression of the French critic François Dagognet, who, in a book called *Écriture et iconographie* (*Writing and Iconography*), speaks of an iconic augmentation of reality. It is this aspect I want to develop.

I do not claim to have offered a study of Bachelard, and for one fundamental reason. He denies the possibility of analyzing poetry. He thinks it is only in epistemology that we can analyze; we must speak poetically of poetry. What bothers me with Bachelard is that he never tries to adjust his epistemology and his poetics. He thinks they must be kept separate and that there must be no concordance. Either we poeticize or we do science. If, though, we could find in poetic language some specific procedures similar to those of a logic of discovery, perhaps we could bridge this gap. For Bachelard the cleft is unbridgeable between the procedures of imagination in poetry and in science. It's mainly against this claim that I want now to develop the analysis of the different strategies of language that display images and by displaying images open new ways of looking at things. I want to develop this potential ontology.

I shall raise two problems, and I shall address myself to the first one in this lecture and to the second in the following lecture. The first problem will be: how does language generate images. What kind of connection is there between the productive aspect of language and the productive capacities of imagination? What is the structural relation between these two modes of productivity? In the present lecture I shall discuss the movement from language to image by the procedures of metaphor. In the next lecture I shall discuss the problem: how does productive imagination shape or reshape reality. This problem I have coined by the expression of productive reference or, as I said, of iconic augmentation. With this second topic the correlation between model and metaphor will occur, and then we will have a transition from the poetic imagination to what I call the epistemological imagination. They have an intersection in the theory of models to the extent that metaphor is to poetic language what the model is to epistemology.

The central problem of metaphor is analysis of the way in which likeness or similarity works. It is here that imagination plays its role. I shall use as an epigraph to this study the famous statement by Aristotle in his *Poetics*, when he says that to metaphorize well (*eu metaphērein*) is to have an insight into resemblances (*to to homoion theōrein*) (Aristotle 1973, 703, 1459a 6–7), to have the intellectual seeing of the similar. I shall discuss this notion of insight into resemblances. I shall try to show that there is something here that can be analyzed and not merely expressed in poetical terms as reverberation, which is a merely a metaphor. There is what I call a strategy of language that can be analyzed. It's possible to show the articulation between discourse and language in the specific case of metaphor. In other words, it's possible to link a psychology of the image to a semantics of discourse. In a sense, this analysis provides a way of returning to Frege, Husserl, and Price, who all said it is impossible to go from the image to the concept, that we must proceed from the concept to the image. As I said in the last lecture, however, this approach remains too narrow, because it is linked to naming only; it tries to analyze how an image cashes the meaning of a name. But what is interesting in the modern theory of metaphor is precisely that it has broken with a theory of naming; it shifts emphasis to the use of odd predicates from that of deviant names.

To explain this development, let me briefly recall the history of rhetoric. In its rhetorical phase, the theory of metaphor remained caught in the same narrow framework. Even in Aristotle's *Poetics*, the definition of metaphor was the following: to give to a thing the name of another thing because of the similarity between these two things (1973, 699, 1457b 6–9). The word *meta-phora*, which means transfer or transport, was a transfer of names on the basis of the similarity between the bearers of the names. The trick of metaphor was merely a substitution of names. In fact this more appropriately describes metonymy, which is really a name for a name, met-onymy. Because in metonymy there is a relation of contiguity, we construe the metaphor on the model of metonymy by substituting similarity for contiguity. It is the same shifting from name to name on the basis of a certain association, an association here not by contiguity but by similarity. In this description of metaphor, the metaphor brings no fresh information. It tends to be merely decorative. That explains why on this basis we have mainly theories of metaphor as emotional.

What has been questioned, both by semanticists such as Max Black in *Models and Metaphors* and by literary critics such as I. A. Richards in *The Philosophy of Rhetoric*, is the initial presupposition that metaphor is only a deviation in naming, a deviation, in the vocabulary of Wittgenstein, in the language game of giving names. For these analysts the framework of metaphor is the whole sentence. In the next lecture, when we turn to the problem of the referent, we shall see that the framework of metaphor is in fact the whole poem. For the present lecture, we may say, as Monroe Beardsley does in his *Aesthetics*, that the metaphor is a poem in miniature (1958, 144). We treat the poem in its miniature form before dealing with it next time writ large. The framework of the sentence is sufficient to raise the problem of the role of imagination in the emergence of a new meaning. The framework of the whole poem will be necessary to raise the problem of the new reference. To use the terminology of sense and reference, we shall speak in this lecture only of sense, not of reference.

The main idea here is that the productivity of the metaphor relies on the use of odd predicates rather than deviant names. The odd predicates implicate the whole sentence. When I say with Shakespeare that time is a beggar, the metaphor lies in none of the words but in the whole sentence. The metaphor is a sentence; we have then to speak of metaphorical statements and not of metaphors as names. If we lay the stress on this predicative structure, we see that the metaphor is produced by the interplay of all the parts of the sentence. It's not the substitution of names that is important but the tension between subject and predicate. I consider the metaphor from the point of view of the reader of metaphor. Following Bachelard, we are the reader of images. For the reader's first reading, there is in the metaphoric sentence a semantic incongruence; the sentence violates a semantic code of appropriateness. We cannot say, for example, that a triangle is blue, because colors are inappropriately applied to these logical entities. Therefore, the initial condition for the metaphor is the collapse of the consistency of the sentence for a first reading, which we may call literal, in the sense that it employs only those uses of the words that are lexically registered, that is, the current meanings. It's only for an interpretation that there is a metaphor, an interpretation that first fails when it uses only the resources of ordinary meanings. The metaphorical meaning emerges from the ruin of the literal sense by building a new compatibility beyond the inconsistency. A French author, Jean Cohen, has introduced here the term *semantic impertinence*, playing on the two senses of the word *impertinence*.[4] We hear those two senses in English, too: the impertinent is both arrogant and inappropriate. So there is both inappropriateness and also a kind of shock linked to the semantic clash we perceive. We then understand how the problem of the words arises, because to rescue the meaning of the sentence, to make sense with inconsistent and incompatible terms, we have to exert a twist on our words. Beardsley has spoken of a metaphorical twist to describe this action; we extend the meaning of our words beyond their ordinary use. There is a fight at the borderline of the lexicon in order to make use of the unheard and unsaid possibilities of a word.

At this point I must say something about the functioning of words in ordinary language. It is well known in ordinary language that words have flexibility. If we open a dictionary, a word has more than one meaning. This is the great difference between ordinary language and scientific language. In scientific language there is univocity, for one word one meaning. But in ordinary language there is polysemy, and this polysemy is open-ended. The word is the result of a cumulative process. It has a historical dimension projected in the synchrony. In the synchrony, in its state in the dictionary, the word has only an actual, a present sense. But the word's history is projected on the surface of the semantic field. Since a word may retain previous meanings, it may also receive new meanings without losing the previous ones. There is an expansion of polysemy. And it's by expanding the polysemy that the metaphoric sentence makes sense. Therefore, it's not false that metaphor concerns the use of words. But this extension of meaning in metaphor is required by the attempt to rescue the meaning of the whole sentence. That is why there are no metaphors in the dictionary. It's in the actual use by an actual poet that there is a lived metaphor.

Of course, when a metaphor has been accepted, it becomes a cliché. When we speak of old age as the evening of life, it's a cliché, but it could have once been a good metaphor. When it is a cliché, we no longer perceive the previous categorizations that prevented the mixing of the two ideas. With the cliché, an accepted metaphor becomes a dead metaphor and perhaps finally a literal sense. In this last stage, the meaning belongs to the actual polysemy of a term. This is the case with the foot of the chair, the foot of the hill, and so on. The metaphor has become intralexical, whereas in its first use it was extra-lexical.

Metaphoric creativity consists of two things. First, it offers a response

Fiction (2): Metaphor 237

to the challenge of inconsistency by the emergence of a new predicative statement. Second, this semantic innovation is supported by the extension of semantic fields on the basis of their previous polysemy. There is an interplay between sentence and word. In *Models and Metaphors*, Max Black has expressed this by saying that the metaphor implies both a frame and a focus. The frame is the sentence; the focus is the word and its polysemy (1962, 28). The theory of metaphor may focus on the word but that's because first a literal interpretation has failed. We must take the detour of the sentence before returning to the word.

On the basis of this analysis we now may say something about imagination. Imagination has to be linked to the role of likeness in the production of a new meaning, a new sentential meaning, a new predicative meaning. This problem of likeness is very difficult, because we are always tempted to return to a concept of likeness as a likeness provided by an original. It is very difficult to elaborate a logic of likeness, because we have a first concept of likeness that we must forget, the idea that things are already alike and because they are alike, then we may transfer their names. There is no productivity there, since we proceed from a given likeness in things to a substitution of names in our language. In a substitution theory, likeness is unproductive. It's also a weak argument, because two things are alike from one point of view and different from another point of view. We must say in what respect they are alike. Then the issue is the rationale for the likeness, and we are sent back to the existence of a previous conceptual unity, a sameness ruling the similarity. The problem is more interesting when we don't possess this sameness, this conceptual identity that provides us with the rationale for the likeness in the things. I keep returning to this issue: as long as we proceed with a theory of imagination ruled by an original, we have only the image as a copy, more or less dependent. The same occurs with likeness; the likeness must be first in the original, then in our language. The mimesis is copying.

The situation is quite different in a tension theory. The tension is twofold. First, there is a tension between subject and predicate because they don't go together. There is an incongruity in their semantic coexistence. Second, there is also a tension between two interpretations, the literal interpretation that states the collapse of the meaning and the interpretation that takes into account the extended meanings of the words. My hypothesis is that imagination plays a role in the transition from literal incongruence to metaphorical congruence, in the birth of a new pertinence, a new appropriateness. Likeness here has nothing to do with the association of ideas. We must forget the mechanical model of balls hitting one another, as in the Newtonian model of the association of ideas. That is not at all an association by resemblance. There is no parallelism between similarity and contiguity. In metaphor we try to derive likeness from the functioning of an odd predicate and derive imagination from likeness.

Consider what happens when two semantic fields are suddenly put together. We may say that a logical distance has been abolished. In the vocabulary of ordinary language, which often has an insight into the functioning of things, we may speak of the nearness of ideas just as before we could have spoken of the ideas as remote. I wonder whether the notion of logical space that Wittgenstein introduces at the beginning of the *Tractatus* (1961, 1.13) is not appropriate here, because likeness has to be interpreted dynamically as this rapprochement. It's the production of a proximity. We construe likeness by generating a new kinship between things that were not akin. This is what is implied in the notion of *meta-phora*; it's a transfer. I interpret transfer precisely in spatial terms, in the logical space, as two ideas that are brought together that have nothing in common. It's in this move that changes the logical distance from the far to the near that there is a transfer. The likeness is the product of the transfer, the move. Could we then not say that the place of productive imagination lies in the insight into the nascent likeness? To see here is to produce, to produce seeing the likeness.

When we speak of seeing or insight, this doesn't exclude thought. On the contrary, it demands the greatest thought to restructure semantic fields. Although, as I have said, I like Price very much, we are far here from his examples, because he never goes further than to give an instance to a concept. In contrast, the problem in productive imagination is to produce a new concept on the basis of new instances. There's a restructuration of semantic fields. The productive imagination is not something irrational; it must be categorial in order to be transcategorial. By transcategorial I mean that we cannot have metaphors if we do not already have a categorization of reality that we violate. There must be laws before there can be a violation of laws. It's in a world already ordered categorically that we may proceed to these transfers, these moves. In some cases the new insight even has a logical structure. Aristotle offers the example in the *Poetics* of what he calls analogical metaphor, metaphor by proportion, when we say that A is to B what C is to D. When I say that the cup of Dionysus is what the shield is to Ares, the God of war, then I may speak of the shield of Dionysus by a kind of shortcut between the second and the fourth term. We speak of the shield of Dionysus or of the cup of Ares as abbreviations (1973, 699, 1457b 16–22). But the insight is also there, the instantaneous grasp of the combinatory possibilities offered by proportionality. Even when there is not the structure of proportion with four terms, which perhaps is a reconstruction after the fact, we can speak in general terms of predicative assimilation instead of similitude. It's not a similitude that is given but an as-similation that is

Fiction (2): Metaphor 239

produced. We make similar. I chose the expression predicative assimilation because it emphasizes first that it's always within predication that this occurs and second that the similarity here is an operation, a move, a change of logical distance. It's always in the expression X is Y that there is a metaphor, where the *is* means *is like*, but the *like* is not a relation elaborated for itself as it is in the simile. The simile is an expanded or displayed metaphor. The metaphoric insight sees immediately the X in the Y and the Y in the X.

What is imaginative in this predicative assimilation? Here the imagination works like the schema in Kant. As we discussed in the first lecture on Kant, the schema is a rule for providing an image for a concept. In predicative assimilation too we have a rule. The rule concerns the logic and, more precisely, the paradoxical structure of this assimilation, since in this assimilation there is a certain contrast—a certain tension or fight—between a previous categorization that resists and a new categorization that does not reach the level of a new concept. We are in a nascent phase of a new categorization built on the ruins of a previous categorization. The logic of likeness here is the emergence of a new sameness in a difference or despite difference. In the metaphor there is, in Ryle's terms, a category mistake when we present the facts of one category in the terms of another category (1949, 16–18). It's a clever and intended category mistake in the sense that the new rapprochement runs against a previous interdiction to connect subject and predicate in that way. In *Languages of Art*, Nelson Goodman says that in metaphor there is a connection that yields while protesting (1968, 69). There is no metaphor if I no longer perceive the old order in the new. In this discrepancy between a nascent categorization and an old categorization that resists, we have this insight into likeness that is not yet sameness.

At this stage imagination, which is not yet full imagination but the schema, is very close to language. It's the competence to produce new genres by assimilation but not yet above the specific differences. By contrast, we have a concept when we give a name to the rule when it is abstracted from its material. With imagination, it's in the difference and despite the difference that we perceive a possible sameness. Imagination is the stage in the production of concepts where the generic kinship has not yet reached what we could call the point of rest or peace of the concept but remains caught in the interplay between remoteness and nearness. I owe this suggestion to Gadamer, who writes in the third part of *Truth and Method* of the general metaphoricity of language (1989, 429–31). We can speak of the general metaphoricity of language if we say that in a sense all our concepts are born in the restructuration of previous categorization. Metaphor as a figure of speech has the advantage of presenting us this restructuring as a stylistic device. The metaphoricity of language is concealed in the process of thought, whereas the metaphor in poetic language becomes a strategy that is obvious and can be described. By extension, what we know as a metaphor in poetic language allows us to cast a glance into the fabric of new concepts, because in the case of poetry the movement toward the concept is suspended and blocked at the level of the image.

We have made a move from likeness to the schema and may now take a step further, from the schema to the image. Here we approach, in Bachelard's vocabulary, the enigma of reverberation: how is the schema reverberated in image? Perhaps we could say that an element of depiction is implied in predicative assimilation. The moment of the image arises when we have not only the intellectual insight into the new appropriateness but we read this new appropriateness in a certain picture of the relation. The relation is depicted in pictures. Something appears in which we read the new connection. It is this complex link between the verbal and the visual that presents the great difficulty for a theory of imagination. How is the appearance of a quasi-visible linked to a verbal element, to a semantic element? Here too our ordinary language has a kind of wisdom of its own since the word *sense*, at least in Indo-European languages, exhibits this ambiguity. We speak of the sense of a sentence, but we also speak of the five senses. Between sense and senses there is a linguistic affinity that may betray something, an intercourse between the two that makes the concreteness of metaphor. For example, very often in literary criticism to inquire into the metaphor of an author is to inquire into his or her images. But the relationship between the verbal and the visual remains without solution as long as we treat the image as a mental picture, as the replica of an absent thing. The obstacle lies in our theory of the image as the image of something. As long as we treat the image as a picture of an absent thing, then the image must remain exterior to predicative assimilation as a kind of associated image. So many authors speak of associated images as though between speaking and seeing, between the linguistic element of the metaphor and the pictorial element of images, there were a logical gap.[5] But precisely we have to discover an element of seeing that is a part of speaking. Can we not say that it is by producing images that we schematize what I call predicative assimilation? By displaying a body of images, we initiate changes of logical distance. We generate rapprochement. We read the rapprochement in a corresponding image. The image is the concrete milieu in which we see resemblances.

This suggestion is supported by a trait of metaphor of which I have not yet spoken that a mere logic may overlook but literary criticism has better recognized. I. A. Richards says that the metaphor is the relation between what he calls a tenor and a vehicle. (The word *tenor* comes, if I'm correct, from George Berkeley when he speaks of the tenor of our idea, its intellectual content.[6]) Richards contends that in the metaphor there is another tension that is not only between the terms, not only between two interpretations, but between two levels. It's a way of seeing something as something else, but something that is a logical relation in terms of something that is a visual presentation. There is a connection between a new semantic connection and an imaginary space within which this new connection is expanded. It's very difficult to speak of this without metaphors about the metaphor. The vocabulary of metaphor is itself metaphorical. The word *metaphor* is a metaphor, since it is a metaphor of space. All the metaphors of metaphors are, precisely, spatial metaphors, because the function of the metaphor is to display the verbal element in a mental space. For example, some speak of seeing a relation through the screen of an image or of seeing something through a lens. Scientists in the nineteenth century spoke of stereoscopic vision: we see the depth of the third dimension by a discordance between two pictures in the second dimension. It's to see something through something else. Here we really hit on the iconic element of the metaphor, which is not at all a mental picture of something but the display of the meaning by way of a depiction. In his article on "Metaphor," Paul Henle says that the icon is not physically presented but linguistically depicted and described (1958, 177).[7] "[W]hat is presented is a formula for construing icons" (178). The difference between the icon and the picture of an absent thing is that the icon presents similarities that are as yet unsaid and unheard, are related to qualities, to structures, to feelings, and so on. Each time the new connection at which we are aiming our thought grasps what the icon describes or depicts. We give to ourselves a presentation of what we are trying to think. We iconize, if we may say, the new relations between things that we are discovering.

A phenomenology of reading, of what we do when we read, could very well support this analysis. The experience of reading presents oscillating levels of depiction. When we read quickly, even if it's a novel with very concrete elements, we don't take time to develop images. The images we have are only light supports of our thoughts, and then the schematic images are not expanded. They are merely nascent and fading illustrations of the new facts, the new events, the new relationships between things. Sometimes, though, we have more concrete representations, but which are always bound by their sense. Marcus Hester, a Wittgensteinian, has written on this topic. In *The Meaning of Poetic Metaphor* he uses abundantly the vocabulary of *seeing as* but applies it to examples other than the ones given by Wittgenstein, who remains always in the field of perception. In Wittgenstein's examples, such as the picture of the duck/rabbit, there is nothing productive. Hester applies the notion of *seeing as* in metaphor to the verbal element (1967, 169–70). We *see as* what we *think as* (187–88). To *think as* and to *see as* are correlative. Then

Hester speaks of the implied images or the bound images, images that are aroused by the verbal element and controlled by it (see, for example, 189). This is the ordinary level of imagination. The image escapes the control of the intellectual reading, the reading of the meaning, the reading of the sense. The reverberation here consists in this arousal of all the sensory fields, all the traces of perception. They are images and not merely traces, because they are controlled by the process of reading itself as an intellectual phenomenon. It's only when we stop or interrupt reading that we have the kind of images that Sartre describes, images that fascinate us and that may become delusive attempts to possess magically some absent things, mainly some absent bodies and persons. This last stage represents a relaxation of the tension of reading and a relaxation of the semantic tensions implied by reading. Then there is a shift from the bound image, which is a part of the meaningful process of reading, to the wild image, which has a life of its own and which represents more an interruption of the process than its depiction. The image no longer depicts the relations that we are following but interrupts them to display its own rule, which is the rule of fascination, of delusion.

The most interesting stage, the one that raises the most interesting philosophical questions, is the intermediary stage between the mere schema and the disrupting image that is more parasitic on the process of reading. This intermediary stage corresponds more accurately to Bachelard's notion of reverberation and is, I think, what he had in mind when he spoke of the term. The image is the echo of the sense. This is more or less what Hester describes as the bound image. We have a fusion between sense and senses, sense and images, that constitutes the poetic image. What is specific to the poetic image is that it's an intellectual process of metaphor but one that emerged in the process of depicting the relationships conceived and perceived intellectually. The image here is not merely an appendix, it does not have this parasitic role that I denounced because it brings into the process of thinking its two dimensions, the likeness and the negation. The negation appears because the image places the sense in the dimension of suspension, of *epochē*, of fiction. At the same time, though, it provides the element of quasi-observation that we may retain from Sartre. We quasi-observe what we are thinking, what I call the element of depiction in thought. The meaning is depicted under the *feature of*. This is the concrete manner of poetic diction. We may say that meaning is not only schematized but depicted, and we may read the sense in the depicted image. All the residual impressions that psychology calls images are incorporated through this process. Just as in the dream, as Freud told us, there are day residues, there are day residues and perhaps also dream residues in the poetic image.[8] The important fact is not their presence but their involvement in the process of semantic innovation. The dialectic is between semantic innovation and depiction.

When I said in the last lecture that there were two main domains in which we could study productive imagination, I should have said that there are in fact at least four. The first two domains are the subject of the present lectures: the productive imagination in the poetic dimension and in the epistemological dimension. A third domain is the current subject of a separate set of lectures on ideology and utopia. The topic there is the dialectics of imagination in cultural, social, and political life. We should not break the theory of imagination into a split between sociology and psychology. The fourth field, which I do not now address, would be the domain of religious symbols. There should be a specific approach to the functioning of symbols as depictions also of certain kinds of meanings.

In lecture 17 I shall discuss the functioning of metaphor as providing new references and then introduce the relation between metaphor and model and the transition to the epistemological imagination.

17

Fiction (3): Painting

In this lecture I proceed a step further in the attempt to elaborate a theory of fiction in which the negative element is the key to the referential power itself. As I have said, the paradox of fiction is that it's not merely absence but, thanks to its negativity, it discloses new dimensions of reality. It is this capacity for a transfiguration of experience and, through experience, for a transfiguration of reality itself that I shall try to develop on the basis of a certain number of approaches borrowed from different aspects of experience—literary, artistic, and scientific. To make a whole I would need to add religious and political approaches, but here I shall give examples only from the three fields named. I speak in other lectures on ideology and utopia as also structures of social action.

It's not without difficulty that we try to speak of a productive reference linked to the fictional aspect of imagination, because there are many obstacles. Some are general and linked to our philosophical tradition, and some are more specific to poetic language. As concerns the obstacles that proceed from our philosophical tradition, let me recall only the general orientation of Kant's philosophy concerning productive imagination. We owe to him the main distinction between reproductive and productive imagination, and I try therefore to follow the line of the latter. Yet remember that the theory of productive imagination in Kant's third *Critique* was linked fundamentally to the reflective judgment. Productive imagination there does not involve a determination of the thing, since the determination of reality is complete with the cognitive element and therefore under the rule of the categories of the understanding. It is only in reflection that we exert the judgment of taste. It is within the judgment of taste that we assess and appreciate the work of art. The universal element in the judgment of taste has nothing to do with something objective but only with the character of our pleasure in a work of art, a pleasure that is essentially communicable. The communicability of pleasure is the only universal element, and it's not borrowed from reality. Gadamer shows that because Kant's aesthetics places the concept of the beautiful under the judgment and therefore before the tribunal of the subject, it then blocks the way to an ontology of the image. The theory of genius that completes the Kantian theory of art also has a subjective element, since in genius, it's nature that gives rules to the mind, to what Kant calls the *Gemüt*, the spirit.[1] There is something fundamentally subjective in the theory of genius, as Richard McKeon has very well shown in an article in his book *Thought, Action, and Passion* concerning the history of the concept of imitation in aesthetics. McKeon establishes that it's the decay in the concept of imitation that paved the way for the concept of genius (1954, 152–53). For Aristotle mimesis was not at all a way of copying a thing. It was a creative reconstruction of reality, as when the tragedy expresses the truth about human action because it's a *muthos*, a plot, a fable. This notion of creative mimesis has been completely lost, because in the tradition of imitation, imitation has been understood not as an imitation of nature, in this creative sense, but as an imitation of previous models of other artists. Imitation becomes a concept of conformity in a tradition, not a creative reconstruction of what is. The aesthetics of genius in the eighteenth century replaced this dying aesthetics of imitation. We are more or less still under the spell of this condemnation of imitation, even in our translation of Aristotle, where mimesis translated as imitation immediately takes on a bad connotation. We also tend to say that there is no longer imitation in art, since art is no longer figurative. We tend to identify the imitative with the figurative, and therefore we say that because abstract art is not figurative, it's not mimetic. We have lost the concept of the mimetic through this tradition. This is one formidable obstacle to breaking through to a concept of productive reference.

We could also say that the philosophy of imagination in both Ryle and Sartre does not help us to make this breakthrough. As I said in the introduction to this third part of the lectures, for example, the psychology of delusion in Sartre closes the way to an ontology of fiction. What Sartre calls the imaginary life is a desperate attempt to possess the thing in its absence. It's not at all a transfiguration of reality but a magic of mock possession: my freedom is signified only in imagination, not in a dimension of reality. In this sense Sartre's philosophy of imagination reinforces the subjective trend of Kant's *Critique of Judgment*. Such are the general philosophical difficulties preventing us from developing an ontology of fiction.

Besides these philosophical problems are difficulties proper to poetic language. It's not only the development of abstract painting but also the aesthetics of poetry that, in modern criticism, is anti-ontological, and for good reasons. These obstacles are not merely prejudices but constitute real difficulties that we have to deal with and fight against. We have to meet the counterexamples. Poetry is itself a kind of counterexample to an ontology of fiction. Why? Because it seems that in poetry, language is directed not toward reality in a descriptive way but toward itself. I use here an important analysis of the poetic function, Roman Jakobson's essay on linguistics and poetics.[2] In his model, language is based on a certain number of factors to which correspond functions. There is a speaker, message, and hearer, a physical or psychological contact, a code, and a situation. According to Jakobson, each act of communication combines more or less all these elements. What is of present interest for us here is the place of poetry in this schema, because there are different modes of discourse depending on the factor that is emphasized. It's not that some modes of discourse use only one element—that's impossible—but the emphasis may be placed on one or the other element. For example, in some forms of discourse that he calls emotive—a cry or an interjection—the speaker is emphasized. Or the hearer may be emphasized, and here it's the imperative, what Jakobson calls the conative, because we influence the other. The element of contact is not very important for our purpose and is the kind of expression—hello, goodbye—we speak only to preserve the communication for itself. Jakobson calls these expressions phatic, because we speak for the sake of speaking. There is also what Jakobson terms a metalinguistic function, and it occurs not only when we do linguistics. Even in ordinary language, we may speak of our language instead of speaking of reality. For example, when we give a definition, we don't add anything to our knowledge of reality, but we extend our language. All the procedures by which the child extends his or her vocabulary—for example, by asking what do you call that—are metalinguistic. In what Wittgenstein calls the language game of naming, or in learning definitions, synonyms, or a foreign language, all of these inquiries are metalinguistic. In learning a foreign language, for instance, we ask how something is said in the new language; we compare elements of two vocabularies. The important discussion for us arises in Jakobson's claim that language is directed toward a situation in the world when it is referential. He tends to identify the referential with the descriptive; language is referential when it describes reality and then adds to our information about reality. By contrast, the poetic function is identified with its message. This may occur in poetry or prose, whenever the message is accentuated for its own sake. There is a cleft between sign and thing, between language and world, as if we enjoyed the fullness of language for its own sake.

This linguistic definition of poetry is confirmed by considerations borrowed from literary criticism. There is a reinforcement and conjunction in linguistics and literary criticism tending toward the same conclusion:

that in poetry there is a suspension of reference, that in poetry language is about itself. In the prior lecture, we offered arguments that led toward this conclusion when we insisted on the display in poetry of images under the control of words. This reverberation of language into images isolates the poem as a self-contained text. Language appears as a sculpture closed in on itself. Earlier critics had emphasized the conjunction in poetry between a poem's sense and sounds. To the extent that the sense adheres to the sounds, it is not directed outward. The sense is encapsulated within the phonetic form and also within the world of images displayed by language. To the extent that there are, as Hester said of poetry, bound images, images tied to language, this tie is reciprocal in the sense that the sense too is tied to these images. Therefore, the imaginative surrounding of language in poetry tends to provide an *epochē* of reality thanks to this adherence between sense and sound.

Many metaphors express how poetic language is a thing in itself. For example, the French poet Paul Valéry compares prose to walking, whereas poetry is a kind of dance.[3] To walk is to go somewhere, while dancing goes nowhere. In poetry there is movement for its own sake and not for the sake of accomplishment. By contrast, the accomplishment of walking is compared to the reference of descriptive language. We may say too that by walking we describe space, whereas in dancing we describe only the movement and the rhythm.

The modern critic who went the furthest in this denial of the referential function of poetic language is Northrop Frye in his book, *Anatomy of Criticism*. In the first part of this book, Frye sets strongly in opposition two directions of language, what he calls an outward direction typical of descriptive language and an inward or centripetal direction which is that of poetry (for example, 1966, 73–89, 113). This is another way to say with Jakobson that in poetry language exists for its own sake, not for the sake of what it says. There is in poetry a suspension of reference. This is taken for granted by an important majority of critics who in fact merely corroborate a positivist epistemology. The claim is that only scientific language has an informative function, and poetry finally has only an emotional function. Poetry does not say anything about what is but only what we feel. A poem is the inner structure of a mood and not at all a description of anything. This is sometimes expressed by critics in a vocabulary that philosophically is very questionable, the opposition between denotation and connotation. This opposition does not correspond to the terms' use in logic but is typical of the vocabulary of literary criticism. It is said that only scientific language is descriptive or denotative; these words are taken more or less as synonymous. In poetry, on the other hand, language is celebrated for its own sake and so has only connotative meaning, that is to say, it develops some associated emotions on the basis of images associated with the kernel of linguistic symbols or, more precisely, linguistic signs.

From all these arguments, I conclude that we cannot proceed directly from a theory of metaphor to a theory of productive reference. We need some roundabout approach to pave the way for the recovery of a second order reference beyond the collapse of a first order reference, the reference of descriptive language, in order to say that the problem of reference is not closed by the absence of a descriptive reference. The two detours I propose to take will be, on the one hand, a reflection on painting and, on the other, a reflection on models in epistemology. After these detours, a transfer from model to metaphor will be possible. In a way, metaphor introduces models when we remain at the level of sense. But the movement is from model to metaphor at the level of reference. I shall try to explain why when I take up this problem in the next lecture. To anticipate, I would say that as long as we remain only with isolated sentences, we cannot see the referential dimension of poetic language. It's not the single metaphor that says something; it's the poem as a whole. We must place the metaphor within the broader framework of a work to see this. Precisely with painting on the one hand and models on the other there is a metaphorical complex, a work of art or a work of thought. But I shall return to this problem in the next lecture.

In the present lecture I shall develop the first example, that of painting, because it paves the way for a concept of productive reference. I take what happens in painting as the paradigm for all kinds of transfigurations of reality through iconographic devices. I use the terms *icon*, *iconic*, and *iconicity* in the sense framed by French epistemologist François Dagognet in his book *Écriture et iconographie*. This book is directed against the thesis coming from Plato's *Phaedrus* that writing and pictures in general impoverish reality because they are themselves less than real, are mere shadows as compared to real things. (My own use of Dagognet here is limited to his argument about pictures.) It's interesting to return precisely to the oldest tradition about the image. Perhaps we are always under the spell of this theory of the image coming from Plato, where the image is always less than. For example, we could say that there is something Platonic still in Hume, where we have first an impression, something that has vividness, intensity, and plentitude. By contrast, Hume considers the image as less vivid, less living. The copy is always less than the model. This relationship between original and copy that I fight against is extremely important in the Western tradition and is in fact a Platonic model. The relation between an original and a copy is the Platonic root of our philosophy of the image. In Plato, painting is an image of an image, a shadow of shadows, since the originals for painting are themselves shadows of the pure models, which are Ideas. And even the Ideas are, if not shadows, at least less than the origin, which is light, the sun, the Idea of the Good, and so on. McKeon has also developed this in his article on imitation, showing that the concept of mimesis in Aristotle was already directed against this notion of the shadow (1954, 112–13, 215). There is no trace in Aristotle of the notion that the *muthos* of tragedy is the shadow of human life. On the contrary, the *muthos* has a power of disclosure concerning reality that is the contrary of a shadow. Whatever may be the case in the relation between Aristotle and Plato, the predominant tradition relating original and copy is the fundamental obstacle behind even the subjectivism of Kant.

The thesis developed in Dagognet's small book is that the images created by the skill of the artist are not less than real but more than real, because they increase reality (1973, 49).[4] It is this notion of increasing reality that I want to develop. Dagognet speaks of iconic augmentation (for example, 48, 73) to express this power of both condensing and expanding reality. He opposes this iconic increase or augmentation to the mere reduplicative function of the shadowy images. Using the vocabulary of the second law of thermodynamics, he says that shadowy images express the entropic trend, which stands for the equalization of energies, the annihilation of differences, of levels (65). Dagognet relies here on the functioning of ordinary perception, which by habit tends to blur the contrasts, the edges of things, and to reduce tensions in perception. There is a loss of energetic differences in the process of perception. Dagognet's idea is that iconic activity may be described as an attempt to take the approach of a negative entropy, a fight against the death of differentiations and contrasting patterns. This is a very interesting way of putting the old problem of productive and reproductive imagination into a broader framework. It implies, though, a series of important decisions concerning the phenomenology of creative imagination, and I want to elaborate this conceptual framework and then to apply it to cases other than poetry.

The first decision, the first presupposition, is to take a point of departure quite different from the classical psychology of imagination, which adhered to the model of the mental image. There the problem was what is it to have an image, something that is supposed to be interior and private. The first step taken in the alternative is to choose as a starting point an image that is public because exterior. This is another way of preferring the picture to the mental image. We saw how the classical theory always oscillated between starting from one of those two poles, either from the picture—for example, the photograph—or from the mental image. Is the mental image a kind of picture or is the picture a kind of mental image on the basis of a neutralized perception? Even the picture, though, is not a sufficient starting point, be-

Fiction (3): Painting 251

cause it's not a work. Here the decisive move is to start from a picture that is a work. The notion of a painting as a picture is quite different from that of a photograph, which is defined by the function of copying.[5] The painting is a fictional work, and the fictional work must be completely distinguished from that of a picture which is the picture of. Of course, some paintings have more or less the character of being a picture of—in the tradition of the portrait, landscape, and so on. There the figurative element is an aspect of the picture; we preserve something of the picture as picture of. But what is important is that the painting is a work. This will be very significant when we try to place the metaphor within the poem as a work.

Through the notion of a work, we introduce some specific categories that don't belong in the first instance to language but to the category of *technē*, production. Language, too, has to be produced as a work and therefore according to certain *technē*, certain techniques. Among the categories of production of a work is to give a form to a matter, a notion of organization, of structuration. Second, general rules that appear in language as literary genres have their parallel in painting as the genres of portraits, landscapes, religious painting, and so on. More important, these genres are not merely classificatory devices but generative tools to produce singular entities. A style is the form of an individual work produced intentionally.

The first step, then, in the phenomenology of creative imagination is to break with the tradition of mental image and even of picture to address oneself to a fictional work. It is exactly at this point that writing and painting raise a similar issue, as Plato discussed. His attack on writing was at the same time an attack against painting, since he compared the external marks of writing to the strokes, lines, and patches of color in painting. Writing and painting have in common the delivery of the creative process to an external bearer, to what he called external marks. The adventure of imagination is here linked to the construction of a material medium that carries the message of fiction. This is already the end of the imagination as shadow, because the exteriorization of the imaginative process places a thought outside itself. The promotion of reality linked to this exteriorization starts from the externalization of creativity itself. We have to break with the tradition of the image as a shadow. To a certain extent we even have to break with the tradition of reminiscence, which says that it's only by a process of interiorization of memory that we get within the mind, because it's also by receiving meaning from external works that we increase our capacity of reminiscence. There is a detour by means of exteriority. The promotion of reality of which we shall speak is the consequence of this externalization of human purpose and creative insights into a material medium.

The second implication of this phenomenology of iconic augmentation is that the augmentation, the increase of reality, is linked not only, as in my first point, to the choice of a material medium but to the creation of an alphabet—a structural screen—used for abbreviating and condensing the pertinent traits of reality, enabling a choice of pertinent traits. This aspect is developed at length by Gombrich in *Art and Illusion* (for example, 1969, 73–74, 293). He compares painting to a reading of reality according to a certain hermeneutical rule. Each painter retains from reality what is congruent with his screen, with his abbreviating and condensing tool. I previously considered that a painting is enclosed within a frame. The notion of the frame is itself significant for separating the painting from the wall, from its support, but more than that, it delineates the closedness of the painting. Whereas reality has endless connections, in the painting there is an enclosure of the message within the limits of a small segment of space. It is within this window that a world is expressed in miniature-like fashion. This condensation is not only a question of scale and of size, of a quantitative reduction. There's also a question of parsimony in the choice and use of what I call the pertinent traits. Dagognet compares this parsimony in means to the invention of alphabets for writing (1973, 29–33). There was a long succession of phases from the pictograms and the hieroglyphs through the ideograms finally to the alphabetic spelling of sound (29–31). Dagognet compares the history of painting to this history of the construction of an alphabetic grid for the signifying of our language (47–48). The capacity of an alphabet to express thought through a limited number of discrete units with a rich power of combination can be transposed to the situation of painting. What I just called the process of abbreviation seems to be the condition for increasing the generative power derived from the combinatory resource of a finite set of discrete units (38). In this sense we may speak of the alphabet of a painter (49). In a similar way, all the progress and changes in painting can be linked to inventions comparable to that of the alphabet in terms of conciseness, distinctness, and generative power. The artist too seems to attempt to capture the universe in a network of abbreviated signs (48).

Of course, I don't intend to blur the fundamental difference between verbal and nonverbal messages. Plato did not completely miss this point when he compared writing to painting, nor do we in comparing, in a reverse way, painting to writing. The main difference between the two has been studied by Nelson Goodman. In chapter 4 of *Languages of Art*, Goodman distinguishes between the functioning of what he calls the dense or thick symbols of painting and the discrete symbols of language. But what is particularly interesting in Goodman is that he ultimately places linguistic and nonlinguistic symbols within a common framework (1968, 252–55), because both display not only a connotative but a denotative function (245), thanks to their condensation, abbreviation, composition, and so on (for example, 230–31). The obvious differences between the dense symbols of painting and the discrete symbols of language fall under a general function of iconicity. The structure of this general function is here the issue.

What could be the concrete procedures of painting that might be compared to the abbreviation of the alphabetic set? I should like to take two or three examples in the history of painting which show that it's by breaking with reality that we express reality. A first example is the reversal of the value of colors at points throughout painting's history. Already in the archaic kind of painting in the Byzantine tradition, for example, the sky is represented as gold whereas we perceive it as blue. Painting the sky as gold displays the value of the sky not in its presentation for an initial description; it's the celebration of light as completely overwhelming all the other characteristics of the atmosphere. We have a redescription of the sky as gold by the choice of this expressive tool. On the opposite side, we could say that blue may be the truth of non-blue objects. Nelson Goodman developed the notion of a metaphoric blue (1968, 83–84), when we say that it's not the blue of the thing that we perceive as blue. I return nearly every week to Chicago's Art Institute to see the blue Picasso there. In this blue period, in this miserabilist representation of a shabby character, an old man playing guitar, it's the blueness of his life as the sadness of his life that is properly depicted, that is redescribed as blue. It's no longer the sky that is blue but the old guitarist who is blue. Consider also the use of colors in the history of landscape. The luminosity of red is used to express distance and depth, while the coldness of blue is appropriate to express the proximity and the thickness of things (Dagognet 1973, 71). In many Constables, the forefront of grass is not green but blue and sometimes brown. The history of color with Paul Cézanne, Paul Gauguin, and Vincent Van Gogh (71) is the conquest of the redescriptive value of colors for expressing the qualities of things.

A more technical example, developed at greater length by Dagognet, is the example of the invention of oil painting by Dutch painters in the fifteenth century (1973, 64–68). By mixing color pigments with oil and therefore by selecting a new range of material means, they could meet the challenge constituted by the erosion of colors' oppositions in ordinary vision (65). When we look at the extraordinary and wonderful Dutch painting, we see that the colors of the world are restituted, all these colors that tended to neutralize one another, to blur their edges, to shed off their contrasts. Dagognet calls this a negentropic strategy (65). It's a very technical problem. For example, there is use of light in the painting by the combination of the deep refraction of light with the mere reflection on the surface, a combination of surface luminosity and thick refraction. In that way they have recreated the luminosity of the universe (66).

The relation between art and the science of the time is an interesting one. As in Dagognet's Dutch example, we may find at least a scientific attitude toward artistic materials. Panofsky has written the story of the invention of pigments in oil painting.[6] And then the use of perspective is linked to optical physics. The great Italian artists of the Renaissance—Michelangelo, Leonardo da Vinci—surely had the idea that they now were telling the truth about nature. Between Francis Bacon and artists such as da Vinci there was a kinship mentality, to explore nature with boldness. Perhaps this should be called an ideology, an ideology of naturalism. It belonged to an age of the discovery of nature. But I would not say for other artists that a scientific attitude toward the tools, the means, the materials, has to be extended to the vision itself. And Gombrich has shown very well in *Art and Illusion* that in fact perspective is something artificial, because it presupposes that there is only one point in space from which all the lines converge toward the vanishing point (1969, 247–57). In all his work Gombrich fights against the idea that art is truer and truer as if we approach nature more and more closely (for example, 87–90). For us after Impressionism, Cubism, and the knowledge of Chinese painting, we know that naturalism is simply one syntax.

We may in fact take the art of Impressionism at the time of the invention of photography as yet another example of the use of painting procedures that break with reality in order to express it in new ways. In its least imaginative use, photography merely transposes the objective dimensions of the exterior world. I know that is not an accurate portrayal of photography, since the choice of angle, the light, the moment of the day, and so on introduce creative elements. Nevertheless, when photography was invented in the nineteenth century, it was mainly for the purpose of having copies of fleeting realities and preserving memories. It was mainly imitative in the sense of reproductive. Painting had to disconnect itself from photography because it could no longer be a *re*presentation of reality since we had photography. In his work on painting, Baudelaire develops at length a fight against photography (Dagognet 1973, 58–64). For him photography was a disaster. His idea was that it merely transposed the objective dimensions, proportions, shapes, and colors of things, and this was the awful model of reproductive imagination. Impressionism tried to beat photography where the latter cannot work by creating a new alphabet of colors capable of capturing the transient and the fleeting with the magic of hidden correspondences. Once more, reality was remade, with an emphasis on atmospheric values and light appearances.

It is in these senses that painting is mimetic. It is an imitation of real-

Fiction (3): Painting 255

ity but under the condition of creating the *medium* of the mimesis exactly as the tragic poet creates the medium of mimesis by controlling the plot. There is a kind of plot here of colors and lines that is a condensed network in exactly the same way that the tragedy is more dense than life, has only the essential structures of life. In the tragedy's condensation in space, time, and meaningful action, only the pertinent traits of tragic situations are retained. In exactly the same way there is creative imitation in painting.

I want to insist, though, on a third and even more important implication of the notion of creative imagination. I have emphasized, first, that we trust a material medium; we externalize in this material medium our creative capacities. Second, it's by construing an alphabet that screens pertinent traits that we can do that. The third and final implication can be expressed in the form of a paradox: the more imagination deviates from what is called reality in ordinary vision and in ordinary language, the closer it comes to the core of reality that is no longer the world of manipulable objects. In terms of painting, the paradox is that when painting is no longer figurative, it displays its most mimetic function. As long as we may raise the question of what the painting represents, then we transfer the productive into the reproductive; we keep asking questions about the relation between the copy and the model. Even with a certain education in the examination of paintings, we try first to see the title of the work and then to see what is represented. We are directed to the things depicted. This is the case particularly in portraits and landscapes. I should say that now it's through the nonfigurative painting that we have to look at figurative painting, because when we can give no names in the ordinary world to the "things" depicted, then we have to do with unseen and unheard objects and, in fact, with no objects. At the same time, it's some nonobjective qualities of reality that are depicted. Could we not say that it's precisely when painting is no longer figurative that it's completely fictional and then that it orients us toward aspects of our way of inhabiting this world according even to the nonfigurative vision? I love the art of Piet Mondrian, for example, and all the networks of lines in his work without any object. In Mondrian we are caught in the peaceful intertwining of lines and colors and then directed toward a peaceful way of dealing with people, with things, and toward living according to the peaceful message of the painting. But it is a subtle, indirect ontology, not the kind of direct and still pictorial ontology of figurative painting. When we can no longer name objects in painting, then what are expressed are some fundamental tensions that relate us to the world as a whole. It's when we can no longer identify manipulable objects that we are directed toward a world, the kind of world within which we are thrown by birth and in which we can orient ourselves. In the Heideggerian vocabulary, there is *Befindlichkeit*—we find ourselves somewhere—when there is *Verstehen*, when we can orient ourselves and project some possibilities.[7] It is in this relation between *Befindlichkeit* and *Verstehen*, between being thrown and orienting oneself, that we develop some fundamental possibilities that are depicted by painting. It's to our relation to reality before its objectification, before it is objectified in the form of the recognition of objects that we can control, that I think that painting is addressed.

This is why I have tried to prepare the parallelism with painting: it's when a descriptive reference is abolished that a more fundamental reference is displayed. It's not a reference to a something, to objects, or to things but to a pre-objective situation of our existence. Only through some imaginative variations may we reach this fundamental situation, and each painting is an imaginative variation concerning a mode of relatedness to the world. Here, despite its philosophical weakness, there is something true in the idea that in painting we have nothing denotative but connotative, if we discover that in the connotative itself there is something ontological. We should reflect on what is a feeling or a mood. If we say that a painting develops only a mood or a feeling but a feeling is no less objective in a new sense of the word, then we are no less related to reality through emotions. It's strange that Sartre was more ontological in his philosophy of emotions than in his philosophy of imagination, because for him we have only a kind of anti-world in imagination, whereas in fear, joy, and all the fundamental feelings, we are in the world. In fear we perceive the world as fearful, and so on. We could say that each painting develops a feeling, a mood, which had no name before this painting. We had no place in our vocabulary for these feelings, because they are created by the painting. Nature is a landscape because of landscape painting. The Western painting of landscape is relatively recent. The first Western landscapes appear in the background of Renaissance painting before coming to the foreground with English painting and then French Impressionist painting.[8] The invention of landscape painting is at the same time a new way of looking at nature as a landscape. There is an augmentation of our world.

What here is difficult not only to understand but to accept is that we have to question our concept of reality. We have to question not only the tradition of the image as a shadow of something but also a frozen concept of reality. We tend to call reality what we know already as reality, what has been agreed upon as reality. Mainly under the influence of science we tend to say that reality is only what can confirm or falsify, that is, empirical statement. There is a circular relation between the notion of an empirical statement and what gives it a truth value. The capacity of giving truth value to empirical statements is what we tend to call reality. But under the shock of fiction, our concept of reality itself becomes problematic. We try to elude this disquieting questioning by saying that reality is what science declares to be real. When the literary critics keep repeating that poetry is only emotional, they ratify a concept of reality that is not their own concept of reality. They take reality as already framed not only by science—perhaps science itself has more respect for reality—but by the epistemology and philosophy of science. Then we say that only scientific discourse denotes reality, whereas poetry and painting do not denote but display connotations that have no truth claims.

The idea that fiction redescribes reality implies that we must give up this too easy distinction between connotation and denotation. I very much like Nelson Goodman's *Languages of Art*, because his book is directed against this distinction. For Goodman, reality is made by language and remade by metaphorical discourse. His approach is nominalistic—anti-essentialist. Rather than essences, we have only names, and we can change the names. Names of things are only labels, and labels can be shifted. Metaphor reassigns labels (1968, 69). His nominalistic approach to language allows him to give a denotative function to painting and to poetry. Whatever we may think of his nominalism, he wants to say that we have never finished building reality. Reality is as much construed by painting and poetry as by empirical sense but not for the same purpose. Here we may relate what I say elsewhere on ideology to the extent that the empirical sciences are linked to an interest in control.[9] What is suspended by poetry and art is the interest in control. I don't know whether the theory of interests in Habermas—distinguishing the interest in control from an interest in communication and an interest in liberation—goes far enough. Perhaps we have a radical interest in what is that is more theoretical than practical.

Let me stop here with having developed the notion of the pictorial aspect of reference. In lecture 18 I shall turn to the theory of models to develop the productive reference there and then return in the final lecture to the problem of productive reference in poetic language. Last year, in a course with David Tracy, I discussed models mainly using Mary Hesse's work on her concept of models as heuristic devices for the means of redescription. The issue was the relation in the theory of models between fiction and redescription. This year I shall principally use Donald Schon's *Displacement of Concepts*. As I shall discuss as well, Ian Barbour's *Myths, Models, and Paradigms* also offers a useful bibliography on the comparison between metaphors and models.

18

Fiction (4): Models

To situate the context of the present lecture, let me recall the problematic in this final section of the lectures. I am attempting to distinguish fiction as much as possible from picture, picture being the heir of the reproductive imagination and fiction another name for the productive imagination. As we have seen, picture's referent is ruled by the referent of perception: I imagine that which I could perceive. The criterion for the picture is the possibility of showing the original in another, direct experience. This theory of reproductive imagination is reinforced by most of the modern theories of imagination, since in Ryle as well as in Sartre, the original rules the image. We saw that in Ryle a mock fight presupposes that we know how to fight. Knowing how is the original. We may compare the picture to a quotation in which something is mentioned that already has its own meaning. Mentioning refers the picture back to its original. Similarly with Sartre, the experience of absence is an indirect reference to presence, since the imagined picture of my friend Peter in Berlin refers to an experience of Peter. In all these cases, the picture has no referent of its own. Its referent is that of the original. That is why the image is not an object in itself but another way of being related to objects. Objects are already objects of the world before being imagined. By contrast, the inexistence of the object of fiction allows the fiction to provide its own referent, a referent that is the referent of the fiction and not a borrowed referent, a referent borrowed from the sphere of experience. It is in that sense that imagination is productive, productive not only of its sense but of its reference.

I am trying to develop the concept of a productive reference in several fields to provide a few examples of this multisided productivity. I did not start from the field of poetry because, due to the strategy of language in poetry, the images in poetic metaphors don't seem to have a reference. Here language seems to work for its own sake, to celebrate language itself. Therefore, we have had to postpone the problem of the referent of poetry and take a roundabout way to the subject. In the last lecture I took a roundabout way by means of the case of painting. With the help of Dagognet's theory of iconography, I tried to show that in painting there is an increase of reality. Painting is not a shadow of reality but on the contrary presents an iconic augmentation of reality. In this lecture I shall try to achieve the same point by means of what I call epistemological imagination in the theory of models.

It's very important to have a developed theory of imagination in the sciences, because if we confine creative imagination only to poetry and to literary fiction, we do harm to both science and poetry. This dichotomy between science and poetry is very popular, even among thinkers who make a plea for creativity. They have a self-defeating position; they say that their arguments about imagination do not work in science. For example, in *Philosophy in a New Key*, Susanne Langer opposes the presentational—what I call productive reference—to the discursive—which is the "vehicle of propositional thinking" (1948, 54). For her, only poetry is presentational; what is discursive does not imply imagination (212–13, 116). This does harm to both sides. It confirms the positivistic claim that only science raises truth claims, because it has nothing poetic in it, and on the other side, confirms the emotionalist theories of art for which art has nothing to do with truth. The dichotomy reinforces the positivistic interpretation of science and the emotionalist theory of poetry. My claim is that the advance must be parallel in both fields. It is to the extent that we have a theory of imagination in cognitive and discursive processes that we may understand finally the role of imagination in poetry. What is at stake here is a conception of the mind, of thought at large. To invent by a creative use of imagination is a general mode of the functioning of thought. The universality of productive imagination implies that we find parallels in the functioning of productive imagination on the sides of both poetry and science. Establishing these parallels is the only way for a philosophy of imagination to get beyond the restrictive boundaries of poetics.

There is not only a parallelism in the functioning of productive imagination in the two fields, for the epistemological modes of imagination teach us about poetic imagination. Just as an epistemological mode of imagination is more discursive, more articulated, then all that is thick, dense, and therefore opaque in poetic imagination may be laterally enlightened by the process of epistemological imagination. What mainly may be expected from the effect of one theory on the other is the possibility of solving the paradox of reference in poetry, because it's with the model that we understand better how fiction has a heuristic function. The heuristic dimension—heuristic being the Greek word for the capacity of discovery—is easier to see in the case of models. Through the example of models we see how all creativity in discourse is rewarded by an extension of our concept of reality. The extension of our language is at the same time an extension of our world. By this roundabout way we have a better understanding of the relation between the function of disclosure in poetry and the creativity of language, because in poetry they seem to be disconnected. Language there seems to function for its own sake. By contrast, in the case of the model, language does not work for its own glory but for the extension of knowledge. The cognitive dimension there is easier to identify.

I shall proceed in two steps and shall undertake the first step in the present lecture and the second in the final lecture. In this lecture we shall see how model and metaphor are similar, how they function in the same way in a logic of discovery. In the final lecture I shall consider the truth claims of models and then apply this notion of truth claims to what I want to say finally about the referential function of fictions.

For the present lecture, I introduce briefly the vocabulary of Max Black in *Models and Metaphors* and then rely mainly on Donald Schon's book, *Displacement of Concepts*. I treated Black at length in my course with David Tracy last spring, and I only summarize his vocabulary here because it has been widely adopted. To prepare for Schon's analysis, then, let me recall the definition of models in Black's work. The distinctions that Black introduces are now classic. I shall try to relate them to my vocabulary concerning picture and fiction, because we shall see that in Black's three kinds of models, the first may be referred to picture, the third to fiction, and the second is the turning point between picture and fiction, picture being the picture of in the sense of a copy while the fiction creates its own referent. The first kind of model, which I put on the same level as picture, Black calls "scale models" (1962, 220).[1] Examples include a "ship displayed in the showcase of a travel agency" (219) and all imitations that present the object in a kind of miniature form. There is only a change of scale in the relevant dimensions. The model here is typically a model of something that exists elsewhere. That is why I compare it to a picture. It refers to and shows how a thing looks. It provides help in reading the properties of the original. Already there is an activity of interpretation, which is alluded to by the term "reading" the model (220). When we look, for example, at a scale model of a ship, we forget that it's not the same material as the original and that only a few features of the model are relevant for the reading. Already we have a process of screening (a concept that Schon will much emphasize) that is not the case in a copy. Screening is an activity. "Reading" the model implies some "conventions of interpretation" (220) in order to set aside the irrelevant aspects and emphasize only what is relevant.

Black's second type of model is the "analogue model," such as, for example, "hydraulic models of economic systems" (222) or the kind of models present in psychoanalysis (in the energetical model, the topographical model, and so on). In this model there is a "change of medium" (222) between the original and the model. What is read in the model is the structure of the original. The structural element is less the apparent shape of the original than its rational structure, the relation between parts, between dimensions, and so on. Black speaks here of a principle of isomorphism (222), the similarity of form (iso-morphism). In this model the creative element is more important, since in the progression from a similarity of shape with scale models to a similarity of relations here, there is an abstractive operation. As we shall see, in order for the abstractive operation to be really creative, it requires displacement, but in the analogue model this displacement is not obvious.

The real models, those which really deserve the name of model, are the third type, "theoretical models." An example is James Clerk Maxwell's "representation of an electrical field in terms of the properties of an imaginary incompressible fluid" (Black 1962, 226). The important fact here is that the theoretical model develops its own referent in the form of an imaginary object on which we read certain properties. In a mathematical model there is nothing to see; it's only a mathematical formula. But what is specific to the theoretical model is that the description of the imaginary milieu of the imaginary object provides a formula that is then transposed to reality. As Black says, the important feature of this model is that it is "not literally constructed," as is the model boat displayed in the showcase. It's not even embodied in a new medium. "[T]he heart of the method consists in talking in a certain way" (229). This means two things: first, it's introducing a new language, and second, it's extending this language to a new domain of application. Already we see the parallelism with metaphor introducing a new language, when the metaphor is understood not as a mere substitution of name but as the production of new information by putting together two different semantic fields, by putting two ideas within one structure. Introducing new language creates a movement in language that in turn moves our way of looking at a thing. To summarize, we may say that here the model is not built or constructed but described (229), and it is this description that is transposed.

These two traits, a new language and its transposition, imply several other differences between the pair, the scale and analogue models, and the theoretical model. The dividing line lies between analogue and theoretical models. An analogue is still a picture, if in a more refined way. Only the theoretical model is truly a scientific fiction. In the theoretical model we start from a situation where an original field of investigation has already yielded some facts and regularities but requires further investigation, because the field has become problematic. The emigration outside of a blocked situation constitutes the element of denial that Sartre described as the negative trace of imagination.[2] The problematic character of the situation, the fact that the regular development of observation and explanation is blocked, invites the shift toward the fictional stage. The structure of the situation demands a new device for solving the problem, and for that purpose a "better-organized secondary domain" is conceived, depicted and described. Then "rules of correlation" are used "for translating statements about the secondary field into corresponding statements about the original field" (Black 1962, 230). Therefore, to return to the comparison of these kinds of models and fiction, we see that the translation of the description of the model into the originary domain extends and changes this domain. In that sense the referent of the model provides a new description of reality. In the vocabulary of Mary Hesse, the model provides a redescription of what had already been described but which was no longer describable in the terms of the previous theory (for example, Hesse 1966, 157, 170–71). This transposition according to rules of correlation constitutes what I call the productive reference.

Of the two elements of Black's definition of theoretical model, I shall inquire in this lecture into the first—what do we mean by introducing a new language—and return in the following lecture to the second—what do we mean by transposing description. On the first topic, I am interested in Schon's book, *Displacement of Concepts*, because he relates his notion of displacement to the concept of metaphor. He doesn't seem to use Max Black, so his book is an independent source concerning our problem. Schon raises the following issue: what can be described and explained in the emergence of new concepts? We are working here at a level different from that of poetic language, where language remains at the level not only of ordinary language but uses the potentialities of semantic fields of natural languages. For Schon, the strategic level is that of conceptual language and the level of theories, that is to say, of basic concepts providing rules for describing facts and elaborating laws. It's a second order language. Schon starts by saying that the classical theories respond to the question of the emergence of new concepts in one of two ways. For some, the process is mysterious and therefore unexplainable, so there is nothing to say about it. For others, novelty is illusory in all fields, and therefore it requires no explanation (Schon 1963, 3, 11–15).[3] The presupposition of the inquiry is dead. There is nothing specific about the nature of poetry or science. The approach presents a paradigm of thought in all its extensions.

In order to get out from this blocked situation, we must have a notion of the concept as something less frozen than according to a logical configuration where we represent a concept as having a certain area, an extension with a circumference, a circumference that can intersect with, include, or exclude the circumference of other concepts as understood by rules of implication (5). For Schon, we must start from a concept that allows displacement. In order to be able to speak of displacement, there must be an initial mobility in our concepts. It is because, Schon says, we always speak after the fact (20) that we have a static view of concepts. Perhaps he is too pragmatist, but in his development here, Schon refers mainly to the school of John Dewey and all those who say that a concept is not something that we see in a kind of intellectual intuition, but it's more a tool "for coping with the world, for solving problems" (5). It's essentially a tool for solving problems. Even a fixed concept like the concept of a chemical body is a summary of expectations. I expect that if I do something to it, the chemical body will behave in a certain way. To say, for example, that the chemical body is an acid is to awaken these expectations (5–6). The concept of expectation is very important for Schon. A theory of the concept as the object of intuition in the tradition of Frege or the early Husserl is not completely alien to this approach. If we apply the notion of an intuition, it implies some protention and some retention. There is this temporal element even in an intuitive tradition. The intuition itself is not by necessity something immutable, something fixed. It has a memory, and it implies a shorthand of expectation. But let us assume Schon's pragmatic theory of the concept in order to retain from it the notion that the function of a concept is always to structure a certain situation (8). This could also be taken in a Kantian sense to say that a concept is nothing as long as it is not applied. We could draw upon the concept of *Anwendung* (application) in Kant and his theory of judgment. It's not the concept finally that is important but the judgment, the activity of applying. We shall see that it's precisely in the process of applying the concept that we shall discover the element of displacement.

In turn, we must say that there is no object or situation that is not already structured. The old approach to the problem of abstraction, starting from the assumption that we first have impressions, then impressions provide images, and these images by means of association provide concepts, this way of proceeding from below upward is very naive (15). Rather, there is a permanent adjustment between some conceptual expectations and the previous structuration of reality. And it is the interplay between a situation already structured and expectations belonging to concepts already available that may present a problem. When the mutual adjustment of available concepts and already structured situations no longer works, there is a conflict between new situations and old concepts. It is in this discrepancy between old concepts and new situations that a process similar to the metaphorical process in poetic language may be found. Therefore, we have already narrowed down our inquiry. If Schon's task is to explain the emergence of new concepts, we may now formulate more clearly the problem: how may we use old concepts to cope with new situations unless under the assumption that when we speak of a new situation it has been already structured (22–23)? The sedimented situation is related to sedimented concepts. I introduce here Merleau-Ponty's vocabulary of sedimentation, but it's proper to speak of this vocabulary in the context of the problem of novelty, because novelty is precisely the contrary of this sedimentation.[4]

Schon considers what he deems inappropriate solutions, all the ways in which we try to elude the problem of novelty by a mere refinement of the old (1963, 22–34). In my language, this would correspond to all the attempts finally to reduce fictions to pictures. For example, Hume said that a new idea is only a complex idea made of simple ideas that are not new, since new ideas proceed by combination; they are merely the echo of an impression (Schon 1963, 13). The notion of the complex idea was always a way of eluding the problem of novelty in thought. Schon undertakes a review of partial solutions that offer something but that finally miss the point. Another example is to proceed by the classical concept of comparison, "the juxtaposition of one thing and another" (23). Schon offers as an illustration a comparison of the Soviet Union and the United States in terms of size, population, industrialization, and so on and discovering that they have something in common, that they result from violent revolutions (23–25). Suddenly I see the United States through the lens of the other, recognizing that the Soviet Union too proceeded from a violent revolution. We discover that one "is an instance of a concept which we had applied before only to the other" (24). This is the usual manner of comparison, by juxtaposition and the discovery of some similar traits. We transfer something from the one to the other; sometimes the transfer is reciprocal. But the comparison generates nothing really new, because all the concepts that we have used—size, population, industrialization, and even violent revolution—are not new concepts. They are concepts already in use, even if applied in another way. Here we don't go very far beyond the concept of application in the sense of putting a new instance under a previous concept (25). There is no displacement of concepts. Rather, we see some individual in a new way by applying an available concept. If I discover that my friend is a Mason (9), I see him in another way, knowing now that he has a secret or parallel life and so on, but I do not have a new concept of the Mason as such. I have a new concept of my friend as *this*. Schon makes the distinction between having a new concept as a concept and having a new concept of something (28). I see something in a new way.

Schon also refers to Charles Sanders Peirce's notion of error in the sense of a productive error. Peirce is more or less affiliated with the same family of minds as Dewey; there is a certain instrumentalism in the theory of concepts. Peirce, says Schon, defines error as a way of "treating different things as though they were similar" and similar things "as though they were different" (26). It's in the process of correcting our errors that we discover things. A classical example is Columbus since he was looking for one thing and found something else. In the history of various kinds of discoveries, many were searching for one thing and discovered something else. The novelty appears in the discrepancy between the expectation and the discovery. The newness of the discovery has as its background a frustrated expectation. Something turns out not to behave as was forecast. I was interested in this section because in the theory of metaphor we have something similar. There are those who say that a metaphor is a category mistake. The term is borrowed from Ryle in *The Concept of Mind* (for example, 1949, 16–18), discussing how we may speak of something in terms of a category that fits something else. There is a certain displacement in the error itself (Schon 1963, 27). We speak of something in terms that are not convenient, and by mistake we displace concepts. The important aspect, says Schon, is the process of correction (27). It's not the error as such that is productive but the correction. We must have a proper theory of correction which will be precisely that of displacement.

The main conception against which Schon fights is the relation between concept and instance (27–29). The ruling theory about the relation between a concept and reality is that something is put under a concept. The notion of putting under is the kernel of the notion of subsumption in Kant, because to subsume is to put under. We tend to identify application with subsumption. We may have a suspicion that in Kant application and subsumption are rigorously interchangeable, since application indicates the point of view of the concept applied to, while subsumption indicates the point of view of the instance put under. Thus, there appears to be a reciprocity between application and subsumption. But even in Kant the reciprocity is not quite true, because the interesting case is when subsumption is not immediate, when we don't see immediately under which concept we have to put something. Precisely the theory of schematism shows that we need a procedure to give an image to a concept; it's giving an image to a concept that we apply. Application takes time, and it's a kind of work. It's not something instantaneous but takes time. And it's precisely in this temporal labor that new concepts emerge. What is overlooked in the notion of a concept applied to an instance or an instance put under a concept is that we do not modify our conceptual scheme. We merely order things in terms of the available conceptual scheme. Strictly speaking, if we speak of an instance of a concept, it's only the perception of the thing that has changed, not the category. We recognize a new instance of a concept, but we don't produce a new concept.

The case of recognition (Schon 1963, 27–28) offers another context for assessing the relation between concept and instance. (The problem of recognition was previously discussed by Price in *Thinking and Experience* [Price 1953, 33–87].) When we recognize a friend whom we have not seen for a long time, we have to readjust our image of him. By contrast, when I recognize my dog each morning, there is an adherence between the name and the thing. The notion of recognizing is itself very ambiguous, then. It may designate something instantaneous and not creative at all, or on the contrary may require a complete readjustment of our perception. My friend's appearance after several years is at first quite different from my memory of him, but then I rediscover the same traits in him despite the changes due to aging. It's also my image of him that I must remodel in order to cover his whole history and not just the earlier period of his life when I last knew him. There is a mutual adjustment between my friend and my image of him. The notion of mutual adjustment helps make more sense of the notion of the extension of concepts. Schon proceeds step by step from comparison to correction of error, to application of a concept to an instance, to the extension of concepts.

We move closer to the issue of displacement when Schon considers the extension in the concept of such ordinary words as a *drum* (30). I may have a very narrow notion of a drum as having, by necessity, a certain hollow structure and a membrane that being hit produces an echo within the internal, empty space. But I may also apply the word *drum* to a room with a thin metal wall that reverberates when hit. In this experience in physics, all the materials are different from what I know of a drum as an instrument of music. We have here what Max Black calls an analogue model, since there is an isomorphism that plays on not merely the similarity of shape or appearances. That I have to include an instance that is on the border of my experience, enlarging my previous experience, implies that I extract the pertinent traits in a more rigorous way. The extension of the concept is a reduction of the number of pertinent traits. It's not important that there is a membrane that vibrates the drum and covers the drum top. We already have the process of metaphor here, since we may say by further extension that a person driving a meeting is a drum (32).

For Schon the concept of extension is not itself a solution resolving how new language emerges, because it's the name of the result. Our concept has been extended. He prefers to speak of displacement to designate the process and extension to designate the result. I myself use the concept of extension in the case of metaphor in a dynamic way, but Schon has always in mind the notion of extension in formal logic (7). In that context, the extension of a concept is something given; the concept has the capacity to cover a certain set of instances. In this vocabulary, then, of course the concept of extension is too special and not dynamic enough. That is why Schon prefers to call displacement the process by which the extension is changed (31). The interesting cases arise, therefore, when the application to a new kind of instance requires changes in the concept that go beyond its relation to the previous instances. Then we may say, to speak like Max Black, that we have changed our language and at the same time we have changed our world. Schon says, "All formation of new concepts, all changes in concepts, involves discovery of the world" (34). We shall see later that the second aspect, discovery of the world, is the counterpart of the formation of concepts.

After having reviewed the improper accounts of displacement, Schon turns to compare displacement with analogy and metaphor (35–52). His relatively negative approach to the historical treatment of metaphor comes from the fact that he relies on a classical theory of metaphor as a mere substitution of words. Therefore he has no difficulty concluding that these classical theories do not satisfy the concept of displacement. Nevertheless, he shows the kind of semantic change that occurs in metaphor when it's not merely a way of giving to a thing a name that belongs to something else. He quotes from Roger Brown's *Words and Things*, an author whom I did not know. Metaphor is not merely substitution; in metaphor, as I also try to show, one word has several references at the same time (Schon 1963, 36). It has the reference of its previous application and the new reference. There is a conflict of references. This is a good way of stating the matter, since in the case of the word *drum*, for example, we keep in mind the drum as a musical instrument and its application to something that seemingly has nothing to do with music; it's only the structure that is fitted to both. There is an oscillation in my mind between the old use and the new use. This tension between the two uses makes the metaphor. There is still a comparison here, something Schon had considered an inappropriate account of displacement.

What Schon denies in the theory of metaphor is the interpretation according to which—as in Roger Brown—we have in mind before the comparison a superordinate category that allows the comparison to occur (1963, 36–37). What is creative in the metaphor is precisely that we do not have the second order category that can encompass the old case and the new case. The higher category emerges from the process of comparing. Then we have a productive metaphor and a displacement of concepts, since a new concept emerges from the application of the word. This is no longer a case of the relation between concept and instance, which would suppose that the new use was already included in an overarching concept more or less already in my mind. The point is the creation of the concept itself, which after the fact makes sense of the rapprochement between old and new use. The rapprochement between old and new use provokes the emergence of the concept, and the new concept after the fact legitimates the rapprochement.

Schon treats the problem of analogy similarly (37–40). We may take the notion of analogy also in two senses. In a classical theory of analogy, the analogy differs from a comparison in the sense that a comparison is between two things, while in analogy the similarity is drawn between two relations. If we say that A is to B what C is to D, the relation A–B is similar to the relation between C and D. This is the classical theory of analogy as a proportion. There is nothing creative, because we know the ratio that makes possible the comparison. The problem is whether we knew the similarity before doing the comparison, or whether, in analogy's second sense, it is by displacing analogically a relation that now a new proportion, a new ratio, appears between things.

All these discussions lead Schon to his own concept of displacement (53–64). He structures his concept of displacement in the following way. First, his definition: A displacement is a "shift of old concepts to new situations. . . . [T]he old concept is not applied to the new situation, as a concept to an instance, but is taken as a symbol or metaphor for the new situation" (53). He retains from the metaphor what is most creative. He defines his concept of displacement in terms of metaphorical transfer. The concept of transfer that is essential to metaphor is preserved in his concept of displacement. As I have previously mentioned, the Greek word *metapherō* means precisely displacement. *Pherō* is the Greek word for a change in space of something mobile that is displaced from one place to another place, a change of place by transportation. What is different in the metaphor of the metaphor from the metaphor of application is that in the latter it's at the same place that we apply a concept to an instance, whereas here we displace. As I have tried to say about the theory of metaphor, we always want a logical space where two ideas that are remote, far apart from one another, then look close. There is approximation, reduction of logical distance. Schon tries to speak of this in terms of a process (54–58), and this part is perhaps too didactic and analytic. What is fundamental in this is Schon's effort to analyze a case where some say there is nothing to analyze and others say that it cannot be analyzed. For Schon, the description that follows below is the kernel of a logic of discovery that would not be only, as Popper calls it, a logic of the *confirmation* of a hypothesis, but a logic of *making* a hypothesis. What is usually called a logic of discovery is the logic of verification or falsification of what has been already discovered. It's not a logic of discovery in the sense of the process itself of discovery (Schon 1963, 92–94).

For Schon the first step in the process of displacement is a leap, the irrational element, "the first establishment of a symbolic relation" (54). He offers as an example the first time that someone used the term *cold war* (54). This is the *making* of metaphor that we see in poetry, when someone for the first time says this or that. There is "the first establishment of a symbolic relation between old and new" (54). Schon says that the process of transposition is not of a single concept but a cluster, a theory (54), if we call a theory the complex of rules for using single concepts. In *Languages of Art* Nelson Goodman argues the same, when he says that it's not only one label that is displaced but whole realms (Goodman 1968, 72). When, for example, we transpose the world of colors to the world of sounds, then there's an immigration, as Goodman says, of a whole host in a new country (73). (It is a very puzzling problem that we always speak metaphorically of metaphor. Derrida discusses this issue and draws from it that we are caught in the process in such a way that there is no outside and no possibility of looking from outside.[5] No philosophy of metaphor would be possible. I don't think that this is true, because the language in which we describe something is taken literally in its use for describing something else. I return to this point toward the end of the lecture in discussion of Schon's fourth phase.)

The first phase is a mysterious element, because suddenly we see something *as*. It's the *seeing as* that is decisive. For the first time an expression fits the new situation. Schon calls the "symbolic relation" (1963, 58) that occurs at this first stage an act of intimation (59). Intimation is the way in which the similarity becomes a kind of order: we see this thing *as*, look at this in that way, find the old things X in the new Y. It's like a riddle (62–63); suddenly we have an insight into the restructuration of the situation. All the analysis that we undertook with Wittgenstein about *seeing as* would fit here. Schon writes:

> We can say, then, that an old theory, A, is in a symbolic relation to a new situation, B, when:
> 1. There is an intimation that B is A-like.
> 2. A is taken as a condensed programme for exploration of B.
> 3. In carrying out this programme, expectations from A are transposed to B as projective models.
> 4. For each of these projective models, aspects of B are seen to be related in A-like ways, where we had not been attentive to those relations in A before. (64)

We had not perceived this relation. There is an intimation that B is A-like. An intimation is a kind of insinuation, a suggestion. Exactly as in a riddle, we have all the elements of the puzzle and now must establish a good form,

Fiction (4): Models 271

a good pattern, a good gestalt. We must find the gestalt that would make sense of the intimation. "Intimation," says Schon, "is a word for feelings. It has a touch of mystery in it" (59). We see something even though there is somewhere a place where we can no longer speak. If we could say what really happens at the moment of discovery, then everybody would be a genius. There would be rules for doing good poetry, for being Newton, and, why not, for being Einstein. But there is something that resists that. It's the first phase; after that the transposition, symbolic relation, or intimation has already occurred (54). What is meant at the moment of transposition is always something more than the application of an existing concept. Schon's permanent concern is that we don't return to the mere relation between a concept and its application to an instance. The symbolic relation is more than an extension; it's a transposition.

After transposition, a second, distinguishable phase of displacement is interpretation (55). This phase is easier, because we have made the jump, the leap. Once we have the hint, the intimation of the relation, then we must say in which respect it applies (55). This is the selective element, the screening element. The metaphor that has been intimated has to be elaborated by assigning the appropriate elements of the old concept to the appropriate aspects of the new situation. We interpret, for instance, how the appropriate elements of the old concept fit within the appropriate new aspect. Here again I refer to Wittgenstein, now for his notion of seeing an aspect: seeing an aspect in a face, in the example of my friend whom I have not seen for a long time. I have to isolate the specific aspects that fit with the appropriate context. I must answer the question, what aspects of the new situation can be assigned to what aspects of the old concept.

The third phase Schon calls correction (55–56). He retains something from the theory of mistake—something has been mistakenly called this or that—to describe the adjustment, the process of mutual adaptation, between the old theory and the new situation. When this adjustment is complete, Schon says, the metaphor is dying, because now it's a part of our vocabulary; the word now means this and that (56). If we had long used the word *drum* as a name for those running committees and so on, it would have become part of the word *drum*. It would no longer be a strange use but a figurative use. In the dictionary, there is a place for those nearly dead metaphors that already belong to a vocabulary. This is what we call figurative use. A figurative use is no longer a metaphor and not yet a part of the literal sense. The figurative use is the metaphor on the way toward its death.

We could say the same of painting. As I have mentioned, the invention of landscape painting led to a new way of looking at nature. We are accustomed now, though, to see landscape paintings in museums; they constitute a part of our vision. When a metaphor has been received in ordinary language, it has extended the polysemy of our world. In the same way, we could say that through landscape painting the polysemy of our vision, of our perception, has been extended, at least in a world of culture. The more we have seen landscapes in museums, the more we see nature as a landscape. There were no landscapes before painting, but now there is a kind of adjustment. As Schon indicates, when the adjustment between old concepts and new situation is complete, there is no longer this tension. When the tension completely disappears, the metaphorical has become literal. In that sense the metaphorical vision of landscape has become a literal vision, and now tour books speak of the "beautiful landscape" of an area, and so on. Abstract painting has to shatter the tradition of representational painting. The renewal of vision is now linked to the nonfigurative.

We can, though, keep returning to the museum and love Constable, because for us the tension remains between ordinary landscapes and painted landscapes. We are in this intermediary stage where we have assimilated the message which is no longer a shock and, on the contrary, we take pleasure in reasserting the kind of values we have already assimilated despite that they remain marginal to our ordinary life. The pleasure we have in works of art keeps providing the contrast with everyday life without puzzling us too much. It is a mixed pleasure. (I try to describe what I feel myself in the pleasure of recognizing.) We return to the works that we love. The kind of shock we receive is not disquieting but comforting, because it's a part of our identity. Our identity is preserved also by this cultural media. We have a kind of fictional identity too that is not exhausted in our social roles. We want to preserve this reserve of being that is documented by works that have become familiar without belonging to everyday life. The problem of the onlooker is not the same as that of the creator. Someone who tries to paint today has a very difficult problem, precisely because he or she cannot repeat what Constable did before.

Schon reserves as the fourth and last stage of the displacement of concepts what he calls the working out or spelling out of the relation (56–57). This is the phase of theorizing, where we say not only under which aspect but under which new category we may place the two terms that are in relation. The movement is from what was still metaphorical to what would constitute the new literal language. Here Schon raises the problem that if we undertake the spelling out by means of a vocabulary that is metaphorical—and this the case, when even mathematics employs the figurative elements of, for example, screens—then "we never come to the literal bed-rock" (57). Schon says that this is not circular, we are not speaking metaphorically about metaphors, because the difference between the literal and metaphorical lies not in the claim that there is nothing figurative in literal use but in "a distinction in function; for a given metaphor, the literal language is similarly what is used to spell it out" (57). This is a good answer to Derrida's paradox about the circularity of metaphor, the metaphoricity of language about metaphor. When we use a language to spell out a relation, we must differentiate two functions of language, one that is operative and the other thematic. This distinction had been offered by Husserl and also by Fink, in his famous article on the two kinds of concepts, the operational and the thematic.[6] The argument is that we cannot thematize everything, because to thematize is to reflect on certain concepts while employing other concepts that then are only used and therefore are not themselves thematic. We think through them, but we don't think about them (Fink 1981, 59). There are concepts through which we think and then the concepts about which we think. At any one time it is impossible to think about all our concepts. There are always some that are implicitly used. We could say that these are the literal as opposed to the thematized metaphors. I don't know to what extent this solves the problem.

There is a kernel of opacity that is the transposition itself. But if there is an ultimate element that can't be analyzed, at least it's not something that makes thought impossible. On the contrary, it acts as the dynamism of thought, since the three other operations are rational in the sense that to interpret, to correct, and to elaborate are something rational. There is an intrinsic implication of the opaque element of transposition in the more analyzable phases. The transpositional insight provides the possibility of the discursive. We should not oppose the intuitive and the discursive. More than that, we could say that a real intuitive element is pregnant with discursive procedures. We must have a dynamic concept of intuition, not a sense of intuition as a kind of dead glance on something and that's all. That would be the end of language. The dynamic intuition provides the possibility of speaking, or to use the expression of Kant about aesthetic ideas, we have to say more and to think more after that.[7] It's this possibility of thinking more that makes of the opaque element of transposition the birthplace of a new language.

19

Fiction (5): Poetic Language

In this final lecture I shall devote attention to the problem of productive reference, my principal topic concerning fictions. At the beginning of this section of the lectures on fiction, I asked whether it is not the case that most of our creations are fictions, because they are not under the rule of an original. As fictions, they can react on reality and expand our vision of things. The central paradox of fiction is that the lack of a direct referent presents the possibility for having an indirect referent and therefore to increase reality, as we said with the case of painting. Until now, we have reserved the problem of poetic language, because it implies a difficulty of its own. Here language seems to work for its own glory; it's language for language. According to the expression of Jakobson, poetic language works for the sake of the message and not of the referent. Therefore we used the roundabout way of the models to prepare the last stage of the referential value also of poetic language.

This roundabout way had an additional benefit. We could plead for another fundamental claim, that there is a unity in the functioning of thought in both poetic language and in science. There is not on the one hand science, which tells the truth, and on the other poetry, which expresses only our emotions. The question of the unity of thought is at stake. If we can show that imagination is creative in the same way in models and in poetry, then we have a unifying view of the way in which thought in general is capable of novelty. Another field raising the same issue of creativity is social action, which also has its pictures and its fictions, its pictures as ideologies and its fictions as utopias. There is therefore a unity in the problem of semantic innovation, in knowing, in acting, and so on. This is a possible approach to the problem of creativity, which is so opaque.

The parallelism between models and metaphors may be extended to the problem of reference beyond the first stage of the discussion of productive imagination considered in the last lecture, which pertained only to the functioning of imagination in extending our concepts. The first stage concerned the similarity of processes between semantic innovation in metaphor and the displacement of concepts in scientific thought. What I want to show in this lecture is that this displacement of concepts is at the same time an extension of the reality, of the world, in which we live and orient ourselves. In other words, if imagination is the intimation of new connections, it's also an intimation of new dimensions of reality. Therefore, the second stage of this inquiry into epistemological imagination will be addressed to the notion of the extension of our concept of reality itself. It's only now that we come to grips with the paradox of productive reference. As I keep saying, fiction does not reproduce previous reality as does the picture; it opens new reality. The paradox of fiction is that the more remote it is from the usual way of dealing with reality, the greater is its capacity for opening, for disclosing, for extending reality.

To support this paradox we shall proceed in the present lecture from model to metaphor and not the other way around. We could have proceeded from metaphor to model in order to isolate the opaque moment of transposition. Recall in the analysis of Schon that there was something irreducible in the novelty, in the step forward, of thought that suddenly sees a new connection. This element of transfer in scientific uses of imagination is similar to the *meta-phora*, the transfer, the transposition, proper to metaphor. Here it's metaphor that enlightens the model. We now have to proceed in the other direction for a fundamental reason. The truth claim of the model is easier to read in the context of scientific innovation, whereas poetic language presents the further difficulty of seeming to close language within itself because of the specificity of poetic discourse. In that sense, it's the model that provides a clue for solving the problem of reference in nonscientific uses of metaphor, since the model is defined by its truth claim. (The model's truth claim is the center of scholarly discussion. Here I present only a schema of this discussion's present state.) The term *model* says more than the term *displacement of concepts* that we used previously, because the displacement of concepts concerns what happens within thought. It's within thought—if *within* makes sense—that an old concept is extended to cope with a new situation. The extension of the concept occurs within the conceptual realms. But with the model we have the notion of a model *for*. As we said with Max Black, the model offers not only the introduction of a new language but its application to a new domain of reality. If we say that something is the model *of*, then it's a picture, as a scale model is a model *of* something. But with the theoretical model, we have an imaginary structure that we describe and then transpose to change the way in which we structure a thing. This is a model *for*. It has a heuristic function, a capacity for discovery. Models *of* are pictures, whereas models *for* are scientific fictions.

The distinction between picture and fiction may be expressed in the duality between model of and model for.

As to the truth claim of models, I rely mainly on works by Mary Hesse and Ian Barbour that describe a complex scholarly discussion. Let me say in very simple terms that there are two schools of thought. On the one hand, there are those who claim that models apply literally. For the fundamental reason this "naive realism" (Barbour 1974, 34–35) is very often the spontaneous philosophy of scientists—not of epistemologists, not those engaged in the theory of science, but the scientists themselves.[2] They tend to think about the domain of application in terms of the model. A realistic commitment lies in the use of the model. When these scientists use their model to describe, they describe reality in what they think is a non-metaphorical and literal way. This is what Colin Turbayne calls the myth of metaphor, when the metaphor becomes a mythified reality. Fictions—the models—once more become pictures. It's very difficult to think in terms of heuristic fictions without returning always to a pictorial concept where the models are replicas of reality, pictures of reality.

Most of the objections against a realistic view of models are convincing to the extent that models are taken as pictures. By necessity our pictures are adjusted to the size of human existence between the infinitely small and the infinitely large. Our images have a mediate size and as long as this homogeneity in size is not destroyed or shattered, then these fictions can be taken as pictures. This was the case to a certain extent in an example discussed at length by Mary Hesse concerning the extension of the concept of the wave (Hesse 1966, 11–56). It was extended from waves in fluids to sound waves and then to light waves with the hypothesis of a medium that would be to light what water and air are to other waves. All the mechanical models are picturable in this sense. This "predilection for picturable . . . models" was undermined by quantum theory, "which has shown that the atomic world is very unlike the world of familiar objects" (Barbour 1974, 35). Pictures remain in the vicinity of familiar objects. If we fail to make the distinction between a theoretical model and a scale model, then the attack against the literalist interpretation is conclusive, since models are not pictures. As they are not pictures, the argument goes, they are not replicas of reality.

The opposite trend has been called by different names, such as *fictionalism* (Barbour 1974, 37)—here in the sense of a dream, a false fiction, a fiction without any ground—or *conventionalism*, which is a better term. (I prefer the term *conventionalism* since I try to use the term *fiction* in a more positive way.) For this school of thought, models "are neither true nor false, but only more or less useful mental devices" (37). There is an important kinship of this approach with instrumentalism and, more generally, pragmatism. Once

278 IMAGINATION AS FICTION

models have done their job, they may be discarded. The, process of thought. As Barbour notes, the French physici..n't belong to the models are "'props for feeble minds'" (37). And Braithw..hem says that well known among English-speaking epistemologists, says ..o is more only a "'convenient way of thinking about the structure of the ..els are They speak of models as useful fictions rather than as having tru..).

Between these two extreme positions perhaps there is room for .. realism" (Barbour 1974, 37) that would take into account the parado. structure of the heuristic fiction. On the one hand, the heuristic fictı is a form of realism in the sense that its models are not only useful, but a new aspect of reality corresponds to its extension of our concepts. Reality itself looks differently. The world itself is described in another way. This element of realism preserved here is closer to the phenomenology of the scientist and to the realistic intent of scientific work. No scientist would be committed to his or her work, to the task, if not convinced that all that the work does and says concerns reality. Through the use of the model, the heuristic fiction, not only is the scientist's language changed but a new dimension of reality is acknowledged, recognized, and witnessed to. On the other hand, something from conventionalism must also be retained. What is true of conventionalism is that the realistic intent is symbolic of reality, it's an indirect grasp of reality, since we see things through the lens, through the screen, of the model. We think *about* things but *through* models. In this tension between the *about* and the *through*, there is a very subtle balance between constructive and descriptive aspects of models. The model is description through construction. This is also what we learned from the history of painting. Painting is a permanent struggle to grasp new aspects of our world but always through a certain selective apparatus. Gombrich raises the question, why did Western painters not represent landscapes before, let us say, the sixteenth century, when everyone had always seen the country? His answer is that they had no alphabet, no available tool of depiction for representing and in fact for presenting reality as a landscape.[3] It's always through an available syntax that we may grasp reality.

There is no alternative, then, either to saying that since a heuristic fiction is a construction, it's neither true nor false, or saying that in order that it be true, it must not be a construction. In a theory of fiction and, more specifically, in a theory of the relation between the heuristic function of the fiction and the descriptive capacity of the construction, there is a dialectics that is perhaps the kernel of the difficulty. This has been expressed in other vocabulary. In a long tradition that comes from Hans Vaihinger and German neo-Kantianism, some speak of models as the *as if* or the *as though* (the *als ob*). Among scientists from Germany, there is often the language of the

The distinction between picture and fiction may be expressed in the duality between model of and model for.

As concerns the truth claim of models, I rely mainly on works by Mary Hesse, Max Black, and Ian Barbour that describe a complex scholarly discussion.[1] We may say in very simple terms that there are two schools of thought. On the one hand, there are those who claim that models apply literally. For one fundamental reason this "naive realism" (Barbour 1974, 34–35) is very often the spontaneous philosophy of scientists—not of epistemologists, not those engaged in the theory of science, but the scientists themselves.[2] They tend to think about the domain of application in terms of the model. A realistic commitment lies in the use of the model. When these scientists use their model to describe, they describe reality in what they think is a non-metaphorical and literal way. This is what Colin Turbayne calls the myth of metaphor, when the metaphor becomes a mythified reality. Fictions—the models—once more become pictures. It's very difficult to think in terms of heuristic fictions without returning always to a pictorial concept where the models are replicas of reality, pictures of reality.

Most of the objections against a realistic view of models are convincing to the extent that models are taken as pictures. By necessity our pictures are adjusted to the size of human existence between the infinitely small and the infinitely large. Our images have a mediate size and as long as this homogeneity in size is not destroyed or shattered, then these fictions can be taken as pictures. This was the case to a certain extent in an example discussed at length by Mary Hesse concerning the extension of the concept of the wave (Hesse 1966, 11–56). It was extended from waves in fluids to sound waves and then to light waves with the hypothesis of a medium that would be to light what water and air are to other waves. All the mechanical models are picturable in this sense. This "predilection for picturable . . . models" was undermined by quantum theory, "which has shown that the atomic world is very unlike the world of familiar objects" (Barbour 1974, 35). Pictures remain in the vicinity of familiar objects. If we fail to make the distinction between a theoretical model and a scale model, then the attack against the literalist interpretation is conclusive, since models are not pictures. As they are not pictures, the argument goes, they are not replicas of reality.

The opposite trend has been called by different names, such as *fictionalism* (Barbour 1974, 37)—here in the sense of a dream, a false fiction, a fiction without any ground—or *conventionalism*, which is a better term. (I prefer the term *conventionalism* since I try to use the term *fiction* in a more positive way.) For this school of thought, models "are neither true nor false, but only more or less useful mental devices" (37). There is an important kinship of this approach with instrumentalism and, more generally, pragmatism. Once models have done their job, they may be discarded. They don't belong to the process of thought. As Barbour notes, the French physicist Duhem says that models are "'props for feeble minds'" (37). And Braithwaite, who is more well known among English-speaking epistemologists, says that models are only a "'convenient way of thinking about the structure of the theory'" (37). They speak of models as useful fictions rather than as having truth claims.

Between these two extreme positions perhaps there is room for a "critical realism" (Barbour 1974, 37) that would take into account the paradoxical structure of the heuristic fiction. On the one hand, the heuristic fiction is a form of realism in the sense that its models are not only useful, but a new aspect of reality corresponds to its extension of our concepts. Reality itself looks differently. The world itself is described in another way. This element of realism preserved here is closer to the phenomenology of the scientist and to the realistic intent of scientific work. No scientist would be committed to his or her work, to the task, if not convinced that all that the work does and says concerns reality. Through the use of the model, the heuristic fiction, not only is the scientist's language changed but a new dimension of reality is acknowledged, recognized, and witnessed to. On the other hand, something from conventionalism must also be retained. What is true of conventionalism is that the realistic intent is symbolic of reality, it's an indirect grasp of reality, since we see things through the lens, through the screen, of the model. We think *about* things but *through* models. In this tension between the *about* and the *through*, there is a very subtle balance between constructive and descriptive aspects of models. The model is description through construction. This is also what we learned from the history of painting. Painting is a permanent struggle to grasp new aspects of our world but always through a certain selective apparatus. Gombrich raises the question, why did Western painters not represent landscapes before, let us say, the sixteenth century, when everyone had always seen the country? His answer is that they had no alphabet, no available tool of depiction for representing and in fact for presenting reality as a landscape.[3] It's always through an available syntax that we may grasp reality.

There is no alternative, then, either to saying that since a heuristic fiction is a construction, it's neither true nor false, or saying that in order that it be true, it must not be a construction. In a theory of fiction and, more specifically, in a theory of the relation between the heuristic function of the fiction and the descriptive capacity of the construction, there is a dialectics that is perhaps the kernel of the difficulty. This has been expressed in other vocabulary. In a long tradition that comes from Hans Vaihinger and German neo-Kantianism, some speak of models as the *as if* or the *as though* (the *als ob*). Among scientists from Germany, there is often the language of the

Fiction (5): Poetic Language 279

als ob or the *as if*, and this has joined the vocabulary of conventionalism, which was more influenced in the United States by the pragmatist trend. There is then a conjunction between neo-Kantianism and pragmatism in conventionalism. Barbour has a good way of expressing the dialectic when he says that even in the most remote heuristic fiction "[t]here is a referential intent and a necessity of experimentation which are not present in pure mathematics" (1974, 47). On the basis of these kinds of assessments arises the pleading for a critical realism (47).

I would like to try to transfer this conclusion about the dialectics of heuristic fiction from the domain of epistemology to the domain of poetic language. I would like to try, therefore, to equate the relation between *muthos* and *mimesis* in Aristotle with the similar relation between heuristic fiction and description and redescription, to use the vocabulary of Mary Hesse (for example, Hesse 1966, 157, 170–71).[4] As I have said previously, the concept of mimesis coming from Aristotle's *Poetics* was a source of misunderstanding. The word was interpreted as meaning imitation, and imitation was understood to be a simple copy of reality. Applying my own distinction between fiction and picture, mimesis was mainly interpreted in terms of picture. If, however, we interpret mimesis in terms of fiction, its meaning and implication are quite different. We may speak not of a reproductive mimesis but of a productive mimesis, a creative mimesis. This is precisely what was intended by Aristotle in the *Poetics*. If we see the context in which he used this notion of a mimesis, he said that poetry—and for him poetry was mainly Greek tragedy—is a mimesis of human action (Aristotle 1973, 682, 1451b 27). But under which conditions is tragedy a mimesis of human action? To the extent that the poet has built a framework, which is conceptual. *Muthos* offers more than metaphor. While a metaphor may occur in a simple sentence, *muthos* includes composition and a network of thoughts surrounding characters and events. There is a *dianoia*, a work of thought, in the tragedy in the construction of the plot or fable, as the word *muthos* has been variously translated. Therefore, it's to the extent that poets have bracketed or suspended their apprehension of ordinary life that they can compose a plot or fable that follows certain rules of composition. Aristotle was very precise concerning the rules of composition (which became more and more a burden in the history of drama), and these rules represented the attempt to use the *muthos* precisely as a model. So we must put together this notion of the *muthos* in drama with the model. They both display what Stephen Toulmin, describing models in *Philosophy of Science*, calls a "systematic deployability" (1960, 39).

I insist on this point because in the introduction to this third part of the lectures, I said that as long as we don't introduce the category of work, we don't see how fiction works. What is lacking in the picture is any invention;

there is no work of thought at all. Recall how Sartre described imaginative life as a life without work, since it's an attempt to magically possess the absent thing. We may oppose the magic of possession in picture to the work of invention in fiction. In painting too there is a work, since the artist must deal with pigments, brushes, different canvases, and so on. There is even an element of craftsmanship. The counterpart of this craftsmanship in the work of language is precisely the constructive element, what Aristotle called *taxis*, which is to impose a certain, dramatic order, with some important turning points, such as the moments of recognition, crisis, and denouement. The relation between crisis and denouement and the sudden discharge of the tension from crisis to denouement is the work of the poet. In all these networks, there is something parallel to what we said about the model. Just as models are constructs, so too the poet's plot or *muthos* is a construct. If we interpret *muthos* in this complex way, not in the sense of a fancy but precisely as a model *for*, then mimesis too has no longer reproductive but productive meaning. It's mimesis through *muthos*, just as we said that the model is descriptive through the construct.

It's true that in contemporary art and literature, there is an attack on the notion of the work. There is a tendency, for instance, to say that art must no longer be a work. Artists do something and then destroy it, or there is no framework, or they put together objects of junk and say this is a work. There is a derision of the work and the rise of the anti-work. What is at stake is the concept of a durable work that can be displayed. There is a critique of the concept of a museum. The tradition is attacked at its roots because even in the transition from figurative to nonfigurative art, there was still the continuity of the concept of a work that must be achieved, must be complete. There is an attack against this sense of completion, claiming that this is still Platonist. A similar attack against the notion of a composed work may be found in poetry and literature. At stake is the notion of a composition itself with a beginning and an end, a story, a poem. There are stories, for example, where we cannot say that they start or that they stop; there is no crisis and no denouement; the stories seem an arbitrary section in a tape of sequences. There are attacks on grammatical and syntactic consistency. This has some Nietzschean overtones, Nietzsche having attacked grammar as the shadow of the gods since it's still a logos, still a rule.[5] There's a plea for chaos or for the unleashing of chaotic forces. Parallels can be drawn from my work elsewhere on ideology and utopia. Some utopias shatter the conventions of morality or of our social life. The notion of anti-work there is one of anti-power, an objection to bureaucracy and technocracy. There is an attempt to return to nature. Charles Fourier is an example of the explosion of a mad diffusion of passions against form. Some speak of the anti-work as the death of art.[6] Transposing a remark by Althusser asking whether the death of philosophy is itself a philosophical death, I wonder whether the death of art is an artistic death.[7] I don't know whether the anti-work will lead to the death of an art. I don't think so, finally, because we see an aggressive return to a very descriptive form of painting in the careful paintings of Wyeth and others and in the naive style of painting. We can never forecast.

But let me return to the descriptive and constructive character of mimesis. To extend other vocabulary to the situation, consider Nelson Goodman's denial in *Languages of Art* of the distinction between the denotative and the connotative (for example, 1968, 245–52). In literary criticism the denotative is the descriptive, and the connotative is merely the evocative, only emotions or subjective associations and merely interior. We must say that mimesis is the denotative dimension of the drama. It's not a way of dreaming besides reality but a taking hold of the essence of reality through the fiction itself. I have previously alluded to the following paradox of Aristotle, who can never be accused of irrationalism. He says in the *Poetics* that poetry is more true than history (Aristotle 1973, 682, 1451b 5). He has a notion of history as more or less a sequence of events without a structure. For him, there is more structure in poetry than in history, since history remains at the surface of events. All the accidents of life are recorded by history, whereas poetry deals only with what is fundamental in human action, the interplay of passions and their mortal implications. There is something fundamental in poetry, while history treats the anecdotes of the changes of power, the accidents of power. The modern historian would disagree, but it's interesting to see that once, at least, the referential dimension of mimesis, of poetry, was recognized.

The example of mimesis is perhaps the easiest because of its narrative support. It's easier to show that fictional narratives have a certain denotative function—a function of description and redescription—because the narrative structure of the drama has a certain homogeneity with the narrative structure of existence. The narrative structure has an immediate denotative function because of its isomorphism with life. Of course, this isomorphism has to be invented in order to be discovered, and we discover it to the extent that we invent it, but narrative structure falls between scale models and theoretical models. We may transfer the structure of the drama to life, because the narrative structure works as a model for reading ordinary life. (A problem deserving full treatment, which I shall take up in lectures next year, is that of the narrative: Why do we tell stories and why do we write histories?[8] Why have people always told stories, from folktales to histories? I have already studied this issue in the context of the small stories of the biblical parables.[9])

There is of course also an element of play in mimesis, since it plays with possibilities. A drama is a play; we play the drama. All the issues of play discussed by Gadamer in the first part of *Truth and Method* would have to be taken into account here. But we should have to say that nothing is more earnest than play if play is also an exploration of reality by imagination. Although there are degrees of pretending, Ryle's concept of pretending doesn't work here, because his concept of pretending once more belongs to the realm of picture and not to that of fiction. It is a mere reproduction of what people do. Children playing with dolls or playing bears—examples from Ryle—are involved in an exercise in the imitation of life. Here the imagination is more reproductive. It's not by chance that Ryle uses the prefix *mock* to say that playing bears is a "mock-performance" (1949, 259–60). I would not say, though, that a theory of play is exhausted by the notion of mock-performance, because in that context the element of make-believe is still on the side of the picture and not on the side of the fiction. When play is more fictional than pictorial, it is exemplary. It delineates some hidden or some unemployed possibilities of reality. It displays the potential of human life. When Heidegger says that *Verstehen* (understanding) is finally the project of our own possibilities, that applies very well to this concept of play.[10]

I have reserved for the end of the discussion the most difficult case, that of lyric poetry, which seems to be the ultimate retreat of language for itself. I wonder, though, whether we cannot proceed from models to drama and from drama to poetic lyricism, because in the latter the denotative function is much more concealed and much more indirect. It's indirect because the suspension, the *epochē*, of the descriptive function of ordinary language is more prominent. It is as though language has retreated into itself to expand its possibilities of connecting sense and sound, sense and images, and therefore to elaborate a closed world of fancy protected against reality by this solidity of language appearing as a sculpture closed in on itself. There is surely something true in the idea that in poetry, in the expression of Northrop Frye, language is inwardly oriented. Frye says that from this language then emerges a mood that is an inner feeling created by the poem.[11] What is a mood when created by the poem if not a model for feeling accordingly? Most feelings in our culture are literary productions. There are models not only for seeing but for feeling. The mood displayed by the poem is not a feeling that we had already but the emotional aura of the poem itself, just as we say that what is represented by a Mozart minuet is exactly what is in the minuet. The minuet displays its own mood. We must start from the inward orientation of the poem precisely to extend in the most extreme way the tension between the fictional and the denotative, since here the fictional is at its extreme. There is nothing to see; nothing is shown, noth-

Fiction (5): Poetic Language 283

ing is described. But is it not to the extent that the movement of language is the most inwardly oriented that it discloses something of our total relation to things? The more inwardly directed it is, the more heuristic it is but in a sense that is very indirect. Because of the suspension of care and concern for ordinary objects, we become more attentive to aspects of reality that are not objective—not that they are subjective—in the sense that they do have not the form of an object.

What prevents the recognition of this realm is that the reign of representation—to speak like Heidegger—provides a channel only between subject and object.[12] Paradoxically, feelings are less "idealistic" than representations, because they offer affective involvement without distance. The opposition between exteriority and interiority falls. Feelings are both the most interior and the most ontological. Poetic schemas of interior life are at the same time depictions of modes of appearance of reality. What is shattered here, then, is our relation to the world as a subject/object relation in a Kantian sense, where there are objects for us when they are structured according to the conceptual network of our categories. We dwell in the world in a more primitive way than this subject/object relation; the subject/object relation is itself built on a fundamental participation in reality. It's quite possible that it is poetic language that says something about this fundamental relation to the world, because the subject/object relation has been suspended there. It is the pre-objective that is poetically said. We can speak of redescription to express this abolition of the objective for the sake of the ontological. The lack of reference of poetic language may be only the negative condition for another, more fundamental orientation to the world, not in terms of objects and, especially, manipulable objects.

When we read a poem that is not at all descriptive, we are transported in a world of words that extend loose images but that induce us to look at reality in the terms of the nondescriptive. We are addressed to some nondescriptive traits of reality, and this is what happens with emotions. I have mentioned several times Sartre's examples of emotions, because I think that his theory of emotions is more realistic than his theory of imagination, which is more idealistic. For Sartre imagination speaks only of my spontaneity, my freedom, not at all of reality, whereas in my emotions I am directed toward the nondiscursive aspects of the world, the world as fearful, for example. When Bachelard, in *The Poetics of Reverie*, speaks of a world at rest (*au repos*) (1971, 196), this restful, this peaceful, aspect of reality is no less real than the fact that there are books.

If we consider things that have names and then can be placed in propositions with predicates and so on, this articulation in terms of subjects and predicates corresponds to the objective. By contrast, it's only indirectly that

I can aim at the aspect that rules the way in which I dwell in the world. Through poetry I dwell in the world in the sense that the aspects it evokes are no longer foreign, since they have received their language, which is not the language of description but of evocation. We tend to say that this evocation is subjective, because we have completely flattened our concept of reality and reduced it to the enumeration of the population of the world in terms of the objects that have received a status in a descriptive language. But the word *world* itself is not one of these objects. This is one of the main discoveries of Husserl.[13] The *world* is the horizon of objects, a background of objects. We understand the word *world* as not only the sum of objects; it's not an additive concept. On the contrary, the objects are subtractions from this whole. We may be related to reality as a whole before the fragmentation in objects, and it's this whole to which we belong. Once more I return to this expression, to be born is to be born in the world. The word *world* here is related precisely to our birth. Each time that we are born or reborn, it's in the world. There is a relation between birth and world and between dwelling and world. Perhaps there is a kind of language that protects this relationship, because it is the shrine of this relationship. We are not silent about the world as a horizon; it has its language. Poetry is condemned to retreat into interiority because exteriority has been completely colonized by ordinary language. The polarity between ordinary and scientific language is not satisfying. We want also an extraordinary language, because ordinary language is the language of ordinary life, and it is ordinary life that is suspended in poetic language.

To relate this to what I say elsewhere on ideology, we may say in poetry an ideological relation to the world is suspended, since what is suspended is fundamentally our interest in control. The interest in control that rules the subject/object relationship takes the form of an empirical control. The empirical is the aspect of reality that may become the point of application of our manipulation by means of power and control. When this claim of control is lifted, it leads not to the disappearance of the world but perhaps on the contrary to the appearance of the world although no longer as a system of tools and manipulable things. This is very difficult to express philosophically without returning to a kind of mysticism, but a theory of fiction here requires a parallel critique of the concept of the object. As long as we remain under the presupposition that objects are the dimension of reality that are screened and organized under our conceptual network, then we may miss a more ontological dimension that is not objective in the sense of being merely emotional but in the sense of being pre-objective. It's this pre-objective aspect that I should say is said poetically.

I would dare extend to this last aspect of language the concept of redescription. Of course, it's no longer as in science when we redescribe on the

Fiction (5): Poetic Language   285

basis of new objects, but it's the abolition of the objective for the sake of ontological redescription, as if there were a bedrock of reality before the division in objects in our ordinary perception. Is it not possible to say that poetic imagination schematizes this pre-objective apprehension? Here we see all the Heideggerian attempts to speak of being not in terms of objects.[14] We may think also of Gadamer's attempt to speak to our belonging to (*Zugehörigkeit*), our participation.[15] What is important for present purposes is that there is a point where invention and discovery are one and the same. Invention is the aspect of construction; discovery is the aspect of description. The opposition between invention and discovery remains caught in the opposition between subject and object. We say that invention is more subjective, and discovery is more objective, but if we question the subject/object distinction, all the other distinctions ruled by this polarity are also put into question. A theory of productive imagination implies revision of our concepts of reality and of truth, since a concept of truth as adequation belongs to the subject/object relationship, whereas the relation to reality in terms of pre-objective belonging has more to do with a concept of truth as manifestation. We cannot isolate the problem of imagination from a revisionary enterprise that involves our concepts of reality and truth. This could have been forecast from the beginning, because the concept of the picture does not commit us to any revision of this kind since the referent of the picture is already given. No critical implications concerning reality are implied in the picture, since the picture is the reassertion of reality in an image. The image is entirely dependent on an assumed concept of reality, since the reality of the picture is borrowed entirely from that of its original. Because, however, the fiction has freed itself from the rule of the original, it then provides a new aspect, a new dimension to reality. The paradox is that a theory of imagination has to be connected with an ontology.

If I could say what are the main ideas of these lectures, they are, first, that there is a polarity between picture and fiction that has been overlooked by the Western tradition analyzing the imagination. The tradition tends to speak of fiction in terms of picture because of the weight of the traditional inquiry that moves from impression to copy and so on. Second, there is a unity of imagination in its epistemological and its poetic functions. Third, the more the fiction is fictional, the more it has ontological implications. Fictions provide the *model for*. This is the referential claim of fiction in opposition to picture which has no referential claim, since the picture has already its model. It's easier to accomplish a theory of reading than a theory of writing in the sense that in reading we receive the invention and are extended within ourselves by the invention of the other. If there were rules for invention, all of us would be painters, poets, and, by chance, good philosophers.[16]

Notes

Editor's Introduction

1. We will return to the differentiation between productive and creative imagination.

2. See, for example, Jean-Luc Amalric, *Ricœur, Derrida. L'Enjeu de la métaphore* (Paris: PUF, 2006); Amalric, *Paul Ricoeur, l'imagination vive. Une genèse de la philosophie ricoeurienne de l'imagination* (Paris: Hermann, 2013); Amalric, "D'une convergence remarquable entre phénoménologie et philosophie analytique: La lecture ricoeurienne des thèses de Sartre et Ryle sur l'imagination," *Études Ricoeuriennes/Ricoeur Studies* 5, no. 1 (2014): 82–94; Amalric, "L'espace de la fantaisie: Prolégomènes à une approche de l'expérience analytique à partir du concept ricoeurien d'identité narrative," *B@belonline* 8 (2021): 21–44; Amalric, "Evénement, idéologie et utopie," *Études Ricoeuriennes/Ricoeur Studies* 5, n. 2 (2014): 9–22; Amalric, "L'imagination poético-pratique dans l'identité narrative," *Études Ricoeuriennes/ Ricoeur Studies* 3, no. 2 (2012): 110–27; Amalric, "Ricoeur, Castoriadis: The Productive Imagination between Mediation and Origin," in *Ricoeur and Castoriadis in Discussion: On Human Creation, Historical Novelty, and the Social Imaginary*, ed. Suzi Adams (London: Rowman and Littlefield International, 2017), 77–110; Amalric, "Le statut de l'utopie dans la philosophie de l'imagination de Ricœur," in *Penser l'utopie aujourd'hui avec Paul Ricœur*, ed. Sébastien Roman (Paris: Presses Universitaires de Vincennes, 2021), 37–55; Luz Ascarate, *Imaginer selon Paul Ricoeur: La phénoménologie à la rencontre de l'ontologie sociale* (Paris: Hermann, 2022); Patrick L. Bourgeois, *Imagination and Postmodernity* (Lanham, MD: Lexington Books, 2013), 140–41; Maria Gabriela Azevedo e Castro, *Imaginação em Paul Ricoeur* (Lisbon: Instituto Piaget, 2002); Geoffrey Dierckxsens, "The Ambiguity of Justice Revisited: The Narrative and Imaginative Aspects of Social Power and Embodiment in Ricoeur's Philosophy," in *The Ambiguity of Justice: New Perspectives on Paul Ricoeur's Approach to Justice*, ed. Geoffrey Dierckxsens (Leiden: Brill, 2020), 84–87; Jeanne Evans, *Paul Ricoeur's Hermeneutics of the Imagination* (New York: Peter Lang, 1995); James Fodor, *Christian Hermeneutics: Paul Ricoeur and the Refiguring of Theology* (Oxford: Clarendon Press, 1995), 189–91; Michaël Foessel, "Action, Norms and Critique: Paul Ricoeur and the Powers of the Imaginary," *Philosophy Today* 58, no. 4 (2014): 513–25; Foessel, "Introduction: Paul Ricoeur ou les puissances de l'imaginaire," in *Ricoeur: Anthologie*, ed. Michaël Foessel and Fabien Lamouche (Paris: Éditions Points, 2007), 7–22; Saulius Geniusas, "Against the Sartrean Background: Ricoeur's Lectures on Imagination," *Research in Phenomenology* 46, no. 1 (2016): 98–116; Geniusas, "Between Phenomenology and Hermeneutics: Paul Ricoeur's Philosophy of Imagination," *Human Studies* 38, no. 2 (2015): 223–41; Geniusas, "The Stuff That Dreams Are Made of: Max Scheler and Paul Ricoeur on Productive Imagination," in *Hermeneutics and Phenomenology: Figures and Themes*, ed. Saulius Geniusas and Paul Fairchild (London:

Bloomsbury, 2018), 93–105; Richard Kearney, "Between Imagination and Language," in *On Paul Ricoeur: The Owl of Minerva* (Aldershot, UK: Ashgate, 2004), 35–58; Kearney, "Exploring Imagination with Paul Ricoeur," in *Stretching the Limits of Productive Imagination: Studies in Kantianism, Phenomenology, and Hermeneutics*, ed. Saulius Geniusas (London: Rowman & Littlefield International, 2018), 187–204; Kearney, "The Hermeneutical Imagination (Ricoeur)," in *Poetics of Imagining: Modern to Post-Modern* (New York: Fordham University Press, 1998), 142–77; Kearney, "Paul Ricoeur and the Hermeneutic Imagination," in *The Narrative Path: The Later Works of Paul Ricoeur*, ed. T. Peter Kemp and David Rasmussen (Cambridge, MA: MIT Press, 1989), 1–31; Maria Avelina Cecelia Lafuente, "Imagination and Practical Creativity in Paul Ricoeur," in *Life: The Outburst of Life in the Human Sphere, Book II*, ed. Anna-Teresa Tymieniecka (Dordrecht: Kluwer, 1999), 243–61; Mariana Larison, "L'imaginaire et ses lieux communs," *Philosophie* 132, no. 1 (2017): 68–77; Leonard Lawlor, *Imagination and Chance: The Difference Between the Thought of Ricoeur and Derrida* (Albany: SUNY Press, 1992), 66–69, 124–26; Mary Schaldenbrand, "Metaphoric Imagination: Kinship Through Conflict," in *Studies in the Philosophy of Paul Ricoeur*, ed. Charles E. Reagan (Athens: Ohio University Press, 1979), 57–81; Alain Thomasset, *Paul Ricoeur: Une poétique de la morale: Aux fondements d'une éthique herméneutique et narrative dans une perspective chrétienne* (Leuven: University Press-Peeters, 1996); Thomasset, "L'imagination dans la pensée de Paul Ricoeur: Fonction poétique du langage et transformation du suject," *Études théologiques et religieuses* 80, no. 4 (2005): 525–41; Kevin J. Vanhoozer, *Biblical Narrative in the Philosophy of Paul Ricoeur: A Study in Hermeneutics and Theology* (Cambridge: Cambridge University Press, 1990), 43–49; Sophie Vlacos, *Ricoeur, Literature and Imagination* (New York: Bloomsbury, 2014).

3. See, for example, Amalric, *Paul Ricoeur, l'imagination vive*, 13; Bourgeois, *Imagination and Postmodernity*, 141; Castro, *Imaginação em Paul Ricoeur*, 13; Dierckxsens, "The Ambiguity of Justice Revisited," 84; Evans, *Paul Ricoeur's Hermeneutics of the Imagination*, 47–48; Fodor, *Christian Hermeneutics*, 123, 189; Foessel, "Paul Ricoeur ou les puissances de l'imaginaire," 8; Kearney, "Between Imagination and Language," 36; Kearney, "Exploring Imagination with Paul Ricoeur," 187; Kearney, "The Hermeneutical Imagination (Ricoeur)," 143; Kearney, "Paul Ricoeur and the Hermeneutic Imagination," 2; Myriam Revault d'Allonnes, "Avant-propos à l'édition française," in Paul Ricoeur, *L'idéologie et l'utopie*, trans. Myriam Revault d'Allonnes and Joël Roman (Paris: Seuil, 1997), 13; Schaldenbrand, "Metaphoric Imagination," 58–59, 76; Vanhoozer, *Biblical Narrative in the Philosophy of Paul Ricoeur*, 6, 7.

Due to the limited length of the Editor's Introduction, the secondary literature cannot receive the attention it deserves and henceforth the Introduction concentrates exclusively on Ricoeur's own texts. The Introduction also generally restricts itself to Ricoeur's relevant books rather than also drawing from his articles.

4. For a representative sample of Ricoeur's work on the religious imagination as a form of productive or poetic imagination, see *The Symbolism of Evil* [1960], trans. Emerson Buchanan (Boston: Beacon Press, 1967); "The Language of Faith" [1963], in *The Philosophy of Paul Ricoeur: An Anthology of His Work*, ed. Charles E. Reagan and David Stewart (Boston: Beacon Press, 1978), 223–38; "Freedom in the Light of Hope" [1968], trans. Robert Sweeney, in *The Conflict of Interpretations*, ed. Don Ihde (Evanston, IL: Northwestern University Press, 1974), 402–24; "Listening to the Parables of Jesus, in *The Philosophy of Paul Ricoeur: An Anthology of His Work*, ed. Charles E. Reagan and David Stewart (Boston: Beacon Press, 1978), 239–45; "Manifestation and Proclamation" [1974], *Blaisdell Institute Journal* 11 (1978): 13–35, republished in *Figuring the Sacred: Religion, Narrative, and Imagination*, trans. David Pellauer, ed. Mark I. Wallace (Minneapolis: Fortress Press, 1995), 48–67; "Philosophy and

NOTES TO PAGES xii–xxxiii 289

Religious Language," *Journal of Religion* 54 (1974): 71–85, republished in *Figuring the Sacred*, 35–47; "Biblical Hermeneutics," *Semeia* 4 (1975): 29–148; "Philosophical Hermeneutics and Biblical Hermeneutics" [1975], in *Exegesis: Problems of Method and Exercises in Reading (Genesis 22 and Luke 15)*, trans. Donald G. Miller, ed. François Bovon and Grégoire Rouiller (Pittsburgh, PA: Pickwick Press, 1978), 321–39, republished in a new translation by Kathleen Blamey in *From Text to Action* (Evanston, IL: Northwestern University Press, 1991), 89–101; "Philosophical Hermeneutics and Theological Hermeneutics," *Sciences Religieuses/Studies in Religion* 5, no. 1 (Summer 1975): 14–33; "L'herméneutique de la sécularisation: Foi, idéologie, utopie, " *Archivio de Filosofia* 46, nos. 2–3 (1976): 49–68, republished in *La religion pour penser: Écrits et conférences 5*, ed. Daniel Frey (Paris: Seuil, 2021), 155–87; "Toward a Hermeneutic of the Idea of Revelation," *Harvard Theological Review* 70, nos. 1–2 (1977): 1–37, republished in *Essays on Biblical Interpretation*, ed. Lewis S. Mudge (Philadelphia: Fortress Press, 1980), 73–118; "Naming God," *Union Seminary Quarterly Review* 34 (1979): 215–27, republished in *Figuring the Sacred*, 217–35; "The Bible and the Imagination," in *The Bible as a Document of the University*, ed. Hans Dieter Betz (Chico, CA: Scholars Press, 1981), 49–75, republished in *Figuring the Sacred*, 144–66; "Poétique et symbolique," in *Initiation à la pratique de la théologie*, ed. Bernard Lauret and François Refoulé (Paris: Cerf, 1982), 37–61.

5. The composition of this Introduction has been assisted by reference to other works I have written while working on the editing of the imagination lectures. Those articles will be cited at appropriate points and also indicate more expansive developments of themes than can be pursued here. The Introduction supersedes an early essay of mine on the lectures, written after an initial review of the transcriptions of the lectures. See George H. Taylor, "Ricoeur's Philosophy of Imagination," *Journal of French Philosophy*, 16 (2006): 93–104.

6. Ricoeur published separately a comparison of Ryle and Sartre on the imagination, an essay based on a 1974 lecture, but his discussion of each in these lectures is much more detailed. Paul Ricoeur, "Sartre and Ryle on the Imagination," in *The Philosophy of Jean-Paul Sartre*, ed. Paul A. Schillp (La Salle, IL: Open Court, 1981), 167–78.

7. For development of the phenomenological insights of the lectures, see George H. Taylor, "The Phenomenological Contributions of Ricoeur's Philosophy of Imagination," *Social Imaginaries* 1, no. 2 (2015): 13–31. It would be a worthwhile endeavor to interrelate Ricoeur's phenomenology in the imagination lectures with his writings on the subject elsewhere, but that topic is beyond the scope of both the present Introduction and the article just named.

8. Ricoeur's references to the "like-real" and elsewhere to the "inexistent" appear inconsistent with the Husserlian notion of the *epochē*'s suspension of judgment. The inconsistency seems to be resolved in Ricoeur's criticism in the lectures, drawing upon Merleau-Ponty, that the suspension of judgment is never complete. I thank Eileen Brennan for discussion of this point.

9. See, for example, Paul Ricoeur, "Philosophy and Religious Language," *Journal of Religion* 54 (1974): 71–85.

10. Ricoeur quotes Kant's *Critique of Pure Reason*, 183; A141/B180–181.

11. Hans-Georg Gadamer, *Truth and Method*, 2d ed., trans. revised by Joel Weinsheimer and Donald G. Marshall (New York: 1989), 140, 143. Jean Grondin has written perceptively on the centrality of the notion of presentation (*Darstellung*) in Gadamer's *Truth and Method*. Jean Grondin, "L'art comme presentation chez Gadamer: Portée et limites d'un concept," *Études Germaniques* 62 (2007) 337–49. A question requiring more research and reflection is to what degree does Ricoeur's theory of imagination and productive imagination itself relate to an inquiry into the nature of presentation (*Darstellung*) and representation (*Vor-*

stellung, Vertretung). Restricting ourselves to presentation, note, for example, that Ricoeur interrelates figuration and *Darstellung*, asserting that it is the task of imagination to figure the Ideas, to give them a *Darstellung*. Paul Ricoeur, "Imagination productive et imagination reproductive selon Kant," in *Recherches phénoménologiques sur l'imaginaire. I.* (Paris: Centre de Recherches Phénoménologiques, 1974), 13. In *Memory, History, Forgetting*, Ricoeur builds on Gadamer to comment that "the ontological structure of *Darstellung* continues to demand its rights" and then asserts: "The whole of textual hermeneutics is thus placed under the theme of the increase in being [that *Darstellung* offers] applied to the work of art." Paul Ricoeur, *Memory, History, Forgetting*, trans. Kathleen Blamey and David Pellauer (Chicago: University of Chicago Press, 2004), 566, n. 81. In the imagination lectures, does productive imagination as depiction provide a more incisive way to recharacterize *Darstellung*? As the index to the present volume indicates, discussion of *Darstellung* and *Vorstellung* does appear as a suggestive subtext of the imagination lectures. For significant discussion of *Vertretung* as representation, see Ricoeur, *Memory, History, Forgetting*, 565–67, n. 81.

12. In other work I question Ricoeur's claims, only tangentially presented in these lectures, that the critical distance positioned at the top of the vertical axis permits an escape from belief and that belief is necessarily distortive. See George H. Taylor, "Imagination and Belief," *International Journal of Social Imaginaries* 1, no. 1 (2022): 66–83.

13. Ideology is generally reproductive but not necessarily so to the extent that it acts as *constitutive* of personal or social identity, which Ricoeur identifies as one form of ideology. In this sense, ideology participates in the symbolic mediation of action, discussed in a subsequent paragraph in the text. For a more extensive discussion of the *Lectures on Ideology and Utopia*, see George H. Taylor, "Editor's Introduction," in *Lectures on Ideology and Utopia*, ix–xxxv.

14. For further elaboration of the relation between Ricoeur's theories of metaphor and ideology and utopia, see Taylor, "Editor's Introduction," xxiii–xxxiv.

15. For more expansive discussion of Ricoeur's theory of utopia, see George H. Taylor, "Delineating Ricoeur's Concept of Utopia," *Social Imaginaries* 3, no. 1 (2017): 41–60.

16. For development of this point, see George H. Taylor, "Prospective Political Identity," in *Paul Ricoeur in the Age of Hermeneutical Reason: Poetics, Praxis, and Critique*, ed. Roger W. H. Savage (Lanham, MD: Lexington Books, 2015), 128–29. David Pellauer insightfully notes that Ricoeur nevertheless continues to employ the vocabulary of reference across all three volumes of *Time and Narrative*. David Pellauer, "Response to Professors Sweeney and Ingbretsen," *Proceedings of the American Catholic Philosophical Association* 62 (1988): 89.

17. Paul Ricoeur, *Time and Narrative* (vol. 3), trans. Kathleen Blamey and David Pellauer (Chicago: University of Chicago Press), 158–59.

18. Paul Ricoeur, *The Rule of Metaphor*, trans. Robert Czerny (Toronto: University of Toronto Press, 1977), 254.

19. For more detailed development of this argument, see Taylor, "Prospective Political Identity."

20. For greater elaboration, see George H. Taylor, "The Deeper Significance of Ricoeur's Philosophy of Productive Imagination: The Role of Figuration," in *Productive Imagination: Its History, Meaning and Significance*, ed. Saulius Geniusas and Dmitri Nikulin (London: Rowman & Littlefield International, 2018), 157–81.

21. Ricoeur, *Rule of Metaphor*, 193.

22. Paul Ricoeur, "The Metaphorical Process as Cognition, Imagination, and Feeling," in *On Metaphor*, ed. Sheldon Sacks (Chicago: University of Chicago Press, 1979), 147.

NOTES TO PAGES XXXiX–13 291

23. Ricoeur, *Time and Narrative*, 3: 184–85.

24. Paul Ricoeur and Cornelius Castoriadis, "Dialogue on History and the Social Imaginary," in *Ricoeur and Castoriadis in Discussion: On Human Creation, Historical Novelty, and the Social Imaginary*, ed. Suzi Adams (London: Rowman & Littlefield International, 2017), 3–20.

25. See, for example, Ricoeur, *Rule of Metaphor*; Ricoeur, *Lectures on Ideology and Utopia*; Ricoeur, "The Function of Fiction in Shaping Reality," in *Man and World* 12, no. 2 (1979): 123–41; Ricoeur, "Creativity in Language," *The Philosophy of Paul Ricoeur*, ed. Charles E. Reagan and David Stewart (Boston: Beacon Press, 1978), 120–33. For development of this argument, see George H. Taylor, "On the Cusp: Ricoeur and Castoriadis at the Boundary," in *Ricoeur and Castoriadis in Discussion*, 23–48.

Chapter One

1. In the initial paragraphs of this first lecture, Ricoeur locates his study of imagination in relation to scholarly trends prevalent in the 1970s when the lectures were delivered: the philosophical literature on imagination was limited; psychology was significantly behavioristic; and the scholarly reputation of the study of creativity was weak. Since that time, substantial changes have occurred in all of these areas. The lectures themselves address changes that were beginning to occur. See n. 3. In this first lecture, Ricoeur will quickly set aside the then contemporary context and turn to his own argument.

2. To minimize endnotes, whenever Ricoeur offers a general reference to a specific text, as here, no endnote is provided, but the complete reference entry is available in the bibliography. No citation is provided where Ricoeur offers only a broad general reference to secondary literature. In the present, introductory lecture, we do not insert endnote citations to topics that Ricoeur will discuss in subsequent lectures.

3. For Ricoeur's acknowledgment of changes in the field, see lecture 4, n.1.

4. As a point of clarification, Ricoeur is explicitly referring to psychological literature here, not to Gilbert Ryle's independent philosophical focus on role-playing. On the psychological literature, see lecture 4, n.1. On Ryle, see lectures 7 and 8.

5. See, for example, Charles Sanders Peirce, *Collected Papers of Charles Sanders Peirce* (vol. 2) (Cambridge, MA: Belknap Press, 1960), 157–58.

6. Full references to the primary texts Ricoeur will be discussing are located in the bibliography in the section on the Course Syllabus.

7. In subsequent lectures, for reasons he will elaborate, Ricoeur's vocabulary will become more precise and prefer instead the term "inexistence." For technical terms such as "inexistence," the Index provides references to Ricoeur's definitions.

8. In his own development of a theory of productive imagination, when he moves away from the image, Ricoeur will argue that productive imagination is better typified not by absence but by the nowhere, something outside current reality.

9. Here and subsequently, Ricoeur is referring to his lectures on ideology and utopia, which he also delivered at the University of Chicago in the autumn of 1975. These lectures were later published as *Lectures on Ideology and Utopia*.

10. Ricoeur is referring to the far left end of the presence/absence axis, as full presence and zero absence would be located there.

11. As carried out, Part II of the lectures does not return to this psychological literature. In lectures 7 and 8, Ricoeur does discuss at some length Ryle's philosophical approach to the role of play. For commentary on the psychological literature, see lecture 4, n.1.

Chapter Two

1. Pagination in the parenthetical references refers first to the text and then to the original Greek, which is provided in the text. See Aristotle, *On the Soul*, trans J. A. Smith, in *The Basic Works of Aristotle*, ed. Richard McKeon, (New York: Random House, 1966), 535–603. Subsequent parenthetical pagination refers to this text.

2. See, for example, Étienne Bonnot de Condillac, *Essay on the Origin of Human Knowledge*, trans. and ed. Hans Aarsleff (Cambridge: Cambridge University Press, 2001), Pt. I, § 2.1.12–13; *Condillac's Treatise on the Sensations*, trans. Geraldine Carr (London: Favil Press, 1930), I.v; II.xi; III.viii.

3. As mentioned in the Editor's Acknowledgments, the edited text incorporates material from Ricoeur's lecture notes where appropriate to amplify his analysis. More rarely, as here, we will refer to lecture notes by means of endnotes, when Ricoeur's notes present important claims, but they are distinguishable from his arguments in the lecture. In the lecture notes for his 1973 course on imagination appears the following at this point in Ricoeur's discussion:

> Aristotle compares the imagination to opinion or belief, as Hume will do also. Why? It is not so much because of the commitment implied by imagination. On the contrary. It is due to imagination's role as anticipation, supposition. In that sense, imagination is a condition of belief as sensation was a condition of imagination ([Aristotle 1966, 587;] 427b 15–16). This analysis has an important philosophical value. We may discern here the first attempt before Kant to isolate productive imagination from reproductive imagination. All of the other features described under the title of imagination versus belief may be considered as anticipations of productive imagination: the arbitrariness of imagination is opposed to belief as bound or necessary.

While Ricoeur's 1975 lectures in this volume do track the general argument in the much shorter 1973 lecture notes, it is not apparent whether they explicitly draw upon the 1973 notes. Ricoeur's unpublished materials at the Fonds Ricoeur in Paris do not include any separate 1975 lecture notes. It is therefore not known whether the lack of the quoted argument in the lectures as presented in 1975 is inadvertent or intentional.

4. Benedict Spinoza, *Treatise on the Emendation of the Intellect*, in *The Collected Works of Spinoza* (vol. 1) (Princeton: Princeton University Press, 1985), § 56.

5. Since in the next sentence in the text Ricoeur refers to Martin Heidegger's *Kant and the Problem of Metaphysics*, he seems to be thinking here of Heidegger's quotation of two passages on the "common root" from Kant's *Critique of Pure Reason* (A15/B29, 61; A835/B863, 655). Martin Heidegger, *Kant and the Problem of Metaphysics*, trans. James S. Churchill (Bloomington: Indiana University Press, 1962), 41.

6. Heidegger, *Kant and the Problem of Metaphysics*, Section Three, Parts B and C ("The Transcendental Imagination as the Root of Both Stems" and "The Transcendental Imagination and the Problem of Human Pure Reason").

Chapter Three

1. See Blaise Pascal, *Pascal's Pensées*, bilingual edition with English trans. H. F. Stewart (New York: Pantheon Books, 1950). Subsequent parenthetical page citations referring to Pascal are to this text.

NOTES TO PAGES 37–64 293

2. See Benedict Spinoza, *Ethics*, ed. James Gutmann (New York: Hafner Publishing, 1957). Subsequent parenthetical page citations referring to Spinoza are to this text.

3. Following customary scholarly practice, citations to Wittgenstein's *Philosophical Investigations* refer to specific paragraphs by number or as here, where paragraphs are not numbered, by page. See Ludwig Wittgenstein, *Philosophical Investigations*, 3rd ed., trans. G. E. M. Anscombe (New York: Macmillan, 1958). For Ricoeur's further development of Wittgenstein, see lecture 9.

Chapter Four

1. At the beginning of this lecture as originally delivered, Ricoeur spent some time presenting details of the course syllabus, which at this point had not yet been distributed to the class due to administrative error. The syllabus is provided in the bibliography to the current volume, so Ricoeur's summary is not replicated here. Ricoeur's few substantive points from these comments are included at appropriate locations elsewhere in the present text.

Deserving of mention at this point are Ricoeur's comments on a section of the syllabus to which he does not return, except in passing. He notes that a final part of the syllabus turns to more recent work in psychology on imagination:

These texts appear not to be known among philosophers, since I know no philosopher who quotes them. After a long silence on imagination in psychology, a number of books on the topic have appeared in recent years. The prohibition on the problem has been lifted. Holt has even written an article on "Imagery: The Return of the Ostracized." Previously the image had been considered as something mental and therefore private and not observable. So there was no place for it in psychology. But there has been a return to imagination through play, through role-playing and so on, and through the experiments on psychedelic experiences and the expansion of the mind. Psychologists discovered the imagination too is a behavior. The behavioral psychologist has had to take into account that there are people who live in the imagination and do something when they imagine. The most interesting text here is Segal, *Imagery: Current Cognitive Approaches*.

It must also be said that after having focused for so many years on learning, perception, and so on, an important development is occurring in psychology concerning cognitive processes. This is part of significant developments in the psychology of motivation, which includes also studies on personality. The attention to cognition is also the influence of Jean Piaget. The problem of imagination returns through the framework of cognitive psychology. In order to show that this is a new field, these psychologists prefer the term *imagery* to *imagination* or the *imaginary*. Authors such as Eric Klinger discuss the structure and function of fantasy.

2. All page references in the text refer to David Hume, *A Treatise of Human Nature*, edited by L. A. Selby-Bigge (Oxford: Clarendon Press, 1965).

Chapter Five

1. Pagination refers first to the Norman Kemp Smith translation and second to the German pagination in the combined A and B editions of the first *Critique*, which is included in

294 NOTES TO PAGES 73–99

the translation. See Immanuel Kant, *Critique of Pure Reason*, trans. Norman Kemp Smith (New York: St. Martin's Press, 1965). Subsequent citations refer to this text.

2. Jean-Paul Sartre, *The Psychology of Imagination* (New York: Philosophical Library, 1948; New York: Washington Square Press, 1966), 127/114. In referencing *The Psychology of Imagination*, the first page citation refers to the 1948 hard cover edition and the second to the 1966 paperback edition. For further discussion, see lecture 13.

Chapter Six

1. See Kant, *Critique of Pure Reason*, trans. Kemp Smith.

2. See Anton Ehrenzweig, "Unconscious Scanning," chap. 3 in *The Hidden Order of Art: A Study in the Psychology of Artistic Perception* (Berkeley: University of California Press, 1967), 32–45.

3. On the relation between Nietzsche and Heidegger on play, see, for example, Jacques Derrida, "Structure, Sign, and Play in the Discourse of the Human Sciences," in *Writing and Difference*, trans. Alan Bass (Chicago: University of Chicago Press, 1978), 278–93.

4. Pagination refers to the Bernard translation that Ricoeur used and then to the pagination of the original German edition. See Immanuel Kant, *Critique of Judgment*, trans. J. H. Bernard (New York: Hafner Press, 1951) and *Kritik der Urteilskraft und Schriften zur Naturphilosophie* (Darmstadt: Wissenschaftliche Buchgesellschaft, 1968 [1790]). Subsequent citations refer to these texts.

Chapter Seven

1. See, for example, Maurice Merleau-Ponty, "Cézanne's Doubt," in *Sense and Non-Sense* (Evanston, IL: Northwestern University Press, 1964, 1–25.

2. As the lectures unfold, Ricoeur does not return to Merleau-Ponty, perhaps because of the lengthy attention given to Sartre, and so we unfortunately do not know in the present pages how Ricoeur's more delineated analysis of Merleau-Ponty would have proceeded.

It is also worth mentioning here that at the beginning of lecture 4, in a brief discussion of the course syllabus the substantive points of which are incorporated in the edited lectures elsewhere where relevant, Ricoeur mentions Gadamer, rather than Merleau-Ponty, as the third author in Continental philosophy who would join his presentation of Husserl and Sartre in the second part of the lectures. Ricoeur mentions that Gadamer's *Truth and Method* has "some interesting pages on *das Bild*, which is closer to the concept of *eikon*," a concept that has been developed in the Byzantine tradition as "the representative of reality." Subsequently, Ricoeur's references to Gadamer in the lectures are few, although he does return to Gadamer's theory of *Bild* in a sentence in lecture 14, a sentence that follows a brief comment on where he will subsequently head in addressing the work of François Dagognet. In the first volume of *Time and Narrative*, Ricoeur briefly adverts positively to Gadamer's recognition in *Bild* of "the power of bringing about an increase in being in our vision of the world which is impoverished by everyday affairs" (81).

It appears that in the present volume, the substantive theme that drew Ricoeur to Merleau-Ponty and Gadamer is taken up in lecture 17, in the third part of the lectures, in Ricoeur's discussion that builds on Dagognet's *Écriture et iconographie*.

3. Gilbert Ryle, *The Concept of Mind* (New York: Barnes & Noble, 1949). Subsequent citations refer to this text.

4. J. L. Austin, "A Plea for Excuses," in *Philosophical Papers*, 2d ed. (Oxford: Clarendon Press, 1970), 123–52.

NOTES TO PAGES 107–136   295

Chapter Eight

1. Ryle, *The Concept of Mind*. Subsequent citations refer to this text.

2. From context it appears that Ricoeur is referencing a more technical understanding of Merleau-Ponty's usage of assumption as a form of protention. However, Merleau-Ponty does not often use assumption (or the analogue, presumption) in this technical manner. If Ricoeur is referring to a broader use by Merleau-Ponty of assumption, this more general sense does appear more frequently, but in English translations of Merleau-Ponty, his usage of *assomption* or *assumer* is more difficult to track. For example, in the final paragraph of the *Phénoménologie de la perception*, Merleau-Ponty writes: "En *assumant* un présent, je ressaisis et je transforme mon passé, j'en change le sens, je m'en libère, je m'en dégage." Maurice Merleau-Ponty, *Phénoménologie de la perception* (Paris: Gallimard, 1945), 519 (emphasis added). As translated, the sentence becomes: "By *taking up* a present . . ." Maurice Merleau-Ponty, *Phenomenology of Perception*, trans. Colin Smith (London: Routledge & Kegan Paul, 1962), 455 (emphasis added); Maurice Merleau-Ponty, *Phenomenology of Perception*, trans. Donald A. Landes (London: Routledge, 2012), 482 (same) (emphasis added).

3. H. H. Price, *Thinking and Experience* (London: Hutchinson's University Library, 1953). Subsequent parenthetical page citations referring to Price are to this text.

4. Kant, *Critique of Judgment* (1951), 52; 217.

Chapter Nine

1. Ludwig Wittgenstein, *Philosophical Investigations*, 3d ed., trans. G. E. M. Anscombe (New York: Macmillan, 1958). Consistent with the practices of Wittgenstein scholarship, citations to Wittgenstein's *Philosophical Investigations* refer either to specific paragraphs— which are cited by number—or, in Part II of the text where paragraphs are not numbered, to page—which are cited as "p. x."

2. Citations to Wittgenstein's *Tractatus* refer to paragraph numbers within the text. See Ludwig Wittgenstein, *Tractatus Logico-Philosophicus*, trans. D. F. Pears and B. F. McGuiness (London: Routledge & Kegan Paul, 1961).

3. As Ricoeur previously observed, he is cognizant of the scientific claim that images are associated with brain activity (118), but his present comments occurred before the advent of contemporary neuroscientific imaging of brain activity. For Ricoeur's subsequent engagement with neuroscience, see Jean-Pierre Changeux and Paul Ricoeur, *What Makes Us Think?* (Princeton, NJ: Princeton University Press, 2000).

4. See, for example, Stephen A. Erickson, *Language and Being: An Analytic Phenomenology* (New Haven: Yale University Press, 1970); George F. Sefler, *Language and the World: A Methodological Synthesis within the Writings of Martin Heidegger and Ludwig Wittgenstein* (Atlantic Highlands, NJ: Humanities Press, 1974).

5. Maurice Merleau-Ponty, *Signs*, trans. Richard C. McCleary (Evanston, IL: Northwestern University Press, 1964), 89–92.

6. See, for example, Martin Heidegger, "The End of Philosophy and the Task of Thinking," in *On Time and Being* (New York: Harper & Row, 1972), 55–73; Louis Althusser, *For Marx* (New York: Pantheon Books, 1969), 28–29; Jacques Derrida, "White Mythology: Metaphor in the Text of Philosophy," *New Literary History*, 6, no. 1 (1974): 74. In lecture 19, Ricoeur will return to discussion of the death of philosophy and will explicitly reference Althusser.

7. Plato, *Meno*, in *The Collected Dialogues of Plato* (Princeton, NJ: Princeton University Press, 1961), 363, 80a.

Chapter Ten

1. The reading of Merleau-Ponty is subsequently not pursued in any substantial way.

2. Ricoeur's discussion of imaginative variations will in fact not occur until lecture 15.

3. See Roman Ingarden, *Controversy over the Existence of the World* (2 vols.), trans. Arthur Szylewicz (Frankfurt: Peter Lang, 2013, 2016). On Ricoeur, see, for example, Paul Ricoeur, "Phenomenology and Hermeneutics," in *From Text to Action*, trans. Kathleen Blamey and John B. Thompson (Evanston, IL: Northwestern University Press, 1991), 25–52.

4. Paul Ricoeur, "The Hermeneutical Function of Distanciation," in *From Text to Action*, 75–88.

5. See, for example, Edmund Husserl, "Second Meditation," in *Cartesian Meditations: An Introduction to Phenomenology*, trans. Dorion Cairns (The Hague: Martinus Nijhoff, 1960), 27–55.

6. Edmund Husserl, *Logical Investigations* (vol. 1), trans. J. N. Findlay (London: Routledge & Kegan Paul, 1970). Subsequent citations refer to this text.

7. See, for example, Husserl, "Second Logical Investigation," Introduction.

8. See, for example, Étienne Bonnot de Condillac, *Essay on the Origin of Human Knowledge*, trans. and ed. Hans Aarsleff (Cambridge: Cambridge University Press, 2001), I, 2, §§ 17, 20, 25, 49; George Berkeley, *A Treatise Concerning the Principles of Human Knowledge*, ed. Colin M Turbayne (New York: Liberal Arts Press, 1957), §§ 33, 65.

9. Husserl's quote comes from John Locke, *An Essay Concerning Human Understanding* (London: Thomas Basset, 1690), § III.iii.11.

10. Martin Heidegger, *Being and Time*, trans. John Macquarrie and Edward Robinson (New York: Harper & Row, 1962), § 44(a).

Chapter Eleven

1. Husserl's *Ideas I* is the first volume in a three-volume text. Consistent with customary practice, Ricoeur will typically refer to this volume simply as "*Ideas.*"

2. Heidegger, *Being and Time*, § 23; Merleau-Ponty, *Phenomenology of Perception* (2012), 81.

3. See Edmund Husserl, *Ideas: General Introduction to Pure Phenomenology*, trans. W. R. Boyce Gibson (New York: Collier Books, 1962). Subsequent parenthetical citations to Husserl refer to this text.

4. The term "in person" appears sometimes in the Gibson translation of *Ideas* that Ricoeur uses (for example, § 1, p. 46) but less frequently than in other English translations. See Edmund Husserl, *Ideas Pertaining to a Pure Phenomenology and to a Phenomenological Philosophy—First Book: General Introduction to a Pure Phenomenology*, trans. Fred Kersten (The Hague: Martinus Nijhoff, 1982); Edmund Husserl, *Ideas for a Pure Phenomenology and Phenomenological Philosophy—First Book. General Introduction to Pure Phenomenology*, trans. Daniel O. Dahlstrom (Indianapolis: Hackett, 2014). In § 43, for example, the Kersten and Dahlstrom translations each uses "in person" three times (92–93; 76), while Gibson uses the terms "bodily" or "embodied" (123). Husserl's original term is "*Leibhaftigkeit*" or a variant. Edmund Husserl, *Ideen zu einer Reinen Phänomenologie und Phänomenologischen Philosophie—Erstes Buch: Allgemeine Einführung in die Reine Phänomenologie* (The Hague: Martinus Nijhoff, 1950), 98–99. In Ricoeur's French translation of *Ideas*, the term is "*corporéité*" or a variant. Edmund Husserl, *Idées directrices pour une phénoménologie*, trans. Paul Ricoeur (Paris: Gallimard, 1950), 138–39.

NOTES TO PAGES 159–186 297

5. See, for example, Merleau-Ponty, *Phenomenology of Perception* (2012), 147, 169.

6. See Paul Ricoeur, *A Key to Edmund Husserl's "Ideas I,"* trans. Bond Harris, Jacqueline Bouchard Spurlock, and Pol Vandevelde (Milwaukee: Marquette University Press, 1996), 96 (note on Kersten translation page 75, line 5; German pagination [which is referenced in Ricoeur's French translation], page 65, Ricoeur's first note); 99 (note on Kersten translation page 86, line 2; German pagination, page 73, Ricoeur's second note).

7. See, for example, Merleau-Ponty, *Phenomenology of Perception* (2012), 5–7, 54.

8. See, for example, Heidegger, *Being and Time*, § 7(C); Merleau-Ponty, *Phenomenology of Perception* (2012), lxxvii.

9. Karl Jaspers, *Philosophy*, trans. E. B. Ashton (Chicago: University of Chicago Press, 1970), vol. 2, Bk. 2, Pt. III, chap. 7.

Chapter Twelve

1. Jean-Paul Sartre, *Imagination: A Psychological Critique*, trans. Forrest Williams (Ann Arbor: University of Michigan Press, 1962).

2. Jean-Paul Sartre, *The Psychology of Imagination* (New York: Philosophical Library, 1948; New York: Washington Square Press, 1966). In quoting *The Psychology of Imagination*, the first page citation refers to the 1948 hardcover edition and the second to the 1966 paperback.

3. William James, "The Stream of Thought," in *Principles of Psychology*, 1: 224–90. 2 vols. (New York: Henry Holt & Co., 1890).

4. In his original lecture, Ricoeur interjected at this point:

Unfortunately, there is a mistake in the translation here. When the text says that the analysis "has pointed out to us what may be called the static nature of the image" (19/17), it's not the static nature of the image that has been analyzed but the statics of the image. The French original says "*la statique.*" It is the method that is static. A few pages later Sartre returns to the point, saying: "But as yet we know only the statics of the image" (21/20). Here the translation is exact.

Ricoeur's quotation of the French edition is drawn from Jean-Paul Sartre, *L'imaginaire: Psychologie phénoménologique de l'imagination* (Paris: Gallimard, 1940), 27.

Chapter Thirteen

1. Sartre, *The Psychology of Imagination*. As noted in the prior lecture, in quoting *The Psychology of Imagination*, the first page citation refers to the 1948 hardcover edition and the second to the 1966 paperback.

2. See Jean-Paul Sartre, *Being and Nothingness*, trans. Hazel E. Barnes (New York: Washington Square Press, 1966), 12–15. There Sartre writes of the nonthetic consciousness as follows:

The necessity of syntax has compelled us hitherto to speak of the "non-positional consciousness of self." But we can no longer use this expression in which the "*of self*" still evokes the idea of knowledge. (Henceforth we shall put the "of" inside parentheses to show that it merely satisfies a grammatical requirement.) (14)

As translator Hazel Barnes indicates, the French syntactical construction is "*conscience (de) soi.*" Since English does not require the "of," she translates Sartre's term as self-consciousness (14, n. 4). The contrast between the French and English illuminates the nature of nonthetic consciousness.

3. See, for example, Husserl, "Fourth Meditation," in *Cartesian Meditations*, §§ 38–39.

4. Husserl distinguishes between an "adequate perception of the universal" and "an intuitive image, an analogon, of the universal we are intending ... [D]oes not an ordinary rough drawing function analogically in comparison with an ideal figure, thereby helping to condition the imaginative character of the universal presentation?" Edmund Husserl, "Sixth Logical Investigation," in *Logical Investigations* (vol. 2), trans. J. N. Findlay (London: Routledge & Kegan Paul, 1970), § 52, p. 801.

Chapter Fourteen

1. Sartre, *The Psychology of Imagination*. As previously mentioned, in quoting *The Psychology of Imagination*, the first page citation refers to the 1948 hardcover edition and the second to the 1966 paperback.

2. In a footnote, Sartre indicates that he is quoting Descartes, "First Meditation," *Meditations*, but provides no pagination. For a common English translation of this passage, see René Descartes, *Meditations on First Philosophy*, ed. Stanley Tweyman, trans. Elizabeth S. Haldane and G. R. T. Ross (London: Routledge, 1993), 46–47.

3. Sigmund Freud, "Mourning and Melancholia," *The Standard Edition of the Complete Psychological Works of Sigmund Freud*, ed. James Strachey (London: Hogarth Press, 1975), 243–58.

4. See, for example, Henri Bergson, "The Possible and the Real," in *The Creative Mind*, trans. Mabelle L. Andison (New York: Greenwood Press, 1968), 107–25.

5. Ricoeur's comment here marks his first reference in the lectures to Dagognet, whose analysis of iconic augmentation in *Écriture et iconographie* (1973) becomes central to Ricoeur's analysis in lecture 17. The prior lack of mention of Dagognet and his lack of inclusion in the course syllabus (provided in the bibliography) might raise the question whether Ricoeur came across Dagognet's text during the autumn of 1975 while the lectures were being delivered. Ricoeur references Dagognet's text, however, in two unpublished sources in 1974. The first came in the third lecture of a set of lectures entitled "On Imagination: From Picture to Fiction." This lecture was revised and later published as "That Fiction 'Remakes' Reality" and, almost identically, as "The Function of Fiction in Shaping Reality." The second mention of Dagognet came in lectures at the University of Chicago given the autumn of 1974 on Kant and the Problem of Imagination in the Three Critiques. Full bibliographic information appears in the "Chronology of Ricoeur's Works on Imagination" in the bibliography.

Chapter Fifteen

1. In fact, the term's origin may lie instead in William James. See, for example, William James, "Philosophical Conceptions and Practical Results," *University Chronicle* 1, no. 4 (1898): 307; James, *Pragmatism: A New Name for Some Old Ways of Thinking* (New York: Longmans, Green, and Co., 1907), 53, 74, 86, 90, 200; James, *The Meaning of Truth, a Sequel to "Pragmatism"* (New York: Longmans, Green, and Co, 1909), v, 119, 208. See, generally, George Cotkin, "William James and the Cash-Value Metaphor," *Et cetera: A Review of*

General Semantics 42 (1985): 37–46. It is not apparent whether Price knew of James's usage of the term. No reference to James (or to Dewey) appears in the index to Price's *Thinking and Experience*, nor is there reference in the book to the term's lineage.

2. See, for example, Husserl, *Ideas*, § 99.

3. The course was entitled Analogical Language and was offered during the spring quarter of 1975.

4. Gaston Bachelard, *The Poetics of Reverie*, trans. Daniel Russell (Boston: Beacon Press, 1971).

5. In his oral presentation of lectures 15 and 16, Ricoeur appeared to be himself translating directly from the French original of *La poétique de la rêverie* (though not of *La poétique de l'espace*). Since Ricoeur's general practice throughout the lectures is to quote the published English translation of cited material and since there appears to be no particular substantive reason Ricoeur himself translates the French, we follow his general practice and cite the published translation, so that readers may more easily trace the text of the translation as published.

6. Gaston Bachelard, *The Poetics of Space*, trans. Maria Jolas (Boston: Beacon Press, 1969).

7. See Eugène Minkowski, *Vers une cosmologie* [1936] (Paris: Payot, 1999): 101: "C'est comme si une source se trouvait à l'intérieur d'un vase clos et ses ondes, en venant se répercuter toujours à nouveau aux parois de ce vase, le remplissaient de leur sonorité, ou encore, c'est comme si le son d'un cor de chasse, renvoyé de toutes parts par l'écho, faisait tressaillir, dans un mouvement commun, la moindre feuille, le moindre brin de mousse, et transformait toute la forêt, en la remplissant jusqu'aux bords, en un monde sonore et vibrant."

Chapter Sixteen

1. Bachelard, *The Poetics of Reverie*.

2. Martin Heidegger, *Discourse on Thinking: A Translation of "Gelassenheit,"* trans. John M. Anderson and E. Hans Freund (New York: Harper & Row, 1966).

3. Bachelard, *The Poetics of Space*.

4. Jean Cohen, *Structure du langage poétique* (Paris: Flammarion, 1966), 114.

5. See, for example, Michel Le Guern, *Sémantique de la métaphore et de la métonymie* (Paris: Larousse, 1973), 21.

6. See, for example, George Berkeley, *An Essay Towards a New Theory of Vision* (Dublin: Aaron Rhames, 1709), § 120, 138.

7. Paul Henle, "Metaphor," in *Language, Thought, and Culture*, ed. Paul Henle (Ann Arbor: University of Michigan Press, 1958), 173–95.

8. The "psychical 'day's residues'" are "currently active psychical material" composed of "psychical residues and memory-traces . . . left over from the previous day" that help "furnish what is used for the construction of the dream." Sigmund Freud, *The Interpretation of Dreams*, trans. and ed. James Strachey (New York: Basic Books, 1955), 228.

Chapter Seventeen

1. Kant, *Critique of Judgment*, §§ 46–50.

2. Roman Jakobson, "Closing Statements: Linguistics and Poetics," in *Style in Language*, ed. Thomas Sebeok (Cambridge: MIT Press, 1964), 353–56.

300 NOTES TO PAGES 248–278

3. Paul Valéry, "Poetry and Abstract Thought," in *The Art of Poetry*, trans. Denise Folliot (Princeton: Princeton University Press, 1958), 69–72.

4. François Dagognet, *Écriture et iconographie* (Paris: Librairie Philosophique J. Vrin, 1973). Subsequent parenthetical citations to Dagognet refer to this text.

5. As a subsequent paragraph in the lecture will clarify, Ricoeur is thinking here about the more reproductive side of photography, particularly in its early purpose to provide a copy of "fleeting realities and preserving memories" (254). In that later paragraph he more broadly discusses photography's "creative" compositional elements.

6. Erwin Panofsky, *Early Netherlandish Painting: Its Origins and Character* (Cambridge, MA: Harvard University Press, 1966), 1: 151–53, 180.

7. Heidegger, *Being and Time*, §§ 29, 31.

8. E. H. Gombrich, "The Renaissance Theory of Art and the Rise of Landscape," in *Norm and Form: Studies in the Art of the Renaissance* (London: Phaidon Press, 1966), 107–21.

9. Paul Ricoeur, "Hermeneutics and the Critique of Ideology," in *From Text to Action*, 287–88; Ricoeur, *Lectures on Ideology and Utopia*, ed. George H. Taylor (New York: Columbia University Press, 1986), 219.

Chapter Eighteen

1. Max Black, *Models and Metaphors* (Ithaca, NY: Cornell University Press, 1962). Subsequent parenthetical citations to Black refer to this text.

2. See, for example, Sartre, *The Psychology of Imagination*, 193–94/173–74.

3. Donald A. Schon, *Displacement of Concepts* (London: Tavistock Publications, 1963). Subsequent parenthetical citations to Schon refer to this text.

4. Merleau-Ponty, *Signs*, 89–92.

5. Jacques Derrida, "White Mythology: Metaphor in the Text of Philosophy," *New Literary History* 6, no. 1 (1974): 5–74.

6. Eugen Fink, "Operative Concepts in Husserl's Phenomenology," in *Apriori and World: European Contributions to Husserlian Phenomenology*, trans. and ed. William McKenna, Robert M. Harlan, and Laurence E. Winters (The Hague: Martinus Nijhoff, 1981), 56–70. After developing the differentiation between the operative and the thematic, which Ricoeur will elaborate, Fink goes on to argue that this opposition is one that Husserl's method of phenomenological reduction attends (62–63). It remains the case that Husserl's method, as indeed any philosopher's, employs operative concepts that are not thematized (63–68).

7. Kant, *Critique of Judgment*, § 49.

Chapter Nineteen

1. Consistent with general discussions in the literature that he is referencing, Ricoeur here and henceforth will typically as a form of shorthand use the term *model* rather than *theoretical model*. It will be apparent from context when the latter meaning is intended. In his original lecture, Ricoeur notes that Barbour relies principally on Hesse and Black and also on epistemologists such as Peter Achinstein and E. H. Hutten, whom Ricoeur had only begun to read and did not use for these lectures.

2. Ian G. Barbour, *Myths, Models, and Paradigms* (New York: Harper & Row, 1974). Subsequent parenthetical citations to Barbour refer to this text.

3. Gombrich, "The Renaissance Theory of Art and the Rise of Landscape," 121.

NOTES TO PAGES 279–285 301

4. In his lecture notes, Ricoeur mentions that this discussion draws upon his text *La métaphore vive*, 308–21 (*The Rule of Metaphor*, 244–56).

5. See, for example, Friedrich Nietzsche, *Beyond Good and Evil*, trans. Walter Kaufmann (New York: Vintage Books, 1966), §§ 20, 54; Nietzsche, "'Reason' in Philosophy," in *Twilight of the Idols*, trans. Duncan Large (Oxford: Oxford University Press, 1998), § 5.

6. See, for example, Guy Debord, *La société du spectacle* (Paris: Buchet-Chastel, 1971), translated as *Society of the Spectacle* (Detroit: Black & Red, 1977), §§ 186, 189, 191.

7. Althusser, *For Marx*, 28–29.

8. During the next academic year, 1976–77, Ricoeur did present lectures on narrative. In the autumn of 1976, he offered a course at the University of Chicago on "Theory of Narrative Discourse: Story, History, and Historicity." In the first semester of 1977, he also lectured on narrative as part of a seminar in Paris. Three of these lectures were published together as "Pour une théorie du discours narrative" and a fourth as "Récit fictif—récit historique," all in the book *La narrativité*, which additionally included student papers from the seminar. See Paul Ricoeur, "Pour une théorie du discours narratif," in *La narrativité*, ed. Dorian Tiffeneau (Paris: Centre National de Recherche Scientifique, 1980), 1–68; Ricoeur, "Récit fictif—récit historique," in *La narrativité*, 251–71. For the 1977 origin of these lectures, see *La narrativité*, 1. For information on Ricoeur's 1976–77 courses at the University of Chicago, we thank David Pellauer, and we also thank Elayne Stecher, Special Collections Research Center, University of Chicago Library, for researching this question in the official publications of the University of Chicago for the time period.

9. See, for example, Paul Ricoeur, "Listening to the Parables of Jesus," *Criterion* 13, no. 3 (1974): 19, republished in *The Philosophy of Paul Ricoeur: An Anthology of His Work*, ed. Charles E. Reagan and David Stewart (Boston: Beacon Press, 1978), 240; Ricoeur, "Le 'Royaume' dans les paraboles de Jésus," *Études théologiques et religieuses* 51, no. 1 (1976): 16–17 (1974 presentation), translated as "The 'Kingdom' in the Parables of Jesus," *Anglican Theological Review* 63, no. 2 (1981): 166–67.

10. Heidegger, *Being and Time*, § 31.

11. See, for example, Frye, *Anatomy of Criticism*, 80–81.

12. See, for example, Martin Heidegger, "The Age of the World Picture," in *The Question Concerning Technology, and Other Essays*, trans. William Lovitt (New York: Harper & Row, 1977), 115–54.

13. See, for example, Edmund Husserl, *The Crisis of the European Sciences and Transcendental Phenomenology*, trans. David Carr (Evanston, IL: Northwestern University Press, 1970), § 33.

14. See, for example, Heidegger, *Being and Time*, § 2.

15. See, for example, Gadamer, *Truth and Method*, 262–64, 458–59.

16. This final phrase of the lectures seems an allusion to Bergson's work, *Laughter*, where Bergson writes: "When we feel love or hatred, when we are gay or sad, is it really the feeling itself that reaches our consciousness with those innumerable fleeting shades of meaning and deep resounding echoes that make it something altogether our own? *We should all, were it so, be novelists or poets or musicians.*" Henri Bergson, *Laughter: An Essay on the Meaning of the Comic*, trans. Cloudesley Brereton and Fred Rothwell (New York: Macmillan, 1912), 153 (emphasis added).

Bibliography

The bibliography is divided into four parts: the course syllabus; a chronology of Ricoeur's works on imagination; other Ricoeur works cited; and secondary works cited.

Course Syllabus

Below is the syllabus Paul Ricoeur provided to students in the course originally entitled "Imagination as a Philosophical Problem," delivered at the University of Chicago in the autumn of 1975. The ordering and elements of the original syllabus are unchanged, except for the expansion of bibliographic information, particularly to provide details on the specific editions Ricoeur used, to assist readers in locating his quotations of these texts. The asterisks shown were included in the original syllabus and indicate texts intended for greater course emphasis. The reference to Maurice Merleau-Ponty in section 2 is provided within brackets and indicates a subsequent oral addition to the syllabus during a lecture. (As noted in the Editor's Acknowledgments, Ricoeur's oral comments on the syllabus during the course have been deleted in general for being duplicative of the written syllabus, except where they add substantive points, and these points are included in endnotes.) In his oral comment adding Merleau-Ponty to the syllabus, Ricoeur noted that Merleau-Ponty's text "could be added also in the fifth part on aesthetics, since it's a kind of counterpart or a complement to Gombrich, *Art and Illusion.*"

Readers of the *Lectures* will observe that Ricoeur did not restrict himself to the specific sections of texts listed. He also did not examine several sections of the syllabus, such as on Comparative Religion and on Psychology, with the exception of brief anecdotal comments. He did not return to examine Merleau-Ponty in any detail, nor did he treat some other individual texts listed, such as Hegel's *Encyclopedia* or, except tangentially, Gadamer's *Truth and Method.* It is of interest that in the syllabus Ricoeur does not mention either François Dagognet's *Écriture et iconographie* (1973) or Donald Schon's *Displacements of Concepts* (1963), texts of importance in Ricoeur's own theory of productive imagination developed in the latter part of the course. Their citations are provided later in the bibliography of secondary works cited.

1. SURVEY OF CLASSICAL PHILOSOPHY

Aristotle. *On the Soul* (Book III, chapter 3). Translated by J. A. Smith. In *The Basic Works of Aristotle,* edited by Richard McKeon, 535–603. New York: Random House, 1966.

Pascal, Blaise. *Pascal's Pensées*. Bilingual edition with English translation by H. F. Stewart. New York: Pantheon Books, 1950.

Spinoza, Benedict. *Ethics* (Part II, Propositions 16–17 and Note), edited by James Gutmann. New York: Hafner Publishing, 1957.

Hume, David. *A Treatise of Human Nature* (Book I, Part I, Sections 3–4; Part III, Sections 5–7), edited by L. A. Selby-Bigge. Oxford: Clarendon Press, 1965.

Kant, Immanuel. *Critique of Pure Reason* (A98–110; A137–47; A189–211). Translated by Norman Kemp Smith. New York: St. Martin's Press, 1965.

Kant, Immanuel. *Critique of Judgment* (on the sublime). Translated by J. H. Bernard. New York: Hafner Press, 1951.

Hegel, G. W. F. *Encyclopedia of Philosophy* (Paragraphs 450–58), edited by Gustav Emil Mueller. New York: Philosophical Library, 1959.

2. PHENOMENOLOGY

Husserl, Edmund. *Logical Investigations* (Volume 1) (Investigations 1 and 2). Translated by J. N. Findlay. London: Routledge & Kegan Paul, 1970.

*Husserl, Edmund. *Ideas: General Introduction to Pure Phenomenology*. Translated by W. R. Boyce Gibson. New York: Collier Books, 1962.

Sartre, Jean-Paul. *The Psychology of Imagination*. Translated by Bernard Frechtman. New York: Philosophical Library, 1948. [Paperback edition, with different pagination: New York: Washington Square Press, 1966].

*Sartre, Jean-Paul. *Imagination: A Psychological Critique*. Translated by Forrest Williams. Ann Arbor: University of Michigan Press, 1962.

Gadamer, Hans-Georg. *Wahrheit und Methode*. Tübingen: Mohr, 1965. [Translated as *Truth and Method*. Translation edited by Garrett Garden and John Cumming. New York: Seabury Press, 1975. Second, revised edition; translation revised by Joel Weinsheimer and Donald G. Marshall. New York: Crossroad, 1989.]

[Merleau-Ponty, Maurice. "Eye and Mind." In *The Primacy of Perception*, edited by James M. Edie, 159–90. Evanston, IL: Northwestern University Press, 1964.]

3. ANALYTIC PHILOSOPHY

Ryle, Gilbert. *The Concept of Mind*. New York: Barnes & Noble, 1949.

*Wittgenstein, Ludwig. *Philosophical Investigations*, 3rd edition. Translated by G. E. M. Anscombe. New York: Macmillan, 1958.

*Price, H. H. *Thinking and Experience*. London: Hutchinson's University Library, 1953.

4. COMPARATIVE RELIGION

Corbin, Henry. *Creative Imagination in the Ṣūfism of Ibn ʿArabī*. Translated by Ralph Manheim. Princeton: Princeton University Press, 1969.

Eliade, Mircea. *Patterns in Comparative Religion*. Translated by Rosemary Sheed. New York: Sheed & Ward, 1958.

*Eliade, Mircea. *Images and Symbols*. New York: Sheed and Ward, 1961.

*Geertz, Clifford. *The Interpretation of Cultures* (Chapter 4). New York: Basic Books, 1973.

BIBLIOGRAPHY 305

5. AESTHETICS

*Bachelard, Gaston. *The Poetics of Space*. Translated by Maria Jolas. Boston: Beacon Press, 1969.

Bachelard, Gaston. *The Poetics of Reverie*. Translated by Daniel Russell. Boston: Beacon Press, 1971.

Furbank, P. N. *Reflections on the Word "Image."* London: Secker & Warburg, 1970.

*Gombrich, E. H. *Art and Illusion: A Study in the Psychology of Pictorial Representation*. Princeton: Princeton University Press, 1969.

Goodman, Nelson. *Languages of Art*. Indianapolis: Bobbs-Merrill, 1968.

6. MODELS AND ANALOGIES IN EPISTEMOLOGY

*Black, Max. *Models and Metaphors* (Chapters 3 and 13). Ithaca, NY: Cornell University Press, 1962.

*Hesse, Mary B. *Models and Analogies in Science*. Notre Dame, IN: University of Notre Dame Press, 1966.

Barbour, Ian G. *Myths, Models, and Paradigms*. New York: Harper & Row, 1974.

Leatherdale, W. H. *The Role of Analogy, Model, and Metaphor in Science*. New York: American Elsevier, 1974.

7. PSYCHOLOGY

Freud, Sigmund. *The Interpretation of Dreams*. Translated and edited by James Strachey. New York: Basic Books, 1955.

Horowitz, Mardi Jon. *Image Formation and Cognition*. New York: Appleton-Century-Crofts, 1970.

Klinger, Eric. *Structure and Functions of Fantasy*. New York: Wiley-Interscience, 1971.

*Paivio, Allan. *Imagery and Verbal Processes*. New York: Holt, Reinhart and Winston, 1971.

Richardson, Alan. *Mental Imagery*. New York: Springer, 1969.

*Segal, Sydney Joelson, ed. *Imagery: Current Cognitive Approaches*. New York: Academic Press, 1971.

Sheehan, Peter W. *The Function and Nature of Imagery*. New York: Academic Press, 1972.

Chronology of Ricoeur's Works on Imagination, 1973 Onward

This list contains the significant works by Ricoeur on imagination beginning in 1973, at a time when he was developing his own theory of productive imagination. (For analyses of Ricoeur's earlier consideration of imagination, see the listings in the secondary bibliography below for Jean-Luc Amalric, Richard Kearney, and Mary Schaldenbrand.) The present list comprehends the discussion of imagination broadly to include consideration not only of imagination but of creativity, figuration, iconic augmentation, poetics, and so on.

The listings are in chronological order, with the text listed first in its original language of publication. Where available, translations into English or French are appended to each listing. We provide the names of translators where that information is available.

"Creativity in Language: Word, Polysemy, Metaphor." Translated by David Pellauer. *Philosophy Today* 17, no. 2 (1973): 97–111. Republished as "Word, Polysemy, Metaphor: Creativity in Language." In *A Ricoeur Reader: Reflection and Imagination*, edited by Mario J. Valdés, 65–85. Toronto: University of Toronto Press, 1991.

"Les directions de la recherche philosophique sur l'imagination." In *Recherches phénoménologiques sur l'imaginaire. I.* Paris: Centre de Recherches Phénoménologiques, 1974, 1–8. Ricoeur produced this presentation and the three following from the same volume for a seminar he offered in Paris in 1973–74.

"Imagination productive et imagination reproductive selon Kant." In *Recherches phénoménologiques sur l'imaginaire. I.* Paris: Centre de Recherches Phénoménologiques, 1974, 9–13.

"Husserl et le problème de l'image. I et II." In *Recherches phénoménologiques sur l'imaginaire. I.* Paris: Centre de Recherches Phénoménologiques, 1974, 24–26, 27–30.

"Métaphore et image." In *Recherches phénoménologiques sur l'imaginaire. I.* Paris: Centre de Recherches Phénoménologiques, 1974, 66–72.

"On Imagination: From Picture to Fiction." Translated and edited by R. Bradley De Ford. James Henry Morgan Lectures, Dickinson College, Carlisle, PA, 1974. Three lectures; unpublished in their original form. As later citations indicate, the second lecture was subsequently published in revised form as "Sartre and Ryle on the Imagination," and the third lecture was revised and published as "That Fiction 'Remakes' Reality" and, virtually identically, as "The Function of Fiction in Shaping Reality."

"Kant and the Problem of Imagination in the Three Critiques." Lecture course at the University of Chicago, autumn 1974. Unpublished.

"Listening to the Parables of Jesus." *Criterion* 13, no. 3 (1974): 18–22. Republished in *The Philosophy of Paul Ricoeur: An Anthology of His Work*, edited by Charles E. Reagan and David Stewart, 239–45. Boston: Beacon Press, 1978.

Translated as: "À l'écoute des paraboles: Une fois de plus étonnés." In *Paul Ricoeur: L'herméneutique biblique*, edited and translated by François-Xavier Amherdt, 256–65. Paris: Cerf, 2001.

"Manifestation et Proclamation." *Archivio di Filosofia* 44, nos. 2–3 (1974): 57–76. Republished in *La religion pour penser. Écrits et conférences* 5, edited by Daniel Frey, 191–226. Paris: Seuil, 2021.

Translated as: "Manifestation and Proclamation." Translated by David Pellauer. *Blaisdell Institute Journal* 11 (1978): 13–35. Republished in *Figuring the Sacred: Religion, Narrative, and Imagination*, edited by Mark I. Wallace, 48–67. Translated by David Pellauer. Minneapolis: Fortress Press, 1995.

"Philosophy and Religious Language." *Journal of Religion* 54 (1974): 71–85. Republished in *Figuring the Sacred: Religion, Narrative, and Imagination*, edited Mark I. Wallace, 35–47. Translated by David Pellauer. Minneapolis: Fortress Press, 1995.

Translated as: "La philosophie et la spécificité du langage religieux." *Revue d'histoire et de philosophie religieuses* 55, no. 1 (1975): 13–26. Republished in *La religion pour penser. Écrits et conférences* 5, edited by Daniel Frey, 227–50. Paris: Seuil, 2021.

"Biblical Hermeneutics." *Semeia* 4 (1975): 29–148.

Translated as: "Paul Ricoeur et l'herméneutique biblique." In *Paul Ricoeur: L'herméneutique biblique*, edited and translated by François-Xavier Amherdt, 147–254. Paris: Cerf, 2001.

"Herméneutique philosophique et herméneutique biblique." In *Exegesis. Problèmes de*

BIBLIOGRAPHY 307

méthode et exercises de lecture, edited by François Bovon and Grégoire Rouiller, 216–28. Neuchâtel-Paris: Delachaux et Niestlé, 1975.

Translated as: "Philosophical Hermeneutics and Biblical Hermeneutics." In *Exegesis: Problems of Method and Exercises in Reading (Genesis 22 and Luke 15),* edited by François Bovon and Grégoire Rouiller, 321–39. Translated by Donald G. Miller. Pittsburgh, PA: Pickwick Press, 1978. Republished in *From Text to Action,* 89–101. Translated by Kathleen Blamey. Evanston, IL: Northwestern University Press, 1991.

La métaphore vive. Paris: Seuil, 1975.

Translated as: *The Rule of Metaphor.* Translated by Robert Czerny, with Kathleen McLaughlin and John Costello. Toronto: University of Toronto Press, 1977. New edition (and pagination): London: Routledge, 2003.

"Philosophical Hermeneutics and Theological Hermeneutics." *Sciences Religieuses/Studies in Religion* 5, no. 1 (Summer 1975): 14–33.

Lectures on Ideology and Utopia, edited by George H. Taylor. New York: Columbia University Press, 1986. These lectures were delivered at the University of Chicago, autumn 1975.

Translated as: *L'idéologie et l'utopie.* Translated by Myriam Revault d'Allonnes and Joël Roman. Paris: Seuil, 1997.

Lectures on Imagination. These lectures comprise the present volume. They were delivered at the University of Chicago, autumn 1975.

"Puissance de la parole: Science et poésie." In *La philosophie et les savoirs,* edited by Jean-Paul Brodeur, 159–77. Bellarmin: Montreal, 1975.

Translated as: "The Power of Speech: Science and Poetry." Translated by Robert F. Scuka. *Philosophy Today* 29, no. 1 (1985): 59–70.

"L'herméneutique de la sécularisation: Foi, idéologie, utopie. " *Archivio de Filosofia* 46, nos. 2–3 (1976): 49–68. Republished in *La religion pour penser: Écrits et conférences* 5, edited by Daniel Frey, 155-87. Paris: Seuil, 2021.

Interpretation Theory. Fort Worth, TX: Texas Christian University Press (1976).

"L'imagination dans le discours et dans l'action." In *Savoir, faire, espérer: Les limites de la raison I,* 207–28. Bruxelles: Facultés Universitaires Saint-Louis, 1976. Republished in *Du texte à l'action. Essais d'herméneutique, II,* 213–36. Paris: Seuil, 1986.

Translated as: "Imagination in Discourse and in Action." Translated by Kathleen Blamey. In *From Text to Action. Essays in Hermeneutics, II,* 168–87. Evanston, IL: Northwestern University Press, 1991.

"Ideology and Utopia as Cultural Imagination." *Philosophic Exchange* 2, no. 2 (1976): 17–28. Republished in *Being Human in a Technological Age,* edited by Donald M. Borchert and David Stewart, 107–26. Athens, OH: Ohio University Press, 1979. This article, in part, parallels the first lecture in *Lectures on Ideology and Utopia* and parts of "Imagination in Discourse and in Action."

"Herméneutique de l'idée de Révélation. " In *La révélation,* 15–54. Brussels: Faculté universitaires Saint-Louis, 1977.

Translated as: Toward a Hermeneutic of the Idea of Revelation." Translated by David Pellauer. *Harvard Theological Review* 70, nos. 1–2 (1977): 1–37. Republished in *Essays on Biblical Interpretation,* edited by Lewis S. Mudge, 73–118. Philadelphia: Fortress Press, 1980.

"Nommer Dieu." *Études théologiques et religieuses* 52, no. 4 (1977): 489–508. Republished as "Entre philosophie et théologie II: Nommer Dieu," in *Lectures 3. Aux frontières de la philosophie,* 281–305. Paris: Seuil, 1994.

Translated as: "Naming God." Translated by David Pellauer. *Union Seminary Quarterly*

Review 34 (1979): 215–27. Republished in *Figuring the Sacred: Religion, Narrative, and Imagination*, edited by Mark I. Wallace, 217–35. Translated by David Pellauer. Minneapolis: Fortress Press, 1995.

"L'idéologie et l'utopie." In *Cahiers du Centre Protestant de l'Ouest* 49–50 (December 1983): 3–16. Republished in *Du texte à l'action. Essais d'herméneutique, II*, 379–92. Paris: Seuil, 1986. This article is largely similar to "Ideology and Utopia as Cultural Imagination," above.

Translated as: "Ideology and Utopia." Translated by John B. Thompson. In *From Text to Action: Essays in Hermeneutics, II*, 308–24. Evanston, IL: Northwestern University Press, 1991.

"Image and Language in Psychoanalysis." Translated by David Pellauer. In *Psychiatry and the Humanities* (vol. 3), edited by Joseph H. Smith, 293–324. New Haven: Yale University Press, 1978 [1976 lecture].

"Préface." In Raphaël Celis, *L'Oeuvre et l'imaginaire*, 7–13. Bruxelles: Facultés Universitaires Saint-Louis, 1977. Republished in Paul Ricoeur, *Lectures 2. La contrée des philosophes*, 457–63. Paris: Seuil, 1992.

"Writing as a Problem for Literary Criticism and Philosophical Hermeneutics." *Philosophic Exchange* 2, no. 3 (1977): 3–15. Republished as "Speaking and Writing," *Interpretation Theory*, 25–44. Fort Worth, TX: Texas Christian University Press (1976). Republished in *A Ricoeur Reader: Reflection and Imagination*, edited by Mario J. Valdés, 320–37. Toronto: University of Toronto Press, 1991.

"The Metaphorical Process as Cognition, Imagination and Feeling." *Critical Inquiry* 5, no. 1 (1978): 143–59. Republished in *On Metaphor*, edited by Sheldon Sacks, 141–57. Chicago: University of Chicago Press, 1979.

"That Fiction 'Remakes' Reality." *Journal of the Blaisdell Institute* 12, no. 1 (1978): 44–62. As previously noted, this essay revises the third lecture of an unpublished 1974 set of lectures entitled "On Imagination: From Picture to Fiction." This essay and the one that follows are nearly identical.

"The Function of Fiction in Shaping Reality." *Man and World* 12, no. 2 (1979): 123–41. Republished in *A Ricoeur Reader: Reflection and Imagination*, edited by Mario J. Valdés, 117–36. Toronto: University of Toronto Press, 1991.

"Préface." In Giuseppe Grampa, *Ideologia e poetica*, ix–xiv. Milan: Vita e pensiero, 1979.

"*Ways of Worldmaking* by Nelson Goodman" [Book Review]. *Philosophy and Literature* 4 (1980): 107–20. Republished in *A Ricoeur Reader: Reflection and Imagination*, edited by Mario J. Valdés, 200–215. Toronto: University of Toronto Press, 1991.

"Sartre and Ryle on the Imagination." In *The Philosophy of Jean-Paul Sartre*, edited by Paul A. Schillp, 167–78. La Salle, IL: Open Court, 1981. As noted earlier, this essay revises the second lecture of an unpublished 1974 set of lectures entitled "On Imagination: From Picture to Fiction."

"The Bible and the Imagination." In *The Bible as a Document of the University*, edited by Hans Dieter Betz, 49–75. Chico, CA: Scholars Press, 1981. Republished in *Figuring the Sacred: Religion, Narrative, and Imagination*, edited by Mark I. Wallace, 144–66. Translated by David Pellauer. Minneapolis: Fortress Press, 1995.

Translated as: "La Bible et l'imagination." *Revue d'histoire et de philosophie religieuses* 62, no. 4 (1982): 339–60.

"Mimesis et représentation." *Actes du XVIIIe Congrès des Sociétés de Philosophie de langue française* [1980], 51–63. Strasbourg: Université des Sciences Humaines de Strasbourg, Faculté de Philosophie, 1982.

BIBLIOGRAPHY 309

Translated as: "Mimesis and Representation." Translated by David Pellauer. In *Annals of Scholarship* 2, no. 3 (1981): 15–32. Republished in *A Ricoeur Reader: Reflection and Imagination*, edited by Mario J. Valdés, 137–55. Toronto: University of Toronto Press, 1991.

"The Creativity of Language" [Interview with Richard Kearney, 1981]. In *Dialogues with Contemporary Continental Thinkers*, edited by Richard Kearney, 17–36. Manchester: Manchester University Press, 1984. Republished in Richard Kearney, *On Paul Ricoeur*, 127–43. Aldershot, England: Ashgate, 2004.

"Poétique et symbolique." In *Initiation à la pratique de la théologie*, edited by Bernard Lauret and François Refoulé, 37–61. Paris: Cerf, 1982.

"Poetry and Possibility: An Interview with Paul Ricoeur Conducted by Philip Fried." *Manhattan Review* 2, no. 2 (1982): 6–21.

"Imagination et métaphore." *Psychologie Médicale* 14 (1982): 1883–87.

Temps et récit. Tome I. Paris: Seuil, 1983.

Translated as: *Time and Narrative* (vol. 1). Translated by Kathleen McLaughlin and David Pellauer. Chicago: University of Chicago Press, 1984.

"Can Fictional Narratives Be True?" *Analecta Husserliana* 14 (1983): 3–19.

Temps et récit. Tome II. Paris: Seuil, 1984.

Translated as: *Time and Narrative* (vol. 2). Translated by Kathleen McLaughlin and David Pellauer. Chicago: University of Chicago Press, 1985.

Temps et récit. Tome III. Paris: Seuil, 1985.

Translated as: *Time and Narrative* (vol. 3). Translated by Kathleen Blamey and David Pellauer. Chicago: University of Chicago Press, 1988.

Dialogue sur l'histoire et l'imaginaire social [with Cornelius Castoriadis, 1985], edited by Johann Michel. Paris: Éditions de l'École des hautes études en sciences sociales, 2016.

Translated as: "Dialogue on History and the Social Imaginary" [with Cornelius Castoriadis, 1985]. Translated by Scott Davidson. In *Ricoeur and Castoriadis in Discussion: On Human Creation, Historical Novelty, and the Social Imaginary*, edited by Suzi Adams, 3–20. London: Rowman & Littlefield International, 2017.

"Figuration et configuration. À propos du *Maupassant* de A.-J. Greimas." In *Exigences et perspectives de la sémiotique*, edited by Herman Parret and Hans-Georg Ruprecht, 801–9. Amsterdam: John Benjamins Publishing Company, 1985. Republished in *Lectures 2. La contrée des philosophes*, 420–30. Paris: Seuil, 1992.

"Rhétorique, poétique, herméneutique." In *De la métaphysique à la rhétorique*, edited by Michel Meyer, 143–55. Bruxelles: Éditions de l'Université de Bruxelles, 1986. Republished in *Lectures 2. La contrée des philosophes*, 479–94. Paris: Seuil, 1992.

Translated as: "Rhetoric-Poetics-Hermeneutics." Translated by Robert Harvey. In *From Metaphysics to Rhetoric*, 137–49. Dordrecht: Kluwer Academic Publishers, 1989.

"La 'figure' dans 'L'étoile de la rédemption.'" *Esprit* 12 (December 1988): 133–46. Republished in Paul Ricoeur, *Lectures 3. Aux frontières de la philosophie*, 63–81. Paris: Seuil, 1994.

Translated as: "The 'Figure' in Rosenzweig's *The Star of Redemption*." In *Figuring the Sacred: Religion, Narrative, and Imagination*, edited by Mark I. Wallace, 93–107. Translated by David Pellauer. Minneapolis: Fortress Press, 1995.

"Mimésis, référence et refiguration dans *Temps et récit*." *Études phénoménologiques* 6, no. 11 (1990): 29–40.

"Une reprise de *La poétique* d'Aristote." In *Nos Grecs et leurs modernes*, edited by Barbara

Cassin, 303–20. Paris: Seuil, 1992. Republished in *Lectures 2. La contrée des philosophes*, 464-78. Paris: Seuil, 1992.

"L'expérience esthétique." In *La critique et la conviction. Entretien avec François Azouvi et Marc de Launay*, 257–78. Paris: Calmann-Lévy, 1995.

Translated as: "Aesthetic Experience." In *Critique and Conviction: Conversations with François Azouvi and Marc de Launay*, 171–86. Translated by Kathleen Blamey. New York: Columbia University Press, 1998.

"Jugement esthétique et jugement politique selon Hannah Arendt." In *Droit et Cultures* 28 (1994): 79–91. Republished in Paul Ricoeur, *Le Juste*, 143–61. Paris: Éditions Esprit, 1995.

Translated as: "Aesthetic Judgment and Political Judgment According to Hannah Arendt." In Paul Ricoeur, *The Just*, 94–108. Translated by David Pellauer. Chicago: University of Chicago Press, 2000.

"Pour une herméneutique juridique: interprétation et/ou argumentation." In *Qu'est-ce que la justice?*, edited by Jacques Poulain, 115–30. Paris: PUF, 1996. Republished as "Interprétation et/ou argumentation." In *Le Juste*, 163–84.

Translated as: "Interpretation and/or Argumentation." In *The Just*, 109–26. Translated by David Pellauer. Chicago: University of Chicago Press, 2000.

"Imagination, Testimony, and Trust" [A Dialogue with Richard Kearney]. In *Questioning Ethics*, edited by Richard Kearney and Mark Dooley, 12–17. London: Routledge, 1999. Republished in *Debates in Continental Philosophy*, edited by Richard Kearney, 46–52. NY: Fordham University Press, 2004. Republished also in Richard Kearney, *On Paul Ricoeur*, 151–56. Aldershot, England: Ashgate, 2004.

La mémoire, l'histoire, l'oubli. Paris: Seuil, 2000.

Translated as: *Memory, History, Forgetting*. Translated by Kathleen Blamey and David Pellauer. Chicago: University of Chicago Press, 2004.

Parcours de la reconnaissance. Trois études. Paris: Stock, 2004.

Translated as: *The Course of Recognition*. Translated by David Pellauer. Cambridge, MA: Harvard University Press, 2005.

Other Ricoeur Works Cited

"Freedom in the Light of Hope." Translated by Robert Sweeney. In *The Conflict of Interpretations*, edited by Don Ihde, 402–24. Evanston, IL: Northwestern University Press, 1974.

"The Hermeneutical Function of Distanciation." In *From Text to Action: Essays in Hermeneutics, II*, 75–88. Translated by Kathleen Blamey and John B. Thompson. Evanston, IL: Northwestern University Press, 1991.

"Hermeneutics and the Critique of Ideology." In *From Text to Action: Essays in Hermeneutics, II*, 270–307. Translated by Kathleen Blamey and John B. Thompson. Evanston, IL: Northwestern University Press, 1991.

A Key to Edmund Husserl's "Ideas I." Translated by Bond Harris and Jacqueline Bouchard Spurlock; edited and translation revised by Pol Vandevelde. Milwaukee: Marquette University Press, 1996.

"The Language of Faith." In *The Philosophy of Paul Ricoeur: An Anthology of His Work*, edited by Charles E. Reagan and David Stewart, 223–38. Boston: Beacon Press, 1978.

"Listening to the Parables of Jesus." *Criterion* 13, no. 3 (1974): 18–22. Republished in *The*

Philosophy of Paul Ricoeur: An Anthology of His Work, edited by Charles E. Reagan and David Stewart, 239–45. Boston: Beacon Press, 1978.

"Narrated Time." In *A Ricoeur Reader: Reflection and Imagination*, edited by Mario J. Valdés, 338–54. Toronto: University of Toronto Press, 1991.

Oneself as Another. Translated by Kathleen Blamey. Chicago: University of Chicago Press, 1992.

"Phenomenology and Hermeneutics." In *From Text to Action: Essays in Hermeneutics, II*, 25–52. Translated by Kathleen Blamey and John B. Thompson. Evanston, IL: Northwestern University Press, 1991.

"Philosophy and Religious Language." *Journal of Religion* 54 (1974): 71–85.

"Pour une théorie du discours narratif." In *La narrativité*, edited by Dorian Tiffeneau, 1–68. Paris: Centre National de Recherche Scientifique, 1980.

"Récit fictif—récit historique." In *La narrativité*, edited by Dorian Tiffeneau, 251–71. Paris: Centre National de Recherche Scientifique, 1980.

"Le 'Royaume' dans les paraboles de Jésus." *Études théologiques et religieuses* 51, no. 1 (1976): 15–19 (1974 presentation).

Translated as: "The 'Kingdom' in the Parables of Jesus." Translated by Robert F. Scuka. *Anglican Theological Review* 63, no. 2 (1981): 165–69.

The Symbolism of Evil. Translated by Emerson Buchanan. Boston: Beacon Press, 1967.

What Makes Us Think? (with Jean-Pierre Changeux). Translated by M. B. DeBevoise. Princeton, NJ: Princeton University Press, 2000.

Secondary Works Cited

Achinstein, Peter. "Models, Analogies and Theories." *Philosophy of Science* 31, no. 4 (1964): 328–50.

Achinstein, Peter. "Theoretical Models." *British Journal for the Philosophy of Science* 16, no. 62 (1965): 102–20.

Amalric, Jean-Luc. "D'une convergence remarquable entre phénoménologie et philosophie analytique: la lecture ricoeurienne des thèses de Sartre et Ryle sur l'imagination." *Études Ricoeuriennes/Ricoeur Studies* 5, no. 1 (2014): 82–94.

Amalric, Jean-Luc. "L'espace de la fantaisie. Prolégomènes à une approche de l'expérience analytique à partir du concept ricoeurien d'identité narrative." *B@ belonline* 8 (2021): 21–44.

Amalric, Jean-Luc. "Evénement, idéologie et utopie." *Études Ricoeuriennes/Ricoeur Studies* 5, no. 2 (2014): 9–22.

Amalric, Jean-Luc. "L'imagination poético-pratique dans l'identité narrative." *Études Ricoeuriennes/Ricoeur Studies* 3, no. 2 (2012): 110–27.

Amalric, Jean-Luc. *Paul Ricoeur, l'imagination vive. Une genèse de la philosophie ricoeurienne de l'imagination*. Paris: Hermann, 2013.

Amalric, Jean-Luc. "Ricœur, Castoriadis: The Productive Imagination between Mediation and Origin." In *Ricoeur and Castoriadis in Discussion: On Human Creation, Historical Novelty, and the Social Imaginary*, edited by Suzi Adams, 77–110. London: Rowman and Littlefield International, 2017.

Amalric, Jean-Luc. *Ricoeur, Derrida. L'Enjeu de la métaphore*. Paris: PUF, 2006.

Amalric, Jean-Luc. "Le statut de l'utopie dans la philosophie de l'imagination de Ricœur." In *Penser l'utopie aujourd'hui avec Paul Ricœur*, edited by Sébastien Roman, 37–55. Paris: Presses Universitaires de Vincennes, 2021.

BIBLIOGRAPHY

Althusser, Louis. *For Marx*. Translated by Ben Brewster. New York: Pantheon Books, 1969.

Aristotle. *De Poetica (Poetics)*. Translated by Ingram Bywater. In *Introduction to Aristotle*, 2d ed., edited by Richard McKeon, 668–713. Chicago: University of Chicago Press, 1973.

Ascarate, Luz. *Imaginer selon Paul Ricoeur: La phénoménologie à la rencontre de l'ontologie sociale*. Paris: Hermann, 2022.

Austin, J. L. "A Plea for Excuses." In *Philosophical Papers*, 2d ed., edited by J. O. Urmson and G. J. Warnock, 123–52. Oxford: Clarendon Press, 1970.

Austin, J. L. *Sense and Sensibilia*, edited by G. J. Warnock. Oxford: Clarendon Press, 1962.

Bachelard, Gaston. *La poétique de l'espace*. Paris: Presses Universitaires de France, 1958.

Bachelard, Gaston. *La poétique de la rêverie*. Paris: Presses Universitaires de France, 1960.

Barfield, Owen. *Poetic Diction: A Study in Meaning*. 2d ed. New York: McGraw-Hill, 1964.

Beardsley, Monroe C. *Aesthetics: Problems in the Philosophy of Criticism*. New York: Harcourt, Brace and World, 1958.

Beardsley, Monroe C. "The Metaphorical Twist." *Philosophy and Phenomenological Research* 22 (1962): 293–307.

Bergson, Henri. *Laughter: An Essay on the Meaning of the Comic*. Translated by Cloudesley Brereton and Fred Rothwell. New York: Macmillan, 1912.

Bergson, Henri. "The Possible and the Real." In *The Creative Mind*, 107–25. Translated by Mabelle L. Andison. New York: Greenwood Press, 1968.

Berkeley, George. *An Essay Towards a New Theory of Vision*. Dublin: Aaron Rhames, 1709.

Berkeley, George. *A Treatise Concerning the Principles of Human Knowledge*, edited by Colin M. Turbayne. New York: Liberal Arts Press, 1957.

Bourgeois, Patrick L. *Imagination and Postmodernity*. Lanham, MD: Lexington Books, 2013.

Brown, Roger. *Words and Things*. New York: Free Press, 1959.

Castro, Maria Gabriela Azevedo e. *Imaginação em Paul Ricoeur*. Lisbon: Instituto Piaget, 2002.

Cohen, Jean. *Structure du langage poétique*. Paris: Flammarion, 1966.

Condillac, Étienne Bonnot de. *Condillac's Treatise on the Sensations*. Translated by Geraldine Carr. London: Favil Press, 1930.

Condillac, Étienne Bonnot de. *Essay on the Origin of Human Knowledge*. Translated and edited by Hans Aarsleff. Cambridge: Cambridge University Press, 2001.

Cotkin, George. "William James and the Cash-Value Metaphor." *Et cetera: A Review of General Semantics* 42 (1985): 37–46.

Dagognet, François. *Écriture et iconographie*. Paris: Librairie Philosophique J. Vrin, 1973.

Debord, Guy. *La société du spectacle*. Paris: Buchet-Chastel, 1971.

Translated as: *Society of the Spectacle*. Detroit: Black & Red, 1977.

Derrida, Jacques. "Structure, Sign, and Play in the Discourse of the Human Sciences." In *Writing and Difference*, 278–93. Translated by Alan Bass. Chicago: University of Chicago Press, 1978.

Derrida, Jacques. "White Mythology: Metaphor in the Text of Philosophy." *New Literary History* 6, no. 1 (1974): 5–74.

Descartes, René. *Meditations on First Philosophy*, edited by Stanley Tweyman. Translated by Elizabeth S. Haldane and G. R. T. Ross. London: Routledge, 1993.

Dierckxsens, Geoffrey. "The Ambiguity of Justice Revisited: The Narrative and Imaginative Aspects of Social Power and Embodiment in Ricoeur's Philosophy." In *The*

Ambiguity of Justice: New Perspectives on Paul Ricoeur's Approach to Justice, edited by Geoffrey Dierckxsens, 72–96. Leiden: Brill, 2020.

Ehrenzweig, Anton. *The Hidden Order of Art: A Study in the Psychology of Artistic Perception*. Berkeley: University of California Press, 1967.

Erickson, Stephen A. *Language and Being: An Analytic Phenomenology*. New Haven: Yale University Press, 1970.

Evans, Jeanne. *Paul Ricoeur's Hermeneutics of the Imagination*. New York: Peter Lang, 1995.

Fink, Eugen. "Operative Concepts in Husserl's Phenomenology." In *Apriori and World: European Contributions to Husserlian Phenomenology*, 56–70. Translated and edited by William McKenna, Robert M. Harlan, and Laurence E. Winters. The Hague: Martinus Nijhoff, 1981.

Fodor, James. *Christian Hermeneutics: Paul Ricoeur and the Refiguring of Theology*. Oxford: Clarendon Press, 1995.

Foessel, Michaël. "Action, Norms and Critique: Paul Ricoeur and the Powers of the Imaginary." *Philosophy Today* 58, no. 4 (2014): 513–25.

Foessel, Michaël. "Introduction: Paul Ricoeur ou les puissances de l'imaginaire." In *Ricoeur: Anthologie*, edited by Michaël Foessel and Fabien Lamouche, 7–22. Paris: Éditions Points, 2007.

Fourier, Charles. *Design for Utopia*. Translated by Julia Franklin. New York: Schocken, 1971.

Frege, Gottlob. "Sense and Reference." *Philosophical Review* 57, no. 3 (1948): 209–30.

Freud, Sigmund. *Beyond the Pleasure Principle*. Translated by James Strachey. New York: Bantam Books, 1959.

Freud, Sigmund. *The Interpretation of Dreams*. Translated and edited by James Strachey. New York: Basic Books, 1955.

Freud, Sigmund. "Mourning and Melancholia." In *The Standard Edition of the Complete Psychological Works of Sigmund Freud* (vol. 14), edited by James Strachey, 243–58. London: Hogarth Press, 1975.

Freud, Sigmund. "The Unconscious." In *The Standard Edition of the Complete Psychological Works of Sigmund Freud* (vol. 14), edited by James Strachey, 159–216. London: Hogarth Press, 1975.

Frye, Northrop. *Anatomy of Criticism: Four Essays*. New York: Athenaeum, 1966.

Geach, Peter. *Mental Acts, Their Content and Their Objects*. London: Routledge & Paul, 1957.

Geniusas, Saulius. "Against the Sartrean Background: Ricoeur's Lectures on Imagination." *Research in Phenomenology* 46, no. 1 (2016): 98–116.

Geniusas, Saulius. "Between Phenomenology and Hermeneutics: Paul Ricoeur's Philosophy of Imagination." *Human Studies* 38, no. 2 (2015): 223–41.

Geniusas, Saulius. "The Stuff That Dreams Are Made of: Max Scheler and Paul Ricoeur on Productive Imagination." *Hermeneutics and Phenomenology: Figures and Themes*, edited by Saulius Geniusas and Paul Fairchild, 93–105. London: Bloomsbury, 2018.

Gombrich, E. H. "The Renaissance Theory of Art and the Rise of Landscape." In *Norm and Form: Studies in the Art of the Renaissance*, 107–21. London: Phaidon Press, 1966.

Grondin, Jean. "L'art comme presentation chez Gadamer: Portée et limites d'un concept." *Études Germaniques* 62 (2007): 337–49.

Hannay, Alastair. *Mental Images: A Defence*. London: George Allen & Unwin, 1971.

Hegel, G. W. F. *Phenomenology of Spirit*. Translated by A. V. Miller. Oxford: Oxford University Press, 1977.

Heidegger, Martin. "The Age of the World Picture." In *The Question Concerning Technology, and Other Essays*, 115–54. Translated by William Lovitt. New York: Harper & Row, 1977.

Heidegger, Martin. *Being and Time*. Translated by John Macquarrie and Edward Robinson. New York: Harper & Row, 1962.

Heidegger, Martin. *Discourse on Thinking: A Translation of "Gelassenheit."* Translated by John M. Anderson and E. Hans Freund. New York: Harper & Row, 1966.

Heidegger, Martin. "The End of Philosophy and the Task of Thinking." In *On Time and Being*, 55–73. Translated by Joan Stambaugh. New York: Harper & Row, 1972.

Heidegger, Martin. *Kant and the Problem of Metaphysics*. Translated by James S. Churchill. Bloomington: Indiana University Press, 1962.

Heidegger, Martin. "What Is Metaphysics?" In *Existence and Being*, 325–49. Translated by R. F. C. Hull and Alan Crick. Chicago: Regnery, 1949.

Henle, Paul. "Metaphor." In *Language, Thought, and Culture*, edited by Paul Henle, 173–95. Ann Arbor: University of Michigan Press, 1958.

Heraclitus. *Heraclitus: Fragments*. Translated by T. M. Robinson. Toronto: University of Toronto Press, 1987.

Hester, Marcus. *The Meaning of Poetic Metaphor*. The Hague: Mouton, 1967.

Holt, Robert R. "Imagery: The Return of the Ostracized." *American Psychologist* 19, no. 4 (1964): 254–64.

Hutten, E. H. "The Role of Models in Physics." *British Journal for the Philosophy of Science* 4, no. 16 (1954): 284–301.

Husserl, Edmund. *Cartesian Meditations: An Introduction to Phenomenology*. Translated by Dorion Cairns. The Hague: Nijhoff, 1960.

Husserl, Edmund. *The Crisis of the European Sciences and Transcendental Phenomenology*. Translated by David Carr. Evanston, IL: Northwestern University Press, 1970.

Husserl, Edmund. *Ideas for a Pure Phenomenology and Phenomenological Philosophy—First Book. General Introduction to Pure Phenomenology*. Translated by Daniel O. Dahlstrom. Indianapolis, IN: Hackett, 2014.

Husserl, Edmund. *Ideas Pertaining to a Pure Phenomenology and to a Phenomenological Philosophy—First Book: General Introduction to a Pure Phenomenology*. Translated by Fred Kersten. The Hague: Martinus Nijhoff, 1982.

Husserl, Edmund. *Ideas Pertaining to a Pure Phenomenology and to a Phenomenological Philosophy—Second Book: Studies in the Phenomenology of Constitution*. Translated by Richard Rojcewicz and André Schuwer. Dordrecht: Kluwer, 1989.

Husserl, Edmund. *Ideas Pertaining to a Pure Phenomenology and to a Phenomenological Philosophy—Third Book: Phenomenology and the Foundations of the Sciences*. Translated by Ted E. Klein and William E. Pohl. Dordrecht: Kluwer, 1980.

Husserl, Edmund. *Ideen zu einer Reinen Phänomenologie und Phänomenologischen Philosophie—Erstes Buch: Allgemeine Einführung in die Reine Phänomenologie*. The Hague: Martinus Nijhoff, 1950.

Husserl, Edmund. *Idées directrices pour une phénoménologie*. Translated by Paul Ricoeur. Paris: Gallimard, 1950.

Husserl, Edmund. *Logical Investigations* (vol. 2). Translated by J. N. Findlay. London: Routledge & Kegan Paul, 1970.

Husserl, Edmund. *Logische Untersuchungen* (vol. 2). Tübingen: Max Niemeyer, 1968.

BIBLIOGRAPHY 315

Ingarden, Roman. *Controversy over the Existence of the World* (2 vols.). Translated by Arthur Szylewicz. Frankfurt: Peter Lang, 2013, 2016.

Jakobson, Roman. "Closing Statements: Linguistics and Poetics." In *Style in Language,* edited by Thomas Sebeok, 350–77. Cambridge: MIT Press, 1964.

Jankélévitch, Vladimir. *Henri Bergson.* Paris: Alcan, 1931.

Translated as: *Henri Bergson,* edited by Alexandre Lefebvre and Nils F. Schott. Translated by Nils F. Schott. Durham, NC: Duke University Press, 2015.

James, William. *The Meaning of Truth, a Sequel to "Pragmatism."* New York: Longmans, Green, and Co, 1909.

James, William. "Philosophical Conceptions and Practical Results." *University Chronicle* 1, no. 4 (1898): 287–310.

James, William. *Pragmatism: A New Name for Some Old Ways of Thinking.* New York: Longmans, Green, and Co., 1907.

James, William. "The Stream of Thought." In *Principles of Psychology,* 1: 224–90. 2 vols. New York: Henry Holt & Co., 1890.

Jaspers, Karl. *Philosophy* (vol. 2). Translated by E. B. Ashton. Chicago: University of Chicago Press, 1970.

Kant, Immanuel. *Kritik der reinen Vernunft.* Hamburg: Felix Meiner, 1956.

Kant, Immanuel. *Kritik der Urteilskraft und Schriften zur Naturphilosophie.* Darmstadt: Wissenschaftliche Buchgesellschaft, 1968.

Kearney, Richard. "Between Imagination and Language." In *On Paul Ricoeur: The Owl of Minerva,* 35–58. Aldershot, UK: Ashgate, 2004.

Kearney, Richard. "Exploring Imagination with Paul Ricoeur." In *Stretching the Limits of Productive Imagination: Studies in Kantianism, Phenomenology and Hermeneutics,* edited by Saulius Geniusas, 187–204. London: Rowman & Littlefield International, 2018.

Kearney, Richard. "The Hermeneutical Imagination (Ricoeur)." In *Poetics of Imagining: Modern to Post-Modern,* 142–77. New York: Fordham University Press, 1998.

Kearney, Richard. "Paul Ricoeur and the Hermeneutic Imagination." In *The Narrative Path: The Later Works of Paul Ricoeur,* edited by T. Peter Kemp and David Rasmussen, 1–31. Cambridge, MA: MIT Press, 1989.

Lafuente, Maria Avelina Cecelia. "Imagination and Practical Creativity in Paul Ricoeur." In *Life: The Outburst of Life in the Human Sphere, Book II,* edited by Anna-Teresa Tymieniecka, 243–61. Dordrecht: Kluwer, 1999.

Langer, Susanne K. *Philosophy in a New Key: A Study in the Symbolism of Reason, Rite, and Art.* New York: Mentor Books, 1948.

Larison, Mariana. "L'imaginaire et ses lieux communs." *Philosophie* 132, no. 1 (2017): 68–77.

Lawlor, Leonard. *Imagination and Chance: The Difference Between the Thought of Ricoeur and Derrida.* Albany: SUNY Press, 1992.

Le Guern, Michel. *Sémantique de la métaphore et de la métonymie.* Paris: Larousse, 1973.

Locke, John. *An Essay Concerning Human Understanding.* London: Thomas Basset, 1690.

McKeon, Richard. "Imitation and Poetry." In *Thought, Action, and Passion,* 102–221. Chicago: University of Chicago Press, 1954.

Meinong, Alexius. *On Assumptions.* Edited and translated by James Heanue. Berkeley: University of California Press, 1983.

Merleau-Ponty, Maurice. "Cézanne's Doubt." In *Sense and Non-Sense,* 1–25. Evanston, IL: Northwestern University Press, 1964.

Merleau-Ponty, Maurice. *Phénoménologie de la perception*. Paris: Gallimard, 1945.

Merleau-Ponty, Maurice. *Phenomenology of Perception*. Translated by Colin Smith. London: Routledge & Kegan Paul, 1962.

Merleau-Ponty, Maurice. *Phenomenology of Perception*. Translated by Donald A. Landes. London: Routledge, 2012.

Merleau-Ponty, Maurice. *Signs*. Translated by Richard C. McCleary. Evanston, IL: Northwestern University Press, 1964.

Merleau-Ponty, Maurice. *The Visible and the Invisible*, edited by Claude Lefort. Translated by Alphonso Lingis. Evanston, IL: Northwestern University Press, 1968.

Minkowski, Eugène. *Vers une cosmologie* [1936]. Paris: Payot, 1999.

Moore, G. E. "A Defence of Common Sense." In *Contemporary British Philosophy* (2d series), edited by J. H. Muirhead, 193–233. New York: Macmillan, 1925.

Nietzsche, Friedrich. *Beyond Good and Evil*. Translated by Walter Kaufmann. New York: Vintage Books, 1966.

Nietzsche, Friedrich. *The Birth of Tragedy, and The Case of Wagner*. Translated by Walter Kaufmann. New York: Vintage Books, 1967.

Nietzsche, Friedrich. *Twilight of the Idols*. Translated by Duncan Large. Oxford: Oxford University Press, 1998.

Panofsky, Erwin. *Early Netherlandish Painting: Its Origins and Character*, 2 vols. Cambridge, MA: Harvard University Press, 1966.

Peirce, Charles Sanders. *Collected Papers of Charles Sanders Peirce* (vol. 2), edited by Charles Hartshorne and Paul Weiss. Cambridge, MA: Belknap Press, 1960.

Pellauer, David. "Response to Professors Sweeney and Ingbretsen." *Proceedings of the American Catholic Philosophical Association* 62 (1988): 88–94.

Plato. *The Collected Dialogues of Plato*, edited by Edith Hamilton and Huntington Cairns. Princeton, NJ: Princeton University Press, 1961.

Plato. *Gorgias*. Translated by W. D. Woodhead, 229–307. In *The Collected Dialogues of Plato*, edited by Edith Hamilton and Huntington Cairns. Princeton, NJ: Princeton University Press, 1961.

Plato. *Meno*. Translated by W. K. C. Guthrie, 353–84. In *The Collected Dialogues of Plato*, edited by Edith Hamilton and Huntington Cairns. Princeton, NJ: Princeton University Press, 1961.

Plato. *Phaedrus*. Translated by R. Hackforth, 475–525. In *The Collected Dialogues of Plato*, edited by Edith Hamilton and Huntington Cairns. Princeton, NJ: Princeton University Press, 1961.

Popper, Karl. *The Logic of Scientific Discovery*. New York: Basic Books, 1959.

Proust, Marcel. *Remembrance of Things Past*. Translated by C. K. Scott Moncrieff. New York: Random House, 1934.

Revault d'Allonnes, Myriam. "Avant-propos à l'édition française." In Paul Ricoeur, *L'idéologie et l'utopie*, 13–16. Translated by Myriam Revault d'Allonnes and Joël Roman. Paris: Seuil, 1997.

Richards, I. A. *The Philosophy of Rhetoric*. Oxford: Oxford University Press, 1936.

Ryle, Gilbert. "Phenomenology versus 'The Concept of Mind.'" In *Collected Papers* (vol. 1), 179–96. London: Hutchinson, 1971.

Sartre, Jean-Paul. *Being and Nothingness*. Translated by Hazel E. Barnes. New York: Washington Square Press, 1966.

Sartre, Jean-Paul. *L'imaginaire: Psychologie phénoménologique de l'imagination*. Paris: Gallimard, 1940.

BIBLIOGRAPHY 317

Sartre, Jean-Paul. *Sketch for a Theory of the Emotions*. Translated by Philip Mairet. London: Methuen & Co., 1962.

Schaldenbrand, Mary. "Metaphoric Imagination: Kinship Through Conflict." In *Studies in the Philosophy of Paul Ricoeur*, edited by Charles E. Reagan, 57–81. Athens: Ohio University Press, 1979.

Schon, Donald A. *Displacement of Concepts*. London: Tavistock Publications, 1963.

Searle, John R. *Speech Acts*. London: Cambridge University Press, 1969.

Sefler, George F. *Language and the World: A Methodological Synthesis within the Writings of Martin Heidegger and Ludwig Wittgenstein*. Atlantic Highlands, NJ: Humanities Press, 1974.

Spinoza, Benedict. *Theologico-Political Treatise*. In *The Collected Works of Spinoza* (vol. 2), 65–356. Translated and edited by Edwin Curley. Princeton: Princeton University Press, 2016.

Spinoza, Benedict. *Treatise on the Emendation of the Intellect*. In *The Collected Works of Spinoza* (vol. 1), 7–45. Translated and edited by Edwin Curley. Princeton: Princeton University Press, 1985.

Strawson, P. F. *Individuals*. Garden City, NY: Doubleday, 1959.

Taylor, George H. "The Deeper Significance of Ricoeur's Philosophy of Productive Imagination: The Role of Figuration." In *Productive Imagination: Its History, Meaning and Significance*, edited by Saulius Genius and Dmitri Nikulin, 157–81. London: Rowman & Littlefield International, 2018.

Taylor, George H. "Delineating Ricoeur's Concept of Utopia," *Social Imaginaries* 3, no. 1 (2017): 41–60.

Taylor, George H. "Editor's Introduction." In Paul Ricoeur, *Lectures on Ideology and Utopia*, edited by George H. Taylor, ix–xxxv. New York: Columbia University Press, 1986.

Taylor, George H. "Imagination and Belief." *International Journal of Social Imaginaries* 1, no. 1 (2022): 66–83.

Taylor, George H. "On the Cusp: Ricoeur and Castoriadis at the Boundary." In *Ricoeur and Castoriadis in Discussion: On Human Creation, Historical Novelty, and the Social Imaginary*, edited by Suzi Adams, 23–48. London: Rowman & Littlefield International, 2017.

Taylor, George H. "The Phenomenological Contributions of Ricoeur's Philosophy of Imagination." *Social Imaginaries* 1, no. 2 (2015): 13–31.

Taylor, George H. "Prospective Political Identity." In *Paul Ricoeur in the Age of Hermeneutical Reason: Poetics, Praxis, and Critique*, edited by Roger W. H. Savage, 123–38. Lanham, MD: Lexington Books, 2015.

Taylor, George H. "Ricoeur's Philosophy of Imagination." *Journal of French Philosophy* 16 (2006): 93–104.

Thomasset, Alain. *Paul Ricoeur: Une poétique de la morale: Aux fondements d'une éthique herméneutique et narrative dans une perspective chrétienne*. Leuven: University Press-Peeters, 1996.

Thomasset, Alain. "L'imagination dans la pensée de Paul Ricoeur: Fonction poétique du langage et transformation du suject." *Études théologiques et religieuses* 80, no. 4 (2005): 525–41.

Toulmin, Stephen. *The Philosophy of Science: An Introduction*. New York: Harper & Row, 1960.

Turbayne, Colin Murray. *The Myth of Metaphor*. New Haven: Yale University Press, 1962.

Vaihinger, Hans. *The Philosophy of 'As If.'* 2d ed. Translated by C. K. Ogden. New York: Barnes and Noble, 1935.

Valéry, Paul. "Poetry and Abstract Thought." In *The Art of Poetry*, 52–81. Translated by Denise Folliot. Princeton: Princeton University Press, 1958.

Vlacos, Sophie. *Ricoeur, Literature and Imagination*. New York: Bloomsbury, 2014.

Wittgenstein, Ludwig. *Philosophische Untersuchungen/Philosophical Investigations*. 3rd ed. German text with revised English translation; translated by G. E. M. Anscombe. Malden, MA: Blackwell, 2001.

Wittgenstein, Ludwig. *Tractatus Logico-Philosophicus*. Translated by D. F. Pears and B. F. McGuiness. London: Routledge & Kegan Paul, 196

Index

This index should satisfy most purposes, but readers are also invited to use the Digital Ricoeur website (www.digitalricoeur.org), where free, customizable searches of Ricoeur's corpus, including this volume, are available.

absence, 5, 7, 8, 11, 12, 28, 37, 39, 44, 49, 53, 66, 92, 115, 118, 125, 131, 169, 170, 172, 175, 176, 177, 180, 182, 183, 185, 194, 195, 196, 197, 198, 204, 210, 211, 212
   difference from inexistence, 212
   nothingness of, 218
   as paradigm for nothingness, 207
   phenomenology of, 214, 218
   as reference to presence, 259
   zero degree of, 8
abstraction, 56, 94, 144, 146, 147, 150, 264
   problem of, 1, 2, 5
Achinstein, Peter, 300n1 (chap. 19)
action, 202, 204, 214, 220, 221, 246, 255, 279
   social, 245, 275
   as *technē*, 221
actuality, 28
   philosophy of, 12
adequation
   truth as, 13, 30, 31, 285
aesthetics, 13, 23, 30, 53, 63, 64, 78, 82, 83, 84, 86, 88, 120, 165, 166, 169, 204, 246, 273
affection, 39, 40, 41, 42, 43, 45, 46, 47
   as being affected by external bodies, 39
affectivity, 196, 198

Althusser, Louis, 281
   For Marx, 295n6 (chap. 9), 301n7
analogue, 160, 188, 189, 190, 191, 192, 193, 194, 195, 196, 197, 198, 199, 213–14, 261, 262, 267, 298n4 (chap. 13)
   as imagined, 192
analogy, 76, 193, 226, 238, 268, 269
   as displaying, 227
   as new proportion, 269
   as proportion not creative, 269
   in theological discourse, 227
analytic philosophy, 4, 91, 96, 123, 126, 137, 141, 143, 154, 160, 162, 170, 173, 182, 187, 188, 217, 224
   fear of problem of creative imagination, 97
   juxtaposition with phenomenology, 91–98, 112, 137, 140, 142, 153, 167, 170, 172, 207
anima, 18
animals, 21, 24
animate, 18, 21, 188, 190, 194
Anscombe, Elizabeth, 85
anti-work, 280, 281
   as anti-power, 280
   as death of art, 280–81
anti-world, 203, 220, 230, 232, 256
Apollonian, 85

apologetics
  Christian, 34, 37, 38
apperception, 64, 67, 68, 69, 224
application, 71, 73, 75, 78, 222, 223, 266, 267, 268, 269, 271
  Anwendung, 146, 264
  as putting new instance under old concept, 265
  as work, 266
archetype, 84, 228, 229
Aristotle, 3, 7, 12, 13, 17–31, 33, 34, 35, 39, 40, 47, 56, 60, 61, 65, 96, 99, 160, 189, 246, 250, 279, 280, 292n3
  On the Soul (*De Anima*), 3, 12, 17–30, 142, 292n1 (chap. 2)
  Physics, 29
  Poetics, 6, 114, 220, 234, 238, 279, 281
art, 22, 52, 62, 64, 76, 78, 79, 120, 123, 169, 213, 245, 246, 249, 254, 255, 257, 272
  abstract, 246
  critique of notion of work, 280
  death of, 280–81
  death of as artistic death, 281
  relation to science, 254
  and truth, 260
Art Institute of Chicago, 253
as if, 6, 37, 38, 39, 40, 41, 42, 43, 44, 47, 51, 61, 86, 104, 105, 110, 111, 116, 161, 219, 278–79
  relation between *as if* doing and not doing, 120
association, 1, 57, 58, 61, 64, 66, 67, 74, 81, 235, 237, 264
assumption, 59, 104, 105, 109, 120, 156
as though, 6, 9, 12, 29, 30, 37, 41, 51, 61, 179, 202, 222, 278–79
  contrast with the inexistent, 212
attention, 147, 158–59
augmentation, 256
  of reality, 233
  See also iconic augmentation
Augustine, 35, 37, 53
Austin, J. L., 20
  "Plea for Excuses, A," 99, 294n4 (chap. 7)
  Sense and Sensibilia, 20, 50, 160
authority, 36

awaken
  philosophy as to, 45
axis of imagination
  horizontal, 7–9, 11, 25
  vertical, 7, 9–10, 11, 25

Bachelard, Gaston, 199, 221, 226, 227–33, 235, 240, 242
  Poetics of Reverie, The, 222, 227, 229, 231–33, 283, 299n4 (chap. 15), 299n1 (chap. 16)
  Poetics of Space, The, 227–30, 231, 233, 299n6 (chap. 15), 299n3 (chap. 16)
  poétique de la rêverie, La, 299n5 (chap. 15)
  poétique de l'espace, La, 299n5 (chap. 15)
Bacon, Francis, 254
Barbour, Ian G., 277–78, 279, 300nn1–2 (chap. 19)
  Myths, Models, and Paradigms, 257, 277–78, 279, 300n2 (chap. 19)
Barfield, Owen, 226
Barnes, Hazel, 298n2 (chap. 13)
Baudelaire, Charles, 254
Beardsley, Monroe, 236
  Aesthetics, 235
beautiful, the, 78, 79, 80–81, 82, 83, 85, 246
Beethoven, Ludwig, 214
  Seventh Symphony, 213
Befindlichkeit
  find oneself somewhere, 255–56
behavior, 2, 101, 102, 105, 107, 125
behaviorism, 2, 102, 124, 125, 126, 127, 135, 219, 293n1 (chap. 4)
being, 37, 154, 155, 165, 166, 181, 182, 210, 220, 230, 232, 233, 272, 285
  increase in, 227, 294n2 (chap. 7)
being-in-the-world, 207, 208, 209, 210
belief, 6, 7, 9, 10, 11, 12, 25, 29, 60, 105, 160, 163, 164, 182, 184, 185, 186, 192, 198, 203, 204, 205, 206
  accompanying perception, 161, 164
  in the *as though*, 202
  as bound or necessary, 292n3
  contrast to imagination, 292n3
  deceptive, 7
  imagination as condition of, 292n3

juxtaposition with representation, 26
modality of, 162
neutralization of, 164
not required in imagination, 26
ontological, 161
as positional act, 181
suspension of, 182, 183
uncritical, 6
belonging
pre-objective as truth as manifestation, 285
belonging to
Zugehörigkeit, 285
Bergson, Henri, 38, 173, 210
"Possible and the Real, The," 298n4 (chap. 14)
Laughter: An Essay on the Meaning of the Comic, 301n16
Berkeley, George, 148, 240
Essay Towards a New Theory of Vision, An, 299n6 (chap. 16)
Treatise Concerning the Principles of Human Knowledge, A, 296n8 (chap. 10)
Bild, 3, 4, 63, 69, 129, 212, 294n2 (chap. 7)
biology, 78, 79
bios, 138
birth, 227, 229, 230, 273
relation to world, 284
Black, Max, 261–63, 267, 268, 276, 277, 300n1 (chap. 19)
Models and Metaphors, 191, 235, 237, 261–63, 300n1 (chap. 18)
body, 39–46, 159, 160, 173, 191, 192, 197, 198
boundary limits, 165
bracketing, 102, 104, 184, 185, 279
defined, 156
epochē, 101
brain, 28, 31, 41, 44, 118, 188
Braithwaite, Richard, 278
Brown, Roger, 268
Words and Things, 268
Buddha, 45
bureaucracy
critique of, 280

Byzantine, 294n2 (chap. 7)
icon, 3
tradition, 253

capitalism, 149, 223
care, 232
suspension of, 283
cashing meaning, 93, 95, 115, 117, 118, 119, 142, 143, 146, 149, 223, 234
categories, 19, 65, 68, 69, 71, 75, 78, 136, 239, 268, 272
transcategorial, 238
category mistake, 239, 266
causality, 10, 27, 28, 31, 41, 43, 46, 56, 57, 58, 59, 60, 65, 76, 77, 80, 113, 127, 171, 228
cause
efficient, 27
formal, 27
centaur, 43, 54, 161, 162, 163, 164, 166, 182
Cézanne, Paul, 93, 212, 253
chimera, 161, 182, 183
Christ, 34, 148
Christianity, 34, 35, 37, 46
clarification, 149, 150, 151, 224
cognition, 19, 81, 99
cognitive, 64, 81, 82, 83, 99, 141, 245, 261
and imagination, 260
Cohen, Jean
Structure du langage poétique, 236, 299n4 (chap. 16)
Columbus, Christopher, 266
common sense (*sensus communis*), 80
communication
interest in, 257
composition
muthos and, 279
rules of, 279
concealment, 53
concept, 2, 12, 13, 17, 33, 63, 65, 71, 72, 79, 81, 85, 91, 94, 95, 96, 99, 112, 114, 115, 118, 120, 123, 127, 128, 133, 134, 135, 143, 146, 150, 196, 223, 225, 239, 240, 264
as allowing displacement, 264
conflict between old concept and new situation parallel to metaphor, 264

concept (*continued*)
creation of, 268
displacement as shift of old concept
to new situation, 269
displacement of, 222, 223, 225, 268
displacement of, as movement, 225
dynamization of, 95
emergence of, 269
emergence of new, 263
extensional function of, 146
extension of, 267, 276
extension of, as corresponding to
new aspect of reality, 278
function to structure situation, 264
as intellectual intuition, 264
interrelation with instance, 222–23,
238, 265, 266, 267, 268, 269, 271
mobility in, 264
as name to rule when abstracted from
its material, 239
new instance requiring change in
concept, 268
operative, 273, 300n6 (chap. 18)
put new instance under old concept,
265
relation to application, 264
relation to image, 234
relation to instance, 222, 225, 228
as a rule, 72
as sedimented, 265
structure of, 224
thematic, 273, 300n6 (chap. 18)
as tool for solving problems, 264
universality of, 147
condensation, 253, 270
in iconic augmentation, 252, 255
Condillac, Étienne Bonnot de, 25, 148
Condillac's Treatise on the Sensations,
292n2
Essay on the Origin of Human Knowledge,
292n2, 296n8 (chap. 10)
connotation, 253, 256
contrast with denotation, 248–49, 281
criticism of distinction with denotation, 257
consciousness, 9, 140, 171, 175, 176, 178,
182, 186, 187, 191, 193, 198, 203, 205,

206, 208, 209, 210, 211, 227, 228,
229
Bewusstsein, 177
capability to posit nothingness, 208
as capable of imagining, 207
consciousness (of), 186
as consciousness of, 140, 181, 186, 210
constitutive alternance between real
and unreal, 207
constitutive to have images, 208
freedom of, 209
imaginative, 193
nonthetic, 186, 204, 210, 297n2
(chap. 13)
nonthetic, definition, 186
reflective, 198
as a relation, 177
self-consciousness, 186, 298n2
(chap. 13)
spontaneity of, 186
stream of, 173
transversal, 186
Constable, John, 253, 272
construction, 6, 246, 278, 279
balance with description, 278
as invention, 285
contiguity, 235, 237
control, 256, 284
interest in, 257, 284
interest in suspended in poetry,
284
conventionalism, 277, 278, 279
Copernicus, Nicolaus, 26
copy, 8, 51, 52, 55, 56, 60, 61, 62, 63, 67,
92, 93, 99, 100, 103, 104, 155, 172,
233, 237, 246, 249, 250, 251, 254, 261,
300n5 (chap. 17)
resemblance to impression, 57
correction, 271, 273
cosmogony, 228, 231, 232, 233
Cotkin, George
"William James and the Cash-Value
Metaphor," 298–99n1 (chap. 15)
counterculture, 220
counterfactuals, 161, 173, 201, 202, 207
creative, 2, 17, 33, 38, 62, 63, 69, 74, 78,
84, 97, 220, 223, 224, 225, 226, 227,

230, 231, 233, 236, 246, 250, 251, 254,
255, 260, 262, 268, 269, 275, 279
creativity of language, 229, 261
as displacement, 262
as extension of reality, 260–61
as opaque, 275
as productive imagination, 54
relation with form, 84–85
criteriology, 20, 30
cube, 125, 129, 157, 179
Cubism, 254
culture, 3, 146
sociology of, 13
custom, 43, 58, 59, 224
cybernetics, 149

Dagognet, François, 212, 249–50, 252–
54, 260
Écriture et iconographie, 233, 249,
253, 254, 294n2 (chap. 7), 298n5
(chap. 14), 300n4 (chap. 17)
dance, 203, 204
poetry as a, 248
Dante Alighieri, 33
Darstellung, 85, 133
defined, 4
depiction, 133
presentation, 4, 85, 133, 160
See also presentation
da Vinci, Leonardo, 254
Debord, Guy
société du spectacle, La, 301n6
Society of the Spectacle, 301n6
deception, 7, 13, 19, 21, 29, 30, 34–37, 38,
39, 131, 203–4, 205, 206, 222
delusion, 33, 219, 242, 246
denotation, 253, 256, 257, 282
contrast with connotation, 248–49,
281
criticism of distinction with connotation, 257
as description and redescription, 281
in narrative structure, 281
tension with fiction, 282
depiction, 164, 165, 166, 195, 240, 241,
242, 243, 255, 256, 263, 278, 283
Darstellung, 133

dialectic with semantic innovation,
243
meaning as not only schematized but
depicted, 242
de-realized, 213
Derrida, Jacques, 270, 273
"Structure, Sign, and Play in the
Discourse of the Human Sciences,"
294n3 (chap. 6)
"White Mythology: Metaphor in
the Text of Philosophy," 295n6
(chap. 9), 300n5 (chap. 18)
Descartes, René, 9, 21, 25, 41, 45, 52, 56,
112, 156, 205
"First Meditation," 205
Meditations on First Philosophy, 298n2
(chap. 14)
description, 92, 96, 98, 125, 127, 128, 134,
137, 138, 139, 145, 171, 172, 181, 281,
283
contrast to evocation, 284
contrast to nondescriptive, 283
as discovery, 285
of essences, 154, 185
phenomenological, 92, 118, 143, 194,
223
reflective, 193
as reports, 129, 133, 134
desire, 185, 197, 201, 202, 203, 206, 207,
212, 222, 232
determinism, 171, 187, 192, 209, 210
detour, 237, 249, 251
Dewey, John, 223, 264, 266
diacritics, 119
defined, 135
dialectic, 85, 87, 226, 243, 278, 279
of reason, 82
between resemblance and sameness,
114
between semantic innovation and
depiction, 243
of similarity and negation, 219
dianoia
discourse of reason, 21
as work of thought, 279
Dionysian, 85
disclosure, 31, 245, 250, 261, 276, 283

discourse, 21, 91, 94, 97, 102, 138, 142,
178, 221, 224, 225, 234, 247
oblique, 101, 103, 104, 105, 107, 109
semantics of, 234
discovery, 131, 133, 134, 223, 225, 241, 260,
268, 271, 276, 281
as description, 285
interrelation with invention, 285
interrelation with invention caught
in opposition between subject and
object, 285
logic of, 76, 94, 226, 233, 261, 269
discursive, the
contrast to nondiscursive, 283
versus opposition with intuition,
273
pregnant in the intuitive, 273
displacement, 222, 223, 225, 264, 265,
266, 267, 268, 269, 270, 271
analogical, 269
analyzable phases, 273
in application, 264
as change in language and in world,
268
comparison with analogy and metaphor, 268
of concept, 268
of concepts happening within
thought, 276
of concepts in scientific thought and
similarity to semantic innovation
in metaphor, 276
conceptual, 264
as creative, 262
as extension of reality, 276
interrelation with metaphor, 263
as metaphorical transfer, 269
as mutual adaptation between old
concept and new situation, 271
process by which extension is
changed, 267, 268
as shift of old concept to new situation, 269, 271
as spelling out of relation, 272, 273
as theory of correction, 266
display, 51, 73, 146, 151, 214, 227, 231, 233,
239, 240, 241, 248, 253, 255, 256,
257, 282

displaying before
vorstellen, 151
distance, 23, 52, 139
critical, 7, 10, 11, 12, 25, 139, 208
logical, 238, 239, 240, 269
distanciation, 139
doxa, 25, 30, 35
opinion, 19, 25
drama, 6, 91, 279, 281, 282
dream, 3, 6, 9, 24, 25, 26, 29, 34, 44, 45,
51, 52, 63, 77, 81, 97, 114, 174, 201,
204, 205, 206–7, 211, 222, 277, 281
day residues, 242, 299n8 (chap. 16)
image, 44, 45
as paradigm of ordinary life, 45
world, 231
Duhem, Pierre, 278
Dürer, Albrecht
"Knight, Death, and the Devil, The"
(engraving), 164, 182
dwell
in the world, 283, 284

Ehrenzweig, Anton
*The Hidden Order of Art: A Study in
the Psychology of Artistic Perception*,
294n2 (chap. 6)
eidetic reduction. *See* reduction, eidetic
eidōlon, 3
simulacrum, 172
eikon, 3, 17, 294n2 (chap. 7)
as shadow, 18
as simile or comparison, 17
Einbildung, 3, 77, 131
Einbildungskraft, 3, 83
in Kant, imagination's active process
of mediation, 3, 63, 69
Einstein, Albert, 271
emergence, 228, 229, 230, 231, 235, 237,
239, 263
of new concepts, 265, 269
emotions, 18, 23, 50, 99, 138, 139, 141, 196,
197, 198, 202, 235, 248, 249, 256, 257,
260, 275, 281, 282, 283, 284
Empedocles, 20
empiricism, 1, 5, 56, 64, 93, 94, 96,
99, 113, 114, 142, 143, 146, 148, 151,
159

entity language, 116, 178, 179, 198

Epicurus, 172

epistemology, 1, 2, 5, 12, 23, 25, 33, 35, 37, 38, 56, 63, 93, 94, 95, 113, 115, 143, 149, 150, 154, 169, 233, 234, 248, 257, 279

    models in, 249

    See also imagination, epistemological

epoché, 101, 105, 139, 142, 153, 154, 232, 248

    defined, 139

    as detachment from care, 232

    suspension, 282

    as suspension in fiction, 242

    as suspension of judgment, 139, 153

    See also reduction, phenomenological (*epoché*)

Erickson, Stephen A.

    Language and Being: An Analytic Phenomenology, 295n4 (chap. 9)

essence, 10, 99, 138, 154, 170, 171, 174, 180–81, 185, 188, 193, 194, 198, 204, 220, 225, 257, 281

    analysis of in Wittgenstein, 155

essential difference

    between perception and images, 204

ethics, 9, 10, 12, 18, 33, 34, 83, 86, 87, 88, 138, 139

Europe, 136

evil, 165

evocation

    contrast to description, 284

existence, 35, 40, 100, 102, 153, 156, 157, 162, 175, 177, 180, 181

expectation, 264, 266, 270

experience, 1, 30, 50, 51, 53, 60, 63, 66, 68, 69, 75, 76, 93, 96, 98, 118, 125, 127, 128, 133, 134, 135, 136, 138, 139–40, 142, 144, 150, 153, 154, 155, 162, 163, 259

    interrelation with language, 91, 97, 125, 126, 128, 138

    lived, 137, 138, 139, 142

    psychedelic, 293n1 (chap. 4)

    structure of, 142, 143

    structure of as meaningful, 140

explanation, 118, 127

    reductive, 226

extension, 120, 271

    of concept, 267, 276

    of concepts as corresponding to new aspect of reality, 278

    by displacement, 268

    in formal logic, 267

    of reality, 261, 276

    result of emergence, 267

    of world, 261

falsification, 114, 269

falsity, 6, 21, 22, 24, 25, 26, 29, 30, 33, 34, 46, 119, 203

fancy, 4, 55, 58, 59, 77, 101, 103, 105, 107, 108, 110, 111–12, 131, 145, 163, 164, 217, 219, 280, 282

fancying, 92, 108, 109, 110, 111, 112, 116, 169

fantasy, 4, 25, 63, 92, 293n1 (chap. 4)

fascination, 7, 171, 184, 187, 192, 195, 199, 201, 202, 206, 207, 208, 211, 212, 222, 242

    captured or bound by image, 187

fatality, 171, 176, 187, 192, 204, 206, 207

feeling, 144, 196, 202, 203, 213, 241, 256, 271, 282, 283

    as ontological, 283

Fichte, Johann Gottlieb, 84

fiction, 5, 6, 8, 12, 26, 28, 33, 34, 38, 39, 45, 47, 52, 54, 62, 63, 123, 154, 161, 162, 164, 170, 177, 180, 183, 186, 190, 194–96, 201, 202, 206, 207, 211, 212, 221, 222, 242, 251, 257, 260, 265

    builds its own referent, 218

    capacity for transfiguration, 245

    as capacity of productive reference, 219

    contrast to presence, 197

    contrast to pretending, 282

    as contrast with reality, 6

    creating its own referent, 261

    creative, 58, 199

    disclosing new dimensions of reality, 245

    as disclosing reality, 276

    distinction from picture, 259

    false, 277

    fictional examples in Husserl, 154, 161

fiction (*continued*)

fictional examples in Sartre, 154

fictional examples in Wittgenstein, 155

as framework of reference, 221

freed from original referent opens new dimension of reality, 285

heuristic, 277, 278, 279

heuristic and redescription of reality, 220

heuristic function of capacity of discovery, 260

imagination as, 217

inexistence of object, 259

as inexistent, 218

literary, 6, 31

as model for, 276–77, 285

in models, 260

in models as useful rather than truth claims, 278

the more fictional, the more ontological implications, 285

narrative, 281

negative element as key to referential power, 245

nonfigurative, 255

nothingness as trait of referent, 218

not under rule of an original, 275

ontology of, 231, 246, 247

as opening a new reality, 214

opening of reality by, 53, 276

as without original reference, 220

phenomenology of, 13

poetic, 211

polarity with picture, 285

as producing a new reality, 214

as productive imagination, 259

provides its own referent, 259

as reality remade, 212

as redescription of reality, 212, 257, 278

as reduction to picture, 277

reference, 261

referent as nothing, 213

referential claim, 285

relation to redescription, 279

as shaping the world, 197

shock of, 256

as taking hold of essence of reality, 281

tension with denotative, 282

in theoretical models, 262, 263

theory of requires critique of concept of object, 284

and truth, 220

as utopia, 275

as work, 280

as work of invention, 280

fictionalism, 277

figurative, 246, 251, 255, 272, 273, 280

nonfigurative, 213, 246, 255, 272, 280

synthesis, 70

use as no longer metaphor but not yet literal, 271

Fink, Eugen

"Operative Concepts in Husserl's Phenomenology," 273, 300n6 (chap. 18)

flesh, 10, 35

forgetfulness, 53

form, 3, 63, 69, 78, 79, 80, 81, 82, 83, 84–85, 88, 163, 164, 251, 262, 270, 280, 283

morphē, 189

morphē, defined, 160

formless, 83

Forms, 80

ideal, 19

Fourier, Charles, 280

framework, 117, 119, 123, 150, 169, 221, 224, 225, 235, 249, 279

freedom, 59, 77, 81, 82, 88, 155, 171, 176, 187, 209, 210, 246, 283

as nothingness, 175

Frege, Gottlob, 1, 21, 56, 94, 95, 113, 144, 147, 219, 234, 264

"Sense and Reference," 2, 94

Freud, Sigmund, 3, 6, 34, 35, 36, 86, 232, 242

"Mourning and Melancholia," 206, 298n3 (chap. 14)

"Unconscious, The," 4

Beyond the Pleasure Principle, 43

Interpretation of Dreams, The, 299n8 (chap. 16)

friend Peter (Sartre), 161, 165, 170, 177,

178, 179, 181, 182, 183, 184, 187,
189, 195, 196, 213, 217, 218, 219,
259
Frye, Northrop, 282
Anatomy of Criticism, 248, 301n11
Furbank, P. N.
Reflections on the Word "Image," 3

Gadamer, Hans-Georg, 88, 212, 246, 285
Truth and Method, 79, 239, 282, 294n2
(chap. 7), 301n15
Gauguin, Paul, 253
Geach, Peter
Mental Acts, 111, 141
genius, 88, 98, 246, 271
givenness, mode of, 142, 143, 155, 170,
171, 174, 176, 177, 178, 179, 182, 218
contrast between perception and
image, 155–57, 218
contrast between perception and
imagination, 161, 166
of the image, 155–57
of perception, 155–57
God, 37, 39, 40, 46, 82
Goethe, Johann Wolfgang von, 84
Gombrich, E. H., 62, 84, 278
"Renaissance Theory of Art and the
Rise of Landscape, The," 300n8
(chap. 17), 300n3 (chap. 19)
Art and Illusion, 62, 114, 252, 254
Good, 17, 250
Goodman, Nelson, 253
Languages of Art, 211–12, 220, 239, 252,
257, 270, 281
grammar, 4, 125, 160, 217–18
critique of, 280
as the rule of use, 127
grasping, 151
Auffassung, 150
guess, 25, 26, 28, 31

Habermas, Jürgen, 257
hallucination, 6, 9, 12, 13, 34, 51, 116, 201,
204, 206, 211, 222
Hamlet, 118
Hannay, Alastair, 127
Mental Images: A Defence, 124
harmony, 79, 81, 82

Hegel, G. W. F., 19, 28, 37, 84
Phenomenology of Spirit, 50
Hegelianism, 144
Heidegger, Martin, 19, 30, 53, 77, 126,
140, 151, 154, 161, 208, 210, 232, 255,
282, 283, 285, 294n3 (chap. 6)
"Age of the World Picture, The,"
301n12
"End of Philosophy and the Task of
Thinking, The," 295n6 (chap. 9)
"What Is Metaphysics?," 208
Being and Time, 296n10 (chap. 10),
296n2 (chap. 11), 297n8 (chap. 11),
300n7 (chap. 17), 301n10, 301n14
*Discourse on Thinking: A Translation of
"Gelassenheit,"* 299n2 (chap. 16)
Kant and the Problem of Metaphysics, 70,
292nn5–6
Henle, Paul
"Metaphor," 241, 299n7 (chap. 16)
Heraclitus, 74
hermeneutics, 139, 252
Hesse, Mary, 257, 263, 277, 279, 300n1
(chap. 19)
Models and Analogies in Science, 220
Hester, Marcus, 242, 248
Meaning of Poetic Metaphor, The, 240–
41, 242
heuristic, 220, 257, 277, 278, 279, 283
capacity for discovery, 260, 276
history, 118, 220, 281
poetry as truer than, 220, 281
Holt, Robert, 2
"Imagery: The Return of the Ostracized," 293n1 (chap. 4)
Homer, 20
horizon, 73, 83, 84, 85, 284
Hume, David, 1, 7, 13, 34, 38, 39, 40, 41,
43, 44, 49–60, 61, 62, 65, 69, 73, 74,
76, 84, 93, 100, 109, 119, 125, 136, 155,
159, 172, 173, 181, 190, 205, 227, 229,
249, 265, 292n3
Treatise of Human Nature, A, 49–60,
100, 293n2 (chap. 4)
Husserl, Edmund, 1, 7, 40, 52, 54, 56, 59,
66, 96, 99, 101, 102, 105, 109, 113, 127,
137, 138, 139, 141, 142–51, 153–67, 171,
172, 173, 174, 175, 177, 178, 180, 186,

Husserl, Edmund (*continued*)
187, 188, 189, 223, 224, 226, 234, 264,
273, 284, 294, 300n6 (chap. 18)
"Nachwort," 296n5 (chap. 10)
Cartesian Meditations, 138, 298n3
(chap. 13)
Crisis of the European Sciences, The, 139,
301n13
*Ideas for a Pure Phenomenology and
Phenomenological Philosophy*, 296n4
(chap. 11)
*Ideas: General Introduction to Pure
Phenomenology*, 136, 138, 142, 143,
151, 153–67, 296n1 (chap. 11), 296n3
(chap. 11), 299n2 (chap. 15)
*Ideas Pertaining to a Pure Phenomenology
and to a Phenomenological Philosophy*,
296n4 (chap. 11)
*Ideen zu einer Reinen Phänomenologie
und Phänomenologischen Philosophie*,
296n4 (chap. 11)
Idées directrices pour une phénoménologie,
296n4 (chap. 11)
Logical Investigations, 10, 95, 136, 138,
142, 143, 144–51, 153, 222, 224,
225, 296nn6–7 (chap. 10), 298n4
(chap. 13)
Hutten, E. H., 300n1 (chap. 19)
hylē. See matter (*hylē*)
hypnagogic, 192, 193, 206

icon, 3, 241, 249
Byzantine, 3
contrast to picture, 241
iconize, 241
iconic augmentation, 212, 234, 260
as abbreviation and condensation, 252
abbreviation as condition for generative power, 252
as alphabetic grid, 252
as condensation, 250, 255
as externalization in material medium, 252
as increase of reality, 233, 250, 252
as negative entropy, 250, 253
as productive, creative imagination,
250–56
as structural screen, 252

iconicity, 17, 249, 253
iconography, 260
idea, 40, 50, 52, 55, 57, 58, 60, 69, 84, 86,
87, 148, 265
abstract, 1, 56, 57, 58, 59, 93, 113
aesthetic, 273
Idea, 82, 250
of the Good, 17, 250
idealism, 139, 140, 283
ideality, 2, 19, 94, 113, 147, 149
of meaning, 147
identity, 64, 93, 113, 141, 144, 146, 147,
173, 198, 224, 225, 237, 272
fictional, 272
meaning implies kernel of, 145
ideology, 13, 35, 36, 85, 149, 243, 245,
257, 280
critique of, 140
of naturalism, 254
as picture in social action, 275
poetry suspends ideological relation
to world, 284
idol, 3
illusion, 6, 9, 12, 29, 30, 33, 34, 35, 39, 45,
62, 63, 82, 100, 108, 131, 171, 172, 173,
178, 197, 205, 226, 263
of immanence, 171, 172, 177, 183, 185,
190, 198, 211, 212
illustration, 94, 143, 146, 149, 153, 163,
164, 224, 241
as clarification, 224
Verbildlichung, 146
image, 1, 2, 3, 4, 5, 6, 7, 9, 12, 17, 18, 24,
25, 28, 29, 38, 39, 41, 42, 43, 44, 45,
49, 50, 51, 52, 54, 56, 58, 61, 69, 71,
72, 74, 91, 92, 93, 94, 95, 96, 99, 100,
101, 107, 108, 112, 114, 115, 116, 117,
118, 119, 120, 126, 143, 144, 145, 146,
147, 149, 151, 154, 156, 160, 170, 171,
173, 176, 177, 178, 180, 183, 184, 186,
188, 191, 192, 194, 197, 198, 207, 209,
211, 212, 226, 227, 229, 230, 240, 241,
259, 264, 282, 283
as absent object, 142
as animated, 190
as appearance, 102, 111, 116, 176, 178,
179, 181, 184, 185, 188, 195, 198, 205
as appearance as nothingness, 188

as an *as if*, 42, 43, 44, 61, 161
associated, 240
as augmentation, 233
as *Bild*, 212
bound, 242, 248
as capacity for extension, 120
cashing meaning in absence, 118
commitment in, 9
comparison to picture, 128
constitutive aspect of consciousness, 208
as copy, 8, 93, 237
cosmic element, 231, 233
as deceptive, 203–4
as denial of reality, 212
as depiction of negation, 195
difference from perception in mode of givenness, 218
as dimension of language, 229
as display, 146, 214, 231, 233, 248
as echo of language instead of perception, 227
as echo of the sense, 242
as existing nowhere, 107, 116, 117
family, 160, 163
as function of absence, 8
generation in language, 234
hypnagogic, 206
as illustration, 94, 143, 145, 153
as image of, 4
implied or bound, 242
in (*en image*), 170, 182, 186, 195
as increasing reality, 212
as instrument of critique of reality, 10
as intentional object without existence, 100
as intuitive-absent, 184, 186
isolated, 91, 120, 150, 169, 221, 223
juxtaposition with concept, 234, 240
juxtaposition with imagination, 69
juxtaposition with impression, 51, 100
juxtaposition with operation of thinking, 93–95, 112, 123
juxtaposition with perception, 123, 173, 174–75, 176, 181, 204
juxtaposition with reality, 201
juxtaposition with schema, 72, 73, 239, 240, 266

juxtaposition with trace, 8, 242
juxtaposition with words, 119
as less than, 249
magic of, 171, 184, 203
memory, 8
mental, 5, 9, 22, 34, 92, 99, 100, 102, 112, 114, 115, 117, 123, 124, 125, 134, 141, 143, 145, 160, 188, 189, 190, 191, 192, 193, 194, 196, 211, 250, 251
as mistaken for reality, 9
movement in metaphor from language to image, 234
negativity of, 31
as nonexistent object, 142, 186
as no-thing, 208
nothingness of, 28, 175, 181, 213, 230
as nowhere, 100, 198
ontological and epistemological status, 169
ontology of, 246
as part of language and not of perception, 230
phenomenology of, 185
as picture, 116, 117, 221
poetic, 199, 214, 225, 227, 228, 229, 230, 231, 242
poverty of, 180, 181, 186
as though present, 29
prisoner of, 206
as production, 176
productive function, 120
productive without original referent, 231
psychology of, 229
as quasi-observation, 159, 179
reassertion of reality in picture, 285
as reduction to impression, 50–55
as relational, 178, 184, 185
relationship to language, between verbal and visual, 214
as representation, 56, 87, 153
as reproductive, 212
reverberation of language into image, 248
root, 232
schematic, 241
as shadow, 249, 250, 251, 256
as standing for, 5, 8

image (*continued*)
 statics of, 169, 184, 187, 201, 221, 297n4
  (chap. 12)
 substitutive function, 148, 149
 thinking with or in images, 113, 114, 117,
  123, 142, 143–44, 149, 151, 153, 222
 trying the meaning in, 151
 unreality of, 210, 212
 as weak impression, 1
 what it is to have an image, 217
 wild, 242
 as worked, 221
image family, 169, 170, 177, 182, 184, 185,
  188, 194
imagery, 4, 293n1 (chap. 4)
imaginary life, 169, 170, 171, 176, 183, 184,
  185, 187, 188, 192, 196, 199, 201, 204,
  206, 208, 219, 221, 222, 246
 as escape, 231
 as life without work, 280
imaginatio, 9, 10, 25, 35
imagination. *See also* axis of imagination; imagination, creative; imagination, cultural, social, and political; imagination, epistemological;
  imagination, poetic; imagination,
  productive; imagination, religious;
  imagination, reproductive
 aesthetic, 64
 as anti-world, 203
 as behavior, 293n1 (chap. 4)
 as building framework of reference,
  224
 as capacity for extension, 119–20
 cognitive, 64, 260
 as common root, 30, 70, 292n5
 comparison to memory, 53, 54, 59
 as condition of belief, 292n3
 connecting function of, 49, 55–59, 61,
  63, 65, 68, 71
 as connection between an intuition
  and a concept, 65
 as connection between the verbal and
  the visual, 65
 connection to theory of utopia, 209
 as constitutive, 62, 63
 as contrary of praxis, 203, 204
 contrast to belief, 292n3

contrast to image, 69
contrast with perception, 154, 161–67
contribution to objectivity, 62
critique of, 36
as deceptive, 13, 34–37, 38, 203
derive from likeness, 238
as display of meaning, 146
as distance, 23
as dynamic, 9, 13
as effort, 84, 85
emergence of new meaning, 235
empirical, 66
as escape, 202, 204
as evasion, 203, 214
as exploration of reality through play,
  282
externalization in material medium,
  251
as fiction, 217
as formative, 69
as free, 59, 63
as free movement, 57, 58
as free play, 22, 75–82, 88
fundamental problem as connection
  between not doing and as if doing,
  110
as illusion, 9
as inadequation, 45
as intermediary, 13, 18–20, 21, 33, 61,
  65, 146
as interplay between freedom and
  rules, 88
as interrelated with language, 88
as interrelated with structure, 88
interrelation between procedures in
  poetry and science, 233
interrelation between productive
  aspects of language and imagination, 234
as intimation of new connections, 276
as intimation of new dimensions of
  reality, 276
as invention, 58
as language, 24
as leap into the inexistent, 166
liberty of, 55
as lie, 9
literary, 10

INDEX 331

as magical, 10
material, 228
as mediation, 13, 19, 30, 61, 62, 63, 65, 69, 71
as a method, 72
moralistic approach, 33, 35, 37
as movement, 27–30, 31, 57, 61, 84
negative trace in, 263
as neutralization, 10, 11, 151, 164
as never naked creativity, 78, 84, 88
and new predicative meaning, 237
nothingness of, 28
nothingness of object, 181
ontology of, 37, 228, 285
pathology of, 204
as perceiving resemblances, 114
as *Phantasie*, 63
philosophy of, 1, 2, 56, 83, 153, 246, 256, 260
as play, 13
poverty of, 204
power of, 4, 9, 35, 45
power of as free, 46
power of connection, 55, 56
as pretending, 92
problem of the unity of the field, 3–4, 6, 64, 92, 98, 99, 102, 103, 105, 125, 144, 169, 188, 275, 285
as a procedure, 72
prophetic, 46
psycho-ethical treatment of, 9, 10
in psychology, 293n1 (chap. 4)
psychology of, 250
reconceptualization of interrelation with perception, 93, 112, 120, 123
relation to freedom, 210
relation to theory of metaphor, 226
relation with pleasure, 121
relation with truth, 31
as remaking reality, 143
as reorientation, 214
reproductive, 11
role in scientific thought, 226
as running along, 59, 65, 69, 77, 84
as a scale of faculties, 17
in the sciences, 260
as shadow, 251
social, 10, 13

sophistry of, 37
as source of understanding, 68
as a striving, 83, 84
as suspension of belief, 105
as synthesis, 13, 23, 56, 61, 64–73, 81
theory of, 6
theory of has overlooked polarity between picture and fiction, 285
as third term, 65, 71, 136
transition from literal incongruence to metaphorical congruence, 237
trying the meaning in, 151
unity of in epistemological and poetic functions, 285
as universal function, 68
Vorstellung, 131
as wild, 63, 88
without belief, 26
as work, 91
imagination, creative, 17, 33, 38, 62, 63, 69, 97, 98, 224, 225, 250, 251, 255, 260
as creative in same way in models and poetry, 275
depiction of nonobjective qualities of reality, 255
externalization in material medium, 255
as a general mode of thought, 260
as iconic augmentation, 250–56
as mode of relatedness, 256
as structural screen, 255
imagination, cultural, social, and political
ideology and utopia, 243, 245
imagination, epistemological, 10, 227, 243
as extension of concept of reality, 276
intersection with poetic imagination, 226, 234, 260, 285
as productive, 225
in theory of models, 260
transposition illumined by transfer in metaphor, 276
imagination, poetic, 225, 226, 243
intersection with epistemological imagination, 226, 234, 285
schematizes pre-objective, 285

imagination, productive, 8, 9, 46, 47, 54, 60, 63, 65, 67, 68, 69, 70, 81, 97, 211, 214, 217, 222, 225, 237–43, 255, 260
  absent in Sartre, 212
  absent in Wittgenstein, 241
  arbitrariness of, 292n3
  categorial to be transcategorial, 238
  as conjunction with productive language, 226, 227
  contrast in Kant to fiction, 63
  contrast to reproductive imagination, 250, 292n3
  as creative, 55, 223, 227
  as creative through language, 231
  as depiction, 240
  domains: poetic; epistemological; cultural, social, and political; religious, 243
  emergence of new sameness despite difference, 239
  as enhancement of reality, 212
  as extension of concepts, 275
  as fiction, 259
  as the fictional, 220
  as iconic augmentation, 250–56
  implies revision of concepts of reality and truth, 285
  insight into nascent likeness, 238
  interplay between remoteness and nearness, 239
  interrelation as creative with language as creative, 226
  interrelation with productive language, 227
  in Kant, 245
  as the nowhere, 291n8
  ontology, 232
  ontology displayed by the image, 231
  as opening and changing reality, 220
  and plot, 55
  as predicative assimilation in schema, 239
  producing a world, 212
  as producing new concept from new instances, 238
  productive of its reference, 259
  relation to reproduction, 54

  as reshaping reality, 234, 254
  in schema, not full imagination, 239
  schema as kernel of, 74
  second ontology, 231
  as synthesizing, 63
  tension in categorization, 239
  universality of across poetry and science, 260
  without an original referent, 233
  as a work, 221
imagination, religious, 243, 245
imagination, reproductive, 8, 9, 11, 54, 63, 65, 67, 68, 70, 74, 81, 211, 212, 214, 217, 221, 245, 250, 254, 255, 282
  and the *as though* of presence, 222
  contrast to productive imagination, 292n3
  existing original, 217
  at issue for reflection, 219
  issue of sense and not reference, 219
  marginal as regards reality, 220
  original referent, 231
  original rules images, 259
  as picture, 259
  picture of existing, 217
  in Ryle and Sartre, 219
  in Sartre, 212
  in Spinoza, 47
  as spontaneity only in reflection, 220
imaginative variation, 10, 13, 95, 138, 224–25, 256, 296n2 (chap. 10)
  defined, 10
  as productive and creative, 225
imaging, 4, 31, 92, 101, 102, 105, 107, 108, 109, 111, 112, 114, 115, 116, 123, 142, 169
imaging knowledge
  savoir imageant, 196
imaginieren, 145
imagining, 4, 25, 92, 99, 100, 101, 102, 107, 108, 110, 111, 123, 127, 142, 162, 164, 169, 198, 207, 210
  operation of, 92, 112, 117, 153, 157
imagist theory
  of meaning, 149
  of thinking, 112–13, 114, 115, 142, 144, 148, 149
imago, 3

imitation, 17, 18, 220, 246, 250, 254, 261
  creative, 255
impression, 1, 7, 19, 24, 38, 39, 41, 44, 49,
    50, 51, 52, 53, 55, 58, 59, 60, 61, 62,
    63, 65, 67, 70, 108, 125, 133, 155, 159,
    160, 165, 175, 188, 201, 204, 227, 229,
    242, 249, 264, 265
  image as copy of, 69, 93
  juxtaposition with image, 100, 123
  kinesthetic, 198
  nonintentional, 188
  reduction of image to, 50–55
  relation to copy, 57, 100, 172
  relation with concept, 65
Impressionism, 254
induction, 59, 154, 155, 174, 189, 193
inertness, 171
inexistence, 102, 161, 162, 163, 166, 170,
    177, 190, 194, 208, 212, 213, 218, 259,
    291n7
  defined, 162
  difference from absence, 212
inference, 57, 59
Ingarden, Roman, 139
  *Controversy over the Existence of the
    World*, 296n3 (chap. 10)
instance, 73, 78, 114, 115, 118, 120, 147,
    223, 224, 266, 267
  interrelation with concept, 222–23,
    225, 228, 238, 265, 266, 267, 268,
    269, 271
  put new instance under old concept,
    265
  relation to change in concept, 268
intellectus
  intellectual intuition, 33
intentionality, phenomenological, 27,
    31, 40, 54, 92, 100, 111, 169, 170, 177,
    186, 188, 189, 190, 191, 192, 193, 194,
    195, 196, 198, 209, 210, 211
  consciousness of, 140
  as correlation of act and object, 102,
    116, 140, 141, 142
  defined, 140
  empty, 223
  of feeling, 196
  of imagination, 161
  of perception, 155, 161

as synthetic act, 141
intermediary, 13, 18, 19, 20, 21, 25, 33, 61,
    65, 136, 146, 242
interpretation, 24, 25, 26, 42, 93, 130, 132,
    133, 134, 160, 174, 226, 235, 237, 261,
    271, 273
  Deutung, 150
  mythical, 29
intimation, 270, 271, 276
intuition, 10, 13, 18, 19, 20, 46, 64, 65, 69,
    72, 74, 79, 81, 87, 96, 136, 138, 149,
    184, 191, 196, 209, 210, 264
  dynamic concept of, 273
  image as intuitive absent, 184
  intellectual, 30, 33, 264
  versus opposition with discursive,
    273
  pregnant with discursive, 273
invention, 58, 131, 256, 271, 280, 281, 285
  as construction, 285
  interrelation with discovery, 285
  interrelation with discovery caught
    in opposition between subject and
    object, 285
involuntary, 187
irrational, 83, 97, 142, 226, 238, 270, 281
irreal, 10

Jakobson, Roman, 247, 248, 275
  "Closing Statements: Linguistics and
    Poetics," 247, 299n2 (chap. 17)
James, William, 173
  "Philosophical Conceptions and
    Practical Results," 298n1 (chap. 15)
  "Stream of Thought, The," 297n3
    (chap. 13)
  *Meaning of Truth, a Sequel to "Pragma-
    tism," The*, 298n1 (chap. 15)
  *Pragmatism: A New Name for Some Old
    Ways of Thinking*, 298n1 (chap. 15)
Jankélévitch, Vladimir, 38
Jaspers, Karl, 165
  Philosophy, 297n9 (chap. 11)
Jastrow, Joseph, 129
Judaism, 46
judgment, 21, 22, 23, 27, 30, 62, 63, 65, 71,
    75, 105, 139, 175, 177, 264
  as activity of application, 264

judgment (*continued*)
  aesthetic, 13, 86
  modality of, 160
  of perception, 160, 174
  power of, 78
  as putting an intuition under a concept, 65
  reflective, 78, 79, 80, 88, 245, 246
  suspension of, 139, 153
  of taste, 64, 79, 81, 245
Jung, Carl, 228, 232
justice, 36, 37, 83

Kant, Immanuel, 3, 12, 19, 30, 34, 46, 49, 56, 59, 60, 61–88, 96, 98, 112, 120, 136, 141, 146, 196, 211, 219, 239, 245–46, 250, 264, 266, 273, 278, 283, 292n3
  Critique of Judgment, 3, 12, 13, 22, 30, 31, 47, 56, 64, 75, 78–88, 121, 245, 246, 294n4 (chap. 6), 295n4 (chap. 8), 299n1 (chap. 17), 300n7 (chap. 18)
  Critique of Pure Reason, 3, 13, 23, 47, 61–78, 80, 81, 85, 292n5, 293–94n1, 294n1 (chap. 6)
  Kritik der Urteilskraft und Schriften zur Naturphilosophie, 294n4 (chap. 6)
Kepler, Johannes, 26
Kierkegaard, Søren, 47
kinesthetic, 197–98
Klinger, Eric, 77, 293n1 (chap. 4)
knowledge, 13, 26, 35, 38, 46, 50, 64, 65, 68, 69, 78, 191, 192, 196, 261, 297n2 (chap. 13)
  connaissance, 196
  imaging, 196
  savoir, 196

landscape, 114, 212, 256, 271, 278
  tension between ordinary and painted, 272
Langer, Susanne
  Philosophy in a New Key, 225–26, 260
language, 13, 96, 98, 99, 101, 107, 110, 112, 125, 126, 128, 132, 137, 138, 139, 140, 141, 143, 160, 167, 184, 199, 230, 234, 248, 259, 273
  birth of new in, 229

  birthplace of new language in thinking more, 273
  conceptual, 263
  as creative, 231, 233
  creative procedures of, 226
  creative use of described and analyzed, 226
  creativity in, 229, 261
  disclosive capacity of what does not have the form of an object, 283
  disclosive capacity when most inwardly oriented, 283
  as discourse, 91
  displacement as change in language and in world, 268
  as display of image, 233
  emergence of new in, 228, 230
  of evocation, 284
  extension of as extension of world, 261
  extraordinary, in poetic language, 284
  and generation of images, 234
  as giving images, 229
  image as dimension of, 229
  image as part of and not of perception, 230
  imagination as belonging to, 24
  imagination as close to, 51
  imagination as interrelated with, 88
  interrelation as creative with imagination as creative, 226
  interrelation as poetic with imagination as creative, 227
  interrelation as productive with imagination as productive, 227
  interrelation between productive aspects of language and imagination, 234
  interrelation with experience, 91, 97, 125, 126, 128, 138
  as inwardly oriented, 282
  limits of, 124, 125, 126, 132, 133, 134–35
  metaphoricity of, 239
  misuse of, 126
  movement in, 262
  movement in metaphor from language to image, 234
  as operative, 273

ordinary, 98, 111, 116, 172, 178, 224, 236, 238, 240, 247, 255, 263, 272, 282, 284
poetic, 123, 233, 234, 240, 245, 248, 263, 265, 275, 276, 279–84
poetic, lack of reference as negative condition for productive reference, 283
poetic as display of image, 214
poetic as nonreferential, 246, 248, 249, 275, 276
poetic as productive reference, 257, 275, 279, 283
poetic as suspension of ordinary life, 284
productive, 226
as redescription, 284
relationship to image, between verbal and visual, 214
in relation to use, 127
scientific, 248, 284
as sedimented, 135, 136
strategy of, 234
as *technē*, techniques, 251
as thematic, 273
theoretical models as new, 262, 263
as a work, 251
work of, 280
language game, 40, 95, 103, 128, 132, 135, 136, 161, 221, 223, 231, 235, 247
law, 36, 81, 82, 85, 238, 263
legitimation, 36
Le Guern, Michel
Sémantique de la métaphore et de la métonymie, 299n5 (chap. 16)
Leibniz, Gottfried, 9, 25
lens, 241, 265, 278
liberation
interest in, 257
likeness, 93, 99, 104, 111, 147, 237
comparison to schema, 240
contrast to sameness, 93, 146, 239
emergence of new sameness despite difference, 239
as fundamental in imagination, 101
interplay between presence and absence, 120
interplay with absence, 120, 143, 220

interplay with negation as remaking reality, 220
interplay with the not, 115, 125, 219, 242
nascent, 238
as production of proximity, 238
relation with metaphor, 234
resemblance, 93, 134
role in production of new meaning, 237
linguistic analysis. *See* analytic philosophy
linguistics, 247
literal, 236, 237, 270, 271, 272, 273, 277
difference from metaphor, 272–73
as the lexical, 235
no longer tension between old concept and new situation, 272
literary criticism, 25, 78, 240, 247, 248, 257, 281
literature
critique of notion of work, 280
Locke, John, 52, 56, 112, 148
Essay Concerning Human Understanding, An, 148, 296n9 (chap. 10)
logic, 94, 95, 112, 113, 125, 144, 145, 147, 149, 150, 162, 240, 248
of discovery, 76, 94, 226, 233, 261, 269
of discovery as process of discovery, 269
formal, 267
intensional, 111
modal, 111, 182
philosophy of, 94, 95, 111
logical space, 149, 238, 269
logos, 138, 230, 280
love, 35

magical, 10, 171, 184, 202, 203, 204, 207, 211, 212, 222, 242, 246, 280
as opposite of work, 222
make-believe, 37, 92, 103, 105, 108, 173, 282
manifestation
truth as, 285
manifold, 64, 65, 66, 67, 68, 69, 70, 71, 81, 82, 136
Marx, Karl, 36, 85

Marxism, 35, 149
material, 92, 172, 178, 189, 190, 193, 194, 221, 239, 253
  imagination, 228
material medium, 252, 255, 262
  imagination as externalization in, 251, 255
mathematics, 272, 279
matter (*hylē*), 163, 166, 172, 188, 189, 190, 192, 193, 198
  defined, 160
Maxwell, James Clerk, 262
McKeon, Richard, 25
  "Imitation and Poetry," 246, 250
meaning, 94, 96, 114, 129, 139–40, 141, 144, 145, 146, 148, 151, 153, 154, 158, 163, 224, 232, 235, 237, 242, 243
  absurd, 146, 162
  exists nowhere, 147
  fluctuating, 224
  ideal, 149
  ideality of, 147
  metaphorical, 236
  occasional or fluctuating, 150
  relation with representation, 151
Meinong, Alexius, 59, 94, 113, 144, 147
melody, 157
memory, 8, 45, 53, 54, 55, 58, 67, 69, 117, 130, 141, 162, 163, 205, 251, 264, 267, 300n5 (chap. 17)
  comparison to imagination, 53, 54, 59
Merleau-Ponty, Maurice, 93, 109, 127, 135, 137, 143, 154, 155, 159, 161, 164, 265, 294n2 (chap. 7), 296n1 (chap. 10)
  "Cézanne's Doubt," 294n1 (chap. 7)
  "Eye and Mind," 93
  Phénoménologie de la perception, 295n2 (chap. 8)
  Phenomenology of Perception (1962), 295n2 (chap. 8)
  Phenomenology of Perception (2012), 295n2 (chap. 8), 296n2 (chap. 11), 297n5 (chap. 11), 297nn7–8 (chap. 11)
  Signs, 295n5 (chap. 9), 300n4 (chap. 18)

Visible and the Invisible, The, 232
metamorphosis, 232
metapherō
  displacement, 269
metaphor, 13, 119, 123, 199, 223, 227, 234–43, 249, 257, 267, 268, 269, 270, 272, 273, 276
  analogical, 238
  application of seeing as to verbal element, 241
  beyond substitution, 234
  as category mistake, 266
  circularity, 273
  comparison to models, 226, 234, 243, 257, 261, 262, 275
  consequences of for theory of imagination, 226
  as creative, 236–37, 268
  dead, 236
  difference from literal, 272–73
  as display, 241
  as display of images, 51, 214
  dying, 271
  frame and focus, 237
  as iconic display by depiction, 241
  as insight into resemblance, 234
  interrelation with displacement, 263
  as less than plot (*muthos*), 279
  lived, 236
  and logic of discovery, 261
  metaphorical twist, 236
  as metaphor of space, 241
  movement from language to image, 234
  myth of, as picture, 277
  no superordinate category, 268
  parallel to conflict between old concept and new situation, 264
  as perceiving resemblance, 114
  philosophy of, 270
  poetic function in, 169
  as predication, 225, 234
  as predicative assimilation, 238
  productive, 268
  productivity due to odd predication, 235, 238

as reduction of logical distance, 269
as relation between tenor and vehicle, 240
relation to poetic language parallels models to epistemology, 234
seeing relation through screen or lens, 241
strategy of language in, 227, 230, 234
as tension, 237
as transfer, 234, 238
as transfer (*meta-phora*), as transposition, 276
transfer, as displacement, 269
as transfer, enlightens scientific transposition, 276
metaphoricity, 273
of language, 239
metaphysics, 53, 82, 173
metaxu
the mixed, 19
method, 72, 91, 95, 97, 99, 124, 153, 154
differential, 22, 30
functional, 184, 188, 221
genetic, 49
imagination as a, 72
metonymy
as contiguity, 235
Middle Ages, 40, 94, 113, 165, 232
mimesis, 220, 221, 237, 250, 254, 255, 279, 281
as copy, 279
as creative, 220
as creative reconstruction, 246
as denotative, 281
as fiction, 279
as imitation, 220, 279
narrative support of, 281
as picture, 279
play with possibilities, 282
through plot (*muthos*), 280
as productive, 280
as productive and creative, 279
as productive reference, 220
referential dimension, 281
as reproductive, 279, 280
as taking hold of essence of reality, 281

mind, 2, 5, 39, 40, 42, 43, 45, 50, 51, 57, 60, 62, 69, 88, 99, 100, 101, 113, 124, 126, 128, 147, 170, 171, 173, 177, 178, 183, 185, 188, 190, 192, 251, 260
as ghost in the machine, 98, 102, 171
See also philosophy of mind
Minkowski, Eugène, 229
Vers une cosmologie, 299n7 (chap. 15)
modality, 151, 160, 161, 163, 165, 166, 182
of belief, 162
models, 13, 30, 60, 62, 99, 123, 150, 169, 202, 211, 223, 226, 227, 249, 255, 257, 260, 261–63, 275, 276, 282
as the *as if* or *as though*, 278
comparison to metaphor, 234, 243, 257, 261, 262, 275
as conventionalism, 277
defined by truth claim, 276
as description through construction, 278
descriptive through the construct, 280
energetical, 262
for feeling, 282
fiction in, 260
function as screen to think through, 278
heuristic function for capacity of discovery, 260
kinship with imagination, 226
literal application, 277
and logic of discovery, 261
mechanical, 58, 237
as offering new aspect of reality, 278
parallel to work in language, 280
as productive of a new reality, 214
as redescription, 257
as redescription of reality, 214
as reduction to picture, 277
relation between fiction and redescription, 257
relation to epistemology parallels metaphor to poetic language, 234
relation to *muthos* (plot), 279
as systematic deployability, 279
topographical, 262
truth claim, 261

models (*continued*)
    as useful fictions rather than truth claims, 278
    as witnessing new dimension of reality, 278
    See also models, analogue; models, scale; models, theoretical
models, analogue, 191, 267
    contrast to theoretical models, 262
    creative element, 262
    as isomorphism, 262, 267
    in structure, 261
models, scale, 277, 281
    contrast to theoretical models, 262
    as model of, 276
    model of something existing elsewhere, 261
models, theoretical, 277, 281, 300n1 (chap. 19)
    comparison to metaphor as introducing new language, 262
    description of imaginary milieu of imaginary object, 262
    develops own referent, 262
    as extending new language to new domain, 262
    as model for, 276
    as new description that is transposed, 262
    as new language, 262, 263
    referent as redescription, 263
    as scientific fiction, 262, 263
    as transposition to reality, 262, 263
models for, 280
    capacity for discovery, 276
    as fiction, 276–77
    provided by fiction, 285
    as scientific fiction, 276
models of
    as picture, 276–77
Mondrian, Piet, 255
mood, 256, 282
    poetic, 248
Moore, G. E., 139
morality, 86, 280
morphē. See form: *morphē*
movement, 18, 27, 28, 29, 31, 41, 84, 140, 197

in language, 262
in presentation, 87
in thought through predication, 225
Mozart, Wolfgang Amadeus, 282
music, 99, 109, 110, 213, 267, 268, 301n16
muthos (plot), 220, 246, 250, 279
    as composition and network of thought, 279
    defined, 6
    mimesis through, 280
    as model for, 280
    as more than metaphor, 279
    relation to models, 279
mystery, 97, 226, 263, 270, 271
mysticism, 97, 138, 284
myth, 2, 29
    of metaphor, 277

name, 93, 95, 223, 225, 234, 235, 237, 257, 262, 283
naming
    language game of, 95, 234, 235, 247
narrative, 55
    denotative function, 281
    isomorphism with life, 281
    lecture course on, 281
    structure as model for, 281
    structure falls between scale and theoretical models, 281
    structure of existence, 281
    support of mimesis, 281
naturalism, 254
    ideology of, 254
nature, 27, 37, 58, 69, 74, 78, 80, 82, 86, 87, 88, 147, 254, 256, 271, 272, 280
negation, 39, 182, 184, 195, 203, 209, 219, 242
    interplay with likeness as remaking reality, 220
negative, 9, 12, 28, 38, 42, 43, 44, 104, 139, 170, 183, 197, 203, 211, 245, 263, 283
negativity, 9, 28, 37, 75, 136, 245
    of the image, 31
    scale of, 8
neo-Kantianism, 144, 278, 279
neo-Platonic, 46
neutralization, 10, 164, 165, 166, 167

of belief, 164
imagination as, 10, 11
of presence, 136, 218, 219
of reality, 151
newness, 227, 228, 229, 230, 231, 266
ontological bearing, 230
Newton, Isaac, 58, 59, 61, 79, 237, 271
Nietzsche, Friedrich, 34, 36, 77, 280,
294n3 (chap. 6)
"'Reason' in Philosophy," 301n5
Beyond Good and Evil, 301n5
Birth of Tragedy, The, 85
noema, 96, 142, 162, 175, 209
defined, 7, 142
noesis, 9, 142, 165
defined, 7, 142
nominalism, 56, 75, 99, 102, 134, 257
nondescriptive, 283
as nondiscursive, 283
nonexistence, 6, 40, 42, 45, 53, 100, 111,
140, 182, 183, 186, 195, 218, 219
in fiction, 182
nonfigurative, 213, 246, 255, 272, 280
non-instantiative particulars, 115, 117,
118, 143
nonintentionality, 159, 188, 210
defined, 159
nonthetic consciousness, 186, 204, 210,
297n2 (chap. 13)
defined, 186
nothingness, 31, 102, 111, 155, 162, 181,
182, 183, 186, 187, 188, 194, 195, 207,
208, 209, 210, 211, 219, 231, 233
absence as paradigm, 207
as the absent, 182, 195, 218, 219
as the existence elsewhere, 182, 183,
195, 218
as fiction, 182
freedom as, 175
of the image, 28, 175, 230
of imagination, 28
includes both absence and inexistence, 208
negative condition for remaking
reality, 211
as neutralized existence, 182, 183, 195,
218, 219
no intuition of, 210, 211

as the nonexistent, 182, 195, 218, 219
of object in imagination, 181
trait of referent in fiction, 218
of the unreal, 195
noticing an aspect, 132, 148, 271
nous, 18, 19, 142
novelty, 227, 228, 230, 231, 263, 265,
266, 275, 276
as contrary of sedimentation,
265
nowhere, 100, 116, 117, 118, 147, 176,
183, 198, 209, 213, 214, 291n8
as utopia, 118

object, 5, 7, 22, 41, 62, 63, 64, 97, 113,
124, 140, 141, 157, 158, 170, 176–77,
178, 183, 198, 202, 220, 255, 256, 259,
283, 284, 285
absent, 169, 170, 185, 189, 201, 207,
218, 219
bracketing of, 102
critique of concept of, 284
fictional, 212, 218
ideal, 2
ideal structure of, 113
imaginary, 262
inexistent, 161, 162, 194, 212, 218, 259
intentional object without existence,
100
intentional relation between act and,
40, 102, 116, 140
manipulable, 126, 212, 221, 232, 255,
283, 284
nonexistent, 6, 111, 140, 142
no object, 220, 255
nothingness of, 181, 187, 218
phantom, 203
spatial, 213
temporal, 213
in thought, 2
unreal, 208
objectification, 63, 256
objective, 22, 283, 285
abolition of in poetry, 283
objectivity, 13, 62, 63, 69, 78
object language, 124
obliqua oratio, 101
logic of quotation, 218

observation, 158, 159, 174, 179–80, 181, 184, 186
one and the many, 64
ontology, 6, 37, 38, 40, 53, 88, 100, 126, 131, 139, 140, 153, 155, 161, 169, 172, 175, 179, 186, 218, 228, 233, 246, 255, 256
  anti-ontological, 246
  connected to theory of imagination, 285
  displayed by the productive imagination, 231
  in feeling, 283
  of fiction, 231, 246, 247, 285
  of imagination, 232
  of nothingness, 208
  pre-objective dimension, 284
  redescription, 283, 285
opacity, 138, 142, 178, 260, 275
  kernel of in transposition, 273, 276
opinion, 19, 22, 23, 25, 26, 33, 37, 292n3
order, 76–77, 78, 79, 80, 81, 82, 88, 270
  dramatic (*taxis*), 280
orders
  of greatness in Pascal, 35
ordinary language philosophy, 20, 137
organization, 133, 251
original, 194, 195, 211, 212, 214, 217, 219, 220, 231, 233, 237, 249, 250, 259, 261, 262, 275
  referent, 285

pain, 64, 85, 86, 124, 128, 132, 139
painting, 70, 84, 93, 104, 143, 153, 169, 212, 213, 219, 221, 246, 249–56, 257, 260, 281, 285
  as abbreviation, 253
  abstract, 272
  Chinese, 114, 254
  as creative imitation, 255
  Dutch, 253
  English, 256
  extension of polysemy of vision, 272
  as fictional work, 251
  figurative, 255
  French Impressionist, 256
  as grasping through selective apparatus, 278

as iconic augmentation, 260
as imaginative variation, 256
interplay with writing, 252
landscape, 256, 271
as mimetic, 254
nonfigurative, 213, 255, 272
paradigm for transfiguration through the iconic, 249
as picture, 251
in Plato as image of an image, 249
relation to reality before its objectification, 256
Renaissance, 256
representational, 272
as a work, 251, 280
of Andrew Wyeth, 281
Panofsky, Erwin, 254
  Early Netherlandish Painting: Its Origins and Character, 300n6 (chap. 17)
Pantheon, 73, 198
parable
  biblical, 281
paradigm, 17, 22, 29, 34, 37, 44, 45, 49, 61, 62, 99, 102, 103, 108, 144, 161, 162, 169, 176, 177, 180, 185, 189, 190, 195, 207, 222, 224, 249
  philosophic problematic as choice of, 64
paradox, 1, 19, 71, 82, 97, 100, 111, 112, 117, 118, 125, 128, 133, 134, 141, 143, 155, 173, 179, 181, 184, 185, 186, 220, 228, 233, 239, 245, 255, 260, 273, 275, 276, 278, 281, 285
particulars, 115, 148, 170, 195
Pascal, Blaise, 9, 10, 20, 33–37, 38, 39, 46, 61, 203
  Pensées, 12, 33–37, 292n1 (chap. 3)
passions, 23, 46, 49, 50, 280, 281
  theory of, 33
passivity, 10, 19, 39, 46, 63, 108, 159, 173, 186
Peirce, Charles Sanders, 265
  Collected Papers of Charles Sanders Peirce, 291n5
perception, 1, 6, 7, 9, 17, 20, 21, 23, 24, 26, 27, 28, 29, 30, 31, 33, 38, 39, 40, 41, 42, 44, 45, 50, 51, 62, 63, 64, 67, 68,

77, 101, 108, 109, 110, 114, 123, 132,
150, 153, 154, 155, 156, 163, 170, 171,
173, 174, 178, 179, 180, 181, 183, 185,
186, 188, 189–90, 191, 195, 197, 203,
205, 206, 213, 219, 227, 229, 230, 241,
242, 250, 267, 272
and belief, 161, 164
as belief in reality, 160
contrast to seeing as, 133, 135
contrast with imagination, 154,
161–67
contrast with the image, 154–61, 163
difference from image in mode of
givenness, 218
division in objects, 285
false, 29
fancied, 105, 107, 108, 143
image as part of language and not of
perception, 227, 230
imagination as belonging more to
language than to perception, 24
impressional element, 159, 160
intentionality of, 155
involvement in being, 154
juxtaposition with image, 173, 174–75,
176, 181, 204
meaning as element of, 140
neutralized, 166–67, 250
nonintentional element, 159
phenomenology of, 141, 155–61
philosophy of, 154
psychology of, 20, 70, 160
reconceptualization of interrelation
with imagination, 93, 112, 120, 123
referent for picture, 259
relation with thinking, 109, 135, 136
perspective, 254
phantasia, 3, 7, 12, 17, 18, 19, 25, 27
Phantasie, 3, 4, 63, 145, 164
imagination as free, wild, 63
phenomenological description. *See*
description: phenomenological
phenomenological reduction. *See* reduction, phenomenological (*epochē*)
phenomenology, 13, 18, 28, 44, 66, 80,
91, 97, 102, 104, 110, 112, 116, 117, 118,
120, 124, 126, 136, 137–42, 144, 153–
57, 173, 184, 217, 218, 228, 229, 278

of absence, 203, 208, 214, 218
analysis of condition of possibility of
having images, 207
of creative imagination, 250, 251
defined, 138
of desire, 203
as discourse, 138
of discovery, 223
and essential analysis, 171
of fascination, 206, 222
of fatality, 204
of feeling, 196
of fiction, 13, 219
fiction as element of, 155
as grasp of essential meaning, 154
of iconic augmentation, 251
of the image, 155, 185
image as image of, 51
of imagination, 45, 58, 142, 201, 228
as inquiry into meaning, 140
juxtaposition with analytic philosophy, 91–98, 112, 137, 140, 142, 153,
167, 170, 172, 207
juxtaposition with philosophy of
mind, 95–96
linguistic, 99
of newness, 227
nothing as feature of the imaginary,
181
of perception, 141, 155–61
of perception and nonintentional
element, 159
of the poem, 229
of reading, 241
of recognition, 223
of reverie, 231
of the work in fiction, 222
philosophy
death of, 136
death of as philosophical death, 281
philosophy of imagination, 1, 2, 56, 83,
153, 246, 256, 260
as interplay between spontaneity and
giving form, 78
rebuilding unity between cognitive
and aesthetic, 64
Romantic, 69
philosophy of logic, 94, 95, 111

philosophy of mind, 93, 94, 95, 96, 113, 188

juxtaposition with phenomenology, 95–96

philosophy of perception, 154

photography, 254

creative aspect, 300n5 (chap. 17)

reproductive aspect, 300n5 (chap. 17)

physics, 27, 29, 61, 157, 171, 254, 267

Piaget, Jean, 293n1 (chap. 4)

Picasso, Pablo, 253

picture, 4, 5, 11–12, 22, 26, 92, 96, 99, 100, 102, 104, 107, 111, 115, 116, 117, 124, 127, 128, 133, 134, 143, 160, 163, 164, 166, 178, 183, 188, 194, 212, 217, 221, 224, 240, 251, 262, 265, 277, 282

as absent work of thought, 280

contrast to icon, 241

as copy, 261

distinction from fiction, 259, 285

existing reference, 259, 285

as ideology in social action, 275

as magic of possession, 280

mental, 24, 101, 128, 134, 193, 240, 241

and mimesis, 279

as model of, 276–77

no referent of its own, 259

public because exterior, 250

reference of perception, 259

reproducing previous reality, 276

as reproductive imagination, 259

as scale model, 261

as a work, 251

Plato, 3, 17, 18, 19, 21, 25, 26, 30, 34, 35, 45, 53, 64, 80, 82, 85, 225, 249–50, 251, 252, 280

Gorgias, 37

Meno, 295n7 (chap. 9)

Phaedrus, 249

Platonism, 144

play, 2, 13, 77, 103, 107, 108, 131, 143, 188, 206, 222, 282, 291n11, 293n1 (chap. 4), 294n3 (chap. 6)

as exploration of reality by imagination, 282

as fiction delineating unemployed possibilities of reality, 282

free, 76, 78, 81, 82, 88

free, of imagination, 13, 22, 75–82, 88

interrelation with rule, 76, 81, 88

in mimesis, 282

as project of our possibilities, 282

pleasure, 22, 50, 64, 79, 80, 85, 86, 120, 121, 245, 272

plot, 6, 55

as disclosure of reality, 250

as medium of mimesis, 255

as model for, 280

muthos, 220, 246, 250, 279

poetic, 169, 226, 229, 230, 231, 232, 233, 247, 260

diction, 226, 242

fiction, 211

image, 199, 214, 225, 227, 228, 229, 230, 231, 242

imagination, 225, 226, 234, 243, 260, 285

language, 123, 234, 240, 245, 246, 248, 249, 257, 263, 265, 275

metaphor, 259

poetics, 233, 247, 260

poetry, 82, 225, 228, 232, 233, 240, 246–47, 248, 257, 259, 260, 261, 263, 270, 271, 275, 279, 282–84

as accentuation of message for its own sake, 247

as anti-ontological, 246

appearance of world through, 284

criticizing dichotomy with science, 260

as a dance, 248

deals with what is fundamental, 281

as depiction of modes of appearance of reality, 283

disclosure in, 261

as *epoché* of reality, 248

images without reference, 259

looking at reality in terms of non-descriptive, 283

lyric as nonreferential, 282

lyric as suspension of descriptive function, 282

as mimesis of human action, 279

productive imagination in, 260

referential dimension, 281

retreating into interiority because

exteriority colonized by ordinary
language, 284
shatters subject/object relation, 283
suspension of ideological relation to
world, 284
as suspension of reference, 248
as truer than history, 220, 281
poiēsis
as creation, 227
polysemy, 224, 236, 237, 272
of vision, 272
Pope, 148
Popper, Karl, 76, 269
portrait, 3, 4, 11, 12, 62, 92, 143, 156, 164,
166, 188, 189, 190, 193, 194, 195, 197,
211, 212
mental, 22, 178
posit, 70, 77, 164, 165, 166, 173, 181, 182,
183, 184, 186, 187, 205, 208, 210, 211,
219
positional act, 181–82, 183, 186, 187, 204,
208
defined, 181
thetic, 204
positivism, 260
possibility, 73, 221, 273, 282
of thinking more as birthplace of new
language, 273
power, 10, 34, 36, 63, 86, 159, 230, 281,
284
anti-power, 280
creative in imagination, 63
of imagination, 4, 9, 35, 45, 68, 74,
88, 203
pragmatism, 264, 277, 279
praxis, 132, 203
precomprehension, 19
predicative assimilation, 240
metaphor as, 238
as a rule, 239
pre-objective, 256, 285
belonging as truth as manifestation,
285
said poetically, 283, 284
presence, 5, 6, 7, 8, 9, 11, 38, 39, 41, 42, 43,
44, 45, 118, 125, 161, 162, 172, 190,
191, 192, 195, 196, 198, 206, 212, 213,
218, 219, 222, 259

affective-kinesthetic, 198
as if of, 38, 39, 44
as though of, 222
contrast to fiction, 197
false, 38, 40, 203
ghostly, 203
negative, 197
neutralization of, 136, 218, 219
ontological, 140
philosophy of, 38
shadow, 181
presentation, 81, 83, 84, 85, 87, 161, 163,
241, 260, 298n4 (chap. 13)
aesthetic, 88
compared to representation, 87, 278
Darstellung, 4, 85, 133, 160
interplay with representation, 87
as movement, 87
and ontology, 88
pre-aesthetic, 88
present in schematic way, 4
visual, 241
pre-Socratics, 20, 45, 74, 142
pretending, 92, 99, 101, 102, 103, 104, 105,
107–8, 109, 110, 111, 112, 123, 132, 143,
167, 169, 188, 217–18, 219, 229
as picture, 282
as reproductive imagination, 282
Price, H. H., 59, 95, 98, 100, 102, 105, 107,
111, 112–20, 123, 134, 137, 143, 144,
145, 146, 147, 149, 150, 151, 174, 179,
184, 198, 222–23, 226, 234, 238
Thinking and Experience, 95, 97, 107,
112–20, 143, 153, 222, 267, 295n3
(chap. 8), 299n1 (chap. 15)
proposition, 56, 94, 95, 111, 112, 113, 144,
260
protention, phenomenological, 109,
158, 264
defined, 157
Proust, Marcel, 8, 203, 233
pseudo, 7, 37
pseudo-evidence, 139
pseudo-presence, 38
psuchē, 18
psyche, 142, 227, 228, 232, 233
psychoanalysis, 85, 135, 148, 230, 232, 262
psychologism, 2, 144

psychology, 2, 5, 6, 9, 12, 13, 18, 21, 25, 28, 45, 49, 53, 63, 66, 69, 70, 93, 96, 98, 113, 114, 127, 134, 135, 142, 144, 146, 147, 149, 154, 155, 159, 160, 173, 197, 210, 227, 230, 232, 242, 243, 247, 291n4, 291n11
  behavioral, 2, 293n1 (chap. 4)
  cognitive, 293n1 (chap. 4)
  of delusion, 246
  experimental, 194
  French, 172
  gestalt, 133
  of the image, 229, 234
  of imagination, 250
  on imagination, 293n1 (chap. 4)
  inductive, 189, 193
  of inspiration, 229
  of motivation, 293n1 (chap. 4)
  of perception, 20, 70, 160
  phenomenological, 154
  as a science, 154
  of the will, 187
  Würzburg, 196
Ptolemy, Claudius, 26
purposiveness, 78, 79, 86, 88

quasi, 7, 37, 111, 151
  modality of, 151
quasi-being, 165
quasi-existence, 111
quasi-experience, 120
quasi-fulfillment, 151
quasi-instance, 115, 119, 120, 123, 142, 149, 151, 222, 223, 226
quasi-instantiative particulars, 115, 119, 143, 151, 222, 223
quasi-object, 218
quasi-observation, 159, 179, 181, 184, 186, 203, 219, 242
quasi-perception, 165
quasi-presence, 30, 38, 40, 44, 111, 119, 151, 185, 204, 207, 222
quasi-purposiveness, 79
quasi-reality, 212
quasi-seeing, 162
quasi-visible, 240
quotation, 103, 104, 107, 218
  theory of, 101, 259

rationalism, 37, 45, 156
rationality, 273
reading, 180, 230, 242, 261
  phenomenology of, 241
  theory of, 226, 285
realism, 139
  critical, 278, 279
  naive, 277
reality, 6, 7, 8, 9, 10, 13, 26, 43, 44, 147, 158, 163, 165, 175, 195, 202, 203, 204, 205, 206, 207, 208, 212, 219, 222, 223, 231, 232, 247, 255, 277, 278, 300n5 (chap. 17)
  absence as characteristic in, 180
  absent as case of, 195
  aspects of that do not have the form of an object, 283
  augmentation of, 233
  before division in objects, 285
  belief in, 160
  break with to express new, 253, 254
  capacity to retreat from, 75
  concept of as flattened, 284
  concept of revised by productive imagination, 285
  confusion with image, 9
  connection with unreality, 211
  as construct of judgment, 62
  contrast to image, 201
  contribution of fiction to, 212
  critical distance to, 10
  disclosure of, 250
  enhancement of, 212
  epochē of, 248
  expansion of, 233
  expansion of through iconic augmentation, 250
  exploration of by imagination through play, 282
  extension of, 261, 276
  fiction as opening a new reality, 214
  fiction as producing a new reality, 214
  fiction not belonging to, 195
  fiction not ruled by, 180
  gap with image, 173, 175
  iconic augmentation as increase of, 252

iconic augmentation of, 260
image as mistaken for, 9
image as shadow of, 18
increase of, 260, 275
mimesis as creative reconstruction of, 246
mimesis of, 220
model as redescription of, 263
models as productive of new, 214
mythified, 277
neutralization of, 151
new dimension in fiction, 285
nondescriptive traits of, 283
nonobjective qualities of, 255
opened in fiction, 53, 276
our concept of as problematic, 257
poetic depiction by, 283
posited as existing, 186
productive imagination as opening and changing, 220
productive imagination as reshaping, 234
promotion of, 251
questioning our concept of, 256
reassertion of in picture, 285
as redescribed, 278
redescription of, 220
redescription of by fiction, 212, 257
relation to as pre-objective belonging, 285
relation to before its objectification, 256
relation to through emotions, 256
as remade, 254
as remade by language, 257
as remade by metaphorical discourse, 257
remaking, 211, 212, 220
remaking or restructuring, 143
reshaping, 214
restitution of aspects of, 212
structuration of, 264
symbolic structure of, 88
taking hold of essence of through mimesis and fiction, 281
theoretical models transposed to, 262
transfiguration of, 245, 249

unemployed possibilities delineated in play, 282
unnoticed aspects of, 212
what imagination adds to or subtracts from, 53
reason, 21, 35, 36, 50, 60, 61, 78, 82, 83, 85, 86, 87, 88
dialectic of, 82
practical, 82
Vernunft, 82
recognition, 114, 119, 130, 133, 134, 150, 151, 174, 222, 223, 224, 256, 267, 283
phenomenology of, 223
as synthesis, 23
redescription, 31, 212, 214, 220, 253, 257, 281
abolition of objective for ontological redescription, 284
of reality, 263
relation to fiction, 279
as transposition, 263
reduction, eidetic, 155, 161, 163
defined, 154
as reduction to essences, 154
reduction, phenomenological (*epoché*), 138–40, 161, 300n6 (chap. 18)
defined, 138
as suspension of judgment, 139
as transcendental reduction, 154
of what, 139
to what, 139–40
reference, 20, 161, 162, 170, 178, 183, 185, 195, 213, 217, 218, 221, 224, 235, 243, 245, 247, 248, 256, 260, 262, 279
absence of original in fiction, 220
conflict of, 268
contrast to sense, 146, 178, 219
dimension of in mimesis and poetry, 281
in fiction, 249, 261
fiction as providing a new, 214
fiction as providing its own referent, 259
first order, in descriptive language, 249
more fundamental, 256
movement from model to metaphor, 249

reference (*continued*)
  pictorial aspect of, 257
  poetic as without reference, 259
  reference of perception for picture,
    259
  suspension of in poetry, 248
  in theoretical models, 263
  See also reference, productive
reference, productive, 220, 230, 234, 245,
    246, 249, 257, 259, 260, 275, 276
  as capacity to open new insights into
    reality, 219
  as increase of reality, 275
  as problem for which name is offered,
    219
  as transposition, 263
reflection, 88, 177, 181, 182, 186, 193, 198,
    218, 219, 220, 221, 245
religion, 34, 138, 139, 243, 245, 251
reminiscence, 53, 251
Renaissance, 232, 254, 256
reports, 96, 97, 110, 111, 112, 115, 117, 120,
    124, 126, 127, 128, 129, 130, 131, 132,
    133, 137, 138, 172, 207, 217
  as descriptions, 129, 133, 134
repose, 232, 283
representation, 4, 8, 38, 51, 52, 53, 64, 66,
    67, 71, 72, 76, 77, 79, 81, 133, 135, 148,
    162, 163, 192, 193, 197, 198, 241, 254,
    255, 262, 294n2 (chap. 7)
  as channel between subject and
    object, 283
  compared to presentation, 87, 278
  as image, 56, 87
  juxtaposition with belief, 26
  relation with meaning, 151
  as *Repräsentation*, 148
  as signifying, 148
  singular, 151
  as *Stellvertretung*, 148
  universal, 151
  as *Vorstellung*, 2, 4, 56, 85, 94
resemblance, 52, 57, 60, 93, 113, 134, 147,
    237, 240
  dialectic with sameness, 114
  imagination as perceiving of, 114
  metaphor as perceiving of, 114, 234
  See also copy

restructuration, 238, 239, 270
retention, phenomenological, 158, 162,
    264
  defined, 157
reverberation, 227, 230, 233, 234, 240,
    242, 248
retentissement, 229
reverie, 222, 231, 232
revolution, 265
rhetoric, 17, 34, 37, 101, 234
Richards, I. A., 240
  Philosophy of Rhetoric, The, 235
Ricoeur, Paul
  "Analogical Language" (1975 course),
    299n3 (chap. 15)
  "Function of Fiction in Shaping Real-
    ity, The," 298n5 (chap. 14)
  "Hermeneutical Function of Distan-
    ciation, The," 296n4 (chap. 10)
  "Hermeneutics and the Critique of
    Ideology," 300n9 (chap. 17)
  "Kant and the Problem of Imagina-
    tion in the Three Critiques," 298n5
    (chap. 14)
  "'Kingdom' in the Parables of Jesus,
    The," 301n9
  "Listening to the Parables of Jesus,"
    301n9
  "On Imagination: From Picture to
    Fiction," 298n5 (chap. 14)
  "Phenomenology and Hermeneu-
    tics," 296n3 (chap. 10)
  "Pour une théorie du discours narra-
    tive," 301n8
  "Récit fictif—récit historique," 301n8
  "'Royaume' dans les paraboles de
    Jésus, Le" 301n9
  "That Fiction 'Remakes' Reality,"
    298n5 (chap. 14)
  "Theory of Narrative Discourse:
    Story, History, and Historicity "
    (1976 course), 301n8
  Key to Edmund Husserl's "Ideas I," A,
    297n6 (chap. 11)
  Lectures on Ideology and Utopia, 8,
    13, 36, 85, 243, 245, 257, 280, 284,
    291n9, 300n9 (chap. 17)
  métaphore vive, La, 301n4

Rule of Metaphor, The, 301n4
Time and Narrative, 294n2 (chap. 7)
What Makes Us Think? (with Jean-
    Pierre Changeux), 295n3 (chap. 9)
role-playing, 2, 13, 291n4, 293n1
    (chap. 4)
Romanticism, 69, 84
rule, 72, 73, 74, 75, 76, 77, 78, 105, 120,
    147, 226, 239, 242, 245, 251, 263, 270,
    271, 275, 280, 285
    and concept, 71, 72
    interrelation with free play, 88
    interrelation with play, 76, 81
    as movement, 72
    as structure, 78
    understanding as faculty of, 76
    of use, 127
Russell, Bertrand, 21, 94, 113, 125, 144
Ryle, Gilbert, 75, 92, 96, 98–105, 107–12,
    115, 116, 117, 118, 120, 123, 124, 132,
    134, 137, 143, 167, 169, 171, 178, 179,
    181, 188, 217–18, 219, 239, 246, 259,
    282, 291n4, 291n11
    Concept of Mind, The, 4, 98–105, 107–
    12, 266, 282, 294n3 (chap. 7), 295n1
    (chap. 8)

Saint Peter's Basilica, 84
sameness, 113, 140, 144, 145, 146, 147, 171,
    183, 218, 225, 237
    contrast to likeness, 93, 147, 239
    dialectic with resemblance, 114
    emergence of despite difference, 239
Sartre, Jean-Paul, 28, 66, 73, 75, 92, 98,
    99, 100, 102, 105, 112, 127, 136, 137,
    143, 151, 153, 154–55, 158, 159, 160,
    161, 165, 166, 167, 169–99, 201–14,
    217, 219, 220, 221–22, 233, 242, 246,
    259, 263, 280, 283, 294n2 (chap. 7)
    Being and Nothingness, 175, 186, 202,
    297n2 (chap. 13)
    *imaginaire, L': Psychologie phénomé-
    nologique de l'imagination,* 297n4
    (chap. 12)
    *Imagination: A Psychological Cri-
    tique,* 92, 153, 170–76, 185, 297n1
    (chap. 12)
    Psychology of Imagination, The, 10,

92, 160, 169, 170, 171, 175, 176–99,
    201–14, 221, 294n2 (chap. 5), 297n2
    (chap. 12), 298n1 (chap. 13), 298n1
    (chap. 14), 300n2 (chap. 18)
    Sketch for a Theory of the Emotions, 141,
    202
Schelling, Friedrich, 69
schema, 71–74, 75, 114, 196, 239, 240,
    242, 285
    as display in images, 73
    juxtaposition with image, 73, 240
    as kernel of productive imagination,
    74
    as a method, 72
    as a procedure, 72
    rule for giving images for concept,
    120, 239
    as rule of synthesis, 72, 73
schematism, 68, 71–74, 136, 146
    as an art concealed, 74
    as giving an image to a concept that
    is applied, 266
Schiller, Friedrich, 84
Schon, Donald, 261, 263–73, 276
    Displacement of Concepts, 222, 225, 226,
    257, 261, 263–73, 300n3 (chap. 18)
science, 25, 50, 58, 59, 65, 79, 83, 85, 118,
    123, 126, 142, 156, 194, 226, 233, 236,
    241, 254, 256, 257, 260, 263, 275, 276,
    277, 284
    criticizing dichotomy with poetry, 260
    imagination in, 260
    philosophy of, 257
    productive imagination in, 260
    psychology as, 154
screen, 84, 178, 241, 252, 255, 261, 271,
    272, 284
    as abbreviation and condensation
    tool, 252
    as alphabet and syntax, 278
    think through the screen of the
    model, 278
Searle, John, 187
sedimentation, 136, 265
    as contrary of novelty, 265
    "seeing," 101, 103, 104, 109, 181
seeing an aspect, 271
    parallels with noticing an aspect, 148

seeing as, 42, 93, 112, 123, 126, 129–36, 143, 144, 241, 270
  correlative with thinking as, 241
seeming to see, 101, 102, 104, 105, 107, 108, 116, 179
Sefler, George F.
  Language and the World: A Methodological Synthesis within the Writings of Martin Heidegger and Ludwig Wittgenstein, 295n4 (chap. 9)
Segal, Sydney Joelson
  Imagery: Current Cognitive Approaches, 293n1 (chap. 4)
self, 297n2 (chap. 13)
self-consciousness, 186, 298n2 (chap. 13)
semantic fields, 3, 148, 236, 237, 238, 262, 263
semantic impertinence, 236
semantic innovation, 237
  dialectic with depiction, 243
  in metaphor and similarity to displacement of concepts in scientific thought, 276
  unity in problem of, 275
semantics, 237
  of discourse, 234
semiotics, 139
sensation, 12, 18, 19, 21, 23, 24, 25, 27, 28, 29, 30, 40, 50, 108, 109, 159, 160, 188, 198
  as condition of imagination, 292n3
sense, 21, 23, 27, 29, 30, 33, 58, 61, 65, 82, 84, 87, 235, 241, 242, 248, 249, 257, 259, 282
  contrast to reference, 146, 178, 219
  interrelation with senses, 240, 242
sense data, 62, 93
sensibility, 21, 29, 64, 65, 69, 70, 71, 80, 86, 193, 203
serenity, 139
  Gelassenheit, 232
shadow, 7, 18, 100, 101, 108, 149, 181, 233, 249–50, 251, 256, 260, 280
  as reproductive imagination, 250
Shakespeare, William, 33, 118, 235
shatter, 81, 126, 272, 277, 280, 283
shock, 236, 256, 272

signs, 1, 139, 148, 149, 156, 247, 249, 252
  indicative, 150
  ostensive, 150
  as standing for, 5, 52
  substitutive, 149
similarity, 114, 135, 147, 148, 219, 234, 235, 237, 239, 262, 267, 269, 270
simile, 17, 239
sin, 10, 35, 53
  original, 35, 37
skepticism, 36, 75, 103, 125, 134, 136
sociology, 243
  of culture, 13, 165
Socrates, 23, 121, 128, 136
sophistry, 21, 37
soul, 18, 27, 39, 40, 50, 74, 82, 87, 161, 228, 232
  as animating, 18, 21
  as movement, 18
space, 39, 64, 73, 149, 157, 177, 198, 224, 241, 248, 255
speech act, 187
spelling out, 272, 273
  as elaboration, 273
Spinoza, Benedict, 7, 9, 10, 12, 25, 26, 29, 34, 35, 37–47, 49, 51, 61, 82, 210
  Ethics, 12, 33, 37–47, 82, 293n2 (chap. 3)
  Theologico-Political Treatise, 46, 82
  Treatise on the Emendation of the Intellect, 46, 292n4
spirit, 18, 35
  Gemüt, 246
spontaneity, 64, 69, 78, 88, 171, 172, 175, 176, 178, 180, 184, 186–87, 191, 201, 204, 221, 231, 283
  as bound, 211
  reflective versus creative, 220
  spellbound, 207
statics
  of the image, 169, 184, 187, 201, 221, 297n4 (chap. 12)
Stoicism, 139, 153
Strawson, P. F., 21, 195
structuralism, 119
structuration, 19, 251
  of reality, 264

INDEX 349

structure, 78, 144, 185, 193, 196, 198, 224, 232, 234, 238, 241, 245, 262, 264, 265, 268, 281, 283
  always already, 264
  of experience, 142, 143
  imagination as interrelated with, 88
  kinesthetic, 198
  of meaningful experience, 140
  symbolic, 88
subjective, the, 7, 9, 77, 86, 87–88, 133, 196, 246, 281, 283, 284, 285
subjectivism, 250
subjectivity, 79, 228
subject/object relation, 283, 285
  as interest in control, 284
  shattered in poetry, 283
  suspended in poetry, 283
sublime, 78, 80, 82–88
  dynamically, 83, 84, 86–88
  mathematically, 83–86, 87
substance, 56
substantives, 101, 141, 179, 181
substitution, 2, 5, 115, 117, 134, 141, 148, 149, 189, 196, 197, 233, 234, 235, 237, 262, 268
subsumption, 71, 78, 266
  relation with application, 71, 266
supersensible, 84, 86, 88
surplus value
  of authority, 36
suspension, 105, 139, 195, 232, 257, 279, 284
  of belief, 182, 183
  of care, 283
  epoché, 242, 282
  of judgment (epoché), 139, 153
  of ontological belief, 161
  in poetry of ideological relation to world, 284
  of reference, 248
  of subject/object relation in poetry, 283
symbolic relation, 270, 271
  as transposition, 271
symbolic structure of reality
  as symbolizing the ethical order, 88
symbols, 95, 269, 270

as depictions, 243
of painting and language, 252
religious, 243
synthesis, 13, 23, 56, 61, 64, 65, 66, 67, 68, 69, 71, 72, 73, 81, 141, 157, 179
  affective, 197
  figurative, 70
  intellectual, 70

taste, 64, 79, 81, 84, 245
technē, 221
  production, 251
technocracy, 280
theology, 10, 227
thetic, 186, 204
things themselves, 157
  die Sachen selbst, 96
thinking, 20, 21, 22, 23, 95, 118, 120, 145
  as activity, 222
  as correlative with seeing as, 241
  and displaying before (vorstellen), 151
  image in relation to operation of, 93–95, 112, 117, 123
  with or in images, 113, 114, 142, 143–44, 149, 151, 153, 222
  imagist theory, 112–13, 114, 115, 142, 144, 148, 149
  possibility of thinking more, 273
  relation with perception, 109, 135, 136
  in seeing, 134
  speculative, 21
  verbalistic theory, 113
thought, 19, 20, 21, 23, 39, 50, 64, 66, 176, 221, 223, 226, 238, 239, 241, 242, 260, 276, 279
  contrast to thinking as activity, 222
  displacement in, 276
  dynamism of, 273
  image as illustration of, 153
  movement in through predication, 225
  unity in functioning in poetic language and in science, 275
  work of, 280
time, 40, 41, 42, 43, 44, 53, 64, 77, 186, 255
Toulmin, Stephen
  Philosophy of Science, 279

trace, 1, 7, 8, 11–12, 28, 40, 41, 43, 44, 45, 47, 51, 54, 103, 108, 227, 230, 242, 263
  contrast to fiction, 12
  contrast to image, 242
  deriving image from perception, 44
  image as, 31
  as reproductive, 9, 11
Tracy, David, 227, 257, 261
tragedy, 246, 250, 255, 279
  fictional, 220
  Greek, 6, 23, 279
  poetic, 220, 255
transcendence, 86, 155, 170, 188
transcendental, the, 65, 66, 67, 68, 69, 70, 71, 72, 76, 154, 193, 207–8
  defined, 63
transfiguration
  of reality, 245, 246, 249
translation, 263
transparency, 142, 176, 178
transposition, 229, 262, 263, 270, 271
  kernel of opacity, 273
  in metaphor, 276
  as opaque, 276
  possibility of thinking more, 273
  as productive reference, 263
  providing possibility of the discursive, 273
triangle, 73, 94, 113, 117, 125, 131, 145, 147, 235
truth, 17, 18, 19, 20, 21, 22, 23, 24, 25, 26, 29, 30, 33, 34, 37, 46, 118, 155, 162, 220, 256, 257, 275
  as adequation, 13, 30
  as adequation belongs to subject/object relation, 285
  alētheia, 53
  and art, 260
  claim, 261, 276, 277, 278
  concept of revised by productive imagination, 285
  imagination and, 12, 31
  as manifestation, 285
  and science, 260
  as unconcealment, 31
Turbayne, Colin, 277

unbelief, 7, 11
unconcealment, 31
  as *a-lētheia*, 53
unconscious, 176, 186
understanding, 49, 68, 69, 70, 71, 72, 73, 75–76, 78, 79, 80, 81, 82, 83, 86, 136, 148, 245
  Verstand, 82
  Verstehen, 282
universal, the, 2, 20, 21, 29, 62, 68, 72, 80, 93, 94, 113, 115, 144, 145, 146, 147, 149, 151, 181, 209, 245, 260, 298n4 (chap. 13)
unmasking, 34, 35, 36
unreality, 6, 9, 75, 143, 147, 189, 191, 192, 194, 195, 201, 202, 203, 204, 205, 206, 207, 208, 209, 210, 211, 213, 214, 218, 222
  connection with reality, 211
  fiction as part of, 195
  of the image, 212
  as nonexistence of referent, 218
unrealizing, 203, 213
unthinkable, 83
use, 111, 126, 127, 129, 130, 268
  figurative, 271
  relation to grammar, 127
  tension between old and new in metaphor, 268
utopia, 8, 10, 13, 36, 231, 243, 245
  connection to theory of imagination, 209
  as escape, 214
  as fiction, 275
  as the nowhere, 118, 209
  parallel to critique of work, 280
  as redirection of action, 214
  as shattering, 280

Vaihinger, Hans, 278
Valéry, Paul
  "Poetry and Abstract Thought," 248, 300n3 (chap. 17)
Van Gogh, Vincent, 253
verb, 101, 107, 108, 116, 141, 179, 181, 198
verbal, the, 241, 242, 252

interrelation with visual, 65, 214, 226, 240

verbalistic theory
of thinking, 113

verification, 31, 114, 269

Verstehen
orienting oneself, 256
understanding as project of our possibilities, 282

violence, 42, 50, 86, 112, 133

visual, the
interrelation with verbal, 65, 214, 226, 240

visualization, 150

volition, 99

voluntary, 187

Vorstellung, 4, 56, 94, 145
defined, 2, 4
displaying before, 151
imagination, 126, 131
to place before, 151
See also representation

will, 116, 140, 187
philosophy of, 187

Wittgenstein, Ludwig, 20, 93, 95, 96, 103, 112, 121, 123–36, 137, 138, 143, 148, 180, 235, 241, 247, 270, 271
Philosophical Investigations, 42, 93, 123–36, 138, 223, 293n3 (chap. 3), 295n1 (chap. 9)
Tractatus Logico-Philosophicus, 124, 150, 238, 295n2 (chap. 9)

work, 62, 92, 120, 150, 221, 222, 225, 249, 251, 266, 280
of art, 249
contrast to dream, 222
critique of, 280
critique of against form, 280
of discourse, 221
fictional, 251
as giving form, organization, structuration, 251
imagination as, 91
of language, 280
as opposite of magical, 222
parallel to models, 280
of the poet, 280
productive imagination as a, 221
as *technē*, production, 221, 251
of thought, 279, 280
See also anti-work

world, 123, 197, 208, 210, 212, 220, 228, 231, 232, 233, 252, 255, 256, 268, 272, 278, 283, 284
appearance of through poetry, 284
extension of, 261, 276
as horizon of objects, 284
suspension of ideological relation to in poetry, 284

writing, 226, 249, 251
interplay with painting, 252
theory of, 285

Wyeth, Andrew, 281